The management research handbook

What constitutes good research in management and the associated social science fields? How should this research be conducted? *The Management Research Handbook* makes a timely contribution to the debate in management about the appropriateness of different assumptions and forms of social science research. It reviews concerns about traditional research approaches and examines the more diverse approaches which have been increasingly recognized as useful in tackling some of the more important research problems in management. Rather than advocate a single research approach, Smith and Dainty acknowledge the strengths and weaknesses of different approaches and urge more meaningful management research through a more complete understanding of the research process and of the need for appropriate methodologies.

Exploring the whole process of research, the editors have put together a compilation which should serve as an important source-book for active researchers, academics as well as students. The focus on the research process ranges from issues of epistemology to the more practical issues of interview strategy and working on group research projects. This different perspective results in a guide to research methodology which looks at the 'why' and 'where' as well as the 'how' of management research.

The *Handbook* is structured in keeping with the research process. The essays on the theoretical underpinnings of social science research help the reader decide on a research perspective. From this position on the nature of management research, the reader may then review a variety of research methods and techniques, such as the case study, ethnomethodology, repertory grid, and surveys. Finally, the opportunity and constraints of the research context are explored, in essays on doctoral research, group research, action research and on research in developing countries. Throughout, the international collection of contributors communicate the sense of research as an exciting and worthwhile craft. The comprehensive survey points the serious academic researcher towards a successful research outcome.

N. Craig Smith is Visiting Associate Professor of Marketing at the School of Business Administration, Georgetown University, Washington DC. **Paul Dainty** is Senior Lecturer at the Graduate School of Management, University of Melbourne, Carlton, Victoria.

The management research handbook

Edited by
N. Craig Smith and
Paul Dainty

London and New York

To Roger, Ruth, Maura and Fiona

First published 1991
by Routledge
11 New Fetter Lane, London EC4P 4EE

Simultaneously published in the USA and Canada
by Routledge
a division of Routledge, Chapman and Hall, Inc.
29 West 35th Street, New York, NY 10001

Preface, Introduction and introductions to Part I, II, and III
© 1991 N. Craig Smith and Paul Dainty
All other chapters
© 1991 the individual author

Typeset by Michael Mepham, Frome, Somerset
Printed and bound in Great Britain by
Biddles Ltd, Guildford and King's Lynn

British Library Cataloguing in Publication Data
The Management Research Handbook.
1. Management. Research
I. Smith, N. Craig 1958– II. Dainty, Paul 1953–
658.072

Library of Congress Cataloging-in-Publication Data
The Management Research Handbook / edited by
N. Craig Smith and Paul Dainty.
p. cm.
Includes bibliographical references and index.
1. Management—Research. I. Smith, N. Craig, 1958–
II. Dainty, Paul, 1953–
HD30.4.M363 1991

90–27224
CIP

ISBN 0–415–04341–7

Contents

Contributors   ix

Preface   xi

Introduction   xiii

Part I Research perspectives   1

1 Alternative perspectives in the organizational sciences: 7
   'inquiry from the inside' and 'inquiry from the outside'
   Roger Evered and Meryl Reis Louis

2 Multiple paradigm analysis: a methodology for management   23
   research
   John S. Hassard

3 The case for the natural science model for research in   44
   organizational behaviour and organization theory
   Orlando Behling

4 Meaningful management research: the meaning of science   57
   and the meaning in science in relation to management research
   Paul Dainty

5 What is management research?   67
   Roger Bennett

Part II Research methods   79

6 How is management research carried out?   85
   Roger Bennett

7 Research methodology in organizational studies 104
Philip M. Podsakoff and Dan R. Dalton

8 Ethnomethodology and organization: an introduction 132
John S. Hassard

9 The case-study: a vital yet misunderstood research method 145
for management
N. Craig Smith

10 Management field research using repertory grid technique: 159
problems and possibilities
Paul Dainty

11 Choosing a survey method in management research 174
David Jobber

12 Designing and using mail questionnaires 181
Paul B. Cragg

13 A first-time user's guide to the collection and analysis 190
of interview data from senior managers
Susan J. Hart

Part III Research contexts **205**

14 The context of doctoral research 215
N. Craig Smith

15 Learning to do research 227
Estelle M. Phillips

16 Understanding supervisory relationships 237
Paul Jeffcutt and Alan Thomas

17 Writing up the doctoral thesis 245
Norman Clark

18 The social process of research: some reflections on 252
developing a multi-disciplinary accounting project
Cyril Tomkins, David Rosenberg, and Ian Colville

19 Researching in teams: lessons from experience 278
M. King, R. Lee, J. Piper, and J. Whittaker

20 Politics and ethics in action research 289
Andrew Kakabadse

21 Data collection for management research in developing
  countries   300
  Kavil Ramachandran

  Index   310

Contributors

Orlando Behling is Professor of Organizational Behavior in the Department of Management, Bowling Green State University, Bowling Green, OH 43403, USA.

Roger Bennett is an independent consultant and a part-time professor at the International Management Centre, Buckingham, England.

Norman Clark is at the Science Policy Research Unit, University of Sussex, Brighton, England.

Ian Colville is at the School of Management, University of Bath, Bath, BA2 7AY, England.

Paul Cragg is Senior Lecturer in Management at the Department of Management, University of Waikato, Private Bag, Hamilton, New Zealand.

Paul Dainty is Senior Lecturer at the Graduate School of Management, University of Melbourne, Carlton, Victoria 3053, Australia.

Dan R. Dalton is at the School of Business, Indiana University, Bloomington, IN 47405, USA.

Roger Evered is an Associate Professor at the Naval Postgraduate School, Monterey, CA 93940, USA.

Susan J. Hart is a Lecturer in Marketing at Strathclyde Business School, University of Strathclyde, Stenhouse Building, 173 Cathedral Street, Glasgow, G4 0RQ, Scotland.

John S. Hassard is Director of the Centre for Graduate Management Studies, University of Keele, Keele, ST5 5BG, England.

Paul Jeffcutt is Lecturer in Organisational Analysis at the Department of Business Studies, The School of Management, University of Stirling, Stirling, FK9 4LA, Scotland.

David Jobber is a Senior Lecturer at the University of Bradford Management Centre, Bradford, BD9 4JL, England.

Andrew Kakabadse is Professor of Management Development, Cranfield School of Management, CIT, Cranfield, Bedford, MK43 0AL, England.

Malcolm King is at the Business School, Loughborough University, Loughborough, Leicestershire, LE11 3TU, England.

R. Lee is at the Department of Management Studies, Loughborough University, Loughborough, Leicestershire, LE11 3TU, England.

Meryl Reis Louis is Associate Professor of Organisational Behavior at the School of Management, Boston University, 621 Commonwealth Avenue, Boston, MA 02215, USA.

Estelle M. Phillips is a Lecturer at the Department of Occupational Psychology, Birkbeck College, University of London, Malet Street, London, WC1E 7HX, England.

J. Piper is at the Department of Management Studies, Loughborough University, Loughborough, Leicestershire, LE11 3TU, England.

Philip M. Podsakoff is an Associate Professor of Personnel and Organizational Behavior in the School of Business, Indiana University, Bloomington, IN 47405, USA.

Kavil Ramachandran is an Associate Professor at the Indian Institute of Management, Vastrapur, Ahmedabad, India.

David Rosenberg was at the School of Management, University of Bath, Bath, BA2 7AY, England.

N. Craig Smith is Visiting Associate Professor of Marketing at the School of Business Administration, Georgetown University, Washington DC 20057, USA.

Alan Thomas is a Lecturer at Manchester Business School, University of Manchester, Manchester, England.

Cyril Tomkins is Professor of Accounting and Finance at the School of Management, University of Bath, Bath, BA2 7AY, England.

J. Whittaker is at the Department of Management Studies, Loughborough University, Loughborough, Leicestershire, LE11 3TU, England.

Preface

The Management Research Handbook is a comprehensive review of the research process for those conducting research in management and associated social science fields. It is aimed at the serious management researcher wishing to think broadly about the research activity and the issues which arise, with a view to producing a meaningful research output. Its focus on the research process rather than research techniques makes it complementary to traditional research texts. Rather than advocate one model of research, the book offers a variety of research perspectives and methods, acknowledging diversity and the strengths and weaknesses of different approaches. The reader can survey the options and thereby gain some appreciation of the alternative approaches chosen by other researchers. In examining research contexts, it is recognized that the circumstances of research influence its form and output. So there are chapters, for example, on the research process within doctoral research and research teams.

The source for much of the material here is *Graduate Management Research (GMR)*, a journal about the ideas, issues, and problems in the research process – the 'how' and 'why' of academic management research. One impetus for this book was the desire to secure wider dissemination of some of the unique and valuable contributions to *GMR*, many of which have been substantially reworked to meet this book's purpose. The editors are grateful to the book's reviewers for their insightful comments which helped the selection, editing, and revision of these papers, as well as for the additional input from the authors. To provide more complete coverage, some additional papers were selected from a variety of other management journals. We are therefore also indebted to these authors, and to the following publications and their editors, for permission to reprint from: *Academy of Management Review, Accounting, Organizations and Society, Journal of Management, Marketing Intelligence and Planning*.

Craig Smith
Paul Dainty

Introduction

This book has three central and unifying themes. First, and foremost, is the urging of meaningful management research. *The Management Research Handbook* was born out of a sense of frustration with much orthodox management research and the belief that a key purpose of education is to question seriously the world we live in. In the search for meaning in management research, we would encourage research in and for the real world of managers and corporate stakeholders. The second theme is the view of research as a process. Clearly, the research task involves a series of steps from, say, specifying the research problem through to proposing a solution. Yet it is also a social process, involving the development of the individual researcher and others, as well as the development of the research topic and knowledge generally. Third is the theme of research as an exciting and worthwhile craft. This introduction explains these themes, together with the book's role, structure, and contents.

Why should the research of management academics have intellectual authority and command the respect and attention of practitioners? A non-cynical response would identify management academics as social scientists and, accordingly, management research as 'scientific'. However, the legitimacy of management research, while imparted by its origins in universities and other 'centers of learning', is more appropriately derived from the way in which it is conducted. Einstein, debunking the mystique of science, said, 'The whole of science is nothing more than a refinement of everyday thinking'. The refinement comes from the methods which scientists employ. So it is the use of the scientific method which confers legitimacy on management research (and, hence, much management teaching) and ensures research findings are meaningful, both theoretically *and* practically within an applied discipline.

Yet this claim to meaning becomes difficult when empirical support is sought by examination of the content of management journals and the research outcomes reported. As Dubin notes:

The ease with which certain research technologies can be used has had a limiting, if not withering, consequence for the knowledge currently produced about people at work. For all its surface appearance of scientism, in the end, worthy knowledge must be produced – not just the claim that whatever is turned out is, at least, 'scientific'.

(Dubin 1982)

Frustration is growing at the dearth of meaning in much of the published research in the management area, accompanied by suggestions for improvements. We define meaningful research as being rigorous, relevant or significant (the researcher has addressed important questions), non-partisan (or not serving a narrow section of society), and conducted with integrity and independence.[1] Debates, particularly about the relevance of research, may be found throughout the social sciences. In management, expressions of concern were being made at least ten years ago, and they continue today. In his presidential address to the 1989 annual meeting of the Academy of Management, in Washington DC, Arthur Bedeian spoke of 'the mindlessness of much of our discipline's research' (Bedeian 1989). He cited the obviousness of this research: 'We have begun our research with hypotheses that are so clearly true, given both our implicit and explicit assumptions, that if all our premises held, then our hypotheses would obviously be true.' He referred to 'our failure to foster a productive interplay between theory and research', and to a discipline that is 'theory thin' and 'method driven', such that: 'We seem to be expert at applying sophisticated data manipulation techniques to data hardly warranting the effort.' Overspecialization was also identified as dysfunctional, because 'our big problems are rarely encapsulated in any one specialty.' Bedeian's conclusion was that without intellectual and social changes in the management discipline there would be 'lean and infertile times in the years ahead'.

The 'scientificness' which characterizes much orthodox management research is too often at the expense of meaning. Bedeian called for a broader definition of scholarship and closer co-operation between academics and practitioners. Because a limiting (if not debilitating) form of management research has become institutionalized, particularly as academic publications are a *sine qua non* for tenure appointments, Bedeian also urged a re-evaluation of the realities of university tenure and promotion systems. We would support his analysis and recommendations.

More meaningful management research could result from a closer acquaintance with management, the discipline's subject of study. Management researchers should not isolate themselves in ivory towers but go out, instead, and talk to managers. It has been our experience that researching with companies and managers can provide a richness of data not otherwise available. Research aimed at producing findings useful to managers would also be more meaningful within an applied discipline. Accordingly, researchers should keep in mind the five key components of research relevance (Thomas and Tymon 1982):

1 Descriptive Relevance – the accuracy of research findings in capturing phenomena encountered by the practitioner in his or her organizational setting.
2 Goal Relevance – the correspondence of outcome (or dependent) variables in a theory to the things the practitioner wishes to influence.
3 Operational Validity – the ability of the practitioner to implement action implications of a theory by manipulating its causal (or independent) variables.
4 Non-obviousness – the degree to which a theory meets or exceeds the complexity of common sense theory already used by a practitioner.
5 Timeliness – the requirement that a theory be available to practitioners in time to use it to deal with problems.

Despite some suggestions to the contrary (for example, Holbrook 1989), managerial relevance and academic scholarship are not mutually exclusive. However, it may be disturbing to find that in the pursuit of relevance, management research is captured by, and serving, a particular section of society. Academic scholarship requires research integrity and researcher independence. Hence, nonpartisan research should be encouraged. So within marketing, for instance, researchers should aim to be neutral social scientists concerned with marketing practice. This would involve, probably predominantly, research to improve practice. However, these improvements would better society as a whole rather than one section (such as managers). This position also allows, for example, research concerned with the impacts of marketing practice, such as consumer and public policy consequences. In sum, we would urge research relevance but also ask, 'relevant for whom?' We favour academic neutrality and attention to multiple perspectives and interests.

Greater relevance would make for meaningful management research, yet there are other ways by which meaning could be enhanced. More than twenty years ago, Rigby commented:

Although business researchers may need to learn even more about techniques, their notable weakness is their inadequate emphasis on the research process. Knowing how to use the tools and techniques of research does not in itself guarantee the effectiveness of an individual in carrying out a scientific investigation.

(Rigby 1965: viii)

This observation remains valid and, accordingly, *The Management Research Handbook* focuses on the research process, rather than on specific techniques of data collection and analysis. We believe that attention to and understanding of the research process is likely to result in a more meaningful research.

At a basic level, the research process can be understood as a series of stages leading from research questions through to research findings. Bennett models the research process in this way in chapter 5 (see figure 5.1, page 71). Importantly, given the above discussion about meaning in research, this prescriptive model highlights the research *problem* as the starting point of research, not research methods. As we and other authors stress throughout the book, research approaches should be dictated by research questions.

Research can also be understood as a social process. Research output is greatly influenced by the researcher and his or her experiences. Figure I.1 is a descriptive model of research. Starting with the researcher, it shows how a research perspective (a theoretical underpinning of the methodology) is formed, with both the researcher and research institution (university) as well as research questions playing a part. Research perspective, in addition to research questions, in turn determines research methodology. The various research contexts, discussed in more detail in the introduction to part III, envelop this part of the process. The model shows how the social process of research leads to research output.

The model reflects the philosophy and structure of this book, acknowledging the impact of research perspectives, research methods, and research contexts on research output. There is a tendency among traditional research texts to give the impression that having the research methodology correct should be the prime concern of the researcher – if the techniques of research are rigorously addressed then everything else will fall into place. We do not question the importance of research methodology, but we do question this emphasis. We believe it is important to take a more holistic approach to the research process, which means not only a concern with research methods but also looking, in particular, at the theoretical basis of the research and the context in which it is conducted.

Consequently, this book is divided into three parts in order to explore and raise awareness of these broader concerns. Each part has a detailed introduction, though a brief outline is provided here to help orientate the reader. Part I, Research perspectives, is concerned with the 'why' and 'what' of research. Its purpose is to encourage the researcher to consider the purpose, theoretical orientation and assumptions underlying research in management. This part starts by examining broad theoretical issues and ends by focusing on issues specific to the management field.

Part II, Research methods, is concerned with ways of actually going about investigating a research problem, the 'how' of research. Our intention here is not to go over methodological issues found in traditional texts but to draw attention to some of the problems which are sometimes ignored or not fully considered, again particularly in relation to management. Part III, Research contexts, highlights our view of research as a social process. Rarely considered in the literature, this part is concerned with the 'where' of research, the different environments and other external influences affecting the conduct of research. Often disregarded by researchers, as well as research texts, the contexts of research can be a major cause of an unsuccessful research outcome, particularly in management. Research contexts have to be understood and managed, as the various contributions to part III explain.

A bold claim is made when 'handbook' appears in a title. We feel the claim is justified with *The Management Research Handbook* because it provides the reader with a source of articles to refer to – and hopefully ideas

Figure I.1 Model of research as a social process

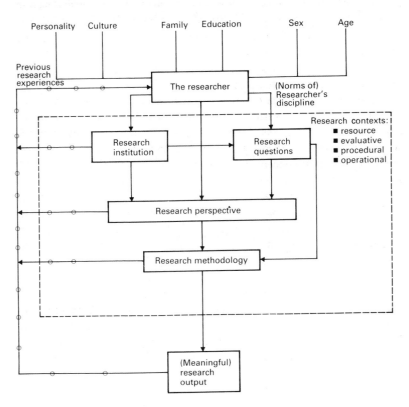

and inspiration – when troubled by the research process. We hope that, used as a sourcebook, it may reduce the trauma of research. We have tried to take an alternative perspective which will help management researchers deal with the reality of research and produce something meaningful. It should in addition be apparent that we, and the other authors represented here, believe research is an exciting and worthwhile activity. The sociologist C. Wright Mills, writing 'On Intellectual Craftsmanship', describes social science as 'the practice of a craft' (1959: 195). In his paper, and in this phrase in particular, Mills captures and conveys a sense of purpose to the research activity. This book, in addressing the meaning and process of management research, aims to help the researcher not only to increase the prospect of successful completion of a research project, but also to achieve a more satisfying outcome.

NOTE

1   This definition attempts to capture the key properties of meaningful research. We would acknowledge that rigour and relevance may often be in conflict. This is discussed, for example, in chapter 9.

REFERENCES

Bedeian, Arthur G. (1989) 'Totems and taboos: undercurrents in the management discipline', *The Academy of Management News* 19, 4.

Dubin, Robert (1982) 'Management: meanings, methods, and moxie', *Academy of Management Review* 7, 3.

Holbrook, Morris (1989) 'Aftermath of the task force: dogmatism and catastrophe in the development of marketing thought', *ACR Newsletter*, September.

Mills, C. Wright (1959) *The Sociological Imagination*, New York: Oxford University Press.

Rigby, Paul H. (1965) *Conceptual Foundations in Business Research*, New York: John Wiley.

Thomas, Kenneth W. and Tymon, Walter G. (1982) 'Necessary properties of relevant research: lessons from recent criticisms of the organizational sciences', *Academy of Management Review* 7, 3.

Part I
Research perspectives

PART I: RESEARCH PERSPECTIVES

As recently as twenty years ago discussion of research perspectives within a social science research text would have seemed unnecessary. The idea that research can have different approaches and views is not new, but there is now far less agreement about what the research process is fundamentally concerned with. In general, research is concerned with a process of inquiry which adds to our knowledge of particular phenomena. However, until quite recently the idea that this process should mirror the approaches adopted within the natural sciences was rarely questioned. Not everyone shared this view, however, and in some areas of human investigation, such as anthropology, there have been different traditions for some time. Nevertheless, in general, the dominance of the natural science model was reflected in texts on research in the social sciences, which tended to start from an assumption of this model.

Now we need to take one step back. The natural science approach to research has received considerable criticism over the years. Other approaches have developed which have highlighted the limitations of the natural science model and constitute viable alternatives. Indeed, there are so many different approaches that confusion rather than a false sense of certainty is more likely. This section should help the researcher to clarify his or her research perspective.

The chapters in part I identify – and encourage the serious researcher to go further in thinking about – the different possibilities, assumptions, values, and paradigms that underlie research. This is what we mean by research perspectives. It is important that the researcher sees the weaknesses and strengths of the different perspectives, looks at ways of limiting those weaknesses, and adopts one or perhaps several approaches which best serve the research purpose. Management teachers often argue that managing any activity demands an understanding of your assumptions about the framework with which you manage. Accordingly, not understanding the assumptions underlying your research approach is at best limiting. At worst it is a strait-jacket which may prevent a successful research outcome.

Part I begins by taking a broad look at different perspectives on research. In chapter 1, Evered and Louis examine some of the critical assumptions and beliefs underlying different approaches to organization inquiry. In one sense they provide a map of the area, albeit one amongst several possible kinds of map. Their map is based on two paradigms which, they argue, exemplify two predominant research approaches which orientate most organization research. One paradigm is described as 'inquiry from the inside' and is characterized by the experiential involvement of the researcher, the absence of a priori analytical categories, and an intent to understand a particular situation. The other paradigm, 'inquiry from the outside', assumes detachment on the part of the researcher, who typically gathers data according to a priori analytical categories and aims to uncover knowledge that can be generalized to many situations.

These two concepts encapsulate a key dichotomy which has been expressed in a number of different ways. Inquiry from the outside can be associated with objective, positivistic, and 'hard' approaches. Inquiry from the inside encompasses more subjective, ethnographic, and 'soft' approaches. However, this chapter is not really about establishing precise definitions, but about challenging assumptions concerning the research process and highlighting differing perspectives. The authors show that greater appreciation of the epistemological differences between the two approaches can help researchers select the mode of inquiry appropriate to the phenomenon under study and to their own abilities and inclinations.

The next chapter also challenges our assumptions. Hassard maintains there are so many paradigm schemes that there is a danger of confusion and inconsistency. But, like the previous authors, he implies that an understanding of paradigm concepts is both possible and necessary to make us aware of our tacit assumptions. Indeed, he goes further than this by demonstrating the very different outcomes that different paradigmatic stances can have.

Using a model by Burrell and Morgan, Hassard explains and develops his notion of 'multiple paradigm research'. The four approaches in the model, those of functionalism, the interpretive position, radical humanism, and radical structuralism, are explained and illustrated by a research study. By using the four different approaches to look at the same organization the chapter shows how the paradigms affect research in practice, what methodologies might be associated with each, and the implications not only of following each of the paradigms, but the richness of using several approaches to give insights into organizational phenomena. Thus Hassard shows how organizational life can be interpreted in qualitatively different ways depending on the type of philosophical assumptions employed as the basis for gathering information while also developing a new approach to organizational research, breaking away from 'mono-methods'. On a positive note he concludes that by examining and using the multiple research approaches of the Burrell and Morgan model we have opportunities to learn the languages and practices of rival communities and develop more suitable approaches for ourselves. Somewhat pessimistically, Hassard doubts whether multiple research approaches will ever be widely adopted by serious researchers, because of the constraints of orthodoxy which were discussed in the Introduction. However, it might be countered that at least some of the benefits of multiple research approaches are realized when different researchers examine the same phenomenon, each using a different approach. In this way, the benefits may be realized through a sharing of ideas within the research community.

One expression of orthodoxy in management research is the use of the natural science model. The natural science approach to research is well known and has been covered in depth elsewhere, so we have not included a detailed review here. However, the criticism that positivistic approaches have received in some quarters might give the impression that the natural science model should be held at a distance rather than embraced. Our purpose is not to encourage people to embrace any single approach, but rather to look critically at various paradigms in the light of their own research purpose. Hence chapter 3 considers the natural science model, but again in a way which prompts a review of our assumptions. Behling, acknowledging the shortcomings of the natural science model for social science research, identifies and responds to five major criticisms. He argues that the natural science model should not be dismissed. In any event, the approach is unlikely to drop from dominance in the near future. Yet there are two key inferences which may be taken from this chapter. First, those rooted in a 'softer' research orientation may usefully review their position. Second, those researchers very favourable to the approach advocated by Behling should understand the constraints and limitations it imposes. Indeed, what matters is not the abandonment of the model but the development of a thorough understanding of the implications of following a particular research path.

In chapter 4, in contrast to Behling, Dainty suggests that the pursuit of a natural science approach within the social sciences is a false pursuit. Exploring the notion of science he argues that science is defined in terms of the method rather than the subject matter under study, and that science is a matter of degree, not of absolutes. Alongside what is or is not science, Dainty considers why the natural science model is still maintained within the social sciences. Assumptions are again questioned. His conclusion is that one should look for methods to investigate a problem, not for a problem to fit acceptable research methods. To understand why this suggestion even needs to be made it is necessary to look not only at assumptions within the social sciences about research but also at assumptions about broader issues than research perspectives alone, such as the status of the management discipline, academic credibility, research funding, and power and politics within universities and more widely.

Some academic researchers may still be wary of the idea of an emphasis on the research problem first and placing methodology second. Doctoral candidates, for instance, have to satisfy examining boards who will not pass a candidate who does not use an acceptable methodology. But we are not arguing that academic researchers use approaches which are not rigorous.

Our concern is that methods used are appropriate to answering a research question rather than trivializing the question by imposing inappropriate, if orthodox, methodologies. The issue is really about balance – to combine the pursuit of a significant research question with methods which will give meaningful conclusions.

It seems, however, that when 'push comes to shove', as many papers in research journals bear witness, there is a tendency to lose sight of the significance of the research topic, and instead to emphasize the methodology, and in a way that suggests this is an acceptable substitute for studying a less than significant topic. Consequently, the importance of the research question is in evident need of greater emphasis. Indeed, in some management environments there is no choice. If you cannot provide answers to the question posed, then you cannot do the research. Management research, of course, is not only about theory building but has a practical purpose, too. Some, in trying to bolster the status of the management discipline, tend to deny the practical problem-solving arena and the range of possibilities within management research. But management is an area where, more so than with many other disciplines, research activity can find immediate outlets.

In chapter 5, the final chapter of part 1, Bennett identifies this range of research possibilities within management. He considers the nature of management research in detail; starting from the notion of solving a problem he highlights how this can have different implications for those pursuing academic research and those more concerned with practical solutions. He shows that while management research is concerned with systematic, careful inquiry of any phenomena associated with management, it may be broader than academic research alone. He distinguishes between approaches aimed at purely academic and theoretical problems, and those concerned with the day-to-day difficulties of management in practice, identifying a continuum from theory-orientated to action-orientated research.

Bennett also challenges assumptions, which are more specific to management research, in this chapter. Nevertheless, some of the important themes raised earlier are also found here. The author argues, for example, that what may yield truth may not be useful, while emphasis on specific problems may not help develop generalizations. More positively, he outlines possibilities, a theme which runs through all the chapters. Reviewing these possibilities helps us to explore our underlying assumptions about research. This may not be an easy process and the different conceptualizations do not always provide obvious answers. Part I does, however, establish the requirement to question assumptions before starting a research project, and certainly before considering research methods in detail. Time spent examining research perspectives might initially seem to be a luxury, but it will assist in yielding more fruitful and rewarding research outcomes.

1 Alternative perspectives in the organizational sciences: 'inquiry from the inside' and 'inquiry from the outside'[1, 2, 3]

Roger Evered and Meryl Reis Louis

Within the broadly defined field of organizational science, a number of different approaches to inquiry are in evidence. Inherent in each approach are basic values, assumptions, and beliefs about the nature of reality and what constitutes valid knowledge. These have, however, remained largely tacit, and as such have given rise to questions of research validity and utility, as well as to controversy and political behaviour within the field. Our aim here is to explicate some critical assumptions underlying the diverse approaches to organizational inquiry and to help bring order to what sometimes resembles a developing chaos in the organizational sciences.

Towards that end, we will identify and contrast two predominant approaches to, or paradigms of, current organizational inquiry. Following Kuhn, we use the term *paradigm* to refer to 'the entire constellation of beliefs, values, techniques, and so on, shared by the members of a given (scientific) community' (1970: 175), that is, the basic configuration of beliefs, strategies, criteria, and exemplars for acquiring knowledge. Most books on behavioural and organizational research, such as those by Kerlinger (1964) and Stone (1978), outline a variety of research approaches, methods, and techniques that constitute 'normal science' but do not directly deal with the fundamental issues associated with the value assumptions underlying the methods advocated. Kaplan (1964) is a notable exception, in that he directly addresses the central role of human values in the scientific enterprise. In this chapter we will deal with two fundamental images (or paradigms) of scientific inquiry rather than with the variety of methods and techniques within either image. A useful discussion of the notion of paradigm in sociology is provided by Ritzer (1975) and by Burrell and Morgan (1979).

We have called the two paradigms 'inquiry from the outside' and 'inquiry from the inside', highlighting what we consider an essential point of contrast. Most organizational research is oriented by one or the other of these two paradigms. Although it may be feasible and at times preferable for researchers to blend or cycle between the two, most organizational researchers seem to have implicitly adopted some particular inquiry-guiding paradigm. We hope our comments will help raise the level of awareness concerning heretofore tacit commitments to particular modes of inquiry. To help explicate the differences, we will present the paradigms as essentially polar extremes. We recognize, however, that there may be a spectrum of approaches in which elements of both are combined.

Our fundamental purpose in contrasting the two paradigms is to increase the general level of understanding and appreciation of epistemological issues in organizational inquiry. Such an appreciation has a number of potential benefits. Articulation of the epistemological differences should foster greater awareness of the appropriateness of different kinds of knowledge for different purposes; it may thereby help legitimate the adoption of alternative and more appropriate knowledge-yielding paradigms in organizational inquiry. It should also help reduce fruitless conflicts within the field, by justifying and providing a basis for tolerance of diversity and multiplicity in research design. Greater epistemological appreciation seems to be an essential prerequisite to developing an appropriate inquiry approach whereby researchers would explicitly select a mode of inquiry to fit the nature of the problematic phenomenon under study, the state of knowledge, and their own skills, style, and purpose. Moreover, appreciation of epistemological issues has implications for the evaluation of research products. It leads to a belief that the quality of a piece of research is more critically indicated by the appropriateness of the paradigm selected than by the mere technical correctness of the methods used.

Our discussion is divided into three parts. First, we introduce the distinction between the two knowledge-yielding paradigms through the use of a mini-case. The mini-case is based on our experience in entering a new organizational setting. It is not meant to represent an ideal, or even typical, method of conducting inquiry, but rather to provide a vivid sense of the distinctions between them. Next, we identify and systematically discuss differences between the paradigms. We conclude by highlighting implications of our thesis for conducting inquiry in the organizational sciences.

A PERSONAL EXPERIENCE

We became aware of the considerable difference between the two modes of inquiry during our recent experiences in changing jobs. When we joined the new organization, our initial experience was one of wanting to make sense of the associated confusion, uncertainty, and apparent lack of order. We felt a need to make sense of our surroundings in order to act. As newcomers, our perceptual systems were alert. We noticed things that old-timers seemed not to notice any more. We were there, noticing acutely, and needing to make sense of the organizational events impinging from all around. We had an immediate personal interest in finding out about the organization. We were *not* acting as laboratory scientists looking through a window at an organization from the outside. The detached 'value-free', external observer/scientists that we were trained to be became flesh-and-blood persons, involved in and committed to the immediate situation. We needed to know the nature of our particular organization – how it worked, how to get things done through it, how to recognize the critical features, how to avoid the personally undesirable outcomes, and what the critical language was. In short, we needed to know how to decipher the 'blooming, buzzing confusion' around us in order to act intelligently (James 1918). (For a theoretical treatment of the experience of entering unfamiliar organizational settings, see Louis 1980.)

Several thoughts occurred to us about our experience in this situation. First, most managers, indeed most organizational participants in general, would undoubtedly recognize the experience just described and acknowledge it as an essential ingredient of their normal day-to-day experience. Conceivably, the more creative and productive the manager, and the more turbulent the immediate environment, the more pertinent would be this need to understand in order to act. The desire to understand the particular organizational situation in order to act intelligently and effectively is, presumably, of focal concern in the field of management.

Second, we became aware that little of the published work in the organizational sciences had much relevance for us in trying to comprehend the new organization around us. The few concepts that did shed some light – such as integration and differentiation, theory X and Y, and bases of power – did not result from the classical 'detached observer' type of research. It seemed to us that the more detached the researcher had been in conducting organizational studies, the less pertinent the research findings were for our situation. Conversely, the writings of 'practitioner theorists', such as Fayol, Barnard, Urwick, Townsend, and Bennis, acquired increased saliency.

Third, we became aware that the mode of inquiry we adopted for acquiring knowledge in our organizational situation was markedly different from the academic social science model. We were probing 'in the dark' into the hidden organizational realities around us, in many directions simultaneously. It was a multisensory, holistic immersion. We did not form and test explicit hypotheses, we did not do a literature search, we had no elaborate instruments, and we did not use sample statistics or draw inferences at the '0.05 level of significance'. In comparison to the idealized scientific method, the process we used to make sense of our organization was a messy, iterative groping through which we gradually, though quite rapidly, built up a picture of the organizational system of which we were a part. The critical point is this –

despite our knowledge of organizational research and our training in scientific method, when 'push came to shove' we adopted another process of inquiry, presumably because it was more effective. Ethnomethodology, anthropology, and clinical methods represent systematic approaches to this mode of inquiry, though they generally lack the Campbell-Stanley rigour of traditional from-the-outside science.

Fourth, we came to realize that our roles and purposes as organizational actors-who-must-observe-to-survive were fundamentally different from those of the detached outsider researcher (as well as the participant observer of traditional ethnography). Our purpose as organizational actors was primarily in coping, action-taking, and survival within our organization. In contrast, the central purpose of the outside researcher (and even the participant observer) is in understanding, informing others, and surviving in organizations other than the one under study. We were experientially and existentially rooted in the organizational system (tasks, people, technologies, culture, rewards, etc.) that we were acquiring knowledge of, whereas the traditional researcher is experientially committed to another system (e.g. academia) and is at most a temporary visitor to the subject organization. Our inquiry, from the inside, was critically related to our own immediate organizational experience and therefore, it seemed to us, was likely to yield knowledge that was inherently more valid, useful, and relevant to the purposes of organizational participants.

Fifth, although our 'personal experience' vignette reads like an example of coping and survival, we wish to emphasize its inherent knowledge-yielding character. Inquiry and valid knowledge are fostered by coping activities, which differ from those of traditional from-the-outside science. Knowledge about organizations and management is continuously being articulated by managers (i.e. participants in organizational life). The essential difference between coping/sense-making/survival on the one hand and inquiry/research/science on the other hand is essentially this: the latter requires the coping organizational actors to be willing to tell as best they can what they know and how they came to know it – and to submit it to critical discussion. In addition, the knowledge discovered through coping is directly relevant to the purposes of the organizational actors. Inquiry does not necessarily require that any formal 'scientific method' be followed.

The distinctions we are making between coping and inquiry in relation to insider versus outsider are presented in figure 1.1. At the right side of the figure a spectrum of possible researcher roles is presented. We surmise that the critical aspect of this continuum is the degree of immersion of the researcher in the organization – that is, the extent of experiential involvement in and existential commitment to the organization. Operationally, it may translate into the extent of physical involvement in the setting.

In summary, we had experienced a mode of inquiry in which the knowledge-seeker is immersed and functioning within the organization under study. On reflection, we became aware of critical distinctions between a mode of inquiry from the inside and the more traditional from-the-outside mode.

TWO MODES OF INQUIRY

Inquiry from the inside and inquiry from the outside can both serve research purposes, but in different ways and with different effects. When would either be used? We address this question by contrasting the two modes on a number of analytic dimensions, summarized in figure 1.2.

We begin by comparing the researcher's role and relationship to the setting under the two modes of inquiry, and by identifying the epistemological and validity assumptions underlying the choice of role and relationship. Knowledge and understanding of an organizational situation can be acquired in two ways: (1) by studying, *from the outside*, data generated by the organization (and other organizations deemed to be similar in certain respects), and (2) by becoming a part of the organization and studying it *from the inside*. We can come to 'know' the Ford Motor Company or Texas Instruments by examining annual reports, employment statistics, union announcements, questionnaire results, or observational records; or, alternatively, by functioning within these organizations for a period of time (or talking with those who do).

Inquiry from the outside is characterized by the researcher's detachment from the organizational setting under study. The detachment derives, in part, from the assumption that the thing under study is separate from, unrelated to, independent of, and unaffected by the researcher. Astronomy provides an ideal illustration. The objects of interest are measured with instruments, the data are analysed to determine if logical patterns seem to exist, and rational theories are constructed to integrate, explain, and perhaps predict a multitude of facts. Knowledge is validated by methodical procedure and logic. Underlying the detachment of the researcher inquiring from the outside are critical epistemological assumptions: the researcher is guided by belief in an *external* reality constituted of *facts* that are *structured* in a law-like manner. This is what Habermas (1971), after Husserl, has referred to as the 'objectivist illusion'.

In contrast, inquiry from the inside carries with it the assumption that the researcher can best come to know the reality of an organization by *being there* – by becoming immersed in the stream of events and activities, by becoming part of the phenomena of study. 'Being there' is essentially what Heidegger (1962) means by his term *'Dasein'*. Knowledge is validated experientially. Underlying the immersion of a researcher inquiring from the inside is a very different set of epistemological assumptions from those of inquiry from the outside. Fundamental to it is the belief that knowledge comes from human *experience*, which is inherently continuous and *nonlogical*, and which may be *symbolically representable*. It is close to what Polanyi (1964) has termed 'personal knowledge'. The danger here is normally considered to be that the findings could be distorted and contaminated by the values and purposes of the researcher. This bias has been referred to by Russell (1945) as the 'fallacy of subjectivism'.

The researcher's role in inquiry from the outside can best be characterized as that of an onlooker. The researcher may use a telescope, microscope, or

Figure 1.1 Alternative modes of inquiry

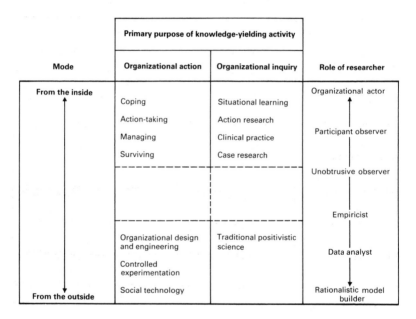

Mode	Primary purpose of knowledge-yielding activity		Role of researcher
	Organizational action	Organizational inquiry	
From the inside	Coping	Situational learning	Organizational actor
	Action-taking	Action research	
	Managing	Clinical practice	Participant observer
	Surviving	Case research	
			Unobtrusive observer
			Empiricist
	Organizational design and engineering	Traditional positivistic science	Data analyst
	Controlled experimentation		
From the outside	Social technology		Rationalistic model builder

any other instrument; the essential feature is looking in from the outside at a selected piece of the world. At the extreme is the pure rationalist, sometimes referred to as a speculator, who needs to collect no data from the world to carry out the task of theorizing.

In inquiry from the inside, the researcher becomes an actor in real situations. The researcher must attend to the total situation and integrate information from all directions simultaneously. The relevant world is the field surrounding the individual actor/researcher.

Another difference between the two modes of inquiry is the *source of the analytical categories* around which data are organized. In a typical piece of outside research, the investigator preselects a set of categories that will guide the inquiry. Hypotheses are phrased in terms of these categories, and only those data pertaining to them are collected. The life in the organizational microcosm under study is viewed through the lens of a limited number of categories, such as centralization and formalization, or commitment and job involvement. At the extreme, this may lead to a form of perceptual 'screening' so that the researcher sees only what is being sought.

Figure 1.2 Differences between the two modes of inquiry

Dimension of difference	MODE OF INQUIRY	
	From the outside	From the inside
Researcher's relationship to setting	Detachment, neutrality ⟷	'Being there', immersion
Validation basis	Measurement and logic ⟷	Experiential
Researcher's role	Onlooker ⟷	Actor
Source of categories	A priori ⟷	Interactively emergent
Aim of inquiry	Universality and generalizability ⟷	Situational relevance
Type of knowledge acquired	Universal, nomothetic: theoria ⟷	Particular, idiographic: praxis
Nature of data and meaning	Factual, context free ⟷	Interpreted, contextually embedded

The a priori categories may have been derived from personal idiosyncrasy, from theoretical formulation, or may have emerged in previous from-the-inside research. In the case of inside research, there are no intentionally prescribed categories to constrain the researcher. Instead, important features emerge through the individual's experience in and of the situation, as figure against ground in a perceptual field. Features are noticed and identified through an interpretive, iterative process whereby data and categories emerge simultaneously with successive experience. The process represents an experiential exploration and is particularly suited to early inquiry into new research territory. Inquiry from the inside is useful for generating tentative categories grounded in the concrete circumstance of a particular situation. Such emergent categories may subsequently be used as the a priori categories guiding the more deductive, hypothesis-testing inquiry from the outside.

A further difference is the *aim of inquiry*. The aim of inquiry from the outside is to generalize from the particular to construct a set of theoretical statements that are universally applicable. The aim is to develop understanding of classes of organizational phenomena, rather than to focus on particular instances in particular settings. Inquiry from the inside, in contrast, is directed toward the historically unique situation, what Lewin (1951) called that 'full reality of the whole, here-and-now individual situation'. The situationally relevant products of inside research serve both practical and theoretical purposes. They can provide guides for action in the immediate situation and inputs in developing hypotheses to guide inquiry from the outside.

The different modes of inquiry are also associated with different *types of knowledge*. The aim of situational relevancy pursued in inside research is served by knowledge of the particular organization under study. This knowledge of the particular is a necessary, but not sufficient, condition for praxis. By *praxis*, we mean a knowledge of how to act appropriately in a variety of particular situations. The aim of generalizability sought by outside research is served by the development of universal knowledge, or theoria (Heidegger, 1962). Habermas (1971) informs us that the original Greek meaning of *theoria* was 'looking on', in the sense of witnessing a particular public celebration. Later, it came to mean 'looking on' in the sense of examining the external order of the natural world and reproducing its presumed logical form. Over time, the meaning shifted focus from the particular to the universal. Praxis, on the other hand, focuses on the particular; it is knowledge that is infused with human organization and human interest, as represented in the situation under study. In the extreme, theoria implies a dissociation of universal knowledge from human interest (Habermas, 1971). And, at the other extreme, praxis implies a preoccupation with the idiosyncratic.

While both modes of inquiry are concerned with understanding everyday happenings in organizations, they differ sharply in what they consider to be *data* and the level at which they consider issues of *meaning*. In inquiry from the inside, the aim of understanding particular situations necessitates that researchers make direct experiential contact with the organization under study. Understanding the events, activities, and utterances in a specific situation requires a rich appreciation of the overall organizational context.

Context refers to the complex fabric of local culture, people, resources, purposes, earlier events, and future expectations that constitute the time-and-space background of the immediate and particular situation. Facts have no meaning in isolation from the setting. Meaning is developed from the point of view of the organizational participant. Inside research yields knowledge that is keyed to the organization member's definition of the situation, what Rogers (1951) has termed the 'phenomenal field' of the person. Researchers involve themselves directly in the setting under study in order to appreciate organizational phenomena in light of the context in which they occur and from the participants' points of view.

In inquiry from the outside, the aim of developing universal principles of organizational life necessitates stripping away the idiosyncrasies of the particular organization(s) studied to reveal what is generally applicable to all organizations. The separation of the universal from the particular is accomplished through several processes. With the aid of sampling, aggregation, and other analytic techniques, the uniqueness of individual organizations is randomized, controlled for, and otherwise 'washed', revealing the kernel of presumed common truths. The validity of such efforts rests on the comparability of measurements across observations, settings, and times, as well as the completeness with which the observational procedures and situations are documented. Hence the concern with instrumentation, specification, and precision.

Outside research is designed to be detached from, and independent of, a specific situation under study in a particular organization. The researcher determines the frequencies of, and associations among, events with respect to a set of hypothesized categories and relationships. Meaning is assigned to events on the basis of a priori analytic categories and explicit researcher-free procedures. Interpretations of the researcher are viewed as inherently confounding. The spectrum of organizational life is filtered through the researcher's pre-set categories; elements related to the categories are selected, coded as data, and simultaneously given meaning by the categories. As a result, data are considered factual when they have the same meaning across situations and settings. That is, they are context-free.

RELATED DICHOTOMIES

Before we discuss the uses of these two contrasting paradigms of inquiry, it may be instructive to comment on the inside/outside distinction in relation to other dichotomies presented in the literature. A surprising consequence of discussing this inside/outside dichotomy with colleagues has been the wide array of parallels that it has evoked.

Included among these were Geertz's (1973) distinction between *thick* and *thin* description; Hall's (1976) *high context* and *low context*; Chomsky's (1965) *deep* and *surface* structure; Pike's (1967) *emic* and *etic*; Kaplan's (1964) *logic-in-use* and *reconstructed logic*; and the distinctions between *acquaintance with* and *knowledge about* as variously construed by James (1918), Dewey (1933), Schutz (1962,1967), and Merton (1972). That there is a fundamental difference between the two modes of inquiry is further suggested by the fact that in many languages there are different verbs to distinguish among different ways of knowing. For instance, French has *savoir* and *connaitre*; German has *wissen* and *kennen*; and Latin has *scire* and *noscere*.

The distinction we have made has commonly (and regrettably) evoked the distinction between *ideographic* research (individual case, situational facts, and particular patterns) and *nomothetic* (general laws, universal variables, large number of subjects), originally made by Windelband and introduced later into the social sciences by Allport (1937). Overall, the ideographic/nomothetic dichotomy has been dysfunctional for the development of the social sciences, because it carries the presumption that only nomothetic research can yield general laws. Even in the early 1930s, both Lewin and Goldstein demonstrated convincingly that nomothetic laws were at best approximations, since they can never characterize any particular event or situation. However, events occurring in the unique or particular situation *are* lawfully connected, and systematic clinical research can extricate these laws by the study of successive cases (Goldstein 1939; Lewin 1931).

Most commonly and naturally, the similarity between from-the-outside inquiry and *positivism* has been noted. There are many varieties of positivism (Susman and Evered 1978); we acknowledge a close correspondence between the kind known as logical empiricism and our description of inquiry from the outside. In one respect, our contribution here is systematically to articulate the positivistic mode of inquiry both by direct description and by contrast with a recognizable alternative.

Our notion of from-the-inside inquiry has evoked a much wider range of analogies. It has been characterized as antipositivistic, phenomenological, enthnomethodological, experiential, existential, ideographic, participative, anthropological, qualitative, dialectic, pragmatic, subjective, intensive, soft, and unscientific. Each of these terms represents a 'high context' notion (Hall, 1976), and each is difficult to define with either brevity or precision. Although the notion of inquiry from the inside undoubtedly has attributes of each of these orientations, we refrain from equating it with any one of them.

The key feature of our description of from-the-inside inquiry is the physical (and therefore experiential) immersion of the researcher within the organizational setting under study. We believe the critical feature that characterizes the various inquiry paradigms is the degree of physical *and* psychological immersion of the researcher, and that other distinctions commonly discussed derive from this.

IMPLICATIONS FOR RESEARCH PRACTICE

As in everyday life, we in the organizational sciences need both ways of knowing and both kinds of knowledge to advance our understanding of organizational phenomena. Most social scientists, however, have typically espoused one or the other mode of inquiry. Inquiry from the inside is widely used by anthropologists, organizational consultants, case writers, and in practicum and apprenticeship programmes, as well as by the FBI. In contrast, inquiry from the outside is the basis for most articles published in the organizational sciences. Notable exceptions include the studies by Barnard (1938), Trist and Bamforth (1951), Mintzberg (1973), Pettigrew (1973), and Van Maanen (1973).

We might speculate on the reasons for the preference in our field for outside research. Perhaps it stems from a desire to have our field be considered a *true* science, which has led us to emulate the hard-science model of research. Despite the success of this model in the physical sciences, its limitations for the social sciences – particularly the management sciences – have become increasingly apparent and of concern in the past decade (see Lindblom and Cohen 1979). Research from the outside systematically overlooks critical features that often render the results epistemologically valueless. Such features include the definition of human *action* in specific settings, the actor's particular *definition of his situation* (world, field), the *human interest* (motives, purposes) of the organizational actor, and the *historical context* of the situation. Such shortcomings can be overcome by inquiry from the inside.

Inquiry from the inside, however, may appear to be so fuzzy that its findings often have dubious precision, rigour, or credibility. But, in turn, these shortcomings can be overcome by inquiry from the outside.

Organizational inquiry is currently characterized by two broad approaches. One is methodologically precise, but often irrelevant to the reality of organizations; the other is crucially relevant, but often too vague to be communicated to or believed by others. We need to find ways to improve the relevancy of the one, and to improve the precision of the other. It follows that we need to identify and refer to exemplars of good research – research that is both methodologically precise and grounded in real-world phenomena.

In addition to improving the quality of both modes of inquiry, researchers should explore ways of combining them, with the aim of securing the strengths of each while avoiding their respective deficiencies. Ways in which this could be done include:

Do both and aggregate Research studies in the organizational sciences require that both approaches be simultaneously pursued, either by different researchers or by a single researcher. Each mode offers distinctive advantages, suggesting circumstances (type of problem, state of knowledge, unit of analysis, researcher's purpose) in which one may be the more appropriate. Inside research is more useful for exploring organizational phenomena and generating tentative concepts and theories that directly pertain to particular organizations. By yielding in-depth knowledge of particular situations, it also more directly serves practitioners' needs. Outside research is more suited to theory-testing and developing universal and timeless-truth statements.

The choice of mode will no doubt depend on the researcher's personal training, cognitive style, and preference. A researcher who scores high S on the Jungian typology scale (sensing, S, vs intuitive, N) and who has had extensive training in statistical inference techniques is not likely to engage in inquiry from the inside. Similarly, a researcher who scores high N on the same Jungian scale and who has extensive training in anthropology is unlikely to embark on inquiry from the outside. Other factors, such as the prevailing reward structure, the particular referents and exemplars that the researcher has available, and the prevailing intellectual vogue, will also influence the choice.

One of the requirements for doing both and aggregating, however, is that good research of either kind should get published with equal facility. This requirement is not currently being met, there being a strong bias toward inquiry from the outside.

Alternate between the two modes In contrasting the two modes of inquiry, we have attempted to discuss the natural limitations associated with different ways of knowing. In the light of these limitations, we believe that to continue the single-minded use of one mode of inquiry that has characterized research in our field for more than a decade will produce feeble results – that is, results that are precise but irrelevant. Our ability to grasp the breadth, depth, and richness of organizational life is hampered by allegiance to a single mode of inquiry. Our efforts to develop comprehensive pictures of organizational phenomena are handicapped when only one (either one) mode of inquiry is sanctioned and practised.

A somewhat stronger approach than aggregation within the field (through journals) is that of alternating between modes. A researcher, or group of researchers, may continuously move back and forth between the two modes, selectively using the relative advantages of each as appropriate. A view is presented in figure 1.3 of the cycling between theory generating and theory testing, to suggest one way in which the two inquiry modes may be synerg-istically linked. Used in tandem, the two modes may help to overcome the natural deficiencies of each.

Develop a new kind of science   What is meant by the term *science* has been in continuous evolution for several centuries. During the late 1800s, a number of scientists, most notably Marx (see Bernstein 1971), Pierce (1931), Husserl (see Kockelmans and Kisiel 1970), and Dilthey (1914), came to realize that there were major epistemological problems in applying the physical science model of Science to the social realm. Dilthey delineated the nature of the 'cultural sciences' (based on historicity and interpretation) to contrast with the material sciences. The distinction between the two realms is most systematically addressed by Radnitzky (1973), who contrasts logical empiri-cism with hermeneutical dialectics.

Figure 1.3 Linking the modes of inquiry

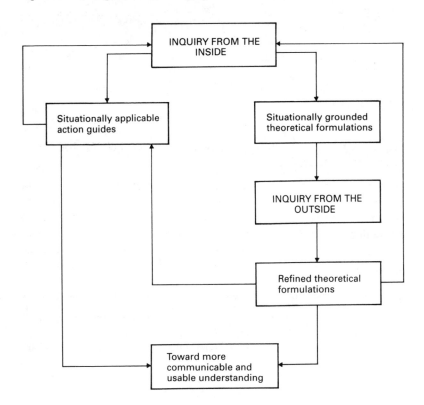

Since 19C0, a number of prominent social scientists have attempted to transcend the epistemological deficiencies of the traditional (from the outside) scientific method. These include Weber (1951), Lewin (1931, 1951), Piaget (1974), Schutz (1970), and Habermas (1971). Each writer has taken a different tack in attempting to reconnect universal knowledge with particular knowledge. However, the issue remains substantially unresolved. We need to develop a new kind of science that combines the rigour and standardization of positivistic science with the relevancy and groundedness of the alternative paradigms now in use.

The new science (human action science) that is gradually emerging is likely to be more actor based, experientially rooted, praxis-oriented, and self-reflective than the current image of (positivistic, objective) science. It is likely to incorporate both the American 'pragmatic' thinking of Peirce, James, Dewey, and Mead and the German 'critical' thinking of Marx, Dilthey, Husserl, Weber, Heidegger, Godamer, and Habermas. It will probably develop from inquiry from the inside and bridge toward the precision and generalizability of inquiry from the outside.

At present, however, there remain differences of the most fundamental kind between the two modes of inquiry. The problem of constructively linking these two modes (and hence the two types of knowledge) is of major significance to the organizational sciences. We hope that this chapter will contribute to the dialogue that aims to relate research more closely with human action.

We have tried to present a balanced view of the two modes of inquiry and to portray fairly their unique benefits and limitations. We hope we have shown why it is critically important for organizational scientists to reexamine continually the inherent epistemological assumptions associated with knowledge-yielding procedures. If we are interested in improving the quality, relevance, precision, and meaning of the knowledge we are producing, then we need to become more self-reflective about what we, individually and collectively, are doing in organization research.

NOTES

1 An earlier version of this chapter was presented at the annual meeting of the Academy of Management, Atlanta, August, 1979. This chapter first appeared in the *Academy of Management Review* 6, 3 (1981). It is reprinted with permission.

2 Support during the writing of this chapter was provided by grants from the Office of Naval Research Foundation Research Program at the Naval Postgraduate School.

3 We thank Phillip Butler, Carson Eoyang, Lou Pondy, and Jerry Porras for their encouragement and insights during the refinement of this chapter.

REFERENCES

Allport, G. W. (1937) *Personality: A Psychological Interpretation*, New York: Holt.

Barnard, C. I. (1938) *The Functions of the Executive*, Cambridge, MA: Harvard University Press.

Bernstein, R. J. (1971) *Praxis and Action*, Philadelphia: University of Pennsylvania Press.

Burrell, G. and Morgan, G. (1979) *Sociological Paradigms and Organisational Analysis*, London: Heinemann.

Chomsky, N. (1965) *Aspects of the Theory of Syntax*, New York: Mouton.

Dewey, J. (1933) *How we Think*, Lexington, MA. : D. C. Heath.

Dilthey, W. (1914) *Collected Works* (Vol 1), Leipzig: Teubner.

Geertz, C. (1973) *The Interpretation of Cultures*, New York: Basic Books.

Goldstein, K. (1939) *The Organism*, New York: American Book.

Habermas, J. (1971) *Knowledge and Human Interest*, Boston: Beacon.

Hall, E. T. (1976) *Beyond Culture*, New York: Doubleday.

Heidegger, M. (1962) *Being and Time*, New York: Harper.

James, W. (1918 [1890]) *The Principles of Psychology* (Vol 1), New York: Dover, p. 488.

Kaplan, A. (1964) *The Conduct of Inquiry*, San Francisco: Chandler.

Kerlinger, F. N. (1964) *Foundations of Behavioural Research*, New York: Holt, Rinehart.

Kockelmans, J. and Kisiel, R. (1970) *Phenomenology and the Natural Sciences*, Evanston: Northwestern University Press.

Kuhn, T. (1970) *The Structure of Scientific Revolutions*, Chicago: University of Chicago Press.

Lewin, K. (1931) 'The conflict between Aristotelian and Galilean modes of thought in contemporary psychology', *Journal of General Psychology*: 141–77 (Also 1935 in *A dynamic theory of personality*, New York: McGraw, pp. 1–42.)

Lewin, K. (1951) *Field Theory in Social Science*, New York: Harper.

Lindblom, C. E. and Cohen, D. K. (1979) *Usable Knowledge*, New Haven: Yale University Press.

Louis, M. R. (1980) 'Surprise and sense-making: what newcomers experience in entering unfamiliar organizational settings', *Administrative Science Quarterly* 25: 226–51.

Merton, R. (1972) 'Insiders and outsiders: a chapter in the sociology of knowledge', in *Varieties of Political Expression in Sociology*, Chicago: University of Chicago Press.

Mintzberg, H. (1973) *The Nature of Managerial Work*, New York: Harper.

Peirce, C. S. (1931–5) *Collected Papers* (Vol. 5; C. Hartshorne and P. Weiss, eds), Cambridge, MA: Harvard University Press.

Pettigrew, A. (1973) *The Politics of Organizational Decision Making*, London: Tavistock.

Piaget, J. (1974) *The Place of the Sciences of Man in the System of Sciences*, New York: Harper.

Pike, K. L. (1967) *Language in Relation to a Unified Theory of the Structure of Human Behaviour* (2nd revised edition), The Hague: Mouton.

Polanyi, M. (1964) *Personal Knowledge*, New York: Harper.

Radnitzky, G. (1973) *Contemporary Schools of Metascience*, Chicago: Henry Regnery.

Ritzer, G. (1975) 'Sociology: a multiple-paradigm science', *American Sociologist* 10: 156–67.

Rogers, C. R. (1951) *Client-centered Therapy*, Boston: Houghton.

Russell, B. (1945) *A History of Western Philosophy*, New York: Simon.

Schutz, A. (1962) *Collected Papers I: The Problem of Social Reality* (M. Natanson, ed.), The Hague: Nijhoff.

Schutz, A. (1967) *The Phenomenology of the Social World*, Evanston, IL: Northwestern University Press.

Schutz, A. (1970) *Reflections of the Problem of Relevance* (R. M. Zaner, ed.), New Haven: Yale University Press.

Stone, E. F. (1978) *Research Methods in Organizational Behavior*, Santa Monica, CA: Goodyear.

Susman, G. I. and Evered, R. (1978) 'An assessment of the scientific merits of action research', *Administrative Science Quarterly* 23: 582–603.

Trist, E. and Bamforth, K. W. (1951) 'Some social and psychological consequences of the longwall method of coal-getting', *Human Relations* February, pp. 3–38.

Van Maanen, J. (1973) 'Observations on the making of police', *Human Organization* 32: 407–18.

Weber, M. (1951) *The Methodology of the Social Sciences* (E. A. Shils and H. A. Finch, trans and eds), Glencoe, IL: Free Press.

2 Multiple paradigm analysis: a methodology for management research

John S. Hassard

INTRODUCTION

During the last twenty years, the literature of organization theory has been replete with assessments of the discipline's paradigmatic status (Silverman 1970, Rose 1975, Reed 1985). Several writers have presented models which outline paradigm formations based either on major theory communities or on prominent methodological approaches (Sanday 1979, Evered and Louis 1981, Clark 1985, Martin 1989). Frequently such assessments, on taking recourse to an historical outline of theory development, have suggested that organization theory, like social science in general, is poly-paradigmatic (Burrell and Morgan 1979, Pondy and Boje 1980, Morgan 1989a). As Kuhn's (1962, 1970) philosophy of science is central here, many analysts have also spoken of a 'crisis' in organization theory, with several paradigms being locked in competition following the decline of the orthodox systems-structure approach (Benson 1983, White 1983, Willmott 1989).

These developments have in fact been part of an explosion of Kuhnism in the social sciences, with Kuhn's model of the history of science, which is based on discontinuous periods of normative and revolutionary activity, being employed as a general framework for explaining changes in social theory (Friedrichs 1970, Bottomore 1975, Ritzer 1975). The popularity of Kuhn's work for social science has stemmed largely from the author's claim that research is validated not only by objective scientific evidence, but also by the consensus judgements of community-orientated practitioners. This is a description which has appealed to sociologists because it appears to question the belief that natural science holds higher authority than social science (Bryant 1975, Heyl 1975, Barnes 1983).

Despite the popularity of importing Kuhn's philosophy into social science, many problems have emerged from the transfer process (Pinder and Bourgeoise 1982). Difficulties have arisen because Kuhn's own statements regarding the paradigm concept have remained ambiguous. Problems of definition have resulted in paradigm schemes being located at numerous analytical levels, this giving the impression of inconsistency and contradiction. Indeed this confusion has provided openings for a wealth of both serious and satirical critiques (Shapere 1964, Masterman 1970, Popper 1970, Watkins 1970, Eckburg and Hill 1979, Mintzberg 1978, Wells and Picou 1981, Eilon 1981, Harvey 1982, Hassard 1988).

However, whereas many of the problems identified by critics give cause for concern, they do not, it is argued here, provide the basis for a complete condemnation either of this borrowing process, or of the development of paradigm schemes. In reply to Pinder and Bourgeoise (1982), one can say that the importing of ideas from philosophy has had a generally positive effect on organizational science, especially through increasing the awareness of epistemological issues. By employing concepts such as paradigm and ontology, organization theorists have developed sophisticated descriptions of community science; and notably through using social philosophy to highlight problems of research practice (e.g. perceptual selectiveness, community images of the subject matter, sociological influence of classic laws/theories). Several writers have noted the power of the paradigm concept for making us aware of the types of tacit assumptions that we, as organizational analysts, bring to the research process (Mitroff and Mason 1982, Carjaval 1983, Dobbelaere 1984, Willmott 1989).

This chapter, then, will consider some of the research implications of models of paradigm plurality. The paper outlines a research programme which has attempted to harness the concept of 'paradigm diversity' as a basis for conducting empirical research. In this study, several theoretical perspectives have been juxtaposed for the purpose of analysing work behaviour in a large public service organization. The aim has been to analyse work organization from a variety of quasi-exclusive perspectives, the goal being to gain a richer understanding of the organization than that which is available from 'conventional mono-method' research designs (Martin 1989). To achieve this, the paradigm model developed by Burrell and Morgan (1979) has been employed as the basis for realizing 'multiple paradigm research'. In the present study, insight into the organization is gained through employing the four paradigms of the model as methodological frames of reference. Results have been obtained by using a theory and methodology from each paradigm as the basis for research.

THE BURRELL AND MORGAN MODEL

Of the many models which have attempted to define paradigms in social and organizational theory, the one developed by Burrell and Morgan (1979) has attracted the most attention (Louis 1983, White 1983, Morgan 1989a).

Burrell and Morgan outline four paradigms for organizational analysis through intersecting subject-object debates in the 'theory of social science' with consensus-conflict debates in the 'theory of society'. Through this process four paradigms are produced: functionalist, interpretive, radical humanist, and radical structuralist (figure 2.1). The authors chart paradigms for organizational analysis by developing a framework which also takes into account major theoretical positions in economics, philosophy, politics, psychology, and sociology.

Figure 2.1 Four paradigm models of social theory

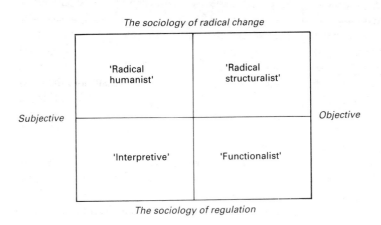

Burrell and Morgan dissect social science by reference to the philosopher's tool-kit of ontology and epistemology. They concentrate upon the metatheoretical assumptions which underpin theoretical statements, and on having identified such assumptions, plot various theoretical positions on their four-paradigm model. Thus, for analysing the 'nature of social science', they suggest that it is useful to conceptualize 'four sets of assumptions related to ontology, epistemology, human nature and methodology' (1979: 1, see figure 2.2). They suggest that all social scientists, implicitly or explicitly, approach their disciplines via assumptions about the nature of the social world and how it should be researched, assumptions being made about 'the very essence of the phenomena under study' (ontology), 'the grounds of knowledge' (epistemology), 'the relationships between human beings'

(human nature), and 'the way in which one attempts to investigate and obtain "knowledge" about the "real world"' (methodology).

Figure 2.2 A scheme for analysing assumptions about the nature of social science

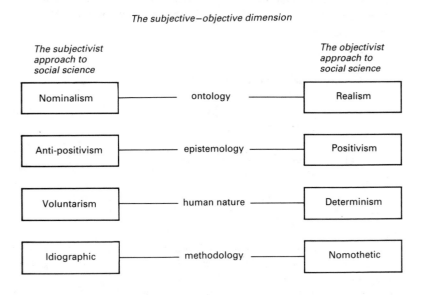

The subjective–objective dimension

The subjectivist approach to social science

The objectivist approach to social science

Nominalism	—— ontology ——	Realism
Anti-positivism	—— epistemology ——	Positivism
Voluntarism	—— human nature ——	Determinism
Idiographic	—— methodology ——	Nomothetic

On the other hand, for assumptions about the 'nature of society', Burrell and Morgan draw upon attempts by earlier social theorists (e.g. Lockwood 1956, Dahrendorf 1959) to distinguish between 'those approaches to sociology which concentrate on explaining the nature of social order and equilibrium... and those... concerned with the problems of change, conflict and coercion' (1979: 10). However, instead of invoking the usual nomenclature of order–conflict or consensus–conflict debates, Burrell and Morgan talk of differences between the 'sociology of regulation' and the 'sociology of radical change'.

Through polarizing these latter dimensions, the 'conservative' functionalist and interpretive paradigms are contrasted with the 'radical' humanist and structuralist paradigms. Conversely, with regard to the nature of social science, the functionalist and radical structuralist paradigms, which adopt an 'objectivist' and 'scientific' stance, are contrasted with the 'subjectivist' emphases of the interpretative and radical humanist paradigms. In presenting the model, the authors argue that these paradigms should be considered 'contiguous but separate – contiguous because of the shared characteristics, but separate because the differentiation is... of sufficient importance to warrant treatment of the paradigms as four distinct entities' (1979: 23). As such, the four paradigms 'define fundamentally different perspectives for the analysis of social phenomena. They approach this endeavour from contrasting standpoints and generate quite different concepts and analytical tools' (1979: 23).

Paradigms

In brief the paradigms can be described as follows:

The *functionalist* paradigm rests upon the premise that society has a real, concrete existence and a systematic character and is directed toward the production of order and regulation. The social science enterprise is believed to be objective- and value-free. The paradigm advocates a research process in which scientists are distanced from their subject matter by the rigour of the scientific method. The paradigm possesses a pragmatic orientation; it is concerned with understanding society in a way which produces useful, usable knowledge.

In the *interpretive* paradigm, the social world possesses a 'precarious ontological status'. From this perspective, social reality, although possessing order and regulation, never realizes an external concrete form. Instead it is the product of intersubjective experience. For the interpretive analyst, the social world is best understood from the viewpoint of the participant-in-action. Here the social researcher seeks to deconstruct the phenomenological process through which shared realities are created, sustained, and changed. For this paradigm the goal of developing a purely 'objective' social science is a specious one.

The *radical humanist* paradigm shares with the interpretive paradigm the assumption that everyday reality is socially constructed and maintained. However, for the radical humanist, this social construction is tied to a 'pathology of consciousness', a situation in which actors find themselves the prisoners of the social world they create. The radical humanist critique highlights the alienating modes of thought which characterize life in modern industrial societies. Capitalism in particular is subject to attack in the humanist's concern to link thought and action as a means of transcending alienation.

In the final paradigm, the *radical structuralist*, we also find a radical social critique, yet this time one at odds with that of the radical humanist paradigm in being tied to a materialist conception of the social world. In the radical structuralist paradigm social reality is considered to be largely independent of the way it is socially constructed. It has a hard external existence of its own. In this paradigm the social world is characterized by intrinsic tensions and contradictions; these forces serve to bring about radical change in the social system as a whole.

Critique

Although the Burrell and Morgan model has been well received within the organization theory literature – so much so that it has formed the basis for conferences on both sides of the Atlantic – those borrowing the model (notably to assess theoretical developments within the social sciences, for example, Griffiths 1983, Hopper and Powell 1985) have often done so with little regard to the model's internal consistency. As such, certain problems have been overlooked.

Pinder and Bourgeoise (1982), for example, note how Burrell and Morgan's application of ontology is misplaced. In a paper on cross-discipline borrowing – in this case organization theory borrowing from philosophy – they argue that Burrell and Morgan have adopted the '"non-standard" use of ontology that has been popular during the last thirty years' (1982: 13). They explain how this use refers to the 'set of existential presuppositions' of a theory, that is, to the set of assumptions that must be made if one is to accept a theory as valid. Pinder and Bourgeoise argue that for the past three centuries ontology has had a relatively stable meaning as 'the study of *qua* being, i.e. the study of existence in general, independent of any particular existing things' (1982: 13). Therefore, in the strict sense of the term, Pinder and Bourgeoise argue that 'it is not a question of ontology to ask whether organizations exist... whether organizations exist is a matter for science to deal with because it concerns the existence of particular things, not the nature of existence' (1982: 13). Pinder and Bourgeoise suggest that instead of talking of the 'ontology of organization theory', we must use the more correct phrase, the 'existential presuppositions of organization theory'.

Another fundamental issue is whether the intra-paradigm perspectives specified by Burrell and Morgan adhere to similar images of the subject matter. Just as Friedheim (1979) has criticized Ritzer (1975) for placing conflict theory and structural functionalism within the same paradigm, one may feel that Burrell and Morgan's placing of the action frame of reference (Silverman 1970) within the same paradigm as Skinnerian behaviourism is problematic. One could argue that the action frame of reference would be far better placed within the interpretive paradigm, despite the arguments the authors make for its meta-theoretical assumptions being 'characteristic of the subjectivist region of the functionalist paradigm' (Burrell and Morgan 1979: 190).

Also, whereas Burrell and Morgan invoke Althusser's (1969) thesis of the 'epistemological break' to divorce Marxian humanism from Marxian structuralism, in social theory this thesis is far from uncontested. For many writers there is in Marx's work an underlying unity, not a gestalt-switch from idealism to materialism (Allen 1975).

Of central concern to us, however, is that because the four paradigms are exclusive entities, we are faced with questions about paradigm incommensurability and relativism and about how inter-paradigm understanding can be achieved (Maruyama 1974, Hassard 1988). Like the majority of neo-Kuhnian models, we are given no indication as to how progress is to be signalled or standards met. We are left in a relativist vacuum: theory communities are pictured in hermetic isolation, and researchers are capable only of talking past their professional enemies. As a result, paradigms are attributed equal status in terms of their ability to explain the organizational world. For inter-paradigm movement, although examples are given of possible epistemological breaks (e.g. by Marx 1867 and, in organization theory, David Silverman 1970) explanation of the change process is never developed beyond a superficial acceptance of the instant-paradigm thesis (see Watkins 1970 on this issue). Indeed in Burrell and Morgan references to inter-paradigm understanding are rather confusing. While initially there is the assertion that 'the four paradigms are mutually exclusive... they offer different ways of seeing' (1979: 25), later there is oscillation between Giddens' (1976) argument that 'some inter-paradigm debate is also possible' (Burrell and Morgan 1979: 36) and their own, rather equivocal, view that 'relations between paradigms are better described in terms of "disinterested hostility", rather than "debate"' (Burrell and Morgan 1979: 36). This equivocation invites Friedheim's (1979) censure abut sociologists arguing for 'paradigm blindness' and 'paradigm bridgers' simultaneously.

MULTIPLE PARADIGM RESEARCH

As noted earlier, the present attempt to operationalize multiple paradigm research is based upon a study of work behaviour in a large public service organization, in this case the British Fire Service. In the main, the study concerns an analysis of work behaviour in one particular division of this organization, which we will call the Lowlands Fire Service. In this study, methods and perspectives characteristic of the four Burrell and Morgan paradigms were used, in systematic fashion, to illustrate the richness of data that can be produced when we deploy a range of philosophical assumptions as the basis for research. In the four studies conducted, the meta-theoretical principles of the model were used to assist the researcher in becoming familiar with four paradigm cultures. The approach to paradigm assimilation was one whereby specific social philosophies were accepted as the basis for immersion into the literature and methods of a theory community. Familiarization with a new paradigm was accomplished by seeking to 'bracket' phenomenologically the assumptions of a learned paradigm in order to accept those of another. The result of this process was a hermeneutic and essentially anthropological research method, the object being to produce authentic paradigm accounts from first-hand experience.

The research process itself saw three major positions adopted as methodological alternatives to the (functionalist) systems theory 'orthodoxy' – i.e. phenomenology (interpretive paradigm), critical theory (radical humanist paradigm), and Marxian structuralism (radical structuralist paradigm). In brief, the research programme commenced with a traditional functionalist investigation (a questionnaire survey) and then was continued, in three stages, by conducting studies representative of the latter paradigms. In terms of the Burrell and Morgan framework, the investigations started in the functionalist box and then continued in a clockwise direction.

However, before any formal research was conducted, one question remained – should the research cover one topic of work organization, or a number of topics? In developing the research design two possibilities were considered: either to focus on one single issue of work organization and to examine this from the four paradigm perspectives, or else to specify four separate research issues, with each paradigm addressing a particular topic.

While the former idea seemed to have merit initially, in that it would allow for straightforward paradigm comparisons, it was later found to raise certain logical and practical problems. The first was that while a particular research issue may count as an admissible problem for one paradigm community, it may not count as such for another. This problem raised logical questions regarding the translation of technical languages and meanings (Hassard 1988).

A second objection was that such an iterative approach would not cover much research ground. While as a methodological exercise it would be interesting – in producing four different accounts of the same topic – as an empirical exercise it would offer only marginal insight into the organization as a whole.

For these reasons, the second option was chosen; that is, for each paradigm to analyse a separate issue of work organization. Thus, four main aspects of work organization were researched: job motivation and design (functionalist paradigm), work routines (interpretative paradigm), training (radical humanist paradigm), and the employment contract (radical structuralist paradigm).

THE FIRE SERVICE STUDY

As each of the four studies was a fairly substantial project, only an introduction will be given here. The analysis will be restricted to explaining the decision processes involved in developing the methodology, and to giving brief introductions to the fieldwork conducted. Comparison of paradigm contributions, and commentary on the research process and the methods employed, is undertaken in the coda (page 36) and the conclusion (page 38). Further details of the fieldwork, plus a more detailed argument for multiple paradigm research, can be found in Hassard (1985, 1988, 1990).

The functionalist paradigm

For the functionalist study, and indeed for all the subsequent studies, the first concern was to choose a theory and a methodology on which to base the field research, and in particular to choose a theory and a method which would be considered faithful to the spirit of the paradigm. In the Burrell and Morgan model the four main theoretical approaches listed as representative of the functionalist mode of analysis are social system theory and objectivism, theories of bureaucratic dysfunctions, the action frame of reference, and pluralism. Of these, social system theory is the approach Burrell and Morgan place at the heart of the paradigm. It represents work characteristic of what Silverman (1970) and others have termed the 'systems orthodoxy' in organizational analysis (see Clegg and Dunkerly 1980, Donaldson 1985, Reed 1985). Indeed, by far the majority of work cited in the functionalist paradigm falls under this heading. This is material typical of that taught on mainstream organizational behaviour courses in business schools and university management departments. It is material that encompasses, for example, classical management theory, human relations, socio-technical systems, and contingency theory, and which is aimed at defining (law-like) relationships between organization design, work motivation, and industrial performance.

As during the access negotiations with the host organization it was agreed that work motivation and design would be considered in at least one stage of the research, it was decided, for both political and pragmatic reasons, to explore these issues as part of the first study, the functionalist investigation.

Research

In line with the above plan, the research commenced with a review of the current theories and techniques available to researchers who undertake this form of work. This review suggested that in the motivation/design field the job characteristics approach was the most prominent development. Notable here was work by Hackman and Oldham (1975, 1976, 1980) on the job diagnostic survey (JDS). Subsequently, the job characteristics approach was chosen as the theoretical basis for the functionalist study, with the JDS the main data collection instrument.

In brief, the research itself involved distributing the JDS to 110 firemen, the sample being differentiated into three groups by age and length of service. The aim was to discover how firemen evaluate the present work design in terms of motivational potential and job satisfaction. From the total of ninety-three responses (85 per cent) which were analysed using analysis of variance and parametric and non-parametric correlations, the research found statistically significant group differences for eight of the twenty JDS dimensions. In particular, the research highlighted a consistent pattern in which levels of reported job motivation reduced with age. Between-group differences were marked for dimensions of 'task identity', 'autonomy', 'feedback', 'experienced meaningfulness', and 'growth satisfaction'.

The interpretive paradigm

Having obtained attitudinal data on motivation, satisfaction, and design, the second stage of research focused on the work process directly. However, in accordance with the research plan, this study analysed work organization from a perspective representative of the *interpretive* paradigm, and thus by way of a phenomenological approach.

The empirical work for this paradigm involved an ethnomethodological study of the daily work process on a fire station. The study examined the main activities of the working day, but specifically how firemen take recourse to context-linked typifications in order to make sense of their activities. The research involved firemen either describing or explaining their work, the ethnography being produced from a data base of tape recordings of unstructured conversational materials collected during a period of non-participant observation. The analysis was based on the premise that only through the speech, gestures, and actions of competent participants can we understand the essence of their work, the aim being to let the participants themselves structure their conversations, descriptions, and analyses. In this way, an inductive approach was developed in which the contextual knowledge of the participants was treated as 'strange' to the researcher. Within the observation period, the researcher employed the phenomenological suspension method of 'epoche' in order to 'bracket' existing personal beliefs, preconceptions, and assumptions (Husserl 1931: 108ff.).

Research

In practice, the research used the methodology developed by Silverman and Jones (1975), in which subjects are required to explain activities in terms of how they are worked through. The fieldwork thus involved accompanying firemen during the working day and asking them to explain their activities before, during, and after each main event, the aim being to appreciate the 'stocks of knowledge' and 'recipes' they employ in making sense of and in (socially) constructing their work (Schutz 1967). The ethnography was presented as a description of the types of routine events which occur during a normal working day.

The analysis noted how routine tasks (which comprise about 95 per cent of total working time – Cunningham Report 1970) are accomplished within a context of perpetual uncertainty, and in particular how an absence of control over immediate future events, which stems primarily from the threat of fire calls, is accepted within a general culture of instability. The analysis found that although in the Lowlands Fire Service there exists an official time schedule to direct non-operational periods, its prescriptions are rarely adhered to. The practice instead is for task routines to be assembled at the discretion of the station officer. This is done so that tasks can be arranged in a manner that will make the day run smoothly without any temporal gaps, the actual process of events rarely being consistent with the official work routine. The research highlighted the 'because' and 'in order to' motives at the heart of this decision-making process (Schutz 1967). In particular the analysis examined those motives which are inextricably linked to the (strategic) relationship between the station officer and the divisional officer – motives which determine how the station officer will assemble the day in terms of the balance between 'real jobs', 'fill-in jobs', and stand-down.

The radical humanist paradigm

In terms of research contributions, the radical humanist is the least developed of Burrell and Morgan's four paradigms. For social theory it includes French existentialism, the anarchistic individualism of Max Stirner, and the critical theory of Gramsci, Lukacs, and the Frankfurt School. For organizational analysis, some steps 'towards an anti-organization theory' are outlined. For this latter area, Burrell and Morgan cite Huw Beynon's (1973, 1986) *Working for Ford* and Stewart Clegg's (1975) *Power, Rule and Domination* as characteristic of a nascent 'critical theory' approach to organizational analysis.

In developing a third research study, the writer attempted to conduct a critical theory analysis. However, in this study the links with social and political theory were made more explicit than in the works by Beynon and Clegg, with Gramsci's concept of ideological hegemony being used to derive interpretations of workplace culture. In line with Gramsci's thesis on 'Americanism and Fordism', the research highlighted the role played by administrative science in cementing organizational 'common-sense' (Gramsci 1977, Adler 1977). Specifically, the research described how administrative science is used to train 'promising' firemen to cross the frontier of control (Goodrich 1920). The research argued that administrative science is a particularly pervasive and influential medium in the hegemony process of fire service training.

In producing this analysis, two arguments were developed. The first was that the cohesion between administrative science and capitalist ideology should be seen as a symbiotic relationship (Baritz 1960, Fleron and Fleron 1972, Nord 1974, Allen 1975, Clegg and Dunkerly 1980). The second was that this symbiosis is fostered by the growth of management training in both the public and private sectors. As Clegg and Dunkerly (1980) suggest that a crucial function of management education is in 'reproducing ideology as well as [creating] middle class careers' (1980: 578), and that this ideology is produced through learning 'modern management techniques' at training institutions, the research wished to explain the ways in which such processes are accomplished in the fire service context. The fieldwork, therefore, analysed management training practices on a course designed to prepare candidates for promotion to first-line supervision, i.e. to the rank of Leading Fireman.

Research

In order to document these processes, the researcher enrolled in a 'Cadre Leading Fireman's' training course, the objective being to gain first-hand experience of in-house training techniques at this level. The research described not only the formal training methods used, but also the processes of presentation. The data base comprised mainly tape recordings of class sessions, especially of discussions between the instructors (fire service training officers) and the 'Cadre' leading firemen.

The research illustrated how the use of supportive educational materials within in-house training programmes allows the organization to keep firm control over both medium and message. Although course members were removed from their immediate working environments (fire stations), in staying within the bounds of organizational influence (training school), they remained subject to normal organizational constraints and conditions. Senior training officers were able to select materials which reinforced the logic of the authority structure. These materials were presented within a context in which established organizational rules were constantly reinforced as 'common sense'. The research demonstrated the ways in which instructors use administrative science to solve problems the answers to which are predetermined in the structures and processes of the organization.

The radical structuralist paradigm

Having analysed the work organization from the functionalist, interpretive, and radical humanist paradigms, the research moved finally to the radical structuralist paradigm, and here to a study of the labour process in fire-fighting.

For contributions to this paradigm, Burrell and Morgan cite the Mediterranean Marxism of Althusser and Colletti, the conflict theory of Dahrendorf and Rex, and the historical materialism of Bukharin. They develop a duality of traditions to show the influence of Marx's work on political economy and the more radical implications of Weber's work on bureaucracy. This duality is later developed into a formal framework for assessing contributions to a 'radical organization theory'. To this end, for 'radical Weberian' approaches, Burrell and Morgan cite works such as Eldridge and Crombie's (1974) *A Sociology of Organizations*, Mouzelis's (1975) *Organizations and Bureaucracy*, and Miliband's (1973) *The State in Capitalist Society*. In contrast, for contributions to Marxian structuralism, Burrell and Morgan draw upon the exemplar of Marx's (1867) *Capital* for analysing the economic structures of capitalism. Here, Baran and Sweezy's (1968) *Monopoly Capital* is joined by Braverman's (1974) *Labor and Monopoly Capital* in setting the scene for developments in labour process theory.

Indeed, following Braverman's (1974) work, the major thrust of research in this paradigm has been a revival of labour process analysis. In the wake of *Labor and Monopoly Capital* there has emerged a wealth of case study material relevant to Braverman's de-skilling thesis (see Zimbalist 1979, Nichols 1980, Wood 1982). However, in recent years the scope of labour process analysis has widened to incorporate *inter alia* issues such as post-Fordism, the sexual division of labour, and capital's use of time (Piore and Sabel 1984, Dex 1986, Nyland 1989). Much recent work in this area has developed longitudinal accounts and especially craft histories with, following criticisms that Braverman's analysis peddles managerial determinism, a stress on the voluntarist initiatives of labour within a control-resistance dialectic (Gospel and Littler 1983, Storey 1983, Thompson 1983).

Research

The aim of the research for the final paradigm was therefore to contribute to labour process analysis. In the present study, the focus was placed upon the development of the employment relation in British fire-fighting, and especially on 'the struggle for a normal working day' (Marx 1867). Research into the history of British fire-fighting, which was accomplished mainly through archive analysis, found the duration of the working period to be the most contentious issue in contractual negotiations between the union, employers, and the State (Blackstone 1957, Fire Brigades Union 1968).

The research focused upon changes in working time from the start of full-time fire-fighting in Britain in 1833 to the last major change in work systems, which followed the firemen's strike of 1977–1978. In explaining such changes, the analysis took recourse to a sectoral assessment by way of the 'fiscal crisis' thesis of O'Connor (1973). Recent contractual issues were pictured against the backcloth of rapid increases in militant state-sector unionism during the 1970s, and the analysis noted how the experiences of firemen were mirrored by workers in other state service sectors (Cousins 1984). The research outlined the mechanisms devised to redress such expressions of conflict, which in the case of the fire service was the development of the 'upper quartile' agreement following the 1977–1978 strike.

CODA: PARADIGM COMPARISONS

The aim of this research programme has been to develop an empirical methodology in which results accrue from several quasi-exclusive domains. To achieve this, the pluri-paradigm model of Burrell and Morgan (1979) has been used as a framework for accessing images consistent with functionalist, interpretive, radical humanist, and radical structuralist modes of analysis. As the Burrell and Morgan model is founded on the premise that a paradigm's reality is unlocked by metatheory, so we have attempted to draw upon a paradigm's most basic assumptions in order to obtain authentic accounts. In so doing, the programme has attempted to develop a new approach to organizational research – one which proposes a break from traditional mono-method forms of enquiry (Martin 1989). The research has shown how organizational life can be interpreted in qualitatively different ways depending on the type of philosophical assumptions we employ as the basis for gathering information. The result has been four studies yielding alternative 'images of organization' (Morgan 1986).

For the functionalist study, the research produced an account which was realist, positivist, determinist, and nomothetic. It adopted a perspective in which psychometric techniques and computer analysis provided a sophisticated understanding of the factual nature of organization. This approach attempted to divorce the role of social values from social research. Explanations were couched in a form promising practical success, especially through defining the concept of organization as a practical activity. The study sought generalizable knowledge of a form acceptable as rigorous, valid, and reliable. The research process drew inspiration from the scientific method, with statistical tests being used to discern those relationships considered significant for future organizational success. In sum, the study epitomized the classical quasi-experimental approach to organizational analysis.

In the interpretive study the form of evaluation changed dramatically. Here we found explanations which were nominalist, anti-positivist, voluntarist, and ideographic. Whereas in the functionalist study we found an 'organized' world characterized by certainty and self-regulation, in this second study we discovered a 'life-world' of social construction (Schutz 1967). Instead of computing statistical correlations, we described a web of human relationships. The analysis outlined how participants create social rules for 'bringing-off' the daily work routine, with personal actions being indexed to a contextual system of meanings (Garfinkel 1967). In sum, the research succeeded in de-concretizing the view of organizational reality created in the first paradigm; it suggested that organization is a cultural phenomenon which is subject to a continuous process of enactment.

In the radical humanist study we found a different mode of explanation again. Although this paradigm, like the interpretive paradigm, views the social world from a perspective which is nominalist, anti-positivist, voluntarist and idiographic, it is committed to defining the limitations of existing social arrangements. The central notion underlying the paradigm is that human consciousness is corrupted by tacit ideological influences. In particular, the common sense accorded to hegemonic practices (e.g. education, the mass media) is felt to drive a wedge of false consciousness between the known self and the true self. Thus, the fieldwork for the third study was concerned to understand how firemen not only create social arrangements, but also how they come, in turn, to experience them as alien, especially with respect to the power dimension which underpins the construction/enactment process. Above all, the research noted how the hegemony of the organization is dependent upon institutionalizing social arrangements which serve to constrain human expression and development.

Finally, in the radical structuralist study we returned to a realist perspective, but one directed at fundamentally different ends to those of functionalism. In this research the focus was upon examples of structural conflict rather than functional integration. The study analysed the strategic relations between capital and labour, especially in regard to the development of the employment relation. The research highlighted crisis points in the fire-fighting labour process, and described the role of state agencies in seeking to mediate contradictory forces and restore equilibrium. Instead of examining the reproduction of hegemony, the radical structuralist study illustrated the concrete actions of labour, capital, and the State in the labour process.

CONCLUSIONS: THE PROSPECTS FOR MULTIPLE PARADIGM RESEARCH

The fire service study represents a first attempt at developing a multiple paradigm analysis of a formal work organization; it has explored some of the empirical possibilities for paradigm heterodoxy in order to demonstrate how differing frameworks contribute to our understanding of the concept of organization; it has illustrated how contrasting images of the subject matter emerge when we base our investigations upon differing sets of meta-theoretical assumptions.

As several writers have described qualitative differences between theory-community perspectives (Silverman 1970, Lincoln 1985, Martin 1989), and many have cited meta-theoretical debate as the root of such differences (Pondy and Boje 1980, Morgan 1986, Willmott 1989), then it can be argued that models such as that by Burrell and Morgan (1979) offer opportunities to learn the languages and practices of rival communities, and in turn to conduct research characteristic of their forms of life (see Maruyama 1974, Hassard 1988). Through developing multiple paradigm research we may be able to realize greater epistemological variety in organizational analysis. Such a spirit of pluralism may indicate a move toward greater methodological democracy. The acknowledgement that in organization theory we possess a range of valid perspectives may signal that the discipline is in a healthy state rather than in crisis. The possession of multiple paradigms seems to imply that organization theory will never serve only one master.

Although we can identify many potential benefits from multiple paradigm research, the question of whether the methodology will develop brings to mind a whole set of problems concerning the institutional nature of academic communities. Whereas many writers have argued for developing 'multi-paradigm enquiry' (Pondy and Boje 1980) or 'multi-plane analysis' (Steinle 1983) through for example 'theoretical blockage' (Driggers 1977) or 'trans-pection' (Maruyama 1974), and although we have recently witnessed an undergraduate textbook which has adopted a more eclectic stance (Morgan 1989b), until now little empirical research has been conducted. Although sociologists have occasionally employed triangulation (cf. Jick 1979, Siehl and Martin 1988), this technique only brings together differing forms of methodology – it does not extend to research based on alternative meta-theories. While Allison's (1971) *Essence of Decision* was a landmark study in adopting alternative frameworks, it has not been capitalized on in terms of any formal social research.

For large-scale empirical projects, one reason preventing paradigm diversity may be that for multiple paradigm analysis we are not simply concerned to design-in *methodological* diversity, but are involved at a stage prior to this, that is, in specifying *meta-methodological* variety in terms of the differing values and beliefs held by theory communities. This may represent a problem in that, when it comes to analysis, research teams may feel pressure to display theoretical consensus rather than to offer a range of paradigm orientations and affiliations. Further, it can be argued that large-scale research projects are in practice conditioned by, for example, the nature of the access agreement, the 'acceptability' of research goals, and the need to produce hard, generalizable, and ultimately publishable results. These factors may act as institutional barriers to protect the more orthodox, positivist and, for organizational analysis, predominantly managerialist positions.

For the individual researcher, the institutional pressures may be even greater. A training in orthodox organizational behaviour may prevent the theoretical eclecticism necessary for transpecting between paradigms. Morgan (1989a) has highlighted the pressures facing researchers considering multiple paradigm exploration, especially in that such diversity may bring about fears over 'fail[ing] to get published and fail[ing] to get tenure' (1989a: 24). Morgan notes the reluctance of doctoral students to be adventurous, especially when faced with the ethos that 'there are few practical alternatives to orthodoxy' (1989: 24). This being so, the skills necessary to achieve transpection may be unlikely to develop as 'the control systems developed by journal and university departments alike, exert a confining, if well-meaning, hold on the jugular of scholarship' (1989a: 24).

Therefore, at present these institutional pressures may militate against the potential for realizing paradigm diversity in organizational research. Mainstream organizational analysis seems to display a tendency for 'monopolarization' and thus for 'psychological dependency on *one* authority, *one* right theory, *one* truth' (Maruyama 1974: 31). Although many writers have argued that in organization theory we require individuals who are specialists in more than one paradigm (Pondy and Boje 1980, Morgan 1986, Hassard and Pym 1989), present institutional constraints seem to reinforce Russell's dictum that 'what men want is certainty not knowledge'. If we argue that paradigm diversity is a desirable objective, we may need to develop academic communities which are capable of supporting a more eclectic approach to organizational research.

REFERENCES

Adler, F. (1977) 'Factory councils, Gramsci and the industrialists', *Telos* 31: 67–90.

Allen V. L. (1975) *Social Analysis: A Marxist Critique and Alternative*, London: Longman.

Allison, G. T. (1971) *Essence of Decision: Explaining the Cuban Missile Crisis*, Boston: Little Brown.

Baran, P. and Sweezy, P. (1968) *Monopoly Capital*, Harmondsworth: Penguin.

Barnes, B. (1983) *T S Kuhn and Social Science*, London: Macmillan.

Benson, J. K. (1983) 'Paradigm and praxis in organizational analysis', *Research in Organizational Behaviour* 5: 33–56.

Beynon, H. (1973) *Working for Ford*, Harmondsworth: Penguin.

Blackstone, G. (1957) *A History of the British Fire Service*, London: Routledge & Kegan Paul.

Boggs, C. (1976) *Gramsci's Marxism*, London: Pluto Press.

Braverman, H. (1974) *Labor and Monopoly Capital*, New York: Monthly Review Press.

Bryant, C. (1975) 'Kuhn, paradigms and sociology', *British Journal of Sociology* 26: 354–9.

Burrell, W. G. and Morgan, G. (1979) *Sociological Paradigms and Organizational Analysis*, London: Heinemann.

Carjaval, R. (1983) 'Systemic netfields: the systems' paradigm crisis', *Human Relations* 36: 227–46.

Clark, D. L. (1985) 'Emerging paradigms in organizational theory and research', in Y. Lincoln (ed.) *Organization Theory and Inquiry: The Paradigm Revolution*, Beverly Hills: Sage.

Clegg, S. (1975) *Power, Rule and Domination*, London: Routledge & Kegan Paul.

Clegg, S. and Dunkerly, D. (1980) *Organizations, Class and Control*, London: Routledge & Kegan Paul.

Cousins, C. (1984) 'Labour processes in the state service sector', paper presented at the *Organization and Control of the Labour Process* Second Annual Conference, Aston University (UK), March 28–30.

Dahrendorf, R. (1959) *Class and Class Conflict in Industrial Society*, London: Routledge & Kegan Paul.

Dex, S. (1986) *The Sexual Division of Work*, London: Wheatsheaf.

Dobbelaere, K. (1984) 'Secularization theories and sociological paradigms: convergences and divergencies', *Social Compass* 31: 199–219.

Donaldson, L. (1985) *In Defence of Organization Theory: A Reply to the Critics*, Cambridge: Cambridge University Press.

Driggers, P. F. (1977) 'Theoretical blockage: a strategy for the development of organization theory', *Sociological Quarterly* 18: 143–59.

Eckburg, D. and Hill, L. (1979) 'The paradigm concept and sociology: a critical review', *American Sociological Review* 44: 925–37.

Eilon, S. (1981) 'Paradigms, gestalts and the obfuscation factor in organization theory', *Omega* 9: 219–25.

Eldridge, J. and Crombie, A. (1974) *A Sociology of Organizations*, London: George Allen & Unwin.

Evered, R. and Louis, M. (1981) 'Alternative perspectives in the organizational sciences', *Academy of Management Review* 6: 385–95.

Fire Brigades Union (1968) *Fifty Years of Service*, London: Fire Brigades Union.

Fleron, F. and Fleron, L. (1972) 'Administrative theory as repressive political theory', *Telos* 12: 63–92.

Friedheim, E. A. (1979) 'An empirical comparison of Ritzer's paradigms and similar metatheories', *Social Forces* 58: 59–66.

Giddens, A. (1976) *New Rules of Sociological Method*, London: Hutchinson.

Goodrich, C. (1920) *The Frontier of Control*, London: Bell & Sons (republished by Pluto Press, 1975).

Gospel, H. and Littler, C. (eds) (1983) *Managerial Strategies and Industrial Relations*, London: Heinemann.

Gramsci, A. (1977) *Selections from the Prison Notebooks*, London: Lawrence & Wishart.

Griffiths, D. (1983) 'Evolution in research and theory: a study of prominent researchers', *Educational Administration Quarterly* 19: 210–21.

Hackman, R. and Oldham, G. (1975) 'Development of the job diagnostic survey', *Journal of Applied Psychology* 60: 159–70.

Hackman, R. and Oldham, G. (1976) 'Motivation through the design of work', *Organizational Behaviour and Human Performance* 16: 250–79.

Hackman, R. and Oldham, G. (1980) *Work Redesign*, Reading, MA: Addison-Wesley.

Harvey, L. (1982) 'The use and abuse of Kuhnian paradigms in the sociology of knowledge', *Sociology* 16: 83–101.

Hassard, J. (1985) 'Multiple paradigms and organizational research: an analysis of work behaviour in the fire service', PhD thesis, Aston University (UK).

Hassard, J. (1988) 'Overcoming hermeticism in organization theory: an alternative to paradigm incommensurability', *Human Relations* 41: 247–59.

Hassard, J. (1990) *Analysing Organizations*, Cambridge: Cambridge University Press.

Hassard, J. and Pym, D. (eds) (1989) *The Theory and Philosophy of Organizations*, London: Routledge.

Heyl, J. (1975) 'Paradigms in social science', *Society* 12: 61–7.

Hopper, T. and Powell, A. (1985) 'Making sense of research into the organizational and social aspects of management accounting', *Journal of Management Studies* 22: 429–65.

Husserl, E. (1931) *Ideas: A General Introduction to Pure Phenomenology*, New York: Macmillan.

Jick, T. (1979) 'Mixing quantitative and qualitative methods: triangulation in action', *Administrative Science Quarterly* 24: 602–11.

Kuhn, T. (1962) *The Structure of Scientific Revolutions*, Chicago: University of Chicago Press.

Kuhn, T. (1970) *The Structure of Scientific Revolutions*, Chicago: University of Chicago Press, 2nd edition (enlarged).

Lakatos, I. and Musgrave, A. (eds) (1970) *Criticism and the Growth of Knowledge*, Cambridge: Cambridge University Press.

Lincoln, Y. (ed.) (1985) *Organization Theory and Inquiry: The Paradigm Revolution*, Beverly Hills: Sage.

Lockwood, D. (1956) 'Some remarks on "The Social System"', *British Journal of Sociology* 7: 134–43.

Marceau, J., Thomas, A., and Whitley, R. (1978) 'Business and the State', in S. Littlejohn (ed.) *Power and the State*, London: Croom Helm.

Martin, J. (1989) 'Breaking up the mono-method monopolies in organizational research', in J. Hassard and D. Pym (eds) *The Theory and Philosophy of Organizations*, London: Routledge.

Maruyama, M. (1974) 'Paradigms and communication', *Technological Forecasting and Social Change*, 6: 3–32.

Marx, K. (1867) *Capital: A Critique of Political Economy*, Harmondsworth: Penguin (1976 edition).

Masterman, M. (1970) 'The nature of a paradigm', in I. Lakatos and A. Musgrave (eds) *Criticism and the Growth of Knowledge*, Cambridge: Cambridge University Press.

Miliband, R. (1973) *The State in Capitalist Society*, London: Quartet Books.

Mintzberg, H. (1978) 'Mintzberg's final paradigm', *Administrative Science Quarterly* 23: 635–6.

Mitroff, I. and Mason, ? (1982) 'Business policy and metaphysics: some philosophical considerations', *Academy of Management Review* 7/3: 361–71.

Morgan, G. (1986) *Images of Organization*, Beverly Hills: Sage.

Morgan, G. (1989a) 'Paradigm diversity in organizational research', in J. Hassard and D. Pym (eds) *The Theory and Philosophy of Organizations*, London: Routledge.

Morgan, G. (1989b) *Creative Organization Theory*, Beverly Hills: Sage.

Mouzelis, N. (1975) *Organizations and Bureaucracy*, London: Routledge & Kegan Paul.

Nyland, C. (1989) *Reduced Worktime and the Management of Production*, Cambridge: Cambridge University Press.

O'Connor, J. (1973) *The Fiscal Crisis of the State*, New York: St Martin's Press.

Pinder, C. and Bourgeoise, V. (1982) 'Borrowing and the effectiveness of administrative science', Working Paper No. 848, University of British Columbia.

Piore, M. and Sabel, C. (1984) *The Second Industrial Divide*, New York: Basic Books.

Popper, K. (1970) 'Normal science and its dangers', in I. Lakatos and A. Musgrave (eds) *Criticism and the Growth of Knowledge*, Cambridge: Cambridge University Press.

Pym, D. (1989) 'Post-paradigm enquiry', in J. Hassard and D. Pym (eds) *The Theory and Philosophy of Organizations*, London: Routledge.

Reed, M. (1985) *Re-Directions in Organizational Analysis*, London: Tavistock.

Ritzer, G. (1975) *Sociology: A Multiple Paradigm Science*, New York: Allyn & Bacon.

Rose, M. (1975) *Industrial Behaviour: Theoretical Developments Since Taylor*, Harmondsworth: Penguin.

Sanday, P. (1979) 'The ethnographic paradigms', *Administrative Science Quarterly* 24: 527–38.

Schutz, A. (1967) *The Phenomenology of the Social World*, Evanston: Northwestern University Press.

Shapere, D. (1964) 'The structure of scientific revolutions', *Philosophical Review* 73: 383–94.

Siehl, C. and Martin, J. (1988) 'Measuring organizational culture: mixing qualitative and quantitative methods', in M. Jones, D. Moore, and R. Snyder (eds) *Inside Organizations*, Beverly Hills: Sage.

Silverman, D. (1970) *The Theory of Organizations*, London: Heinemann.

Silverman, D. and Jones, J. (1975) *Organizational Work*, London: Collier Macmillan.

Steinle, C. (1983) 'Organization theory and multiple plane analysis', *Management International Review* 23: 31–46.

Storey, J. (1983) *Managerial Prerogative and the Question of Control*, London: Routledge & Kegan Paul.

Thompson, P. (1983) *The Nature of Work*, London: Macmillan.

Watkins, J. (1970) 'Against normal science', in I. Lakatos and A. Musgrave (eds) *Criticism and the Growth of Knowledge*, Cambridge: Cambridge University Press.

Wells, R. and Picou, J. (1981) *American Sociology: Theoretical and Methodological Structure*, Washington DC: University of America Press.

White, O. (1983) 'Improving the prospects for heterodoxy in organization theory', *Administration and Society* 15: 257–72.

Willmott, H. (1989) 'Beyond paradigmatic closure in organizational inquiry', in J. Hassard and D. Pym (eds) *The Theory and Philosophy of Organizations*, London: Routledge.

Wood, S. (ed.) (1982) *The Degradation of Work?* , London: Heinemann.

Zimbalist, A. (ed.) (1979) *Case Studies in the Labour Process*, New York: Monthly Review Press.

3 The case for the natural science model for research in organizational behaviour and organization theory[1]

Orlando Behling

One widely accepted view of the role that science plays in organizational behaviour and organization theory is that it functions to:

> establish general laws covering the behaviour of empirical events or objects with which the science is concerned, and thereby enable us to connect together our knowledge of separately known events and to make reliable predictions of events yet unknown.
>
> (Braithwaite 1973: 1)

In the tradition of Campbell and Stanley (1963), Cook and Campbell (1976), and Kerlinger (1973), most advocates of this view hold that good research is characterized by careful sampling, precise measurement, and sophisticated design and analysis in the test of hypotheses derived from tentative general laws. Popper (1964) labels this rigorous search for general laws the *natural science model* because it represents a social science approximation of the approach that serves the natural sciences (such as physics, chemistry, biology) so well. I will use Popper's label throughout this chapter.

Clearly, the authors of mainstream texts in organizational behaviour and organization theory accept the natural science model of good research. Those who include research methods chapters (e.g. Bobbitt *et al.*1978, Hamner and Organ 1978, Jackson and Morgan 1978) clearly follow this approach and generally appear to owe an intellectual debt to Kerlinger, a strong proponent of the natural science model. Some authors are even more definite in their advocacy of the model. First, Luthans quotes Berelson and Steiner (1964):

> Organizational behavior should strive to attain the following hallmarks of a science:
> 1 The procedures are public.
> 2 The definitions are precise.
> 3 The data collecting is objective.
> 4 The findings are replicable.

5 The approach is systematic and cumulative.
6 The purposes are explanation, understanding, and prediction.

(Luthans 1973: 77)

While Berelson and Steiner's points 1, 4, and 6 can be encompassed by all but the most radical definitions of good research, it is clear that points 2, 3, and to a certain extent 5, call for application of the natural science approach. Second, Filley *et al.* (1975) have discussed research methods in terms of 'levels of rigor'. Though they point out the dangers of undervaluing less rigorous research methods for exploratory studies, there is a clear implication in their work that the closer a study approximates the natural science ideal, the better it is. They also organize each of their chapters around a series of 'propositions' or tentative general laws.

Recently, however, questions have been raised regarding the appropriateness of the natural science approach for organizational behaviour and organization theory research. These questions do not arise from the traditional charges that much research on organizational phenomena merely verifies in elaborate and costly ways things that most managers already know (e.g. Gordon *et al.* 1978) or that it simply splits hairs to benefit the egos of theoreticians (e.g. Koontz 1961). Rather, the questioners hold that organizations and the groups and individuals who make them up differ from phenomena of interest to the natural sciences in ways that make natural science methods inappropriate for their study.

Some of the apparent dissatisfaction is implicit – for example, the increasing interest in models such as functionalism as replacements for or supplements to the currently dominant causal models (Behling 1979), and the growing use of intuitive participant–observer methods not merely for exploring new areas but also for drawing conclusions. But the dissatisfaction has also been made explicit by Behling and Shapiro (1974), Argyris (1976), Lundberg (1976), and most provocatively by Mitroff and Pondy, who write:

> We are conditioned by our scientific training to associate progress with greater rigor, greater precision, disintegrative analysis, more empirical documentation of a phenomenon, and the progressive exorcism of value-laden questions in favor of a purer pursuit of 'truth,' that is, a closer and closer fitting of our theories to the one objective reality we presume exists.... If you are spinning off ideas, you are allowed to be intuitive and nonrigorous, so long as you get scientific again when you begin testing your ideas empirically. But we believe that... increased openness toward imprecision extends *beyond* the hypothesis-generation stage. This is not to say that precise, rigorous, empirically testable descriptions and theories are out. But it does mean that looser, nontestable, nongeneralizable descriptions (e.g. poems) of social facts are equally legitimate forms of

> representation and, perhaps,... even more appropriate forms of inquiry than the normal model of science... perhaps 'science' is the wrong strategy for understanding social phenomena.
>
> (Mitroff and Pondy 1978: 145–6)

I share the frustration of Mitroff and Pondy and the other critics with the nitpicking and repeated 'back to the drawing board' retrenchments that accompany natural science methods in some areas of organizational behaviour and organization theory. I feel, however, that those who argue against the natural science approach should not go unchallenged, for two reasons. First, they typically present only one side of the question. Second, they usually consider only one or two of the important issues bearing on the usefulness of the natural science approach to research. Sociologists (Popper 1964), social psychologists (Gergen 1973; Schlenker 1974), and those in other applied social sciences (Campbell 1974) have explored a wide range of issues that deserve discussion in organizational behaviour and organization theory.

In the following paragraphs, working from Brown (1965), Gergen (1973), Homans (1967), Kaplan (1964), Nagel (1961), Popper (1964), and Schlenker (1974), I identify five key objections to the use of the natural science model raised in other social and behavioural sciences that have been or could be raised in organizational behaviour and organization theory, and I explain why they do not rule out attempts to apply the model to solving riddles in the discipline. These objections have been discussed under many different labels; I refer to them as:

1 *Uniqueness* Each organization, group, and person differs to some degree from all others; the development of precise general laws in organizational behaviour and organization theory is thus impossible.
2 *Instability* The phenomena of interest to researchers in organizational behaviour and organization theory are transitory. Not only do the 'facts' of social events change with time, but the 'laws' governing them change as well. Natural science research is poorly equipped to capture these fleeting phenomena.
3 *Sensitivity* Unlike chemical compounds and other things of interest to natural science researchers, the people who make up organizations, and thus organizations themselves, may behave differently if they become aware of researchers' hypotheses about them.
4 *Lack of Realism* Manipulating and controlling variables in organizational research changes the phenomena under study. Researchers thus cannot generalize from their studies because the phenomena observed inevitably differ from their real world counterparts.

5 *Epistemological Differences* Although understanding cause and effect through natural science research is an appropriate way of 'knowing' about physical phenomena, a different kind of 'knowledge' not tapped by this approach is more important in organizational behaviour and organization theory.

These objections are discussed in greater detail in the following sections.

UNIQUENESS

This objection holds that the phenomena of concern to organizational behaviour and organization theory researchers are specific to the organizations, work groups, or individuals in which they occur. If this is indeed the case, then attempts to generalize from a sample, no matter how carefully chosen, will be futile since no organization, group, or individual can represent any other, much less a broad class. If each case is unique, the idea of general laws is meaningless.

The phenomenological premises underlying Weick's concept of the 'enacted organization' (1969) and Pondy and Boje's call for 'bringing mind back in' to the study of organizations (1976) lead almost inevitably to the idea that what any one organization, group, or individual has in common with any other exists only in the shared perceptions of the people who interact with them. More directly, Newell and Simon's (1972) and Dawes's (1975) work on individualized processes in decision-making represents moves in the direction of substituting appreciation of unique entities for the search for general laws.

Much of the apparent uniqueness of phenomena studied in organizational behaviour and organization theory is real, but this fact does not limit the field to the description of singular events. To understand why, it is useful to follow Merton (1949) in differentiating between *empiric generalizations* and *scientific laws*. While both are statements of contingencies of the form 'If A, then B', a scientific law is stated in more abstract form than an empiric generalization, permitting the insertion of specific objects, events, and the like as variables and allowing the prediction of specific 'events yet unknown' from the abstract statement.

The fact that many works published in organizational behaviour and organization theory journals report empiric generalizations (e.g. 'matrix organizations work well in aerospace firms' or 'urban blue-collar workers are less likely to respond to job enrichment than their rural counterparts') rather than scientific laws does not justify the assertion that the field *cannot* yield scientific laws. (Nor should the statement be interpreted as saying that empiric generalizations are valueless; in fact, they serve as bases for practical decisions in specific situations and also serve as a kind of raw material for builders of scientific laws.)

McKelvey (1975, 1978) points out that the key to the development of meaningful generalizations lies in *taxonomy*, a theory of differences among organizations, together with methods of *classification* derived from it. Such an approach leads to two things. First, McKelvey holds, it permits the development of generalizations about important though relatively narrow populations:

> Narrower, more homogeneous populations would limit the generalizability of any single study, but this would be offset by gains in the definitiveness of the findings, the levels of variance explained, and the applicability of the results to the population. In short, solid findings about a narrower population are better than marginal findings of questionable generalizability to a broadly defined population.
>
> (McKelvey 1978: 1,438)

Second, generalizations about narrow populations defined systematically rather than casually can be combined into higher order generalizations. Because such laws must encompass diverse organizations, groups, or individuals, they cannot be as exact or explain as large a portion of the total variance as one might hope. Nevertheless, they represent a form of useful general law.

INSTABILITY

The opponents of natural science methods in organizational behaviour and organization theory hold that phenomena of concern to researchers in the field change frequently, making it extremely difficult to combine data obtained at different times in order to arrive at general laws, as is commonly done in the natural sciences. Mitroff and Pondy, for example, state:

> The phenomenon will never be completely described or understood before it vanishes and some new phenomenon supplants it. That is the guts of our conjecture that *science* is the wrong enquiring system for the social 'sciences'; it converges too slowly relative to the rate of decay and evolution of social phenomena.
>
> (Mitroff and Pondy 1978: 147)

Were this assertion correct, cumulatively developing knowledge about organizations and groups and individuals within them would be well nigh impossible. Instead, organizational behaviour and organization theory would be journalism – the recording and explaining of ephemeral phenomena – rather than science.

But this does not appear to be the case, for two reasons. First, as explained in the discussion of the uniqueness objection, scientific research seeks laws that transcend time and place, not empiric generalizations that often are specific to certain situations. Second, as explained by Gergen (1973) and Schlenker (1974) in their discussions of a 'continuum of historic durability', to assume that *all* phenomena of interest to organizational behaviour and organization theory are ephemeral is as much an error as to assume that even the most specific aspects of them remain constant over long periods. Clearly, some phenomena change more rapidly than others. Relationships with roots in human physiology and those reflecting performance limits of organizational and group forms probably change more slowly than those that are socially determined or simply 'common practice'. Thus, careful consideration of the likely durability of the phenomena studied should be a necessary part of decisions each researcher makes regarding the appropriateness of methods characterized by varying levels of natural science rigour.

SENSITIVITY

Opponents of natural science methods in organizational behaviour and organization theory charge that awareness of hypotheses in the social sciences inevitably changes the behaviours of the persons involved. These changes take two forms. First, such awareness may create *self-fulfilling prophecies* whereby participants change their behaviour to increase the chances of supporting the hypothesis. Behling and Shapiro (1974), for example, point out how researchers' attempts to gain managerial permission to study 'need for A' (which could be anything) in an organization can sensitize the managers to its manifestations. This in turn could lead the managers to reinforce 'A-seeking' behaviour on the part of their subordinates. The research process would thus create rather than measure the importance of 'need for A'.

Second, such sensitivity may take the form of what Nagel (1961) calls *suicidal predictions*. Nagel points out that predictions of a depression immediately following World War II induced business to cut certain prices, which led to increased demand, which made the prediction incorrect. Similarly, I have observed a case in which participants successfully sabotaged a part of a study performed by a researcher they disliked.

Although the sensitivity of some behaviours to the act of studying them is indisputable, this does not rule out natural science methods in organizational behaviour and organization theory for three reasons. First, the sensitivity objection assumes that natural science research is necessarily transparent – that the individuals participating in the study are always aware that they are under study and of the nature of the hypotheses being tested.

The need for informed consent in organizational research does undoubtedly restrict the degree to which researchers can keep participants in the dark, but it does not eliminate the use of unobtrusive measures and other means of increasing the chance that the behaviour of participants in research studies represents their real world actions.

Second, the sensitivity objection assumes that research participants control all dependent variables of concern to organizational researchers. Obviously, participants can change some things quite easily – for example, where they put a checkmark on an anonymous questionnaire; but the likelihood that they could and would change others in an attempt to support or reject the researcher's hypotheses is small. Work behaviour over substantial periods of time, organizational structures, and informal interaction patterns are all examples of important phenomena that probably do not change in response to knowledge of research hypotheses. It seems reasonable to posit a hypothetical 'continuum of discretion and control' to parallel Gergen (1973) and Schlenker's (1974) continuum of historic durability. I suspect that relatively few key dependent variables are close enough to the 'immediately and completely responsive' end of the scale to result in the self-fulfilling prophecies or the suicidal predictions the sensitivity critics fear.

Third, the sensitivity criticism holds only if suicidal and self-fulfilling effects cannot be identified and separated from the 'true' effects of the variables of interest. Even though our abilities to tease out these effects are limited, given reasonably sophisticated experimental designs it is usually possible to do so. Moreover, although a 'theory of reactions to theories' (Schlenker 1974) creates the possibility of a mind-boggling progression of theories of reactions to theories of reactions to theories, even greater ability to predict such phenomena could come with a better understanding of the widely recognized but poorly understood 'Hawthorne effect' and related phenomena.

LACK OF REALISM

Critics of natural science methods in organizational behaviour and organization theory sometimes hold that the study of social phenomena necessarily changes them to such an extent that the researcher cannot generalize from such studies to behaviours of organizations, groups, and individuals in the real world. They hold that such studies are, in a word, unrealistic. Stone (1978: 119–20) lists a series of such charges as part of a survey of the pros and cons of various kinds of research methods. Specifically, seven potential threats to realism can be extracted from his list. The first three apply primarily to laboratory experimentation. The remaining four relate to natural science research in the field as well as in the laboratory:

1 The environments in which laboratory studies are performed are often strange and potentially embarrassing. Thus participants may behave differently there than they would in more familiar circumstances.

2 The laboratory environment may be unrealistic because the researcher may not recognize all of the important aspects of the situation under investigation and thus fail to manipulate or control them or even to include them in the research task or situation.

3 Researchers rarely permit participants to show the full range of behaviours open to them in real organizations. Laboratory 'employees', for example, are almost never allowed to quit or to form labour unions.

4 It may be practically impossible to control or manipulate some key variables – for example, the economic climate in which the researcher performs the study.

5 It may be ethically unacceptable to manipulate other variables such as emotional stress, even though they may be crucial to the study.

6 For both practical and ethical reasons, research manipulations are rarely as strong as are encountered in actual organizations, even when variables can be manipulated. For example, 'pay' is usually a one-shot supplement to the subject's income in research studies, not his or her primary source of support.

7 Dozens of factors may interact in complex patterns to determine the behaviours of individuals, groups, and organizations, but researchers rarely manipulate more than three or four in a single study.

Such criticisms stem in part from a misunderstanding of what a controlled environment for natural science research need be. As Weick points out with regard to laboratory research:

> Because laboratory experimentation is much more flexible than most persons realize, the laboratory can be adapted to exceedingly complex and ambiguous problems. At the same time, many organizational problems are encumbered with extraneous and superfluous details. These details can be removed with little effect on generality.
>
> (Weick 1965: 745)

There are, however, two more important reasons why the lack-of-realism criticism is invalid.

First, three of the objections listed above equate the natural science model with the laboratory, when it is in fact possible to do rigorous natural science research in the field as well. Cook and Campbell (1976), building on previous work by Campbell and Stanley (1963), provide a series of research designs capable of minimizing key threats to validity. They point out:

As the examples in this chapter illustrated again and again, good quasi-experiments and true experiments have been conducted in the field in the past. They have reduced all or most of the threats to internal and statistical conclusion validity, many of the threats to construct validity of effects, and they have even reduced some of the threats to external validity and the construct validity of causes.

(Cook and Campbell 1976: 318)

Second, I believe the criticism is invalid because it assumes that a flawed study – that is, one which does not control all threats to internal and external validity – yields no useful information. In fact, many of the conclusions drawn in the discipline are extracted grudgingly from the weight of evidence from dozens of studies, most of them flawed in one way or another. Campbell has written:

Too many social scientists expect single experiments to settle issues once and for all. This may be a mistaken generalization from the history of the great crucial experiments in physics and chemistry.... Because we social scientists have less ability to achieve 'experimental isolation', and because we have good reason to expect our treatment effects to interact significantly with a wide variety of social factors, many of which we have not yet mapped, we have much greater need for replication experiments than do the physical sciences.

(Campbell 1969: 427–8)

It is likely to be the weight of evidence, not the crucial study that defines scientific law in organizational behaviour and organization theory. Constructive replications, designed not only to verify the results of specific studies within specific contexts but also to test for and overcome threats to internal and external validity, are necessary to establish general laws in organizational behaviour and organization theory.

EPISTEMOLOGICAL DIFFERENCES

Some opponents of natural science methods in organizational behaviour and organization theory argue that understanding in the social sciences should differ from that in the natural sciences and this, in turn, demands different research methods. Advocates of this position hold that natural science strives to generalize about *why* things happen by identifying causes. Social science, on the other hand, seeks to explain the *significance* or *meaning* of phenomena in terms of their implications for the unique social systems in which they occur and as manifestations of important social trends, forces, and conflicts. Max Weber, for example, wrote:

The analysis of the historically given individual configurations of ... 'factors' and their *significant* concrete interaction, conditioned by their historical context, and especially the *rendering intelligible* of the basis and type of this significance would be the next task to be achieved.... 'Laws' are obviously of great value as heuristic means – but only as such. Indeed they are quite indispensible for this purpose. But even in this function their limitations become evident at a decisive point.... The *significance* of a configuration of cultural phenomena and the basis of the significance cannot, however, be derived and rendered intelligible by a system of analytical laws (*Gesetzbegriffin*), however perfect it may be.

(Weber 1949: 75–6, emphasis in original)

Thus, for example, the events at Lordstown should be studied not simply as a chance to build a data base for generalizing about sources of worker demands for things beyond pay, good physical working conditions, and the like. They have meaning as a milestone in a major shift in expectations regarding work.

Although it is difficult, of course, to argue over the relative merits of different kinds of goals for organizational research, comment should be made regarding the methods normally advocated by those who see the identification of significance as a primary goal of research on organizations. Advocates of this approach argue that the best way to learn about complex social phenomena is to immerse the researcher in the organization under study and allow time for the development of intuitive appreciation of its workings. Unquestionably, since the studies of Roy (1952) and the Hawthorne researchers (Roethlisberger and Dickson, 1964), such in-depth observations have affected the course of thought about organizations. Nevertheless, such methods have important limitations. First, as Campbell (1974) points out, such research, improperly performed, is nothing more than a naive phenomenology that discards objective verification in favour of uncritical acceptance of the observer's experiences as reality. In the face of all we know about biases in the perception and interpretation of complex stimuli (e.g. Tversky and Kahneman 1974), it would be foolish to contend that any social research, natural science or not, is totally free of systematic bias. But the natural science approach has built in extensive means for protecting the researcher against personal biases and thus such biases affect the outcomes of natural science research less often than they do those of other methods.

Second, such research generates a highly affective kind of knowledge. Although there are notable exceptions (e.g. Leighton's *The Governing of Men*, 1945), the process of conveying this very personal information, no matter how potent, to others can entail substantial loss of both completeness and richness. Researchers often find themselves resorting to the stand-up comic's cliché, 'Ya hadda be there.'

CONCLUSION

Numerous objections have been raised to the use of natural science methods in organizational behaviour and organization theory. Yet none of the barriers raised is insurmountable. Admittedly imperfect and in need of more thoughtful application, natural science research methods represent an important means of understanding organizations and the behaviours of individuals and groups making them up. My attitude toward the natural science approach can be captured in a paraphrase of Winston Churchill's famous comment on democracy: it is the worst possible way to study organizations – except for all the others.

NOTE

1   This chapter first appeared as an article in the *Academy of Management Review 5*, 4 (1980). It is reprinted with permission.

REFERENCES

Argyris, C. (1976) 'Problems and new directions for industrial psychology', in M. D. Dunnette (ed.) *Handbook of Industrial and Organizational Psychology*, Chicago: Rand-McNally.

Behling, O. (1979) 'Functionalism as a base for midrange theory in organizational behavior and organization theory', in C. C. Pinder and L. Moore (eds) *Middle Range Theory and the Study of Organization*, Leiden, The Netherlands: Martinus Nijhoff.

Behling, O. and Shapiro, M. (1974) 'Motivation theory: source of the solution or part of the problem?', *Business Horizons* 7: 59–66.

Berelson, B. and Steiner, G. A. (1964) *Human Behavior*, New York: Harcourt, Brace & World.

Bobbitt, H. R., Breinholt, R. H., Doktor, R. H., and McNaul, J. P. (1978) *Organizational Behavior*, Englewood Cliffs, N. J. : Prentice-Hall, 2nd edition.

Braithwaite, R. (1973) *Scientific Explanation*, Cambridge: Cambridge University Press.

Brown, R. (1965) *Social Psychology*, Glencoe, IL: Free Press.

Campbell, D. T. (1969) 'Reforms as experiments', *American Psychologist* 24: 409–29.

Campbell, D. T. (1974) *Qualitative Knowing in Action Research*, unpublished manuscript, Society for the Psychological Study of Social Issues.

Campbell, D. T. and Stanley, J. C. (1963) *Experimental and Quasi-experimental Design for Research*, Chicago: Rand-McNally.

Cook, T. D. and Campbell, D. T. (1976) 'The design and conduct of quasi-experiments and true experiments in field settings', in M. D. Dunnette (ed.) *Handbook of Industrial and Organizational Psychology*, Chicago: Rand-McNally.

Dawes, R. M. (1975) 'The mind, the model, and the task', in H. L. Casellon and F. Restle (eds) *Proceedings of the Seventh Annual Indiana Theoretical and Cognitive Psychology Conference*.

Filley, A. C., House, R. J., and Kerr, S. (1975) *Managerial Process and Organizational Behavior*, Glenview, IL: Scott, Foresman, 2nd edition.

Gergen, K. J. (1973) 'Social psychology as history', *Journal of Personality & Social Psychology* 26: 309–20.

Gordon, M. E., Kleiman, L. S., and Hanie, C. A. (1978) 'Industrial-organizational psychology: Open thy ears O house of Israel', *American Psychologist* 33: 893–905.

Hamner, W. C. and Organ, D. P. (1978) *Organizational Behavior: an Applied Psychological Approach*, Dallas: Business Publications.

Homans, G. C. (1967) *The Nature of Social Science*, New York: Harcourt, Brace & World.

Jackson, J. H. and Morgan, C. P. (1978) *Organization Theory*, Englewood Cliffs, N. J.: Prentice-Hall.

Kaplan, A. (1964) *The Conduct of Inquiry: Methodology for Behavioral Science*, San Francisco: Chandler.

Kerlinger, F. N. (1973) *Foundations of Behavioral Research,* New York: Holt, Rinehart & Winston, 2nd edition.

Koontz, H. (1961) 'The management theory jungle', *Academy of Management Journal* 4: 174–88.

Leighton, A. H. (1945) *The Governing of Men*, Princeton, N. J.: Princeton University Press.

Lundberg, C. C. (1976) 'Hypothesis creation in organizational behavior research', *Academy of Management Review* 1: 5–12.

Luthans, F. (1973) *Organizational Behavior*, New York: McGraw-Hill.

McKelvey, B. (1975) 'Guidelines for the empirical classification of organizations', *Administrative Science Quarterly* 20: 509–25.

McKelvey, B. (1978) 'Organizational systematics: taxonomic lessons from biology', *Management Science* 24: 1428–40.

Merton, R. K. (1949) *Social Theory and Social Structure*, Glencoe, IL: Free Press.

Mitroff, I. I. and Pondy, L. R. (1978) 'Afterthoughts on the leadership conference', in M. W. McCall and M. M. Lombardo (eds) *Leadership: Where Else Can We Go?,* Durham, N. C.: Duke University Press.

Nagel, E. (1961) *The Structure of Science: Problems in the Logic of Scientific Explanation*, New York: Harcourt, Brace & World.

Newell, A. and Simon, H. (1972) *Human Problem Solving*, Englewood Cliffs, N. J.: Prentice-Hall.

Pondy, L. R. and Boje, D. M. (1976) *Bringing Mind Back In: Paradigm Development as a Frontier Problem in Organization Theory*, unpublished manuscript, Department of Business Administration, University of Illinois, Urbana.

Popper, K. R. (1964) *The Poverty of Historicism*, New York: Harper Torchbooks.

Roethlisberger, F. J. and Dickson, W. J. (1964) *Management and the Worker*, New York: Wiley.

Roy, D. (1952) 'Quota restriction and goldbricking in a machine shop', *American Journal of Sociology* 57: 430–7.

Schlenker, B. R. (1974) 'Social psychology and science', *Journal of Personality and Social Psychology* 29: 1–15.

Stone, E. (1978) *Research Methods in Organizational Behavior*, Santa Monica, CA: Goodyear.

Tversky, A. and Kahneman, D. (1974) 'Judgment under uncertainty: heuristics and biases', *Science* 185: 1124–31.

Weber, M. (1949) *On the Methodology of the Social Sciences*, Glencoe, IL: Free Press.

Weick, K. E. (1965) 'Laboratory experimentation with organizations', in J. G. March (ed.) *Handbook of Organizations*, Chicago: Rand-McNally.

Weick, K. E. (1969) *The Social Psychology of Organizing*, Reading, MA: Addison-Wesley.

4 Meaningful management research: the meaning of science and the meaning in science in relation to management research

Paul Dainty

INTRODUCTION

This chapter discusses the notion of science and the notion of meaning in relation to management research. It was prompted by two considerations. The first stems from the return to prominence in the United Kingdom of the rather well-worn debate about whether social research, which includes management research, can be considered scientific. This occurred in the early 1980s as a result of the Secretary of State for Education, Keith Joseph, expressing doubt that the social sciences were scientific, as a result of which the major government social research financing body subsequently dropped 'science' from its title. The second, perhaps more important, consideration is whether the present methods we use in our strivings to be 'scientific' do, in fact, have meaning. The treatment of the subject is brief, but its value lies in raising questions about how and what we are really trying to accomplish.

SCIENCE AND SOCIAL RESEARCH

Let us begin by considering whether the word science has any applicability to management research, as management studies are often subsumed under the umbrella of social studies. The question of management science is perhaps a little trickier in that management research has managed to carve a niche where it has difficulty not only in claiming to be scientific, but in some instances, even mildly academic. Nevertheless, management research suffers from many of the difficulties of social research, especially in those disciplines primarily concerned with human behaviour. Thus we can justifiably look at the problems of social research in general because they apply to most forms of management research.

However, before we look at these problems, it is perhaps worth passing a fleeting comment to those wincing at the thought of being confronted with another assessment of the scientific status of social studies. Few new issues are raised here, but the task is worth undertaking because the debate, as implied above, is no longer confined only to the academic community, but has become a symbolic one that some may feel has wider implications for the status of social studies, including management research.

The debate about the nature of scientific study in the social sciences is a tacky one, although on the surface it looks fairly straightforward – formal statements about the nature of scientific research and theory are fairly easy to come by. It is not too controversial, for instance, to argue that the objective of any branch of study is to offer knowledge in the sense of establishing a body of facts in which we can have confidence. Very crudely stated, such knowledge may be of two types: description, in the sense of showing us what a particular area of existence looks like, and explanation, in the sense of offering reasons why one event occurs rather than another. Both description and explanation require the use of a set of concepts and the assumption of a set of propositions according to which the concepts are interrelated. This is usually what is meant by theory which is defined by Roberts as 'an inter-related set of propositions cast in terms of a particular conceptual vocabulary' (Roberts 1973). Additionally, the notion that theory should have a predictive element is often assumed in the definition.

A science can be seen as a discipline which is concerned with establishing such theory. In the natural sciences, there has been little real doubt that this has been frequently accomplished. In the social sciences, of course, there is much less confidence as to whether this has been achieved. There is concern about the 'scientificness' of our disciplines and the literature is riddled with the self-conscious search for ways of bringing the social sciences closer to the natural sciences. To suggest that this soul-searching has a long history would be an understatement. The striving for a positivistic science, in the sense of allowing for the clear, rigorous, and reliable collection of data and permitting the testing of empirical hypotheses in a logically consistent manner, goes back at least as far as J. S. Mill. For some, this striving continues, although for me it has stopped at a position which is exemplified by Mann, who argues that attempts to make comparisons between the natural sciences and the scientificness of the social sciences are sterile. He believes that science is better defined in terms of method rather than the subject matter under study, and that science is a matter of degree rather than an absolute 'is' or 'is not' (Mann 1976). It is true that for the most part the social sciences are concerned with probabilities rather than certainties; but Mann maintains that the fact that you cannot make absolutely definite causal links between factors does not in any way detract from disciplines like ours being a science, as most sciences today are concerned with probabilities rather than certainties.

This, he argues, means that it is possible to carry out scientific work in any field at all so long as scientific method is used. Mann quotes Lundberg, who maintains that all that the term science as applied to a particular field comes to mean is a field which has been studied according to scientific method. He goes on, 'If our knowledge of a certain field has been derived according to this method and if that knowledge is applicable to this field for the purpose of prediction then that body of knowledge may properly be designated a science regardless of the nature of the subject matter'. The test of the thoroughness (or success) with which the method has been applied is found in our ability to predict the behaviour of classes of phenomena under given conditions. Thus, instead of just saying that some fields of enquiry are scientific and others are not, we should say that some may be more scientific than others because of the sophistication of the method used.

Anyone feeling that the statements of the last paragraph wrap the debate up neatly will find their sense of security short lived. The above, of course, is controversial and is far from being a generally accepted principle. Nevertheless, for me it is a plausible position for those in the social sciences to adopt. Perhaps the real difficulties arise when one then attempts to explore further what is meant by scientific method. Mann quotes Pearson who maintains that the person who classifies facts of any kind whatever, who sees their mutual relation and describes their sequence, is applying the scientific method and is a person of science. He adds that to qualify as the scientific study of social behaviour, behavioural disciplines must observe systematically, classify systematically, and interpret systematically. The better they do these three things the more they can claim to be sciences.

However, the problem with this, as some would argue, is that it does not take us any further away from the notions of a positivistic science. It might not be as positivistic as some would like, but it leans in that direction. Yet even this is more normative than what is achieved in reality. The chances of ever establishing an objective, value-free, scientific study of social relationships with something even vaguely close to laws formulated from propositions based on data which is accurate, sensitive, reliable, measurable, and testable, are pretty slim.

THE DANGERS IN POSITIVISM

The reason why such a possibility is fairly remote, as we all know, is because what distinguishes social research from other scientific pursuits is the complex phenomena of human behaviour and experience. This poses many more problems in terms of methods of data collection and hypothesis evaluation in the social sciences than it does in the natural sciences.

However, rather than encouraging social scientists to cast their covetous eyes away from the natural sciences, the problems have merely encouraged some to become more entrenched. The further doubts cast by the political establishment may only serve to strengthen the resolve of some to entrench a little more. This would be misguided for two reasons in particular.

First, much that is passed off as being 'scientific' is actually ideological. This becomes evident if one accepts that no branch of science can be considered a 'pure' science, or notes that the natural sciences are often plagued with problems of uncontrollable variables. Astronomy, for instance, is widely accepted as a science, but measurement, observation, and the manipulation of variables (such as planets) is hardly straightforward. If we resort to the earlier argument, that branches of study should be seen in terms of degrees of scientificness, depending on the extent to which they employ scientific method, then we find further problems. Crick, in the field of politics, argues that methodology is most often a retrospective way of describing what we did to discover truths in particular situations. Science is itself largely a traditional body of knowledge and the modifications by which one theory gradually gives way to a new one are often the product of the imagination and intuition rather than the manipulation of a fixed canon of methods (Crick 1971). It is coming to be realized, argues Crick, that there are no general rules of method that can guarantee the discovery of new and valid knowledge.

While I would not go so far as to argue that there are no criteria by which we should judge research pursuits, nevertheless what comes to be accepted as scientific depends as much on dominant arguments as it does on any absolutes. I am all for engaging in the ideological debate, and all for claiming that my discipline is as scientific as any other, especially if the loss of status means loss of government funding, but it should be seen for what it is. The word 'science' has a high ideological content, but this should not detract from the real search for the understanding and describing of human activity.

That it does detract, and this is the second, more important argument, is evident from the continued need to criticize the influence of positivism. The energy devoted to this should be unnecessary, but positivism is still rooted in the psyche of the academic management establishment as if it is the lodestar of management research. Yet many writers have noted, almost to the point of monotony, that we are often hindered by methodological preoccupations which always disguise and often inhibit actual generalizations. As far back as 1962, Bottomore was complaining of the undesirable growth of trivial, repetitive investigations in which rigour and calculation are equalled only by the futility of the conclusions. The management journals hardly suggest there have been radical changes since then. As Phillips argues, the concern to be regarded as scientific has led to an overemphasis on certain types of research methods to the exclusion of others (Phillips 1971). He is particularly critical of the strong emphasis on the quantification of data and over-utilization of various statistical procedures, which the pursuit of scientificness has generated.

The cling to positivism, especially in management research, has possibly been partly encouraged by the status position of the management discipline. Some of what passes off as serious management research has really little claim to being so. Consequently, I wonder whether some academics have been pushed towards a more positivistic stance in an attempt to distance themselves from some areas of the field. This is unfortunate because the main criticisms levelled against management research have not, necessarily, much to do with the debate raised here. These criticisms are that management research is 'problem solving', and problem solving with the interests of one particular group in mind. In other words, they are criticisms of the objectivity and purpose of research which, presumably, all serious researchers would accept anyway. But this should not be confused with the notion that any move away from positivistic methods means that management research must therefore be more biased, or trivial, or that a slavish adherence to positivistic methods ensures that these problems are overcome.

MEANING AND SOCIAL RESEARCH

A disenchantment with 'scientificness' has led to a greater concern in some quarters with the question of meaning, both on the part of the researcher and on the part of the interviewed. Verbal responses have been criticized, ever since La Piere's (1933) study, as a poor substitute for actually observing behaviour. But verbal responses may also mislead us into believing that because the words used by interviewer and interviewee are the same, then we also have communicated our feelings, beliefs, or attitudes. Obviously, I am not by any means the first to raise meaning as important in management research. There is, of course, the fairly long tradition of the social action approach. But the social action approach, or the importance of understanding meaning, has far from gained ascendency. Yet such an approach, especially in behavioural management research, would seem to be more appropriate than many other approaches.

But are these our main problems? Are the main issues being slightly side-stepped here, and am I dismissing, in a round about way, the importance of reliability and validity in data collection methods, and dodging problems of measurement? For instance, what of the concern of Hauser (quoted in Phillips 1971) and others that perhaps the major block to progress in research in the social sciences is the problem of adequate measurement? Hauser argues that it is inadequate measurement more than inadequate concept or hypotheses formulation that has plagued social researchers and prevented fuller explanations of the variances with which they are confounded. Indeed, he notes that the problems of obtaining precise enough measurements of the items with which we work has probably retarded sociology (for instance) more than the absence of more powerful analytical procedures.

While these problems and those of reliability and validity are discussed in all methodological textbooks, they seldom seem to be given much attention in actual reports of research activities. One of the reasons for this, it would seem to me, is that they are considerations that can be far from easily and mechanically applied to data collection techniques. This is the opposite of the impression sometimes given by some advocates of positivistic research.

Nevertheless, the point is not that measurement is unimportant but that, despite the problems we have with it, measurement has often been emphasized over and above attempts to understand the meaning and significance a respondent attaches to his/her social situation. I am not saying that we should not be attempting to measure, but it would seem to be a little pointless to measure the wrong things. The dominant emphasis is still on quantifying first, and worrying about what we are quantifying secondly.

Let me scotch, before we go any further, any lingering feelings readers might have that I am arguing for the complete abandonment of positivistic notions, or even implying we should ignore the kind of principles I outlined earlier in relation to scientific method. This would not only be unrealistic but also misguided. Rather, my argument is that we should generally accept a greater degree of flexibility in deciding on research approaches, and question, or at least be aware of, some of the assumptions that underly them. This is not the slippery slope to research anarchy, but the only way I see for us to progress. For instance, one of the basic assumptions of positivism is that there is order 'out there', in relation to the phenomenon we study. We may, of course, conclude that there *is* order. But failing to acknowledge that there may not be, or at least acknowledge that order may not be as easily identifiable as some of the simple models produced even by quite eminent researchers (possibly as a result of the pressure to find order) detracts from, rather than adds to, the subject knowledge. If we are on a slippery slope we are often kept there by simple assumptions and even more simple models, the questioning of which does not lead us into anarchy, but away from ignorance.

The problems we face in trying to understand, let us say, organizational behaviour, are so great that without the acceptance of new approaches we are unlikely to make much progress in a number of areas. Let me use as an example my research. My project is concerned with the feelings, experiences, and to some extent work behaviour of managers who are in organizations that are in a state of decline or contraction. Even if one did start from a point of wishing to study the area in a purely positivistic way, the restrictions imposed by the nature of the subject matter make such an approach almost impossible. For instance, it is not possible in the first place to identify easily the population of such managers. Even if the population could be identified, getting access to a random sample would be just as difficult; companies are often reluctant to give researchers access to their managers even in good times, never mind when things are difficult and such companies are experiencing upheaval and change. Even if one does manage to get access to companies in this state, which managers you would want to see and how you are allowed to collect data from them is often further restricted. It is not entirely a case of accepting what you can get, but one's freedom to manoeuvre is far from great. Moreover, case studies may not be possible either, as the number of managers you are given access to in any one company may be too small.

On the basis of the above, even readers with only a tendency toward, rather than full-blooded support for, positivistic notions might doubt whether the subject is researchable. It might be argued that this is especially true for doctoral research, where notions of a research training are often (and rightly so in my opinion) of paramount consideration. But while such notions are important they should not imply a rigid adherence to certain methodologies and approaches. That the researchability of such a subject should be questioned in the first place is because of the generally-held topsy-turvy assumptions about what is important. It seems strange that, in general, the emphasis is on how orthodoxly a subject can be studied, rather than on how important it is as a subject. Certainly the student should be able to demonstrate a knowledge of the 'traditional', but surely the more important consideration is whether he/she can find ways of studying particular important phenomena, not whether he/she can find phenomena of importance to fit traditional methodological moulds.

METHODOLOGY AND CIRCUMSTANCE

I have been particularly critical of notions of positivistic research, of which survey methods perhaps best complement such an orientation. But some of the same criticisms could equally be applied to those who rigidly advocate ethnographic methods. Nevertheless, my main argument, and one which is just as appropriate to research pursuits that contain notions of 'training', is that the methodological approach one should adopt is the one that is best for a particular circumstance. As Sapsford and Evans point out, ideal cases of experimental, survey, or ethnographic studies are moderately rare and are not necessarily the best way of tackling a research question. In practice, research is not one which follows styles, but one which tries to answer questions by the most appropriate means. They accept that the most appropriate means may well be an *ad hoc* combination of methods designed to maximize generalizability and inclusiveness within the available resources and circumstances (Sapsford and Evans 1979).

In my research, the most appropriate method has come to be one that attempts to combine the 'best' of both survey and ethnographic research approaches – an 'ethno-survey' orientation. Consequently, my position has become an amalgamation of two philosophies. The first, underlying survey methods, is what I labelled positivism. The second, underlying ethnographic research, is related to the argument noted by Bynner that at the primitive stage we have reached in social science it is premature to look for precise measurement models for our variables, of the kind employed in natural sciences (Bynner and Stribley 1979). Instead, we should concentrate on exploring the relationships between fairly crude indicators of our variables so that we get a clearer idea of which ones are of most theoretical and practical importance. The philosophical end product underlying my research, then, becomes one where, while models and precise measurement should be sought after, the nature of my subject and the underdevelopment of the social sciences means I have to look for clarification as well. This hybrid philosophy is reflected in the practicalities of my research approach in a number of ways, and can be illustrated if we take as an example my actual data collection methods.

My subjects were managers, most of whom had experienced considerable changes, and some who had experienced some personal shock as a result, for instance, of demotion within their firms. My main methodological tool was a fairly lengthy interview process, but with my starting point the desire to prestructure the process as much as possible. After piloting, I adopted a survey-type approach where a question schedule was used in an attempt to give structured interviews in order to establish a methodology that was consistent between participants and yielded standardized data. Yet I found that in order to explore some areas salient to managers, in order to understand what contraction meant to them, and maintain a relationship that would yield answers, I had sometimes to transform and, indeed, abandon my question schedule, use non-directive techniques, and fit questions into the conversation in the most effective manner. This, of course, was much more ethnographic in character.

The critical reader might argue that one prespecifies one's questions, in survey methods, in order to facilitate the replication of a study, and thus reliability. It might seem that the flexibility I had introduced into my interviews meant the process lacked any reliability.

I do not feel that this is the case. We might recall that the rationale for replication is that it enables us to assess the extent to which the findings of a study were produced by the particular characteristics of the researcher, either through reactivity or bias. But, as an 'ethnographer' would argue, the prestructuring of the research process can only be minimally successful because the researcher has no control over the expectations and interpretations of subjects and respondents. Furthermore, the concept of reliability relates only to personal and not procedural reactivity. Replication, by definition, involves the use of the research procedures employed in the original study and thereby replicates any reactivity involved in the use of these procedures. This may be an important source of systematic error.

My research approach and argument is that if some standardization can be obtained in an interview, then this will help to reduce researcher bias. However, to include a flexible element into the interview process need not necessarily be a drawback if the researcher takes steps to counteract the main problems. Indeed, by using a technique such as reflexivity, an aid in ethnographic research to assess reliability and validity[1], a combination of standard and flexible interviewing methods can be used which seems more valuable than a completely standardized process.

Thus the defence for my hybrid approach comes back to the statement I made earlier, that the approach one adopts can be the best one for the particular circumstances, without straying away from the principles of scientific method and without being constrained by narrow frameworks.

CONCLUSION

I have tried to argue in the first place that the debate about the scientificness of the social sciences is to some extent both futile and ideological. 'Science' is important if our concern is status, or research funding, but its dominant notions sometimes detract from understanding human activity. The argument is that we should not abandon such notions, but give greater place and support, even during periods of 'research training', to finding ways of researching a problem rather than to finding a problem to fit preconceived research approaches. The end result must surely be more meaningful management research.

NOTE

1 Reflexivity is the attempt to render explicit the process by which the data and findings of a project were produced. It demands a continual monitoring by the researcher of his actions and interpretations in the course of the research, and the products of these reflections will provide one of the bases on which he acts in the field in the future. It also requires the researcher to record these reflections alongside the data that has been collected, to provide a basis for later methodological assessment. In addition, the researcher needs to make available to the reader, as far as possible, his reflective account of his own role in the research and the recorded data, which form the basis of his analysis.

REFERENCES

Bottomore, T. B. (1962) *Sociology – A Guide to Problems and Literature*, London: Allen & Unwin.

Bynner, J. and Stribley, K. M. (eds) (1979) *Social Research Principles and Procedures*, London: Longman/Open University Press.

Crick, B. (1971) *American Science of Politics*, Berkeley, CA.

Mann, P. (1976) *Methods of Sociological Enquiry*, Oxford: Basil Blackwell.

Phillips, D. (1971) *Knowledge Form What? Theories and Methods in Social Research*, New York: Rand McNally.

Roberts, G. K. (1973) in P. G. Lewis and D. C. Potter (eds) *The Practice of Comparative Politics*, London: Longman.

Sapsford, R. J. and Evans, J. (1979) *Evaluation of Research*, Block 3 of course DE304, *Research Methods in Education and Social Sciences*, Milton Keynes: Open University Press.

5 What is management research?

Roger Bennett

THE MEANING OF RESEARCH

To ask what is management research may seem irrelevant and unnecessary. Since so many people are doing it, some of them at least must know what it's all about. Yet views seem to differ. Some people consider research to be a cosy and personal activity that can be indulged in from time to time from the safety of an armchair, with access to a pile of books. Such 'research', or *private study/desk research/literature search*, is of immense value in helping us to keep up to date and improve our personal stock of knowledge. It can provide ideas for improving training or establish the basis for the start of a major piece of investigative or empirical research. Whilst some would call this form of research nothing more than 'armchair theorizing', it has a very important part to play in management research by establishing what is already known and therefore not in need of research, unless in a totally different context (for example, researching the effects of applying to the learning situation previously researched motivation models, or of using Western styles of management in different cultures).

For others, the term 'research' is concerned with a *rigorous scientific activity* aimed at developing new bodies of knowledge. It conjures up pictures of the physicist in a laboratory, carefully making sure that nothing changes except what he or she wants to change, and noting the results. This, too, is an important conception of research. Whilst in the social sciences it is difficult to control and change the things we want to in our research, we can set up experiments and simulations which allow us to get close to this scientific approach. We can use models and computer programs to predict the way the economy might move (with well-known margins of error!); we can examine factory loading and space requirements before putting up the building (preventing us finding it is too big or too small); and we can design training courses which use particular methods and compare them with courses for similar managers but using different methods.

Neither extreme is wrong – they simply illustrate that research is not neatly separable from the world in which it takes place and can therefore take on different shapes forged by the 'reality' in which it exists. They do, however, have one thing in common – both are concerned with the *systematic development and acquisition of knowledge*. The first starts with an existing base, the second with the aim of generating or extending the base. What is done with that knowledge is a factor which often distinguishes social scientific research – and particularly management research – from some other research. We are concerned also with its application. Whilst in, say, the scientific engineering field, application is separated from research, this is less true in management. Some forms of research have developed which, as we shall see, embrace within the research process problem-solving and action in the managerial world. This tends to blur the distinction between research, development, and consultancy. But the fact that for some researchers the edges are very indistinct does not mean that the core differences do not exist. They still hold good.

We can derive from such considerations a *definition of research* that fits both the generally held view and the more specific management-related view. Research can be seen as a systematic process of discovering, acquiring, and using knowledge. Put more formally, research is: a systematic, careful inquiry or examination to discover new information or relationships and to expand/verify existing knowledge for some specified purpose.

The 'specified purpose' is usually a problem, and the problem may belong to the researcher or to the manager; it may be academic (i.e. a problem of theory) or applied (i.e. a problem of practice). Since there is nothing more practical than a good theory, academics and managers should have a combined interest in research.

But what is management research? Clearly, it is a systematic, careful inquiry of anything to do with management. Since all enterprises are managed, the scope for such inquiry is very broad. There are processes which are fundamental to management that may be the subject of research. But there are many things which are not 'management' that impinge upon the process of management. They may well be the subject of their own research specialisms but will still contribute to management. Accounting research, for example, may be very specific to accountancy but will still have an impact on management. The collection of basic data on industries may not be classed as management research but can still provide useful information *and* a means of getting research started. External agencies may be willing to fund what appears to be non-management research that can provide routes into research more closely related to the managerial process. There is, therefore, a blurred distinction between what is and is not management research.

THE RESEARCH PROCESS

Understanding research starts with knowing what, in essence, it's all about. As we have seen, the process usually *starts with some form of problem or question.* The problem/question may be the researcher's – for example, a wish to know which learning theory of several is most relevant in explaining certain levels of performance in different situations. The problem may, of course, be initiated by the manager or someone else; perhaps wanting to decide on the best technique for developing greater participation. In either case, the requirement is for some information that will shed light on the problem and help make a decision to solve it. It may be that solutions are not the end result of the research: an outcome might be the development of a new theory or body of knowledge. Whatever the end result, the starting point is represented by an urge to find out, to explore, to evaluate – in short, to do research.

In between these end points exist a number of other steps. Having defined, or at least acknowledged, the problem or area of interest, the researcher may carry out a preliminary study. This will enable him or her to set out the parameters of the problem and to gain some idea of the essential information to be sought. Such *exploratory studies,* free from too much bias or pre-conceived ideas, can be of great value in setting the research in the right direction. For example, the problem being looked at may have been concerned with inadequate commission earnings of sales representatives immediately after finishing training. The temptation here is to blame the training. An exploratory study (usually much less costly than the full treatment) might uncover poor supervision during the first weeks of the job, or lack of understanding of the commission scheme, as possible alternative explanations. If this preliminary work is reasonably thorough, the next stages can be less embracing than might otherwise be the case. From this work the researcher may well set up an *hypothesis,* or a series of hypotheses, which can then be tested against reality. In simplest terms an hypothesis is an imagined answer to a real question. In the example just given, the question would be: 'What causes low levels of commission earnings in immediate post-training periods?' The answer, as we have seen, might be based on guess-work, theoretical inspiration, or an appreciation of the factors involved, or indeed a combination of all three. In our case, the hypothesis might be that, in immediate post-training periods, sales representatives will earn low levels of commission if inadequate supervision persists.

Having framed this hypothesis, the researcher then *seeks information,* or data, which will allow him or her to test its validity. This might mean a decision to check records for low earnings, and see what situations led to them; or the monitoring of earnings and performance levels in two sales forces, one of which had a high ratio of supervision, the other a low ratio. The data collected would then be *analysed* and subjected, possibly, to several statistical tests to determine whether the proposed 'answer' holds true or not and with what degree of confidence or faith it can be accepted. The results of this analysis and deliberation would be *interpreted and communicated* – via reports, seminars, planning groups, or whatever – to the 'client'. This phase can be a difficult one but need not be as inconclusive as so often is the case. The process is shown in Figure 5.1.

It should be stressed that the research process may not necessarily be geared to the testing of hypotheses. Often a researcher will be more interested in the exploratory stage, with a view to developing a number of alternative hypotheses for later testing by himself or herself, or by others. If this proves successful, a useful contribution will have been made to management knowledge.

RESEARCH AND THE MANAGERIAL PROCESS

It is not too difficult to establish the relevance of research to management education in its broadest meaning. We can easily convince ourselves that research and 'teaching' are, or should be, mutually supportive. But what about management practice? Can the same conditions be said to apply?

They can. There is a similarity between the research process and the management process which suggests they need one another. Furthermore, it suggests that managers are, in fact, their own researchers in many circumstances. The good manager is, at least unconsciously, a good researcher too. Both management and research are decision-making processes.

Management and decision-making are both processes concerned with objectives. Problems arise and have to be solved. To do this, information must be obtained, alternative solutions sought and evaluated, and the chosen solution implemented and monitored. Management *is* a decision-making process, as a little self-analysis will demonstrate to even the most sceptical amongst us.

These stages of the managerial decision-making process are virtually the same as those the researcher goes through. Some major differences are concerned with:

1 *Time* The manager is often short of this and may be unable to be as rigorous as needed in collecting and analysing information. Researchers usually have more time and are judged, in part, on the quality of information collected and analysis as well as on the end results.
2 *Experience* Managers are usually very experienced in the problem area and in dealing with the changing complexities of their situation. The

Figure 5.1 Major steps in research processes

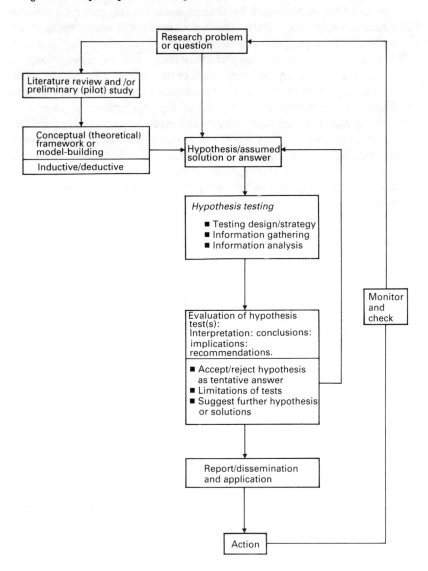

researcher can bring to bear upon that situation considerable research-based experience which can be of value in obtaining and evaluating information.

3 *Urgency* Managerial problems often require solutions in a short time-period, whereas a research-based approach to tackling the problem may have a longer time-horizon. The temptation for the researcher to do a 'quick, cheap job' must be resisted.

4 *Impact* Solving managerial problems usually has implications of major and minor forms for the work of colleagues and of the manager both currently and in the future. The employment fate of people, the profit earned by investors, the result of the next general election ... all can hang on a poorly made decision. At best, the researcher's efforts will provide a base for an exciting new tomorrow (in some small way, usually) and at worst, the research report will rest, unread, on a bookshelf: it can be ignored without any real implications for 'the real world'! It may, and probably does, have an impact on his or her career prospects and reputation.

Despite these differences, research has an affinity with the managerial process and has an important role in helping managers through the application of its techniques and methods to identifying problems, collecting relevant and timely information, and sorting out solutions. We should, however, bear the following points in mind when assessing the role of research in management:

Research and researcher are not infallible.

Managers must be involved in the research if it is to be of use to them.

Researchers must not be hedged in by endless constraints.

Much valuable information and experience exists within the organization itself.

'Packages' or 'ready-made' solutions to managerial problems should be thoroughly evaluated through research.

Researchers should not be seen as replacing the manager as decision-maker.

Researchers should be expected to provide supplementary information to enable the manager to take the necessary decision.

Research methods and techniques can help managers in their own information-seeking activities.

Research can be of indirect help by providing case material, knowledge, issues, and so on about decision-making for the development of managers.

APPROACHES TO RESEARCH

There are, as indicated earlier, a number of different approaches to research. Whilst it is easy to argue (as some do) that research is research, whatever form or shape it takes, there does exist a sharp contrast between those approaches aimed at *purely academic or theoretical problems,* and those concerned more with the 'day-to-day' difficulties of *management in practice.* There is, too, the often-associated difference in the degree of 'scientific method' adhered to in carrying out the research. In the physical sciences, it is much easier to have rigid control over an experiment: to formulate an hypothesis, design a rigorous research project, control all variables, and look for the answer.

In the social sciences generally, and management in particular, this rigid control is rarely achievable. So what form or forms of research are relevant? Let us examine a number of identifiable approaches which might loosely be argued to exist on a continuum going from *'theory-orientated'* to *'action-orientated'*, on the assumption that there are many kinds of research, not just one. This analysis is based on the typology put forward by Clark. He uses three dimensions for establishing the typology:

1 Is the research concerned with clarifying and resolving theoretical issues, or with solving a practical problem in one enterprise?
2 How is the research disseminated and diffused? Through learned journals? Reports to sponsors in the organization?
3 What is the nature of the involvement of the researcher with his audience? Is it a single case, where only one audience exists (e.g. members of the scientific community or the research sponsors), or a multiple case where the researcher is both solving a practical problem and contributing something to our knowledge base?

Combining these dimensions produced five types of research, which are described here together with a sixth and more recent approach which has interest and relevance for management and social science research. This is not a scientific classification, and the boundaries are blurred. It does help, though, to think about the type of research we want to do.

Pure basic research   This form of research arises from the perceived needs for developing a basic discipline. It is concerned with resolving, illuminating, or exemplifying a theoretical issue. Its aims are to enhance knowledge and understanding of the world around us. The findings are published in learned journals for the sole benefit of scientific colleagues and are of a high level of generality. They may take years before they add to our general stock of knowledge or become part of the armoury of practising professionals (e.g. personnel, organizational development, training specialists) in organizations, or even before they become part of the thinking of people concerned with other types of research.

Basic objective research   Here, the research is concerned with tackling a general problem of the application of knowledge which can arise in many contexts but does not aim to solve a particular practical problem. The findings are often published in both learned and professional journals with the aim of transmitting the outcomes of the research to scientists and to the practising professional. Thus, the level of generality is still high and the people receiving the feedback about the research are professionally trained and/or academic. It is usually publicly funded and sometimes written up in a manner which the management teacher/trainer finds easy to pick up and use.

Evaluation research   The purpose of this kind of research is to provide an assessment of some aspect of the performance of an enterprise (e.g. the effects of a change from authoritarian management to management by objectives; the change in behaviour of managers after receiving a three-week programme in human relations; the costs of and social benefits of a United Nations road development programme to the economic activities of, say, a town of India). It is usually concerned with the effectiveness of such change programmes. It is not usually concerned with actually making the change. The problems it tackles are essentially practical (as opposed to theoretical) and the results usually conveyed only to the sponsoring organization through very specific reports (although they may sometimes be published in professional journals to illustrate, for example, the use of a new research technique). Evaluation research is often sought by enterprises looking for a sophisticated method of collecting information with the appearance of 'scientific neutrality' or impartiality. Arguments exist about the role and utility of evaluation research but there can be little doubt that it is an area in which management academics and practising managers can stand together looking at the same problem with mutual interest.

Applied research   This form of research is aimed at solving a specific, practical problem within an enterprise or sponsoring organization. It does so through the application of appropriate knowledge. An example would be the use of our existing knowledge of human motivation to make changes to job/work organization design in order to improve job satisfaction; or to apply our knowledge of human learning to improving training designs for management programmes. The results may or may not be written up: the recipient of the findings is the sponsor. Sometimes the research is published in case-study form in professional journals.

This restricted dissemination usually means that applied work does not contribute to our existing stock of knowledge. It can, in fact, become rather insular, running the risk even of applying knowledge which is known to be inadequate. To effectively carry out applied work, the researcher has to be able to read the learned and professional journals with an eye to spotting theoretical developments and their relevance to applications of the sort in which he or she is interested.

Action research This is a form of research where action (e.g. the solution of a problem, usually regarding some aspect of organizational change and development) is both an outcome of the research *and* a part of the research process. It aims to tackle potential problems which have relevance to theory and to report the findings to the sponsor and scientists/practising professionals via reports and learned/professional journals.

Action research thus has three taskmasters – the sponsor, the behavioural science practitioner, and the scientific community. This imposes many strains upon the research and the researcher. The main purpose of action research is to improve the stock of knowledge for the sponsoring (i.e. client) organization. This can, and does, cause problems in disseminating the findings to a wider audience. However, where sensible, open and trusting collaborative research is carried out, publication of results is usually possible (albeit in a disguised or anonymous form), providing opportunities for adding to our knowledge in general about management in organizations. Its critics argue that, since the researcher is changing what is being researched during the process of the research, the project cannot be replicated. If it cannot be replicated, its findings cannot be tested in other situations. This prevents general knowledge being developed. Thus, it cannot contribute to theory. These points are difficult to refute, unless the notion of action research is changed. However, as a means of improving the utilization of the research carried out, it has a lot to commend it to the management researcher. It is important to bear in mind that the researcher is actually involved in the change process, at least by providing information collected through surveys etc. to a group of organization members, possibly before, during, and after the change. He or she thus loses what some would argue is the key to good research – a critical, detached objectivity.

'New paradigm' research This is a fairly recent addition to the range of approaches adopted for management research. Just as action research developed on a ground swell of enthusiasm from the late 1960s on, so new paradigm research seems set to become a front runner in the 1980s and beyond. As its name implies, it is based on a new model or framework for research. It claims that research can never be neutral and that even the most static and conventional research exposes needs for change. New paradigm research centrally involves inquiry into persons and relations between persons, and is based on a close relationship between researcher and researched.

The research is a mutual activity of a 'co-ownership' form, involving shared power with respect to the process and outcomes of the research. Those being researched can, for example, decide how the research will be done, in what form and with what questions being asked. The researcher is a member of the 'community' and brings to it special skills and expertise. He or she does not dictate what shall happen. In clear contrast to the 'old paradigm' with its emphasis on 'hard', objective, tight, and quantitative research, the new paradigm approach seeks to develop 'a new rigour of softness'. It links knowledge with participation, with action, with qualitative data, with the person as 'a whole', and with values. In short, it states that 'the outcome of research is knowledge. Knowledge is power. The wrong kind of research gives the wrong kind of power. The right kind of research gives the right kind of power. Research can never be neutral.' This is an exciting approach, particularly when put over by one of its enthusiastic adherents. In terms of utility, it clearly has a place in helping research get started in situations where more conventional approaches are difficult (e.g. prisons, mental hospitals), where the real feelings of a person need to be examined (e.g. a manager facing a group decision going against him), and where personal and small group experiential learning is a key focus (e.g. T. Groups). It is clearly action-orientated and might be said to be seeking the ultimate in truth and knowledge in social science. Its rate of adoption will very much depend on availability of the necessary skills among staff in management institutions and its acceptability to practising managers.

A way of summarizing all this is to think of research being concerned both with 'truth' and 'usefulness'. Some research – the theory orientated – seeks what is 'true', to find out exactly what the 'facts' are and, through a process of trying to refute the theory which explains these facts, present the real state of knowledge. However, it is not necessarily 'useful' to know that something is true. Indeed, the reverse may be so. Newtonian physics did not present a 'true theory', as we now know, but it has been immensely useful in enhancing our capacity to build machines that actually work! In management, it may often be impossible to establish that any of one theory represents the truth of management practice, but we can show that some management technologies work well in certain situations. This is useful to those who manage in such situations. Of course, the two are not necessarily exclusive – indeed, what our aim should be is to show through research that usefulness and truth go hand-in-hand – sometimes!

The management researcher has a vital role to play in helping to determine what kind of research is necessary and relevant to the needs of his or her own institution and those of client organizations. Research can no longer be thought of as the 'playground' of the academic: it is in a real sense a 'classroom' where managers and trainers/researchers can combine their knowledge and view of the managerial world for the benefit of both.

Part II
Research methods

PART II: RESEARCH METHODS

Compiling a section on research methods poses a similar problem to that faced by the researcher looking at methods for a research project – namely, where do you start? Even a superficial glance at research methods texts reveals a vast range of possibilities open to the researcher. Indeed, it is a range which may seem overwhelming to first-time researchers. Thus one might ask why it is necessary to provide further contributions on the subject.

There are several reasons for this. First, a predominant amount of published research emphasizes 'traditional' research methods and, indeed, often within a fairly narrow range. We would wish to illustrate the diversity of methods available. Second, much of the research methods literature, whether emphasizing quantitative or qualitative methods, tends to portray an ideal, with little acknowledgement of the constraints. This is not a problem if an ideal research project is being undertaken, but poses more difficulties if the individual is trying to pursue the ideal in a far from ideal world. So provided here are papers which recognize practical constraints. Finally, while within the social sciences there is much material on research methods applicable to management issues, few texts have attempted to select approaches which may be more relevant to management researchers. The contributions here were written specifically for management researchers. In acknowledging these difficulties this section does not attempt to provide a comprehensive review of research methods and omits some areas already well developed, such as experimental methods. But, taken in conjunction with traditional texts, part II helps provide a more realistic understanding of the possibilities and limitations of research methods which employ both the 'hard' and the 'soft' approaches, as earlier described.

The first chapter in this section lays a foundation for looking at research methods. Bennett provides a broad and introductory assessment of those methods which are particularly useful in management research. He deals with levels of research and rigour, criteria for choosing different methods, and an overview of the principal methods used; including historical research, the case study approach, survey, and experimental methods. The chapter provides a framework with which to view the rest of the section, while showing which methods are actually used and why. As we have earlier noted, some of the more positivistic research methodologies – and their over-use – have come in for criticism over the years, yet these methods, and a relatively restricted range of them, are still predominantly used in social science research.

Podsakoff and Dalton reinforce this point, in chapter 7, 'Research methodology in organizational studies'. Although its title would seem to imply a discussion of methodology specific to organization studies, the chapter raises important issues about research methods which apply more generally. Podsakoff and Dalton highlight the limited set of research strategies and analytical procedures found in academic publications and the chapter displays well the possible constraints on researchers seeking academic recognition for their work. They suggest strongly that the constraints largely result from certain gatekeepers' views of 'acceptable' methods. Nevertheless, even the acceptance of this limiting conclusion should not detract from the more positive realization that there are a range of methods which are under-utilized and have considerable potential. Despite the pressure to pursue research methods which are more acceptable to journal reviewers and editors there is a growing acceptance of research based on more qualitative methods. Indeed, most recently, the editors of some management journals have acknowledged earlier over-restrictive acceptance criteria and begun to encourage more diverse contributions, particularly of qualitative research (for example, *Journal of Consumer Research*). This is an encouraging trend.

Hassard, in chapter 8, outlines a technique in this vein. He provides an introduction to ethnomethodology, a method which has grown in stature, though possibly out of proportion to its actual use. It is much more 'research from the inside', in the terms of Evered and Louis (chapter 1, part I), providing subjectivist data from the point of view of the researcher as a participant actor rather than as an outside observer. As well as describing ethnomethodology, Hassard emphasizes that it is impossible to divorce method from theory. Some methods may seem more flexible or adaptable than others, but the assumption, sometimes apparent, that a method is theory-neutral indicates more a lack of critical understanding of the research process than the properties of research techniques.

Criticisms sometimes levelled at ethnomethodological research are that it lacks rigour or representativeness. On occasion these criticisms are related to assumptions about the acceptability (or lack of it) of a particular research paradigm rather than the methodology *per se*. On other occasions such criticisms may not fully take into account the researcher's purpose in using this approach. Certainly concerns of this nature have been expressed about another 'soft' approach, that of the case study method, outlined in chapter 9. Here Smith refutes the notion of representativeness as a valid criticism of the case-study method arguing that the validity of explanations derived from case-studies depends on the logic of the analysis and acknowledgement of *ceteris paribus* conditions, not on how typical the cases may be. The chapter makes recommendations for the conduct of systematic and rigorous case-study research and reiterates the point that research problems should be addressed using appropriate research methods.

One technique which has become widely used in the management area and rarely considered in the standard texts is repertory grid. For some the technique has become an answer to the researcher's prayer, providing hard data yet having a degree of flexibility which makes its applicability broad, both in terms of the conditions under which research is conducted and its theoretical underpinning. In chapter 10, Dainty outlines the basic technique and explores some of the possibilities and areas of usage. The paper encourages greater adoption of the technique, but cautions against inappropriate use. The 'hard' data it provides may push some researchers into using it because of the 'acceptability' of the methodology, rather than whether it is fully appropriate to the research question.

Appropriateness is a theme throughout part II: a research method should be evaluated in terms of its relevance and contribution to understanding the subject under study. We would not, therefore, suggest the methods outlined so far should be pursued at the expense of others, though they are often ignored in favour of other techniques, for reasons already noted. But one 'traditional' approach, used widely in management research, is survey research; it is examined in the last three chapters of this section. Jobber (chapter 11) explains the relative merits of face-to-face, telephone, and mail surveys. A systematic approach to mail surveys which maximizes response rates, is presented by Cragg in chapter 12. The final chapter in part II considers interviewing techniques in face-to-face surveys. Hart's paper (chapter 13) is not a standard review: the chapter takes as its focus industrial markets and senior executives within this arena, who as a group are not normally addressed in the research literature. It also considers other issues, frequently ignored in the literature, such as access. In a fitting conclusion to part II, this paper exemplifies the theme that no matter what, normatively, the researcher might wish to do, the broader context of research cannot be ignored any more than the specific limitations of research techniques.

6 How is management research carried out?

Roger Bennett

Research is concerned with solving problems; with investigating the relationships that exist in the world around us; with building or establishing a body of knowledge that some might refer to as a 'science'. Whilst many people would not regard the body of management knowledge as constituting a science (notwithstanding subject areas such as 'management science' and 'behavioural science'), the investigation of managerial issues, problems, and interests can take on a scientific aura, depending on the methods of research used. In this chapter we shall discuss briefly the main methods used in management research (see Bennett 1983).

First, however, a brief look is required at the different levels at which research can take place and at the levels of rigour involved. This will help place in perspective the nature of management research and the role of key methods in carrying out research. At all times, though, it should be remembered that the main aim of management research is to help improve the practice of management. If this is used as a key criterion in selecting methods, our search and choice will not be fruitless.

LEVELS OF RESEARCH

Not all research takes place at the same level of scientific sophistication. This is because different disciplines or areas of study have established different states of knowledge. They may also have different hoped-for outcomes and uses of research. In those disciplines concerned with space flight and travel, such as physics, the emphasis is placed very much on accurately predicting what will happen and how to control events. This is in contrast with a good deal of research into wildlife, for example, which is focused upon describing and understanding events. The latter is clearly necessary if the former is to be attained. Particular methods will be more relevant to one level than to another. Thus, observation and recording will be important in studying wildlife; experimental design and sophisticated data analysis and modelling in getting someone to the moon. In general, most sciences follow a similar pattern of development and progression. In management we still have our observational studies (e.g. of what managers do), but we also attempt prediction (for example, reactions of group members to different managerial styles). There are, in essence, four levels of research. These levels are not mutually exclusive, they overlap; and neither do they form a rigid hierarchy. For example, it can be argued that classification comes before description, in that we group things and then look for the common properties in each grouping. Usually, however, we start with a description of objects and events, and establish that some are similar to and different from others.

Description This is, perhaps, the most basic level of research. It is concerned with describing what exists around us. An example might be to improve our knowledge of management processes in different countries. To do this it is necessary to describe such processes. Thus, analysis of job descriptions and observational/diary studies would prove helpful. Another example are those studies which have attempted to describe managerial traits, looking for those that characterize the successful or eminent manager (the 'great man' theory approach). Such studies yield information which allows us to draw up a profile of a particular manager – i.e. his or her managerial style. We may then be able to classify managers according to similarities in profile or style. An important starting point (it helps to 'map out' the research terrain), describing 'what is', on the other hand, may not of itself improve our knowledge of management.

Classification Observational research often throws up similarities and differences in what has been studied. It may show, in the case of managerial styles, that democratic styles occur in certain situations in particular countries (but not in others) whilst more authoritarian approaches seem persistent in yet different circumstances. This allows us to classify, or categorize, the things we are studying, on the basis of known, natural characteristics.

Explanation Having reached the stage of being able to fit things into classifications, of being able to document similarities and differences, it is not unnatural for the research to ask 'why?' Why do these differences occur? What causes the similarities and differences? Why do certain approaches to management seem to prevail in some countries, but not in others? How do such styles arise in the first place? Clearly, the interest of the researcher is in seeking to understand what is happening and representing this in theoretical developments, models, propositions, and so on. Thus, descriptive and classificatory work has established a basis on which theory-building becomes a possibility. We are able to describe much of the world around us, and the different forms of life that have existed (using, for instance, a classificatory system known as 'cladograms', which relate certain life forms to each other), but we are still asking the questions 'why' and 'how'.

Prediction The level to which all sciences must aspire but few have reached to any extent, is to be able to 'predict'. Using established theories and formulae, the researcher is able to say 'if X, then Y'. In the physical and advanced sciences, this is the level at which most researchers now operate, although work at other levels is clearly necessary. In the field of management, it is exceptional to find some truly predictive theory. Whilst the testing of hypotheses may take on this predictive form, we are still very much concerned with understanding and explaining what managers do. Our methods of research will be geared to this. It is likely, therefore, to find greater use of field studies and field experiments than the experimental designs of the laboratory scientist. Whilst researchers in particular disciplines, such as psychology, will conduct laboratory experiments, the main focus of management research will, and has to, be in the natural settings of managers themselves, i.e. their work places.

LEVELS OF RIGOUR

Another important consideration in the choice of research method is the extent of rigour involved. The term rigour is used to refer to the extent to which the method employed strictly adheres to the fundamental requirements of research design. Three levels of rigour have been identified (House 1970).

The *first level* of rigour embraces those methods which offer a qualitative and narrative approach to the analysis of variables. Such methods offer minimum scope for classification and enumeration of the variables involved in the study. The methods would include authoritative opinion, the single case-study, and narrative history. Such methods can be used for indicating important variables and hypotheses which might then be tested through the use of more rigorous methods. They should not be ruled out purely on the grounds of their low level of rigour. Their utility lies in a capacity to handle issues which more rigorous approaches may not be able to deal with. This is especially so in exploratory studies.

The *second level* of rigour is one at which measurement, particularly in a more quantitative form, begins to play an important part in the research method. Methods related to this level of rigour would include survey research, longitudinal or time-series analysis, and uncontrolled experimentation. Here the emphasis is changed from illustrating and describing situations and potentially important variables to one of measuring and manipulating certain variables and their relationships to one another. Usually such methods enable us to argue that something is related to something else.

They seldom if ever allow us to establish a causal relationship, i.e. that A causes B, or if A, then B.

The *third level* of rigour takes us much closer to the notion of scientific method as used in the physical sciences. Here the research is concerned with manipulating variables in order to test for a causal relationship, to seek out those variables which have a critical or important impact on what is being studied and the key relationships involved. Thus, if the purpose of the research is to establish why something came about, what caused something to happen, then research methods at this level of rigour are necessary. This involves experimentation in some form or another, either in a laboratory or controlled field setting.

Any research undertaken should clearly be of the highest level of rigour appropriate to the objects and needs of the research itself. Pursuing increased rigour for its own sake is not necessarily an advantage. The quality of information derived from first and second level of rigour methods plays an important part in the development of theory. It is far more effective to carry out controlled experimentation, for example, on variables known to be of importance than on variables which turn out to be trivial. The issue then is not one of deciding which is the one best method, for there is no such thing. There is, however, a method or methods more appropriate than others to the purposes of the research. If our purposes have more to do with description and classification then first and second level of rigour methods would be more likely to be appropriate. If, however, we are seeking to explain and predict, i.e. we are establishing theory, then second and third level of rigour methods would become important. As we have seen in the previous section, it is not possible to explain and predict if the bases of classification and description have not been established.

It is likely that, for much research in the management field, first and second level methods will be of use to the researcher. Experimentation will in most cases be restricted to constructing and verifying theories.

CRITERIA FOR CHOICE

The discussion on levels of research and levels of rigour have illustrated the point that consideration should be given to criteria which govern the choice of research method. Clearly two important criteria are those we have already examined. It is important to know if the research is concerned with exploring what might be, or verifying what is, and to choose methods appropriate to this. There are other points that should be borne in mind when choosing an appropriate research method.

Answering the research questions The method chosen must allow the research questions to be answered. It is clearly important to know and thoroughly understand what questions you are seeking to answer. A clear statement of the research questions will enable both the level of research and level of rigour to be more adequately determined. It will also enable a check to be made on the understanding of the nature of the research problem involved.

Current state of knowledge If little is currently known about the nature of the variables involved in the research problem then it is likely that more qualitative, exploratory research methods will be needed. If, on the other hand, a review of the literature shows that a good deal is already known, it is then possible to isolate the key variables involved. This would then determine the extent to which a hypothesis or hypotheses could be established and made available for testing. This in turn would lead to a choice of method which allowed hypothesis testing to be carried out. However, even where the variables are known in advance their very nature may prevent the use of experimental research methods.

The nature of the variables involved The choice of method will also be governed by the extent to which the variables involved can be manipulated and measured in a controlled way. In the physical sciences it is often possible to make the subject of the research do what you want it to do. In the social sciences this is not always the case. For example, if we are interested in testing a hypothesis concerned with the relationship between managerial style and productivity of employees, we need to be able to control the style adopted and the situation in which it is used. This is often just not possible. The right kind of situations may not arise and even where they do, the people involved in them may not be prepared to allow us to control what they are doing from a research point of view.

PRINCIPAL RESEARCH METHODS

There are a number of quite different methods that can be employed in exploring a problem situation, helping solve a problem, or establishing acceptability or otherwise of a hypothesis. Some of these methods can be used to compliment each other in certain circumstances.

The 'scientific' or conventional approach

Before considering the principal methods applicable to management research, it is necessary to refer back to the major steps of the research process as outlined in chapter 5. This depicts the key steps of the research process as determined by what is known as 'scientific method'. This is usually considered to consist of four logical steps, namely:

1 Setting up an hypothesis.
2 Developing a method.
3 Gathering the data.
4 Drawing conclusions.

These steps assume a problem exists and that something will be done about the problem once conclusions have been drawn from the data gathered. It might be argued that there really is very little difference between scientific method and common sense. Both can develop from the determination or formulation of ways of thinking about the world based on information received and conclusions drawn. There are differences, however, and they hinge on the notions of being systematic and controlled. Common sense usually derives from experience and other people's views. These may or may not be systematically garnered. Scientific method ensures that systematic approaches and procedures are used. Likewise, experiences may not be controlled, in the sense that most people do not deliberately seek to experience certain things simply in order to draw conclusions from them. In scientific method the researcher deliberately sets out to control what is looked at, what is measured, and how it is measured.

Scientific method may be considered as one of *four methods of knowing*. The first may be termed the *method of tenacity*. Here, we know something to be true simply because a lot of people fervently say or believe it is true. The more it is said the more valid the truth becomes. There clearly are dangers here. Many people, centuries ago, held tenaciously to the view that the world was flat!

The second method of knowing is the *method of authority*. If a well-respected and authoritative source says that something is so, then it must be so. The Bible is one such source. Tradition and public sanction can add to the authoritative nature of a statement of truth or belief. Thus, if, for example, a government bases its approach to managing the economy on a well-respected tradition of economics, its commentators may give the impression that such an approach is 'correct'. Whilst such an approach is dangerous from a research point of view, we have to accept that it is an important part of life. If a subordinate asks a manager for advice on how to solve a problem, the manager may well give this from a position of experience and authority. This may be taken for granted. If it were not so, the time taken to solve problems and make decisions would be inordinate.

A third way of knowing is the *method of intuition*, or, as it is sometimes known, the *a priori method*. This is based on the notion that people will reach the truth because their natural inclination will be to do so. It is based on the notion that intuitive propositions should agree with reason and not necessarily with experience. It might thus be termed a 'rationalistic' approach. But whose reason does it agree with? Different people will come to different conclusions using different processes of reason.

The *scientific method* has a key characteristic that none of the previous three methods possess, namely, self-correction. Scientific method has built-in checks which are so conceived and used that they control and verify the researcher's work and conclusions. This helps produce objective, verifiable knowledge. Put another way, theory derived from scientific methods is something more than the researcher alone. The other three methods are very much more subjective and therefore result in theories which involve, to a large extent, the experience, reason, and intuition of the individual.

Methods used in management research will vary in the extent to which they are objective, systematic, and controlled; that is, they will more or less approach the ideals of scientific methods. If scientific method is considered to be the anchor of the third level of rigour considered above, then we have a bench-mark against which to compare and contrast other methods. This does not mean that these other approaches are any less acceptable, useful, or 'correct' than the scientific method.

The reasoning process

In conventional research, as in all research, we seek to obtain facts from which to draw conclusions. Drawing conclusions depends on the researcher's ability to follow a logical reasoning process. Scientific method is itself a step-by-step logical reasoning process but there are two important methods of reasoning which need to be referred to. One of these is known as the *inductive method*. This consists of studying many individual managers or situations in order to develop a generalized conclusion. This is the procedure followed in most research projects, when new facts are being studied, new truths revealed, and new general propositions or theories put forward. An example is the Aston studies on organizational structure, where hundreds of organizations have been studied and general dimensions of structure put forward. There are four conditions necessary for effective induction (Clover and Balsley 1979), namely:

1 Observations must be correctly performed and accurately recorded.
2 Observations must cover cases that are representative of the population from which they are drawn.
3 Observations must cover a sufficient number of cases.
4 Conclusions must be confined only to the statements that are substantiated by the findings and are not over-general or too inclusive.

The other method of reasoning is known as the *deductive method*. Here, reasoning starts from a general principle or rule regarded by most people as fact, and assesses a specific fact or case that seems to fit the rule or principle. This involves reasoning from the general to the particular. For example, the conventional principles of management (planning, controlling, co-ordinating, etc.) might be regarded as general statements about how managers operate and perform. In assessing the effectiveness of several companies, a researcher might use measures to be able to gain information on each company on each 'principle'. The company not operating one of these principles, for example, might then be reasoned to be ineffective, or likely to be so in the future. Two conditions are essential in this type of reasoning: (1) the general principle or rule must be correct, i.e. true; (2) it must also be applied only to those cases that properly come under its scope.

Such reasoning processes are important in helping us to determine cause and effect. In seeking such a relationship we must, however, be sure: that the cause and effect conditions exist; that no other unknown conditions could be the cause of the effect: whether more than two conditions are interacting to bring about the effect; and that we have distinguished correctly between basic and secondary causes. If we follow these relatively simple rules, the conclusions drawn from our reasoning or inferences about our data will stand up to rigorous scrutiny.

Model-building

An important part of the research process is the building of models to represent cause, effect, and other relationships. Whilst the term 'model' is used in many different ways (Emory 1980), it basically refers to a dynamic framework or schema that helps portray the key concepts, propositions etc. of our theory. Models may be highly conceptual or theoretical (theory itself being a model), developed at the start of a piece of research, and then tested through the processes of data gathering, analysis, and reasoning. They may also be the end product of research, with little by way of a conceptual framework having been in existence at the start. Model-building is now a sophisticated process, with computers and advanced statistical procedures being employed, for example, in developing economic models for predicting future movements in the economy and in looking at population growth, and so on. Models have their place, as Helmstadter (1970) argues, but we should not see research only in the light of building models. The gathering of basic facts, for example, can be a most useful exercise in itself.

Let us now turn to the main methods of research that can be used in management research, remembering that they have varying degrees of 'scientific respectability' and that methods of low respectability may still be useful.

Historical research

Whilst in one sense all research is historical (i.e. it is impossible to analyse data at exactly the same time as it is collected and in any event interpretation is based on the past), a particular method of research is the historical approach. The approach may take one of two forms: it may be concerned with a historical problem in management or it may be a historical approach to a current management problem. Where historical problems are concerned, particular problems are faced by the investigator. A key problem is separating out fact from opinion or myth. When the problem under investigation is of more recent historical origin, then data and facts may be available but not collected in the form needed in order to describe and understand the problem.

The problem can be looked at in one of two ways: the researcher may collect data and describe the field at a particular point in time (this is known as a cross-sectional study) or the researcher may describe the development of the managerial problem over a period of time (in this case it is referred to as a longitudinal historical study).

The second form of historical research is concerned with helping to solve current problems through an examination of what has happened in the past. In management education and training we often use the case-study approach in a similar way. Students and trainees look at the historical development of a company, the problems it has faced, and the situation it currently finds itself in, in order to suggest future directions and strategies the company might adopt. In the same sense the literature review carried out prior to a research study may be considered to be a particular use of the historical approach. Often, a literature review will lead to the development of hypotheses which can then be tested through other research methods. Thus, in general, historical research methods can be used as a means of generating hypotheses. They can also be used to test hypotheses through what has been called the 'ex-post-facto' design of research. In such a design the main steps of scientific method appear. However, many of the variables about which information is collected will be historical in nature. Whilst the relationships between a current problem and historical variables might be established it may not be possible to say one has been caused by the other.

There are traditionally three basic steps in the historical method: the collection of data, the criticism of data, and the presentation of data. Whilst these steps occur in any form of research, it will be evident that they are limited by the fact that the events being studied have taken place before the time of the study. Thus in using the information collected, researchers have to exercise their own judgement of the data validity and meaning (Chandler 1962).

The case-study

The term 'case-study' usually refers to a fairly intensive examination of a single unit. Such a unit may be a person, a small group of people or indeed a single company. Case-studies involve measuring, looking at (i.e. studying), what is there and how it got there. In this sense it is historical. It can enable us to explore, unravel, and understand problems, issues, and relationships in a particular situation. It cannot, however, allow us to generalize our research, that is, to argue that from one case-study the results, findings, or theory developed apply to other similar case-studies. The case looked at may be unique and therefore not representative of other instances. It is of course possible to select a number of case-studies which will represent certain aspects or features of management that we are interested in studying. This can lead us to developing an experimental design from which theory and generalizations may flow.

Two types of study can be carried out. *Exploratory studies* seek to establish what is; to discover significant variables and relations between them, and to lay the foundations, perhaps, for more scientific work aimed at testing hypotheses. For example, it might be wondered as to what variables have the greatest influence on effective management: a case-study, probing through discussions with and observations of the people involved, might throw some light on this question. It might then be possible to predict how the variables would be related to each other in certain circumstances and to test this particular prediction. This would take the second form of study, namely *hypothesis testing*, rather than hypothesis generating. Here the researcher would be seeking data, perhaps from a number of different case-study situations, aimed at proving or disproving the validity of the hypothesis.

A key point to note about such studies is that they do not attempt rigorous control. This is both a strength and a weakness. The strength is that we obtain greater realism in the research; the weakness is that things may get out of hand (sudden incidents erupting), destroying the validity of the research. They can be costly and time-consuming and may of course not produce much by the way of shattering conclusions. For a number of management research requirements, however, the results can be rewarding. Where several case-studies are combined within the research design, the label 'field-study' may be used.

It should be noted that the case-study approach, like the historical method, has a dual function. Whilst the intensive investigation of a single manager or group of people or organizations may be carried out for the sole purpose increasing our knowledge of management, more often than not it is carried out in order to make practicable improvements. Any contributions to general knowledge are therefore incidental. The case study approach may therefore have research, consultancy, and management training objectives attached to it.

There are a number of specific steps in using the case-study method. The *first step* is determining the present situation. The research worker may have only a vague impression of the research problem. He or she needs descriptive information which will determine as clearly and accurately as possible the present status and circumstances of the case being investigated. The *second step* is concerned with gathering background information. Such information will be about the circumstances leading to the current situation and will enable an examination to be made of the key variables involved. It helps the researcher to compile a list of possible causes of the current problems. The *third step* has to do with testing suggested hypotheses. The background information collected will have been analysed for possible hypotheses. In this step specific evidence about each of these hypotheses can be gathered. The main aim of this step is to eliminate those possibilities which clearly cannot stand up to the evidence collected, and to gain confidence for the important hypotheses. The culmination of this step might be the development of an experimental design to test out more rigorously the hypotheses developed, or it might be to take action to remedy the problem. Taking remedial action is the *fourth step* of the traditional case-study method. The aim is to check that the hypotheses tested actually work out in practice. Some action, correction or improvement is made and a check carried out on the situation to see what effect the change has brought about.

The survey

This is almost certainly the most widely adopted method in the social sciences, and probably in management research also. Surveys are usually cheaper, quicker, and broader in coverage than most scientific experiments can hope to be. But, on the other hand, they often lack the control and in-depth study of the experiment. They also lack the richness and depth of meaning which can be generated from a case-study approach. Relying in the main on the techniques of sampling, interviewing, and/or the questionnaire, the survey can provide useful information on many problems or issues faced by managers in organizations. For example, managers may have wondered how employees feel about the training provided: what subject matters foremen think should be given priority treatment on supervisory management courses; whether members of the organization think participation is a good thing; or perhaps what young managers think about their career prospects. It may be that basic facts about the make-up of local industry, the distribution of employees, the movement and growth in population, that main sources of wealth/income generation, the centres of key purchasing power, the nature of marketing issues, and so on, are not available locally or nationally. These and other issues can be explored using survey research methods involving research instruments (for example, questionnaires, checklists) which, if constructed and tested adequately, can produce useful information. In short, surveys are based on a very simple principle – if we wish to know what people think about certain things we must ask them.

By their very nature, surveys produce a lot of information. Thought must therefore be given before the data is collected as to how it will be analysed. If this is not done, severe problems can arise causing frustration and even the abandonment of the project. Many excellent techniques of analysis exist – from slogging it out by hand to computer processing – and are described in a number of sources (see, for example, Weisburg and Bowen 1977).

A survey, of course, is not the answer to all research requirements. Used wisely it can produce useful information in a short time but may suffer from problems associated with people not wanting or bothering to respond to the questions; giving false answers where they do; treating it as a joke; misunderstanding its purpose; and a host of other problems. Many of these can be avoided, or certainly reduced in terms of their impact on the results, only if care and attention are applied throughout. Carrying out the survey is not as simple as some people would have us believe, neither is it as difficult and scientifically immoral as others obviously do believe. As with all things in life it has its place – as a planned collection of information, no more or less!

The survey may be used for two quite different purposes. The first is simply to describe current practices and events. As such they may be termed polls. A polling survey is concerned mainly with the distribution of responses or answers to any one particular item.

A second use of the survey is for the purpose of analysis. Analytical surveys go beyond the simple description of the current state of practice. A polling survey of one organization may show us that all its managers exercise an authoritarian style of management, but it enables us to say little else that might be of importance.

The survey can be, and is, widely used to collect information and observations over a period of time. Such longitudinal analysis enables us to identify not only which variables are related to each other but also how that relationship might change with time. If, in addition, it is possible to control the circumstances in which the questionnaire is used or other observations are made, it is possible to test hypotheses. Such control over the variables is very seldom achieved in management research and is a main drawback of longitudinal studies.

A longitudinal study may be turned into an uncontrolled experiment. This can be achieved by collecting information from a number of people at one point in time, making some change to the circumstances and then taking further information at a later point in time. The problem here is again that we seldom have any control over what happens as a result of our introduced change.

The experiment

The classical method used in the physical sciences for many years is the experiment. In most, if not all, physical sciences the researcher aims to set up a situation in which all the variables can be controlled or varied at will. The usual approach is to hold all variables constant except one. By varying this one and monitoring changes in the 'output' the relationship between variables can be carefully studied and documented. In essence, the researcher seeks to vary one of several independent (or input) variables whilst measuring the effects on the dependent (or output) variable(s), keeping intervening variables constant. For example, it would be possible to vary the petrol mixture fed to an internal combustion engine and note the difference in speed or power achieved but at the same time keeping, for example, pressure or load constant and controlling temperature in the laboratory. When dealing with human behaviour, it is not possible to adhere strictly to this approach, although sometimes we can get reasonably close. Such an approach clearly meets the requirements of scientific method. It does not, however, meet all the requirements of management and social research. Experimentation is a particularly desirable method where research questions take the form of hypotheses which state, if A then B follows; rather than those hypotheses which seek to describe a phenomenon or where the primary purpose of the research is to develop or verify theory. It is not especially useful in exploring a field, describing phenomena, and suggesting or generating hypotheses for testing purposes.

Although a true experiment is unlikely in management research, it is possible to develop approaches which come close. For example, it might be possible to vary the instructional techniques used for training managers and to measure the achievements. Here, however, control over intervening variables such as ability, intelligence, orientation, and the like, would be complex. But the use of matched groups (i.e. different groups of managers who have roughly the same I. Q. etc.), undergoing different approaches, would take us a step nearer to the scientific method. We should not delude ourselves, however, by thinking this approach is foolproof – it isn't. We can't control, for example, the activities of managers outside work – their love lives, drinking habits, arguments with spouses, etc. which may well affect performance. We can, nonetheless, attempt to recognize and account for them. In getting close to the true experimental design, the researcher has to attempt to gain complete control over the situation by determining exactly who will take part in the experiment and which participants will or will not receive whatever experimental treatment is given.

A simple example of true experimentation which can be used in the study of human behaviour and particularly in that of management, is the *pre-* and *post-test control design*. Here two groups will be taken. Each group will contain managers who have been randomly assigned to the group. Data is then collected about the individuals (for example, a questionnaire may be administered to establish their attitudes to work, managerial style, biographical details in terms of background, age, etc.). Some form of change is then made in one group, but not in the other. The change might, for example, be to send one group of managers away on a particular training activity. Once the change has been made further observations or data collection are made. The data achieved before and after the change in both groups will be compared. The researcher will clearly be looking for a difference in data in the group which had experienced the training as compared with the group which had not.

Experiments can broadly be considered to be of two types – the *laboratory experiment*, where the problem to be studied is divorced from the real world surrounding it; and the *field experiment*, where attempts are made to study the problem in its real setting and to minimize the influences of seemingly unconnected facets or variables. Whilst most experiments in management research are likely to be field experiments, the existence of training schools, simulators, and so on, make laboratory experiments quite attractive – even though the results may not have much significance in the real setting.

Laboratory experiments

A laboratory can be considered as any setting in which the researcher is able closely to control the conditions under which observations are made. A laboratory may therefore be a training room, a specially designed or set-up part of an organization, or any other setting which gives the researcher more control over the circumstances involved. The aim is to achieve as much control as possible over as many as possible of the influential independent variables not pertinent to the immediate research problem. Thus theoretically relevant variables are isolated and measures taken of the response of dependent variables when either independent or intervening variables are manipulated.

The field experiment

With the growth and development of statistics, the need for a special laboratory for the purpose of experimentation can no longer be regarded as necessary for adequately controlled research. Through the use of replication (i.e. repeating the experiment on several groups), randomization (i.e. assigning participants and/or treatment/changes to groups by a random process), and certain statistical controls (i.e. mathematically adjusting results to account for the affects of uncontrollable variables), field experiments can be carried out with little interference from the normal activity and with several variables being manipulated at once. The use of experimental and control groups is the most common approach to controlling a field experiment. As with the true experimental design, in a controlled field experiment the experimental group would consist of a group of people subjected to the experimental variable or treatment. The control group would consist of a group sufficiently similar to the experimental group to allow comparisons to be drawn between the two, but not subjected to the experimental variables. An example may serve to illustrate. Imagine the data preparation room in a large computer installation and suppose that the managing director of the company believes an authoritarian approach to the management of data preparation personnel will lead to improved performance. A simple field experiment might be developed to test this hypothesis. The data preparation personnel could be randomly divided into two groups: one the experimental group, the other the control group. The experimental variable would be the style of management adopted for each group. In the experimental group it might be changed from authoritarian to democratic and perhaps back again to authoritarian, whilst in the control group it would be held constant at authoritarian. Performance measures would be taken of both groups, before and after the change had been made in the experimental variable in the experimental group. However, as the famous Hawthorne experiments illustrated, it is quite possible in such an experiment that some other variable is influencing performance.

COMBINING METHODS

Whilst for many purposes a single method may be appropriate, the possibility and advantages of combining different methods should be considered. In some situations it may not be possible to carry out research without using a combination of methods. For example, it would be possible to carry out research into the politics of management using several different methods. An experimental design might be established in which two companies were involved. Each company might have a number of different plants managed by general managers. It could be possible to select the companies on the basis of similar technology, size, location, and so on, in order that certain variables could be controlled. The experimental variable might be attitude towards the general manager. Survey research could be used to establish in the first instance what the attitudes were in each of the different plants. In true experimental fashion, a change could be introduced (this might constitute providing additional information in one of the plants but not in the others, or sending three of the managers on a training programme but not another, or other similar changes). A longitudinal study could then be made to monitor the effects, through the use of questionnaires and observational studies, of the changes over a period of time. Historical research methods might be introduced to establish the antecedents from which the political behaviour of the managers in question appear to derive. Clearly, in such circumstances the combination of research methods enables a wealth of rich information to be garnered and for a degree of control to be maintained over the study. However, since each method will have its own problems and limitations they may combine to cause serious difficulties regarding the validity of the research findings.

SOME TECHNIQUES OF RESEARCH

Whilst many texts refer to instrumentation, measurement devices, methods of data collection, and the like to mean the way in which the researcher goes about acquiring information within one of the frameworks just described, a more general term is 'technique'. Some of the other terms are too precise (such as 'instrumentation') or involve the use of terms applied elsewhere (such as in 'data collection method'). In essence, we are talking about 'how' we do it as opposed to 'what' we do or 'why' we do it. Only a brief description of the most general techniques is given here – most are well discussed (if not always jargon-free) in texts on research methods.

Observation

This is the most classical and natural of techniques. It simply involves looking at what is going on – watching and listening. We all do it, most of us badly because we do not know what to look for or how to record it. Work study practitioners are probably the most competent of observers – they have been trained to do it. So, too, are most researchers. Important in being a good observer is to have a wide scope, great capacity for being alert, and the ability to pick up significant events. Here, technology can be helpful, offering services ranging from simple pen and paper, through tape recorders and cameras, to video recorders. If carried out quietly, unobtrusively, and shrewdly, observation can be a useful, if not powerful, technique. It can be used to tell us the difficulties encountered in running meetings; how workers relate to each other; or the effects of tea-breaks on worker activity levels – all of which have managerial implications of one form or another. It does not allow much scope for probing and exploring relationships further, unless used in conjunction with other techniques. The combinational use of techniques is now quite widespread and has much to commend it. Since, however, observation is 'simple' (if time consuming) and opportunities for using it often present themselves, it can be used quite effectively for its purposes – enabling a general picture to be built up. It is, therefore, often a part of naturalistic research methods.

Another approach to observation is known as 'participant observation'. This is a technique which has been adapted by management researchers from cultural anthropologists. It involves the researcher in becoming part of or integrated with the group or organization being studied – usually by becoming a 'proper' employee. The researcher participates in all the activities of the group whilst taking note of the things that were intended to be observed. It is a less structured approach but one that produces good insights into, for example, behaviour and relationships. This approach is much less susceptible to the problems of the more structured ones – the events observed are real and therefore not so much contaminated by the researcher. The participant usually remains unknown to the group as a researcher.

Interviews

It is quite tempting to suppose that the interview was first 'created' by the early observers who couldn't resist asking people why they were doing what they were doing. Whatever its origin, the interview has a fundamental role in management research. It allows for exploration and probing in depth and, if the money and time are available, in breadth as well. The questions asked might stem from periods of general observation – and this is to be preferred to just dreaming up questions in the bath! Interviews can be unstructured and free-ranging, a general discussion, picking up points and issues as they emerge and pursuing them in some depth; or they can be structured around questions and issues determined in advance, based on theoretical principles, pre-conceived ideas, or prior (exploratory) investigation. If the questioning is non-directive and free from biased or loaded questions, if the interviewer is a good, attentive listener (and adept recorder), and if the interviewee is of a mind to 'tell it like it is', the results can be very effective. However, problems of time, cost, and sampling, related to research objectives, may mean that a full-scale interview programme is not possible or necessary. For example, a researcher may wish to gain ideas for the development of a job appraisal form – for this, a small number of 'pilot' interviews would be quite effective. If detailed views on the attitudes of managers to newly trained personnel were required, a wider programme of in-depth interviews could be of use. Remember, too, that for some purposes (e.g. where a 'testing of views' is required), group interviews have a role to play. Whilst they can be a bit more difficult to handle, the end results may provide more useful insights than would the same people interviewed separately.

Whatever sort of interview is relevant, the means of recording information must be thought through in advance: whether to tape-record unstructured group interviews or take notes; how to design an interview schedule (a 'questionnaire' completed by the interviewer) for structured interviews, with maximum ease of recording information but minimum effect on interviewees (such as a feeling of 'not being listened to' when writing copious notes). As with all research matters, a little advance thinking and planning can save a lot of later difficulties.

Questionnaires

Whilst questionnaires are undoubtedly the most used technique – or, more correctly, instrument – of researchers in the behavioural and social sciences, they do pose problems. The major difficulties are associated with response rates, bias, and flexibility.

Since questionnaires are important to the survey researcher (as are interviews) the effect on the results of someone not responding must be considered. Who are they? What are their characteristics? Would they share the views of those who did respond? These are important questions that have to be faced. Even when 'reasonable' response rates (however defined) are achieved, these problems still exist, and in any case the resulting data may be biased.

Bias might be due to the respondent anticipating the answers he or she thinks the researcher wants, or putting down 'socially expected' answers (on the basis of what is 'good', or would be the 'right sort of thing to say'), or simply as a result of finding some form of pattern to the first ten questions and assuming the pattern must be repeated. These and other difficulties can be minimized, if not overcome, by careful design and piloting of the questionnaire.

Flexibility, however, is not so much a design problem (although it can be considerably reduced by poor design), as a function of the nature of the research questions being asked. Answers might range from factual information (e.g. date of birth), through simple 'yes/no' replies (e.g. do you smoke?), to scale-type responses of the agree-disagree form (e.g. training is a waste of time) with a number of possible responses in between. Often, however, the person filling in the questionnaire would like to say 'yes – but!' and has no opportunity to do so. It is the qualifying 'but' that may be important – and an interview would allow it to be explored. For information of a somewhat broad and superficial nature (detail can be obtained, of course, but mostly factual), involving large numbers of people, the questionnaire is a useful technique and is relatively easy and cheap to use. If thought is given to the major drawbacks and to the way in which the data is to be analysed, there is every reason to expect fairly reliable and valid results. If preceded or backed up by interviews or observations, many additional benefits can be derived as well as difficulties minimized.

Other techniques

Many other techniques exist, some of them variations on those briefly described here (for example, the 'diary' technique, a form of questionnaire/self-observation log), others developed for specific purposes. They will not be discussed here since most of them require considerable experience in their design and use. They can be found in many of the texts (see, for example, Helmstadter, 1970), from which special references (e.g. to sociometry, testing, scaling, and projective techniques in psychology) can be obtained. Often such techniques are limited in their application and will probably have restricted value for the management researcher.

REFERENCES

Bennett, R. (1983) 'Management research – guide for institutions and professionals', International Labour Office.

Chandler, A. D. (1962) *Strategy and Structure – Chapters in the History of the American Enterprise*, KIT Press. An interesting piece of work based on historical research. It is based on intensive studies of General Motors, Du Pont, Standard Oil of New Jersey and Seers Roebuck. A brief introduction sets out the strategy and structure including methods used.

Clover, V. T. and Balsley, H. (1979) *Business Research Methods*, Grid Publishing, 2nd edition, chapter 2.

Emory, C. W. (1980) *Business Research Methods*, Illinois: Irwin & Co, 2nd edition, 38–9.

Helmstadter, G. C. (1970) *Research Concepts in Human Behaviour*, Appleton: Century Crofts, 37–8.

House, R. J. (1970) 'Scientific investigations in management', *Management International Review* 4, 5: 139–50.

Weisburg, H. F. and Bowen, B. D. (1977) *An Introduction to Survey Research and Data Analysis*, Freeman.

7 Research methodology in organizational studies[1]

Philip M. Podsakoff and Dan R. Dalton

A few years ago a survey was conducted that, among other things, solicited the opinions of selected members of the Division of Industrial and Organizational Psychology and the Academy of Management on the state of research in their discipline (Campbell *et al.* 1982). Based on the responses and comments generated, the authors of the survey concluded in part that 'the predominant impression is that people are well aware of what is published and are very dissatisfied with it. A very negativistic theme runs throughout the respondent comments.' (1982: 71) This is, of course, a potentially severe indictment. In a somewhat different context, we also provide an overview of the state of research in the following sections. Unlike Campbell *et al.*, however, we do not address the subject matter examined in the organizational sciences. Rather, we focus here on the research methods employed by those interested in organizational questions.

We do not know how those who may read this chapter will respond to the information it contains. To add some perspective to its content, however, it may be useful to consider the profile of what a typical research effort in organizational studies might entail. By *typical*, we mean only the inclusion of those characteristics that a study would most likely have based on the data we report in the following sections. The results of this hypothetical study would be based on:

1 a survey relying on a questionnaire that solicits data from a single sample, or a laboratory study relying on student subjects;
2 conducted at the individual level of analysis;
3 with a sample size of some 372 subjects from the private sector of the economy who are professional/managerial/technical personnel if conducted in the field, or 115 college subjects if conducted in the laboratory;
4 there will be more than one dependent variable and those variables will be attitudinal and/or perceptual;

5 these data will be cross-sectional and analysed by regression techniques or ANOVA;

6 there will be no provision for cross-validation or any hold-out procedures; and,

7 the construct validity of the various metrics, scales, or measures relied on in this study will not be shared with the reader.

Suppose someone – perhaps yourself – who regularly supervises research were approached by a doctoral student with interests in some aspect of organizational studies. You are asked to serve on or chair a dissertation committee and are presented with a formal proposal that is based on the methods and analyses just noted. Although it is possible that a variety of interesting questions could no doubt have been addressed by similar methods, it would have to be fairly acknowledged that no single aspect of this proposed study is consistent with what might be immodestly referred to as the cutting edge of organizational inquiry. Many would be far more comfortable serving on this project if it were, for example, longitudinal as opposed to cross-sectional, or considered some behavioural as opposed to perceptual or attitudinal metric, or would be cross-validated, or – better yet – some combination of these. The information that follows, however, indicates that any of these demands to change the methods of this proposed research made on a doctoral student, or faculty member, or anyone else for that matter, would result in a project that is altogether *atypical* of the current state of organizational research.

The purpose of this chapter is twofold. The first goal is to examine the current literature and provide a much more specific description of the research methods and analyses that are employed in the field of organizational studies. Here we rely on a comprehensive review of all research reported for 1985 in five largely empirical journals dedicated almost exclusively to organizational studies.

The second objective of this report is to propose some explanation for the dynamics that may account in part for the incidence and, at times, persistence of some methods and analytical procedures. Potential causes of the use of specific methods is included as well as a discussion of possible implications for the field of organizational studies as a whole.

AN OVERVIEW

Recently, Sears has noted that 'every science has its own methodological idiosyncrasies' (Sears 1986: 515). Disciplines such as astronomy and physics primarily rely on observation aided by sophisticated apparatus. Mathematicians more often rely on derived proofs that are presumably consistent with the assumptions of the system. Archaeologists, botanists, clinical psychologists, cultural anthropologists, pharmacologists, and members of countless disciplines and subdisciplines also rely to a greater or lesser extent on a relatively small number of methods by which their data are ordinarily collected.

By *data* we do not assume that the information collected or produced by these various methods will be subject to statistical analysis or even hypothesis testing of any sort. Rather, we are more comfortable with the broad interpretation of data provided by Webster's dictionary 'factual information ... used as a basis for reasoning, discussion, or calculation'. We would strongly argue that every scientific endeavour has these data in common. No matter what the discipline, no matter what the method, all systematic inquiry includes the collection, derivation, or production of such information. Even so, the choice of method to pursue this information is actually quite restricted. Kaplan notes some of the dynamics that limit individual discretion in these choices:

> Every discipline develops standards of professional competence to which its workers are subject. There are certain acceptable ways of interpreting a projective test, of carrying out a dig, of surveying public opinion. Case studies, experiments, hypotheses, theories – all must meet certain conditions if they are to be taken seriously by the profession. The conditions are seldom made wholly explicit, and they differ for different disciplines and at different times; but in any case, their demands are likely to be firm and unyielding.
>
> (Kaplan 1964: 4)

The issue of a limited set of research methods is not, in itself, problematic. Indeed, the use of a relatively restricted set of methods may have some substantial benefits, not the least of which is that it permits the accumulation of data in a more efficient manner and allows one to conduct comparative analyses across studies. Recently, however, a mounting number of criticisms of the current 'methods of choice' in the organizational sciences have been expressed.

Some of these criticisms focus on the applicability (or presumed lack of it) of the findings obtained from the use of a relatively restricted range of 'normal science' methodologies to the problems that organizational practitioners face (e.g. Boehm 1980; Gordon *et al.* 1978; Kilmann 1979; McGuire 1986; Morgan and Smircich 1980; Strasser and Bateman 1984; Susman and Evered 1978; Thomas and Tymon 1982). Thomas and Tymon (1982), for example, have identified five different areas where the needs of the organizational scientist using contemporary methods of research may conflict with the needs of the practitioner in organizational settings: descriptive relevance, goal relevance, operational validity, non-obviousness, and timeliness.

Other, related, criticisms focus on the differences in the epistemological and ontological assumptions of researchers who use traditional quantitative methodologies as opposed to managers and those who use non-traditional qualitative methodologies (cf. Guba and Lincoln 1982; Lincoln and Guba 1985; McGuire 1986; Morgan and Smircich 1980; Susman and Evered 1978; Thomas and Tymon 1982), and to the descriptive as opposed to action orientation of the fields of organizational behaviour and organizational theory (Pondy 1972; Thomas and Tymon 1982; Tosi 1979).

Still another set of criticisms focus on the practices used by those who conduct research using the prevailing methods of our time. One part of this criticism is aimed at the general lack of sophistication in the development and refinement of the measures used in the organizational sciences. Schwab, for example, has noted that there has been a disturbing tendency for many researchers in the field of organizational behaviour to examine the substantive validity of a variable before its construct validity has been established. He warns that such practices may necessitate the rejection of much empirical evidence from earlier research efforts (Schwab 1980). This point has also been noted by Cummings (1978), Mitchell (1985), and Venkatraman and Grant (1986). More recently, Phillips and Lord (1986) have argued that many researchers have assumed that the more reliable questionnaires are in terms of estimates of internal consistency, the more valid they are, even though any systematic source of variance (halo effects, implicit personality theories, leniency errors) can produce high internal consistency. Finally, another part of this criticism is aimed at the practices of those members of the research community who conduct studies in laboratory settings, including the artificial laboratory setting, and the use of college students as subjects (Gordon *et al.* 1986, 1987; Sears 1986).

Unfortunately, despite the number of criticisms that have been levelled against the methods used in the organizational sciences, surprisingly little research has been conducted to actually examine the prevailing methods employed in the field or the potential reasons why these methods are used. This is not to say that an examination of the research practices of organizational scientists have been totally neglected. For example, Dipboye and Flanagan (1979), Flanagan and Dipboye (1981), and Muchinsky (1979) have reported some research on the characteristics of laboratory and field studies in the field of industrial and organizational psychology. Similarly, Campbell *et al.* have provided an analysis of the organizational behaviour research literature (examining five peer-reviewed journals over two years) to determine the types of topics and questions asked over the examination period (Campbell *et al.* 1982), and Daft developed a twenty-year retrospective of articles appearing in *Administrative Science Quarterly* with the intent of comparing the complexity of organizational models and the variety of language used to transmit observations about organizations over that period (Daft 1980). More recently, Mitchell has examined the validity of correlational field research conducted in organizational settings (Mitchell 1985). Finally, Rosnow, among others, has attempted to identify some of the causes of the current states of social research methodologies (Rosnow 1981).

Nonetheless, even with the studies cited above, it must be acknowledged that there is at best only a modest tradition of research that has examined the nature of methods employed in organizational studies. We propose, then, to examine the current literature in organizational research and report the nature of the various research methodologies employed by these studies.

METHOD

Journals reviewed

In order to assess the characteristics of the research in the field of organizational studies, all articles published in the *Academy of Management Journal, Administrative Science Quarterly, Journal of Applied Psychology, Journal of Management*, and *Organizational Behavior and Human Decision Processes* during 1985 were obtained and read. The year 1985 was chosen because it represented the most recent, complete year of publication for each of these journals available to the authors at the time of this chapter.

The specific sample of journals was selected with the concurrence of the editors of the *Yearly Review* to meet several criteria. First, they all represent examples of journals that publish peer-reviewed, empirical research. Second, these journals are well respected, highly evaluated (e.g. Coe and Weinstock 1984, Howard *et al.* 1985), and have been used for similar purposes in the past (e.g. Campbell *et al.* 1982, Mitchell 1985). Third, although the studies reported in these journals during this period are certainly not exhaustive, we do feel that they represent a subset of empirical work across a broad spectrum of subdisciplines in organizational studies.

Despite these advantages, however, it should be recognized that quantitative, positivistic, normal science research dominated much of the literature published in these journals in 1985. This is a limitation, and parenthetically a symptom of a potential problem that we intend to discuss in the conclusions of the chapter.

Classification of studies

There were 213 total articles in these journals in 1985. Twenty of these (e.g. conceptual papers, comments, replies, descriptive reviews) were excluded from our review as they did not report empirically based research, leaving

193 articles for analysis. For purposes of this review, twelve coding dimensions were selected for analyses:

1 Primary location of data collection.
2 Level of analysis.
3 Sample size.
4 Type of sample.
5 Occupation of subjects.
6 Primary means of data collection.

7 Type of dependent variable.
8 Number of dependent variables.
9 Type of analysis.
10 Time-frame of study.
11 Nature of results verification.
12 Nature of construct validation procedure.

RESULTS

Primary location of data collection

Table 7.1 reports the primary location from which the data for the 193 studies analysed in this review were derived. It is apparent that nearly 70 per cent of all research conducted in organizational studies reported in 1985 relied on information derived from either survey instruments or laboratory research.

Table 7.1 Primary locale of data collection

Survey	40.0
Laboratory	29.5
Field	14.0
Archival	15.5
Mixed	0.5
Other	0.5
Total	100.0

Level of analysis

Table 7.2 presents the level of analysis of research conducted in organizational studies. Overall, just over 73 per cent of research published is at the individual level of analysis, with organizational level second (14.8 per cent), and the relatively little research conducted at the group level third (6.5 per cent). As would be expected, laboratory research is conducted solely at the individual and group level. There is a modest amount of aggregation of survey research to reflect an organization level focus. Not surprisingly, the majority of archival research is conducted at the organizational level.

Table 7.2 Level of analysis (%)

	Overall	Survey	Laboratory	Field	Archival
			Setting of study		
Individual	73.4	88.4	87.9	57.1	30.0
Organizational	14.8	7.2		25.0	53.3
Group	6.5	1.4	8.6	14.3	3.3
Mixed	3.6	2.9	3.4		13.3
Other	1.8			3.6	
Total	100.0	100.0	100.0	100.0	100.0

Sample characteristics

Sample size Table 7.3 summarizes the characteristics of the samples used in research in the organizational sciences. As indicated in this table, survey data collection procedures on average have larger sample sizes and a far greater range than reported in other types of research settings: conversely, reliance on laboratory protocols apparently results in smaller sample sizes.

Type of sample Overall, over two-thirds (68.26 per cent) of the samples reported in organizational studies consisted of respondents from private sector organizations or student subjects. However, closer examination across research settings indicates that the archival studies reported in 1985 in the examined journals depended almost exclusively (81.5 per cent) on private sector samples (perhaps because many of these studies depend on the financial information that can be obtained from these organizations), whereas the majority of field research reported relied on public sector and not-for-profit organizations (74 per cent), and laboratory research rarely used anything other than student samples (89.5 per cent). Given the general importance accorded to identifying the characteristics of the sample under study, it is somewhat surprising that almost 12 per cent of the empirical studies reported in 1985 did not indicate the nature of the sample.

Occupation of subjects Students represent the single largest percentage of subjects for organizational studies. This results from the very large percentage of laboratory studies (89.5 per cent) that rely almost exclusively on student subjects. Consistent with the findings of Dipboye and Flanagan (1979), professional, managerial, and technical workers, and mixed occupational groupings (including professional, managerial, and technical workers, along with one or more of the other occupational groupings) accounted for the majority of the subjects used in survey and field settings. Also consistent with the results reported for the type of sample, the relatively large percentage of studies (14.7 per cent) that did not report the occupation of subjects is somewhat disturbing. Organizational level studies, however their data is collected, account for the 'not applicable' category. Many of these studies, of course, have no individual subjects at all.

Table 7.3 Sample characteristics of research in organizational studies

Characteristic	Setting of study				
	Overall	*Survey*	*Laboratory*	*Field*	*Archival*
Sample size (N)					
Mean	253.94	372.71	114.78	224.29	271.88
Standard deviation	404.02	540.80	135.17	285.28	290.64
Range	1–3200	20–3200	4–876	1–1020	20–1280
Type of sample (%)					
Private sector	34.96	52.31	5.30	33.30	81.50
Public sector	12.27	16.92		40.70	3.70
Not-for-profit	1.84	1.54		11.10	
Mixed	5.52	10.77		3.70	3.60
Not reported	11.65	18.46	5.30	11.10	11.10
Student subjects	33.30		89.50		
Other	0.61				
Total	100.00	100.00	100.00	100.00	100.00
Occupation of subjects (%)					
Prof/mngrl/tech	18.40	29.00	3.50	22.20	25.90
White collar	4.90	7.20	1.80	3.70	11.10
Blue collar	6.10	11.60		14.80	3.70
Students	33.70	5.80	89.50		3.70
Mixed	12.90	21.70		25.90	7.40
Other	1.20	1.40			
Not reported	14.70	21.70	5.30	14.80	14.80
Not applicable	8.00	1.40		18.50	33.30
Total	100.00	100.00	100.00	100.00	100.00

Means of data collection

Table 7.4 reports the primary means of data collection procedures used in the survey, laboratory, field, archival, and overall studies in the organizational sciences. As is evident from this table, although a variety of different means have been used for collecting data, questionnaires are used as the primary source of data collection in over a third (36.20 per cent) of the studies, and questionnaires, along with laboratory manipulations, account for over half (56.45 per cent) of the procedures used in the organizational studies. Although not reported in this table, only one descriptive review (less than 1 per cent of the articles examined) was reported in the five journals reviewed in 1985. This, coupled with the obvious burgeoning in meta-analytic reviews over the past decade (cf. Guzzo *et al*. in press), suggests that the cautions of possible misinterpretations with the descriptive review format (e.g. Glass *et al*. 1981; Hunter *et al*. 1982; Rosenthal 1984; Sackett *et al*. 1985; Schmidt *et al*. 1985) have apparently been well received.

There has been a long-standing, distinguished tradition of research by cultural anthropologists, and to a somewhat lesser extent by sociologists, that has relied on ethnomethodological procedures. More recently, there have been concerted efforts to introduce its use more widely for organizational applications. Many will recall a special volume of *Administrative Science Quarterly* (1979, 24, 4, J. Van Maanen, [ed.]) dedicated to 'qualitative', 'ethnographic', 'direct' research. Since then, a large amount of related work has described and enthusiastically endorsed this form of inquiry for organizational studies (e.g. Agar 1986; Kirk and Miller 1986; Van Maanen *et al*. 1982).

Table 7.4 suggests that little work of this ethnographic type appeared in the organizational sciences in 1985. No research reviewed here relied on participant observation techniques. There was, however, a modest percentage of studies classified under 'non-participant observation' that may be reasonably included as qualitative, or interpretative research. Nevertheless, however considered, research that could be included even broadly in such a category was rarely seen in these journals during the year examined.

Table 7.4 Means of data collection (%)

Primary data collection procedure	Setting of study				
	Overall	*Survey*	*Laboratory*	*Field*	*Archival*
Questionnaire	36.20	68.00	14.93	30.43	19.15
Laboratory task	20.25	1.00	70.15		
Archival	14.22	9.00	1.49	8.70	63.83
Interview	12.06	12.00	4.48	32.61	12.77
Meta-analytic review	3.87				
Simulation	3.01				
Naturally occurring field experiment	2.58	2.00		6.52	2.13
Field experiment	2.15	1.00		8.70	
Nonparticipant observation	2.15	4.00		6.52	
Behaviour recording	1.29	1.00	4.48		
Nominal group/delphi	0.86	1.00		4.35	2.13
Other	1.29	1.00	4.48	2.17	
Total	100.00	100.00	100.00	100.00	100.00

Characteristics of the dependent variable

Type of dependent variables Almost a decade has passed since Cummings' warning that 'unless OB can increase its performance payoffs, the field may be in danger of losing some of its hard battles for a niche in the curriculum or a moment in the boardroom' (Cummings 1978: 94). Similarly, with reference to organizational strategy research, Hambrick (1980) and Lenz (1981) also argue that the most obvious and useful research questions should address the factors and linkages that influence performance. Schneider, too, is persuasive in endorsing the practical aspects of considering productivity, including both 'rapprochement with other areas of business study and ... educating business, industry, and government to the very large potential benefits of research and intervention...' (Schneider 1985: 598).

Given the usefulness of measuring observable outcomes, the data reported in table 7.5 is perhaps disappointing. Overall, slightly over 18 per cent of the reviewed studies used performance or productivity as the major dependent variables. Other (non-performance) outcomes, including absenteeism, turnover, acquisition and divestitures, among others, accounted for an additional 28.76 per cent. However, taken together, perceptual measures (e.g. perceptions of external environment, supervisory behaviour, leadership style, extent of formalization, standardization, [de]centralization, intentions to act) and attitudinal dependent variables including job satisfaction, self-assessments of certain predispositions (e.g. locus of control, manifest needs) and psychological states (e.g. stress, motivation) account for the majority (52.04 per cent) of the types of measures used in organizational studies.

Table 7.5 Characteristics of dependent variables (%)

Characteristic	Setting of study				
	Overall	*Survey*	*Laboratory*	*Field*	*Archival*
Type of dependent variable					
Performance	18.26	11.11	25.32	11.76	24.24
Other outcomes	28.76	20.20	29.11	23.53	57.58
Perceptual	35.15	41.41	31.65	38.24	12.12
Attitudinal	16.89	26.26	13.92	17.65	6.06
Other	0.91	1.01		8.82	
Total	100.00	100.00	100.00	100.00	100.00
Number of dependent variables					
Single dependent variable	33.11	36.67	22.64	33.33	35.71
Multiple dependent variables	66.89	63.33	77.36	66.67	64.29
Total	100.00	100.00	100.00	100.00	100.00

Here a note of caution might be reasonably well placed. No doubt, Cummings' notion of 'performance payoffs' (Cummings 1978) could be addressed in any number of ways. Also, there is an obvious problem with establishing a baseline. Although it would be a fascinating subject for future research, we admit that we do not know what proportion of research in other disciplines (e.g. social psychology, cultural anthropology) or in the field of the organizational studies in the past relies on behavioural (as opposed to attitudinal, perceptual, etc.) dependent variables. We concede a certain value judgement here, but would add that a case could be made that organizational studies should rely on such variables more often.

Number of dependent variables Table 7.5 also illustrates the incidence of studies that rely on multiple dependent variables. As indicated in this table, two-thirds (66.89 per cent) of the studies reported using multiple rather than single dependent measures.

Types of analyses

Although it is true that multiple dependent variables are commonly used, this in and of itself is of little interest. A review of table 7.6 (types of analyses), however, indicates a potential problem. Some 67 per cent of the research has more than one dependent variable, but only 6.6 per cent of the research relies on analytical procedures (e.g. canonical correlation, MANOVA, MANOCOVA) that simultaneously treat multiple dependent variables.

That such simultaneous treatments have several advantages has been recognized frequently (e.g. Bray and Maxwell 1985; Cohen and Cohen 1983; Kerlinger and Pedhazur 1973; Levine 1977; Thompson 1984). Cohen and Cohen, for example, note that the analytical advantages of such procedures 'in behavioral science hardly needs demonstrating' (Cohen and Cohen 1983: 453). Unfortunately, even though researchers have repeatedly been encouraged to use these simultaneous assessment analyses with multiple dependent variables for over a decade (cf. Baggaley 1981; Tatsuoka 1973; Thompson 1984; Thorndike 1977), it would appear based on this review that less than 7 per cent of eligible studies apply these techniques.

We do not wish to appear overly evaluative. There may be a number of reasons why a study with multiple dependent variables would not necessarily have to rely on a simultaneous analysis. On the other hand, it seems reasonable that multiple dependent measures are normally seen where independent variables are thought to be conceptually related to them. In any case, 7 per cent seems low, although once again we would acknowledge that we have no frame of reference with other disciplines and their analyses.

Table 7.6 Type of analyses (%)

Analytical procedure	Setting of study				
	Overall	Survey	Laboratory	Field	Archival
Correlation	20.53	29.55	17.92	16.67	22.50
ANOVA	18.54	9.09	35.85	12.50	7.50
Multiple regression	14.24	15.91	10.38	12.50	32.50
MANOVA	5.30	2.27	11.32		5.00
Descriptive	5.30	2.27	2.83	8.33	
ANCOVA	4.64	3.03	6.60	6.25	
Crosstabs (contingency)	3.31	4.55	1.89	2.08	2.50
Factor analyses	3.31	5.30	0.94	4.17	2.50
Partial correlation	3.64	6.82	0.94	4.17	5.00
Moderated regression	2.65	3.03	1.89	6.25	
Discriminant	1.66	2.27			2.50
Interpretative	1.66	0.76		6.25	7.50
T-tests	1.66	1.52	0.94	4.17	
Categorical analyses	1.32	2.27			2.50
Repeated measures ANOVA	1.32		3.77		
Canonical correlation	0.99	2.27		2.08	
Non-parametric regression	0.99	0.76		2.08	
Time series analyses	0.99		0.94	4.17	2.50
Change scores	0.66	0.76		2.08	
Cluster analyses	0.66	0.76		2.08	
Curvilinearity tests	0.66	0.76			2.50
Gamma	0.66	1.52			
Lisrel	0.66	0.76			2.50
Network analyses	0.66	1.52			
Multi-dimensional scaling	0.65	0.76	1.89		
Catastrophe algorithms	0.65				
Comparative case-studies	0.33				
Conjoint analyses	0.33		0.94		
Cross-lag	0.33				
Difference of proportions	0.33			2.08	
MANOCOVA	0.33				2.50
Path analyses	0.33			2.08	
Yules Q (contingency)	0.33				
Other	0.33		0.94		
	0.66	1.52			
Total	100.00	100.00	100.00	100.00	100.00

Time frame of study

Several researchers (Bohrnstedt 1975; Fleishman 1973; Kerr and Schriesheim 1974; Kimberly 1976; Liker *et al.* 1985; Sashkin and Garland 1979) have noted the advantage of longitudinal research to the study of social and organizational phenomenon. Such studies facilitate a researcher's attempts to establish causal priorities between variables, as well as the degree of mutual dependence of the relationships between two or more variables. Table 7.7 indicates that about one-fifth (21.24 per cent) of the reviewed studies employed longitudinal as opposed to cross-sectional designs. Interestingly, however, the data in table 7.6 indicate that less than 5 per cent of the studies used change scores, cross-lagged correlation procedures, repeated measures ANOVA, path analyses, or time series analyses; this suggests the possibility that those studies that at times report the collection of 'longitudinal' data do not always analyse the data in this manner.

Table 7.7 Time frame of study (%)

| | Setting of study | | | | |
	Overall	*Survey*	*Laboratory*	*Field*	*Archival*
Cross-sectional	78.76	81.54	79.07	66.67	76.67
Longitudinal	21.24	18.46	20.93	33.33	23.33
Total	100.00	100.00	100.00	100.00	100.00

Results verification

Presumably, researchers should be concerned about the accuracy of their results. We are normally concerned as researchers and reviewers that the results reported are generalizable. Toward that objective, there are any number of procedures researchers can use to assess the predictive robustness and stability of their own results. Cross-validation procedures (e.g. Kerlinger and Pedhazur 1973) and exploratory/confirmatory factor analyses (e.g. Kim and Mueller 1978) are two examples of such techniques.

Table 7.8 provides an illustration of the extent to which these and other

Table 7.8 Nature of results verification (%)

| | Setting of study | | | | |
	Overall	*Survey*	*Laboratory*	*Field*	*Archival*
Cross-validation	4.96	4.35	3.45	3.57	3.33
Sub-group analyses	4.25	7.25		3.57	3.33
Exploratory/confirmatory factor analyses	2.12	1.45	1.72		3.33
Other hold-out group analyses	1.41	1.45	1.72		3.33
Multiple levels of analysis	1.41	1.45			3.33
Multitrait/multimethod	2.83	5.80		3.57	
None reported	82.97	78.26	93.10	89.29	83.33
Total	100.00	100.00	100.00	100.00	100.00

techniques of validation are used. Taken together, less than 5 per cent of the studies attempted to cross-validate their findings, and less than 15 per cent attempted any form of results verification at all. Interestingly, there is some evidence that the current review does not represent an anomalous year. Mitchell (1985) reported a similarly low (5.5 per cent) level of cross-validation/hold-out techniques in correlational field studies for the years 1979–1983 for a number of selected journals, all of which are included in this review.

Construct validation

There has been a continuing concern in organizational studies regarding the extent to which the many constructs that we rely on so heavily are valid, that is, that the values derived from their use are reasonable approximations of some true, but presumably unknown, 'real' value. Many critics (e.g. Churchill 1979; Jacoby 1978; Mitchell 1985; Schwab 1980) argue that little or no effort is committed to determining the extent to which constructs measure what they purport to measure. This point has been made somewhat harshly by one of our marketing colleagues:

> More stupefying than the sheer number of our measures is the ease with which they are proposed and the uncritical manner in which they are accepted. In point of fact, most of our measures are only measures because someone says that they are....
>
> (Jacoby 1978: 91)

Table 7.9 does not provide much in the way of comfort to those who share this opinion. Few of the studies (3.23 per cent overall) that relied on construct measures reported any direct evidence of the discriminant or convergent validity of the measures used. It is notable that a very large percentage of

Table 7.9 Nature of construct validation efforts (%)

	Setting of study				
	Overall	*Survey*	*Laboratory*	*Field*	*Archival*
Reliability	66.67	62.69	76.47	76.92	71.43
Factor analyses	20.43	23.88	11.76	15.38	14.29
Discriminant/convergent/ predictive validity	3.23	4.48			
Interrater validity	2.15	1.49	5.88		
None reported	7.53	7.46	5.88	7.69	14.29
Total	100.00	100.00	100.00	100.00	100.00

studies did report reliabilities (almost exclusively Cronbach's alpha) and factor analyses for the items that constitute the construct scales. However, as noted by Schwab (1980), among others, factor analyses and reports of reliability are not adequate, in and of themselves, for establishing the validity of a construct.

We have essentially provided in the first part of this chapter the frequencies of certain approaches to research in organizational studies. We shamelessly adopt a central caveat provided by Campbell *et al.* (1982) in a slightly different context. They admonish us that there is no necessary relationship between the importance of an area or a subject and its popularity as judged by the frequency with which it is studied. Likewise, the disproportionate presence of a given method, analytical technique, type of sample, or any other relevant dimension is neither an indictment against nor an endorsement for its use. As noted earlier in this chapter, there are certain methods in any discipline that are accepted; they constitute normal manners of inquiry. They are not necessarily 'right' or 'better' than any other means. The use of such means can also be quite persistent, in common use well after many analysts believe they no longer constitute the cutting edge of a discipline. The second part of this manuscript, then, addresses the possible dynamics that may account at least in part for the possible intransigence of some approaches to organizational studies.

WHY ARE RESEARCH METHODS SO RESISTANT TO CHANGE?

We began this paper with a bit of a tease, a scenario where we presented the profile of a 'typical' study with all the characteristics that the results of this review would suggest it would have. Such a design might adequately – even notably – result in a responsible piece of research. As noted, however, it would probably not constitute 'cutting edge' research methods or analysis.

Given that two hypothetical pieces of research are adequate in every other way, few researchers would have any trouble deciding which of the following sets of choices constitutes a 'better' treatment: longitudinal versus cross-sectional; cross-validated versus not cross-validated; organizational sample versus student subjects; performance dependent variable(s) versus non-performance; construct validated versus otherwise. We would venture to say that nearly everyone would choose the first option in virtually every case, all else being equal. Even so, the second options are those that are most commonly reflected in the current literature. Why? Despite the discussions and entreaties to use methods other than those that prevail in the field of organizational studies, why do we continue to see the same traditional methods used over and over again? Why do researchers in the field seem so resistant to change and to the adoption of new (or non-traditional) methods?

We could resort to an often cited authority on why change is so difficult:

> It must be considered that there is nothing more difficult to carry out, nor more doubtful of success, nor more dangerous to handle, than to initiate a new order of things. For the reformer has enemies in all those who profit by the old order, and only lukewarm defenders in all those who would profit by the new order ... who do not truly believe in anything new until they have had actual experience of it.
>
> (Machiavelli 1532 [1952]: 49–50)

Machiavelli was obviously not addressing himself to the issue of some intransigence in research methods. Even so, his admonitions may be well placed. Unfortunately, although we will rely on them in part, they do lack a certain specificity and are not prescriptive.

However, Rogers' classic *Diffusion of Innovations* (1983) provides a far more systematic approach for explaining why some innovations are adopted more easily than others. Rogers applies his work to innovations across a very broad range of disciplines (e.g. anthropology, sociology, education, public health, communication, marketing, geography, organizational studies). We presume here to apply his guidelines to innovations in research methodology as well.

According to Rogers, there are several characteristics common to innovations that help explain their different rates of adoption:

1 *Relative advantage* is the degree to which an innovation is perceived as better than the idea it replaces.
2 *Compatibility* is the degree to which an innovation is perceived as being consistent with existing values, past experiences, and the needs of potential adopters.
3 *Complexity* is the degree to which an innovation is perceived as difficult to understand and use.
4 *Triability* is the degree to which an innovation may be experimented with on a limited basis.
5 *Observability* is the ease with which the results of an innovation can be seen.

An example: meta-analysis vs ethnomethodological inquiry

We noted earlier that meta-analytical techniques seem to have largely supplanted descriptive reviews. At the same time, ethnomethodological study, despite its continuing and impassioned advocacy, still does not appear in the current literature. An examination of Rogers' criteria for adoption of innovations may help explain these developments.

Rogers argues that 'it does not matter so much whether an innovation has a great deal of 'objective' advantage. What does matter is whether an individual perceives the innovation as advantageous' (Rogers 1983: 15). Few would argue that meta-analytic techniques do not have some advantages. True, there may be some continuing controversy about exactly how (technically) to conduct a meta-analysis. But, that aside, it does possess certain advantages over traditional descriptive reviews. (We assume here that there are sufficient studies to conduct a reasonable analysis.)

Meta-analytic techniques also seem compatible with current, mainstream, quantitative, data-analytic approaches. The use of such techniques does not constitute some quantum leap in the philosophy of inquiry. For, like traditional statistical analyses, it provides a summary of data. Does this technique meet the 'needs of potential adopters'? We think the current widespread use of this approach attests to its usefulness in numerous subdisciplines of the field. At the most practical level, we wonder if a current literature review (again, with sufficient studies) could be published in any of these sample journals if it did not rely on meta-analytical techniques.

These techniques also meet Roger's 'complexity' standard: they are not overly complex. Meta-analysis probably requires little additional knowledge or training for most potential users to apply these procedures. 'Triability' is also evident. There is little investment involved in time and effort. Most investigators could try meta-analysis on some group of studies with relative ease and on a limited basis.

Finally, we would submit that Rogers' criterion of 'observability' is also easily met. The results of the meta-analysis innovation are evident to anyone: look at the journals. Meta-analysis works at least to the extent that it results in published work, a presumably salient outcome. For this point Rogers is emphatic, 'The easier it is for individuals to see the results of an innovation, the more likely they are to adopt it' (Rogers 1983: 16).

Ethnomethodological approaches, in contrast, meet few of Rogers' adoption criteria. Undoubtedly, there are any number of advantages to be gained by such 'direct' techniques. But to suggest that these approaches are widely perceived to be better than the more traditional methods that they would in part supplant is, we believe, an overstatement.

Ethnomethodological inquiry may also be viewed as incompatible with the existing values, past experiences, and needs of many of the potential adopters (cf. Guba and Lincoln 1982; Lincoln and Guba 1985; McGuire 1986), not to mention their professional training. Thus it would appear that this method is probably not compatible with the values and norms of many organizational researchers.

Also, qualitative research may be seen as somewhat complex by many observers. For most, perhaps because of their (lack of?) training in this area, it may be difficult to understand and hard to use. Therefore, it is not really subject to 'triability'. To go into the field with a commitment to conduct excellent qualitative work is not something many researchers would consider doing on a limited, trial basis.

Lastly, and perhaps most importantly, qualitative research does not meet Rogers' criterion of observability. As indicated in our review, little research conducted with these methods appeared in the mainstream empirical journals in 1985. As long as there are few exemplars or examples for others to view, the innovation is not likely to be widely adopted.

Given these conditions, Rogers would suggest that this innovation – the use of ethnomethodological techniques – if adopted at all, would be adopted very slowly. The comparisons drawn here between meta-analysis and ethno-methodology should not be interpreted evaluatively. We don't mean to suggest that one or the other of these innovations is better in some overall sense. We claim no special expertise in either technique and apologize if we have treated either too cavalierly. Rather, we suggest only that one is more likely to be adopted than the other because of its diffusion characteristics.

OTHER PRAGMATIC CONCERNS

We do not, of course, mean to suggest that an innovation's diffusion characteristics are the only factors that account for the intransigence in organizational research methodologies. In addition, there are several other pragmatic issues that contribute to the scientific community's persistence in the use of particular methods as well.

People do what they know

Evidence that the training that scientists receive has a substantial impact on the research they conduct and the methods they use has been provided recently by Gieri (in press). He reported that the cognitive resources individuals acquire in their training not only influence the choice of the problems they are interested in, but, more importantly for our discussion, the methods employed to examine the problem of interest. Thus it should not be surprising that young researchers trained in the use of traditional research techniques will rely primarily on these methods in their own research.

People do what they have done

Arkes and Blumer (1985) hypothesized that individuals exhibit a greater tendency to continue an endeavour once they have expended time, money, or effort on the endeavour than when they have not expended such resources, because they have difficulty ignoring these 'sunk costs' in their decision-making processes. In the context of our earlier discussion of training and cognitive resources, however, another possible reason for the tendency to continue to use the same research strategy, even if there is evidence that it is not the most effective one that can be used, is that the transition costs associated with acquiring new cognitive resources may also be perceived to be prohibitively high.

People do what is efficient (easier?)

Anyone who conducts research knows that it takes a considerable amount of time, effort, and money – all of which are limited resources. As a result, the use of those methods that use these resources efficiently are likely to be viewed with considerable favour.

So, for example, it should not be surprising to find that students are widely used in the majority of laboratory studies. Several researchers (Christie 1965, Gordon *et al*. 1986, Higbee *et al*. 1976, Smart 1966) have noted the pragmatic advantages of using college students as subjects. Smart for example, concluded that 'College students are employed so extensively chiefly because of opportunistic reasons. In most university settings they are a captive group of willing subjects anxious to please instructors or complete course requirements by participating in faculty research' (Smart 1966: 120). Similarly, Higbee, Lott, and Graves noted that 'college students are ... the most easily accessible subjects for college professors, who comprise most of the researchers' (Higbee *et al*. 1976: 240). Nor, if recent evidence is any indication, is this trend in the use of college students likely to change in the behavioural sciences in the near future.

Table 7.10 reports summaries of the percentage of studies in social psychology and from the present study that use students as subjects. This table indicates that students are the overwhelming subjects of choice in social psychology, and to a lesser extent are depended on widely in laboratory research in the organizational sciences. Thus, as noted by Gordon *et al*.:

It is unlikely that applied behavioural researchers will reduce their reliance upon college students of their own volition. The availability of undergraduates and university laboratories (expenditures for the latter are often justified by college administrators in terms of their level of use) militate against any significant shift to research in settings to which research findings are intended to apply. Also, in this era of tight budgets

Table 7.10 Percentage of research studies using college students as subjects

Author(s)	Discipline	Journal(s) examined	Year(s) covered	Studies using students (%)
Christie (1965)	Social Psychology	*Journal of Abnormal and Social Psychology*	1949	20
Christie (1965)	Social Psychology	*Journal of Abnormal and Social Psychology*	1959	49
Smart (1966)	Social Psychology	*Journal of Abnormal and Social Psychology*	1963–1964	73
Smart (1966)	Social Psychology	*Journal of Abnormal and Social Psychology*	1963–1964	86
Schultz (1969)	Social Psychology	*Journal of Personality and Social Psychology*	1966–1967	70
Schultz (1969)	Social Psychology	*Journal of Experimental Psychology*	1966–1967	84
Carlson (1971)	Social Psychology	*Journal of Personality and Social Psychology and Journal of Personality*	1968	66
Higbee and Wells (1972)	Social Psychology	*Journal of Personality and Social Psychology*	1969	76
Higbee *et al.* (1976)	Social Psychology	*Journal of Experimental and Social Psychology*	1969	80
		Journal of Social Psychology	1969	53
		Sociometry	1969	69
		Journal of Personality and Social Psychology	1970	70
		Journal of Personality and Social Psychology	1971	86
		Journal of Personality and Social Psychology	1972	75
Higbee *et al.* (1982)	Social Psychology	*Journal of Experimental and Social Psychology*	1978–1979	96
		Journal of Social Psychology	1978–1979	57
		Social Psychology Quarterly	1978–1979	53
		Journal of Personality and Social Psychology	1978–1979	72
		Overall	1978–1979	61
Sears (1986)	Social Psychology	*Journal of Personality and Social Psychology*	1980	82
		Personality and Social Psychology Bulletin	1980	81
		Journal of Experimental Psychology	1980	89
Present study	Individual and Organizational Studies	*AMJ, JAP, JOM, OBHDP, ASQ*	1985	88[a]

Note: [a] Percentage of laboratory studies that included students as subjects.

for education generally, and research specifically, students offer a low cost alternative to investigating nonstudents.

(Gordon *et al*. 1986: 203)

Considerations of limited time, effort, and money are also probably partially responsible for the fact that so many field-studies utilize self-report measures obtained from respondents. In addition to the fact that self-report questionnaires are, in many cases, the most plausible alternative for measuring unobservable constructs such as the attitudes, values, intentions, perceptions, and personalities of organizational participants (Ganster *et al*. 1983), they are also (a) a convenient data collection technique that can be used to gather a relatively large sample with reasonable investment of time and trouble (Sims 1979: 209), (b) relatively easy to use (Ganster *et al*. 1983), (c) less expensive (Kidder 1981; Ganster *et al*. 1983), and (d) faster (Kidder 1981) than other field methodologies available for use.

People do what is rewarded

If publication can be considered rewarding, it seems clear that the use of traditional methods have been generously rewarded. In fact, based on this review, it seems that organizational researchers using the predominant paradigms (which as we noted generally are well articulated and therefore have less ambiguity associated with their use) are likely to be rewarded just as much, if not more, than the researchers who undertake nontraditional research methods. All else equal, it would be difficult to dissuade individuals from conducting research in the same fashion if they continue to be rewarded for it.

There exist, too, the ubiquitous promotion and tenure committees across the country. Is it possible that the typical evaluation from this group is more rewarding of *many* publications relying on traditional methods, as opposed to a *few* ethnographic, or perhaps multiple-year longitudinal, efforts? With all due respect, would you advise a new faculty member to embark on an extended programme of qualitative research? Of course, in the interest of fair reporting, this would not account for the lack of such methods in more senior faculty.

In the meantime, the literature reflects the continued use of traditional methods – cross-sectional, surveys, student subjects, no results verification, limited construct validity. It has been vigorously argued that these methods may not always represent the best means of collecting and analysing organizational data. Given the various dynamics that have been discussed, is it hopeless that changes can be introduced such that other, presumably more robust techniques, are seen relatively more often in our literature?

TOWARDS CHANGE

An obvious, if pedestrian, recommendation is that some people have to be more active in using non-traditional techniques. Kuhn recognizes the importance of 'exemplars' – examples of how to use and work successfully with the research methods and procedures (Kuhn 1974). Rogers, however, adds an important dimension. Exemplars are important to innovation inasmuch as they are the vanguard of new ideas and methods; however, they are a necessary, but insufficient condition for change (Rogers 1983).

There are several prerequisites to become an innovator: substantial resources to absorb your (high probability) losses; ability to understand and apply new, sometimes complex means and technologies; and the ability to withstand a high degree of uncertainty, ambiguity, and risk. Interestingly, these innovators are often not respected by the other members of the social system – here again, their community of colleagues. Indeed, in many cases these people are seen to be radical, as deviant. The role of these persons in persuading others to adopt the change is likely to be quite limited.

In addition to the innovators, Rogers argues that you must have 'opinion leaders' and sometimes 'change agents'. Opinion leaders are simply highly influential persons in the system. Change agents are basically those individuals who influence innovation decisions in a direction that is seen as appropriate by the change agent or by the organization with which the agent is associated. A variety of persons could be classically described as change agents: teachers, consultants, health workers, salespeople. We argue here that there are certainly opinion leaders in most organizational disciplines. Also, editors and reviewers are clearly potential change agents. Beyond that, and more directly, we argue that the only reasonable way that adoption of methodological innovation will be increased is through the practical leadership via publication of these opinion leaders and the intervention of the change agents. This would provide the publication observability that Rogers (1983) suggests is essential.

Increasing methodological diffusion

Whether the use of traditional methods limits our ability to examine complex processes over some extended period of time is, we expect, a debatable issue. However, we do agree with Rosnow that all research methods have their limitations and that there is an apparent need in the organizational sciences, as in social psychology, to explore the use of other research paradigms and procedures (Rosnow 1981). This does not mean that traditional methods of research used presently in the field should be abandoned, or even that the employment of such research should be de-emphasized as the primary strategies for examining organizational phenomenon. It seems clear, however, that any impetus for any change in methodologies should be brought about in large part by the direction of opinion leaders and change agents – ultimately our editors and reviewers. It is here and only here through the journals that the critical 'observability' of any phenomenon can be manifest. Without that observability, the incentive for change by individual researchers seems modest at best. There will always be innovators and strong advocates. A mature argument can be made that these, as previously noted, are necessary, but insufficient conditions for change.

There are, however, some encouraging signs of change toward the use of more diversified methods in the organizational sciences. Witness the inclusion over the past few years of reviewers with more diverse methodological interests on the editorial review boards of many of the journals included in this review, as well as the solicitation of articles using non-traditional methods by the editors of some of these journals. Papers incorporating qualitative methodologies, such as that published by Barley (1986) and those submitted and presented in the Research Methods Interest Group at the 1986 Academy of Management Meeting, are another sign of increased methodological diversity in the field, as are some of the papers appearing in the 1986 *Yearly Review* issue of the *Journal of Management* that were written from a more subjectivist orientation. Similarly, the development of the journal *Dragon*, which publishes interpretive, ethnographic, subjectivist papers, is another sign of the growth of pluralism in research methods in the organizational sciences.

Despite these signs of movement, we admit to some impatience and at some level concede its foolishness. By definition, 'cutting edge' could hardly be cutting edge if it were frequently encountered. Most would agree, though, that additional examination of the practices and potential problems of using the current methods of choice in the field of organizational studies is needed. Mitchell's recent analysis of the potential problems of research conducted in organizational settings using correlational techniques and his attempt to develop a checklist for judging the validity of such research designs is a good example (Mitchell 1985). Similarly, Schwab's (1980) analysis and discussion of construct validity, Phillips and Lord's (1986) treatment of measurement accuracy in leadership research, and Gordon *et al.*'s (1986) and Locke's (1986) somewhat conflicting findings regarding the comparability of the findings from laboratory and field settings all provide valuable suggestions on the types of issues that need to be considered by those using the dominant field and laboratory research paradigms.

Implications for management practice

Certainly the topics, results, and implications of empirical research in organizational studies are of potential interest to the management practitioner. For many, the methods employed to choose or arrive at these reports – given that they are perceived to be responsible – would typically enjoy less attention. We would argue, however, that sound forums on research methods that may range from appreciative to critical contain several key consequences for managers.

We would hope initially that more careful planning for traditional as well as innovative techniques will lead to better questions – questions chosen not from the limitations of methods available, but because the answers meaningfully impact the organization. Also, reliance on sounder methods of organizational study may provide far less equivocal results. Lastly, we would expect that research conducted in this manner would lead to more widespread application in the field.

NOTE

1 This chapter first appeared in the *Journal of Management* 13, 2 (1987). It is reprinted with permission.

REFERENCES

Agar, M. H. (1986) *Speaking of Ethnography*, Beverly Hills, CA: Sage.

Arkes, H. R. and Blumer, C. (1985) 'The psychology of sunk costs', *Organizational Behavior and Human Decision Processes* 35: 124–40.

Baggaley, A. R. (1981) 'Multivariate analysis: an introduction for consumers of behavioral research', *Evaluation Review* 5: 123–31.

Barley, S. R. (1986) 'Technology as an occasion for structuring: evidence from observations of CT scanners and the social order of radiology departments', *Administrative Science Quarterly* 31: 78–108.

Boehm, V. (1980) 'Research in 'the real world' – a conceptual model', *Personnel Psychology* 33: 495–503.

Bohrnstedt, G. (1975, October) 'Structural equations and the analysis of change', Presentation at the 28th annual meeting of the Gerontological Society, Louisville, KY.

Bray, J. H. and Maxwell, S. E. (1985) *Multivariate Analysis of Variance*, Beverly Hills, CA: Sage.

Campbell, J. P., Daft, R. L., and Hulin, C. L. (1982) *What to Study: Generating and Developing Research Questions*, Beverly Hills, CA: Sage.

Carlson, R. (1971) 'Where is the person in personality research?' *Psychological Bulletin* 75: 203–19.

Christie, R. (1965) 'Some implications of research trends in social psychology', in O. Klineberg and R. Christie (eds) *Perspectives in Social Psychology* (pp. 141–52), New York: Holt, Rinehart & Winston.

Churchill, G. A. (1979) 'A paradigm for developing better measures of marketing constructs', *Journal of Marketing Research* 16: 64–73.

Coe, R. and Weinstock, I. (1984) 'Evaluating the management journals: a second look', *Academy of Management Journal* 27: 660–5.

Cohen, J. and Cohen, P. (1983) *Applied Multiple Regression/Correlation Analysis for the Behavioral Sciences*, Hillsdale, NJ: Lawrence Erlbaum Associates.

Cummings, L. L. (1978) 'Toward organizational behavior', *Academy of Management Review* 3: 90–8.

Daft, R. L. (1980) 'The evolution of organization analysis in *ASQ*, 1959–1979', *Administrative Science Quarterly* 25: 623–36.

Dipboye, R. L. and Flanagan, M. F. (1979) 'Research settings in industrial and organizational psychology: are findings in the field more generalizable than in the laboratory?', *American Psychologist* 34: 141–50.

Flanagan, M. F. and Dipboye, R. L. (1981) 'Research settings in industrial and organizational psychology: facts, fallacies, and the future', *Personnel Psychology* 34: 37–47.

Fleishman, E. A. (1973) 'Twenty years of consideration and structure', in E. A. Fleishman and J. G. Hunt (eds) *Current Developments in the Study of Leadership* (pp. 1–37), Carbondale, IL: Southern Illinois University Press.

Ganster, D. C., Hennessey, H. W., and Luthans, F. (1983) 'Social desirability responses effects: three alternative models', *Academy of Management Journal* 26: 321–31.

Gieri, R. N. (in press) *A Cognitive Theory of Science*, Chicago: University of Chicago Press.

Glass, G. V., McGaw, B., and Smith, M. L. (1981) *Meta-analysis in Social Research*, Beverly Hills, CA: Sage.

Gordon, M., Kleiman, L., and Hanie, C. (1978) 'Industrial-organizational psychology: "Open thy ears, O house of Israel"', *American Psychologist* 32: 893–905.

Gordon, M. E., Slade, L. A., and Schmitt, N. (1986) 'The "science of the sophomore" revisited: from conjecture to empiricism', *Academy of Management Review* 11: 197–201.

Gordon, M. E., Slade, L. A., and Schmitt, N. (1987) 'Student guinea pigs: porcine predictors and particularistic phenomena', *Academy of Management Review* 12: 160–3.

Guba, E. G. and Lincoln, Y. S. (1982) 'Epistemological and methodological bases of naturalistic inquiry', *Educational Communication and Technology Journal* 30: 233–52.

Guzzo, R. S., Jackson, S. E., and Katzell, R. A. (in press) 'Meta-analysis analysis', in L. L. Cummings and B. M. Staw (eds) *Research in Organizational Behavior* (Vol. 9), Greenwich, CT: JAI Press.

Hambrick, D. C. (1980) 'Operationalizing the concept of business-level strategy in research', *Academy of Management Journal* 5: 567–75.

Higbee, K. L., Lott, W. J., and Graves, P. (1976) 'Experimentation and college students in social psychology research', *Personality and Social Psychology Bulletin* 2: 239–41.

Higbee, K. L., Millard, R. J., and Folkman, J. R. (1982) 'Social psychology research during the 1970s: predominance of experimentation and college students', *Personality and Social Psychology Bulletin* 8: 180–3.

Higbee, K. L. and Wells, M. G. (1972) 'Some research trends in social psychology during the 1960s', *American Psychologist* 27: 963–6.

Howard, G. S., Maxwell, S. E., Berra, S. M., and Sternitzke, M. E. (1985) 'Institutional research productivity in industrial/organizational psychology', *Journal of Applied Psychology* 70: 233–6.

Hunter, J. E., Schmidt, F. L., and Jackson, G. B. (1982) *Meta-analysis: Cumulating Research Findings Across Studies*, Beverly Hills, CA: Sage.

Jacoby, J. (1978) 'Consumer research: a state of the art review', *Journal of Marketing* 42: 87–96.

Kaplan, A. (1964) *The Conduct of Inquiry*, San Francisco: Chandler Publishing Co.

Kerlinger, F. N. and Pedhazur, E. J. (1973) *Multiple Regression in Behavioral Research*, New York: Holt, Rinehart & Winston.

Kerr, S. and Schriesheim, C. A. (1974) 'Consideration, initiating structure, and organizational criteria – an update of Korman's 1966 review', *Personnel Psychology* 27: 555–68.

Kidder, L. H. (1981) *Selltiz, Wrightsman and Cook's Research Methods in Social Relations*, New York: Holt, Rinehart & Winston.

Kilmann, R. H. (1979) 'On integrating knowledge utilization with knowledge development: the philosophy behind the MAPS design technology', *Academy of Management Review* 4: 417–29.

Kim, J. and Mueller, C. W. (1978) *Factor Analysis: Statistical Methods and Practical Issues*, Beverly Hills, CA: Sage.

Kimberly, J. R. (1976) 'Issues in the design of longitudinal organizational research', *Sociological Methods and Research* 4: 321–47.

Kirk, J. and Miller, M. L. (1986) *Reliability and Validity in Qualitative Research*, Beverly Hills, CA: Sage.

Knapp, T. R. (1978) 'Canonical correlation analysis: a general parametric significance-testing system', *Psychological Bulletin* 85: 410–16.

Kuhn, T. S. (1974) 'Second thoughts on paradigms', in F. Suppe (ed.), *The Structure of Scientific Theories* (pp. 459–82), Urbana, IL: University of Illinois Press.

Lenz, R. T. (1981) 'Determinants of organizational performance: an interdisciplinary review', *Strategic Management Journal* 2: 131–54.

Levine, M. S. (1977) *Canonical Analysis and Factor Comparison*, Beverly Hills, CA: Sage.

Liker, J. K., Augustyniak, S., and Duncan, G. J. (1985) 'Panel data and models of change: a comparison of first difference and conventional two-wave models', *Social Science Research* 14: 80–101.

Lincoln, Y. S. and Guba, E. G. (1985) *Naturalistic Inquiry*, Beverly Hills, CA: Sage.

Locke, E. A. (1986) *Generalizing From Laboratory to Field Settings: Research Findings from Industrial-Organizational Psychology, Organizational Behavior, and Human Resources Management*, Lexington, MA: Lexington Books.

McGuire, J. B. (1986) 'Management and research methodology', *Journal of Management* 12: 5–17.

Machiavelli, N. (1532/1952) *The Prince*, New York: Mentor.

Mitchell, T. R. (1985) 'An evaluation of the validity of correlational research conducted in organizations', *Academy of Management Review* 10: 192–205.

Morgan, G. and Smircich, L. (1980) 'The case for qualitative research', *Academy of Management Review* 5: 491–500.

Muchinsky, P. M. (1979) 'Some changes in the characteristics of articles published in the *Journal of Applied Psychology* over the past 20 years', *Journal of Applied Psychology* 64: 455–9.

Phillips, J. S. and Lord, R. G. (1986) 'Notes on the practical and theoretical consequences of implicit leadership theories for the future of leadership measurement', *Journal of Management* 12: 21–42.

Pondy, L. R. (1972) 'A reviewer's comment', *Administrative Science Quarterly* 17: 408–9.

Price, R. L. (1985) 'A customer's view of organizational literature', in L. L. Cummings and P. J. Frost (eds) *Publishing in the Organizational Sciences* (pp. 125–32), Homewood, IL: Irwin.

Rogers, E. M. (1983) *Diffusion of Innovations* (3rd edition), New York: Free Press.

Rosenthal, R. (1984) *Meta-analytic Procedures for Social Research*, Beverly Hills, CA: Sage.

Rosnow, R. L. (1981) *Paradigms in Transition: The Methodology of Social Inquiry*, New York: Oxford University Press.

Sackett, P. R., Tenopyr, M. L., Schmitt, N., and Kehoe, J. (1985) 'Commentary on forty questions about validity generalization', *Personnel Psychology* 38: 697–798.

Sashkin, M. and Garland, H. (1979) 'Laboratory and field research on leadership: integrating divergent streams', in J. G. Hunt and L. L. Larson (eds), *Crosscurrents in Leadership* (pp. 64–87), Carbondale, IL: Southern Illinois University Press.

Schmidt, F. L., Pearlman, D., Hunter, J. E., and Hirsh, H. R. (1985) 'Forty questions about validity generalization and meta-analysis', *Personnel Psychology* 38: 697–798.

Schneider, B. (1985) 'Organizational behavior', in M. R. Rosenzweig and L. W. Porter (eds) *Annual Review of Psychology* 36: 573–611, Palo Alto, CA: Annual Reviews Inc.

Schultz, D. P. (1969) 'The human subject in psychological research', *Psychological Bulletin* 72: 214–28.

Schwab, D. P. (1980) 'Construct validity in organizational behavior', in B. M. Staw and L. L. Cummings (eds) *Research in Organizational Behavior* (pp. 3–44), Greenwich, CT: JAI Press.

Sears, D. O. (1986) 'College sophomores in the laboratory: influence of a narrow data base on social psychology's view of human nature', *Journal of Personality and Social Psychology* 51: 515–30.

Sims, H. P. jun. (1979) 'Limitations and extensions to questionnaires in leadership research', in J. G. Hunt and L. L. Larson (eds) *Crosscurrents in Leadership* (pp. 209–21), Carbondale, IL: Southern Illinois University Press.

Smart, R. G. (1966) 'Subject selection bias in psychological research', *The Canadian Psychologist* 7: 115–21.

Strasser, S. and Bateman, T. S. (1984) 'What we should study, problems we should solve: perspectives of two constituencies', *Personnel Psychology* 37: 77–92.

Susman, G. I. and Evered, R. D. (1978) 'An assessment of the scientific merits of action research', *Administrative Science Quarterly* 23: 582–603.

Tatsuoka, M. M. (1973) 'Multivariate analysis in educational research', in F. N. Kerlinger (ed.) *Review of Research in Education* (pp. 879–92), Itasca, IL: Peacock.

Thomas, K. W. and Tymon, W. G. jun. (1982) 'Necessary properties of relevant research: lessons from the recent criticisms of the organizational sciences', *Academy of Management Review* 7: 345–52.

Thompson, B. (1984) *Canonical Correlation Analysis: Uses and Interpretation*, Beverly Hills, CA: Sage.

Thorndike, R. M. (1977) 'Canonical analysis and predictor selection', *Journal of Multivariate Behavioral Research* 12: 75–87.

Tosi, H. (1979) 'The need for theoretical development in organizational behavior: or, if the past is prologue in organizational behavior, economics will be replaced as the dismal science', *Exchange: The Organizational Behavior Teaching Journal* 4, 3: 5–7.

Tversky, A. and Kahneman, D. (1974) 'Judgement under uncertainty: heuristics and biases', *Science*, 183: 1124–31.

Van Maanen, J., Dabbs, J. M., and Faulkner, R. R. (1982) *Varieties of Qualitative Research*, Beverly Hills, CA: Sage.

Venkatraman, N. and Grant, J. H. (1986) 'Construct measurement in organizational strategy research: a critique and proposal', *Academy of Management Review* 11: 71–87.

8 Ethnomethodology and organization: an introduction

John S. Hassard

INTRODUCTION

This chapter suggests the use of ethnomethodology as a viable technique for research in management. Its objectives are threefold: (1) to review the central principles of the ethnomethodological position; (2) to outline the main streams of analysis; and (3) to describe how it can provide insight for understanding behaviour in organizations. The aim, overall, is for the chapter to act as a stimulus and resource for students considering the method for doctoral research.

The chapter complements Madut's (1986) recent article on phenomenology, by exploring, further, research possibilities in the 'interpretive' paradigm (see Burrell and Morgan 1979). It seeks to advance the prospects for paradigm diversity by making the method intelligible to the beginning doctoral student. As ethnomethodology is frequently accused of being obscurantist, and as many works in this area are difficult for the lay reader, it attempts to decode the more exotic writings of Bittner, Garfinkel, Zimmerman, and others.

WHAT IS ETHNOMETHODOLOGY?

> we are concerned with the how society gets put together; the how it is getting done; the how to do it; the social structures of everyday activities. I would say that we are doing studies of how persons, as parties to ordinary arrangements, use the features of the arrangement to make for members the visibly organized activities happen.
>
> (Garfinkel 1974: 16)

Ethnomethodology, which has been the subject of great interest in recent years, is essentially the creation of Harold Garfinkel (see Garfinkel 1967, Garfinkel and Sacks 1970) who established the idea that everyday, commonplace, or routine activities are 'accomplished' through the use of a variety of skills, practices, and assumptions. It is an approach to social analysis which is grounded in the detailed study of everyday life; it seeks to treat practical circumstances as topics for empirical enquiry, being concerned to understand the ways in which people order and make sense of everyday activities, and specifically the ways in which they make them accountable to others. The main objective is to analyse how subjects, through social interaction, make sense of verbal and non-verbal cues ('indexicals', see Garfinkel 1967: 3–7) whose meaning is dependent on the context of production. Interactions are regarded as on-going accomplishments in which those involved take recourse to a range of assumptions, practices, and conventions in order to define, sustain, and reproduce everyday situations. These practices and assumptions are what the ethnomethodologists call 'methods'.

Although it is the names of Garfinkel and his colleagues (e.g. Egon Bittner, Aaron Cicourel, Harvey Sacks, Don Zimmerman) that are most readily identified with the approach, their work owes considerable intellectual debt to the phenomenological sociology of Alfred Schutz and the symbolic interactionism of George Herbert Mead and Erving Goffman. From the work of Schutz and Goffman, in particular, comes this concern with understanding encounters in their own terms, and thus with identifying (1) the 'taken-for-granted' assumptions which characterize social situations, and (2) how participants make their actions 'accountable' to themselves and to others. In this understanding process, emphasis is placed upon how subjects make use of 'reflexivity' (see Garfinkel 1967: 7–9) and thus how they characterize situations by looking back at what has occurred previously. Here, ethnomethodology is seen to borrow two of the main pillars of Schutz's analysis – his notions of 'because' and 'in-order-to' motives – as the bases of social action.

Indeed, like Schutz, ethnomethodologists are concerned to account for how actions are given *meaning* in the flow of the 'life-world' (Schutz and Luckmann 1974), and especially how actors are constantly trying to make sense of the world and interpret what is happening. Here, social structure, instead of being a hard facticity 'out there', is something that is continuously generated within the process of social construction. The lay public are seen as attempting social explanation just as social scientists do. In fact, the attempts by lay actors to make sense of the social world are seen as a major way in which social structure is created and sustained.

Ethnomethodology, therefore, places prime importance on analysing the common-sense features of everyday life, the chief concern being to understand things that are known to 'anyman'. As Zimmerman and Pollner note:

In contrast to the perennial argument that sociology belabors the obvious, we propose that sociology has yet to treat the obvious as a phenomenon. We argue that the world of everyday life, while furnishing sociology with its favoured topics of inquiry, is seldom a topic in its own right.

(Zimmerman and Pollner 1971: 33)

ETHNOMETHODOLOGICAL RESEARCH: FORMS AND ORIENTATIONS

[T]raditional empiricism fails to come to terms with the problems of empirically grounded concepts in the life-world. Concepts are irrelevant unless they are grounded in concrete experiences and unless they refer to the realities of men in their life worlds.

(Phillipson 1972: 146)

Ethnomethodology involves analysing social interaction as an on-going practice. In so doing, studies typically concentrate either on conversational analysis (e.g. Sacks *et al.* 1974), or on interactions within a particular organizational setting (e.g. Zimmerman, 1973).

Douglas has produced a useful analytical distinction in his discussion of 'linguistic' and 'situational' forms of ethnomethodology. Linguistic ethno-methodologists (e.g. Cicourel 1972, Schegloff and Sacks 1973) examine the use of language, and particularly how conversations are structured in every-day circumstances. They analyse natural language and especially the shared meanings that words have for members of a particular group. They seek to lay bare the networks of indexical expressions which give situations their meaning, here making much of the 'taken-for-grantedness' in conversations, and of how verbal language conveys more that is made explicit. Thus linguistic ethnomethodologists demonstrate how much information 'goes without saying', messages being conveyed and understood without ever being verbalized (Douglas 1971). Garfinkel argues that to comprehend the meaning of statements, we need to know not just *what* is being said, but *how* it is said (Garfinkel 1967: 24–31); i.e. we must understand the 'rules' participants employ in making sense of verbal interaction.

Situational ethnomethodologists (e.g. McHugh 1968), on the other hand, seek to access a wider range of social activity. The objective here is to understand how participants make sense of, and construct, their immediate social situations. In field-studies, ethnomethodologists often purposefully disrupt commonplace activities so as to reveal the normative processes at work. This is done in order to expose the taken-for-grantedness of everyday situations. They make the point that everyday situations are governed by well-regulated sets of rules, and that these serve as meanings from which to stabilize interaction. Although such rules are a largely tacit phenomenon, they nevertheless provide an agenda from which to conduct research. Through uncovering such practices, ethnomethodologists discern how sense is made out of indexicals.

Ethnomethodology is often seen as being not just a new approach to sociological analysis, but actually an alternative to it. Its writers are found rejecting formal sociological theory, and denying the explanatory power of such theories. Notable here is that ethnomethodologists feel orthodox socio-logical researchers generally neglect the very things they should treat as phenomena worthy of study.

Traditional sociological research is seen to take the phenomena resulting from social processes as given, or else as points from which research should commence. Their goal is to discover correlations between phenomena with-out first attempting to explain why these phenomena are of interest. The problem here is that while professional social scientists share everyday common-sense practices with lay persons, and agree with them about the 'proper' problems to be studied, they nevertheless consider lay accounts as faulty and their own as superior. To ethnomethodologists, however, the two are quite similar, as both represent processes that are of interest as phenomena to be understood in their own right. While lay members and professional sociologists may agree that a certain social phenomenon is a worthy topic for study (e.g. bureaucracy, deviance, kinship etc.), the ethnomethodologist would not treat that phenomenon as a given fact from which to begin research; he would instead see it as a topic for investigation in its own right (see Pollner 1974 on this point). Ethnomethodologists argue that social research should study *process*, rather than accept the effects of process as given and proceed from there.

Thus, many ethnomethodologists strongly resist any attempt to locate their work within the conventional problems and concerns of sociology. They dissociate themselves from what they see as the dominant orientation within academic sociology, that of 'constructive analysis' (see Garfinkel and Sacks 1970), as instead they confine themselves to understanding the 'awesome indexicality' of everyday accounts. The approach is orientated toward em-pirical study, and especially of how social actors make sense of the uniqueness of commonplace events.

However, developing a new approach to social analysis is not an easy task, and as such empirical output has emerged in rather piecemeal fashion. Yet this is not to say that ethnomethodologists have not met their objectives; their research has, for the most part, succeeded in documenting social routines in terms of the kinds of typifications, presumptions, and actions upon which such routines are founded. In so doing, they have demanded a logic quite different to that of the Popperian hypothetico-deductive method, as instead a form of idiographic inductivism has been employed. Although referring specifically to the concept of organization, Bittner summarizes the basic premise of the method when he notes:

> The important point ... is that we must be prepared to treat every substantive determination we shall formulate as a case for exploring the background information on which it in turn rests. By way of defining our task we propose that the study of the methodological use of the concept of organization seeks to describe the mechanisms of sustained and sanctioned relevance of the rational constructions to a variety of objects, events and occasions relative to which they are involved.

> (Bittner 1974: 76)

ORGANIZATIONAL ANALYSIS: BITTNER, ZIMMERMAN, SILVERMAN, AND JONES

> [T]he meaning of the concept [of organization], and of all of the terms and determinations that are subsumed under it, must be discovered by studying their use in real scenes of action by persons whose competence to use them is socially sanctioned.

> (Bittner 1974: 75)

The question remains, however, of how the approach is effected in practice; i.e. what kind of field-work do ethnomethodologists do? At its most basic, we can say that their research interests focus upon two main areas: first, with analysing the language-forms individuals employ in establishing that the actions of peers are acceptable and understandable (e.g. Weider 1974); and second, with the description of concrete situations in formal (mainly work) organizations (e.g. Sudnow 1973). These concerns often overlap in the final research output (e.g. Silverman and Jones 1976).

The research focus of most interest to us is the description of commonplace encounters within formal organizations. Most ethnomethodological studies are in fact of organizations, and the range of accounts is now quite wide, e.g. geriatric hospitals, prisons, welfare agencies, research laboratories, police, abortion clinics, public bureaucracies, and kindergartens. Furthermore, recent years have witnessed not only doctorates awarded for work in this area (e.g. Lynch 1979, Fairhurst 1981), but also the appearance of ethnomethodological papers in mainstream management journals (e.g. Gephart 1978, Fairhurst 1983). Interest in this form of analysis continues to grow, and Garfinkel is presently developing a three-volume manual to assist those wishing to engage in field-work (Garfinkel, forthcoming).

Indeed, as the number of ethnomethodological accounts of organizations has grown, so certain studies have taken on the mantle of landmark contributions, these tending to influence the direction and style of research. This has mainly been where a work has either been the first to discuss a problematic concept (e.g. Bittner 1974), or else where the empirical analysis is considered extremely well crafted (e.g. Zimmerman 1971, Silverman and Jones 1976). Through assessing some of these contributions, we will draw out the main theoretical and empirical characteristics of the ethnomethodological approach to organizations.

As Silverman (1975) notes, ethnomethodological studies of organizations are concerned with:

1 'Attempts to examine the ways in which activities and their outcomes are displayed as in-accord-with-a-rule such that their sensible character may be recognized', and
2 'Examinations of the practices and policies through which the features of the real world are provided for in the activities and accounts (both lay and professional) that routinely arise in socially organized settings' (Silverman 1975: 280).

In denoting these characteristics Silverman is in fact acknowledging a debt to Bittner (1974), who was the first to develop an ethnomethodological treatise with specific reference to organizations. Bittner set an agenda for subsequent field studies, his paper being used thereafter as a bench-mark for evaluating empirical contributions. Although noted for its analytical importance, Bittner's paper is also known for the difficulty of its style. The substance of his thesis is as follows.

Bittner argues that organizations should be appreciated as 'normative idealizations', or language forms, which provide 'a generalized formula to which all sorts of problems can be brought for solution'. He suggests that organization theory tends to define organizations as 'stable associations of persons engaged in concerted activities directed to the attainment of specific objectives', this serving to posit the concept of organization structure as unproblematic. Rather than treat organizations as real structures in their own right, he suggests we should, instead, aim to examine the 'sense of organization structure' with which actors operate. For Bittner, the concept of structure is no more than a common-sense typification constructed by individuals for use within particular contexts. Therefore, to adopt this everyday assumption uncritically, and then to employ it as a basis for organizational analysis, is to engage in a practice beset with problems. Bittner argues that the sociologist who uses the concept so is in fact using it only as a device for explaining organizational activities. Here he is committing a basic error, as such concepts should be the *subject* of inquiry rather than the tool of analysis. By relying on everyday theories of the world, the sociologist confuses the use of organization as 'topic' with its employment as an unacknowledged 'resource' in the development of explanations. Bittner gives warning:

In general there is nothing wrong with borrowing a common-sense concept for the purposes of sociological inquiry. Up to a point it is, indeed,
unavoidable. The warrant for this procedure is the sociologist's interest
in exploring the common-sense perspective. The point at which the use
of common-sense concepts becomes a transgression is where such concepts are expected to do the analytical work of theoretical concepts. When
the actor is treated as a permanent auxiliary to the enterprise of sociological inquiry at the same time that he is the object of its inquiry, there arise
ambiguities that defy clarification.

(Bittner 1974: 70)

Bittner maintains that the most characteristic feature of orthodox
organizational analysis is its over-reliance on common-sense knowledge of
the world. Post-Weberian sociologists are seen to base their explanations on
a whole set of implicit assumptions, these serving to build a shield around
the subject matter. Indeed, Weber is accused of setting a precedent here, his
production of the ideal-type being reliant, primarily, on common-sense
knowledge of 'bureaucracy'. Instead of coming to terms with the everyday
presuppositions of his analysis, Weber offers a partial account which
'glosses' how competent participants make sense of (notions of) 'hierarchy'
and 'office' in the context of their enactment. Bittner suggests that in
attempting to formalize a definition of bureaucracy – by way of everyday
knowledge – Weber has engaged in a theoretical shortcut. Here, the
alternative is to analyse the processes by which competent participants use
everyday knowledge of bureaucracy to account for specific activities in
particular settings. Bureaucracy has no implicit meaning of its own; it exists
only through the socially sanctioned occasions of its use – it does not
determine action (Bittner 1974).

In developing this critique, Bittner suggests that Weber's prime fault lies
in being in collusion with those he seeks to understand. As Zimmerman and
Pollner note, the position is analogous to a person trying to explain his or her
dreams while still being asleep and dreaming – it cannot be done (Zimmerman and Pollner 1971). Bittner notes:

If the theory of bureaucracy is a theory at all, it is a refined and purified
version of the actor's theorising. To the extent that it is a refinement and
purification of it, it is by the same token, a corrupt and incomplete version
of it; for it is certainly not warranted to reduce the terms of common-sense
discourse to a lexicon of culturally coded significances to satisfy the
requirements of theoretical postulation.

(Bittner 1974: 74)

To replace this form of incomplete theorizing, Bittner advances a method for understanding organization as a common-sense construct. The chief concern is for documenting the processes actors invoke in constructing the social world. Bittner treats the actor not as a passive functionary, but as a creative author whose competence lies in using the concept of organization to produce rational accounts. Here, the actor is seen to use the concept as a 'gambit of compliance' whereby certain accepted rules of behaviour are inferred simply by *using* the term. Accounts are developed which illustrate how an idea such as 'formal organization' is used as a 'collaborative reference' for establishing the 'stylistic unity' of everyday interaction. Thus, competent actors employ the concept as a mechanism for producing order and control. Organization is not treated as an object in itself, but rather as a language-category providing for the object-*like* qualities of social interaction; it is a notion called upon for decoding the 'sense' of everyday activities such as bureaucratic routines.

Bittner's paper (which was first published in 1965) represents *the* major ethnomethodological analysis of the concept of organization. As noted, it has served as the main referent for a series of empirical studies conducted during the last two decades. Almost exclusively, these studies have assessed the sense-making strategies of employees in either public services or public bureaucracies (e.g. Bittner 1973, Zimmerman 1970, 1973, Silverman and Jones 1973, 1976, Fairhurst 1983). Here, researchers have suggested that organizations are 'constellations of rules' (Fairhurst 1983), the main analytical focus being on how 'competent' actors account for 'rule use'. Organizations are experienced as networks of rules of conduct regarding what proper actions should take place. These rules situate the meaning of social activities.

In the wake of Bittner, works by Zimmerman and Silverman and Jones can be seen as paradigm cases of the ethnomethodological approach to organizations. Their field-work focuses on how courses of (bureaucratic) action are contingent upon the relevance of particular rules to particular contexts. These studies illustrate many of the characteristic features of this approach to organizational analysis.

Zimmerman's work, in particular, epitomizes this form of research and provides a template for organizational enquiry. In line with both Garfinkel (1967) and Bittner (1974), he focuses on the common-sense rationalities of bureaucratic actors, and especially the ways in which they provide for the features of organization structure (and show rule-governed characteristics) in their everyday activities. These processes are displayed in his most-cited empirical papers: 'Record-keeping and the intake process in a public welfare bureaucracy' (1971) and 'The practicalities of rule-use' (1973). Both pieces result from Zimmerman's work at a district office of a State bureau of public assistance, the former analysing the role of the welfare caseworker, while the latter the role of the receptionist who directs clients to relevant officials.

In 'Record-keeping', Zimmerman describes how welfare caseworkers 'enact sensible intake work', here engaging in a process of interpreting how much of a client's story can be accepted as factual. Before welfare aid can be given, the caseworker needs to make a decision regarding the 'eligibility' of the client in order to be able to justify the decision *vis-à-vis* the official requirements of the welfare programme applied for. Here, documentary evidence is seen as crucial, the case record being of particular importance in 'assembling' the world of the client (Zimmerman 1971).

In accounting for a client's case, however, the intake worker adopts procedures which both make for, and rely upon, a sense of social structure. Here, the issue is not the reliability of these procedures, nor the factual nature of the accounts, but rather the ways in which both *provide* for their 'reliability' and 'factual nature'. The intake worker attempts to assemble the client's case through *post hoc* reconstruction. As such, an 'investigative stance' – an attitude and practice of thorough-going scepticism – is adopted in order to evaluate features which are deemed investigatable (i.e. issues that can be settled through documentary 'evidence'). Within the interview, however, the caseworker invokes stereotypes of actors and situations in order to question and assess the truthfulness of the client's account.

In dealing with applicants, caseworkers rely on an assumption of bureaucratic fiat in order to 'bring off' non-problematic situations. Here, they seek to establish the status of official documents as 'plain facts', certain social activities being *constituted* simply by the process of record-keeping. These documented sets of information are given the status of concrete facticities; they are seen as objective, reliable, and immutable. Thus, for the caseworker the world becomes non-problematic as case records reflect this presupposition. The 'plain facts' position offers no grounds for questioning either the everyday reliability of official documents, or the ordered structure of the world which they both portray and rely upon. As Zimmerman comments:

> The taken-for-granted use of documents ... is dependent on an ordered world – the ordered world of organizations, and the ordered world of society at large. When simply taken-for-granted, the features of these ordered domains are matters of mere recognition for which no accounts are called for or given.
>
> (Zimmerman 1971: 350)

Although the majority of ethnomethodological studies of organization are North American (especially Californian) in origin, the tradition of examining accounting practices in public bureaucracies has been continued in Britain –

most notably by Silverman and Jones (1973, 1976). Their studies succeed in combining both linguistic and situational forms of analysis.

Silverman and Jones focus on the process of staff selection within a large organization, and especially on how power relations are reflected in the forms of language generated. Their main concern is how interviews are built around verbal/non-verbal exchanges in which candidates (in this case final-year undergraduates applying for junior administrative posts) are assessed by way of typifications (e.g. 'abrasive', 'acceptable') which serve to make intelligible the reasons for known outcomes. Here, candidates either succeed or fail according to their 'displays' of acceptability, the process only becoming problematic when selection outcomes are unknown, and therefore where situations arise in which forms of behaviour to be considered 'acceptable', or the parameters of 'abrasiveness', are ill-defined. The interview comes to represent an accounting process driven by the need to make 'authoritative reports' which are themselves capable of being made accountable to others. As a basis for explanation, Silverman and Jones argue:

> an account of any reality derives its rationality *not* from its direct correspondence with some objective world, but from the ability of its hearers (readers) to make sense of the account in the context of the socially organized occasions of its use (and thereby *to treat it* as corresponding to an objective world).
>
> (Silverman and Jones 1973: 63–5)

From the interview materials:

> we came to the conclusion that 'acceptability' [and 'abrasiveness'] did not picture a set of possible actions, such that we could predict how any given action would be defined. [Rather their role was in] explaining (but not producing) courses of action. Like 'reasons' in general, they provide a rhetoric through which outcomes are made accountable.
>
> (Silverman and Jones 1976: 60)

These studies by Zimmerman and Silverman and Jones typify the form of research carried out by ethnomethodologists in formal organizations. The emphasis is placed firmly on treating practical activities as the topics for investigation. They give to everyday, common-place events the status usually accorded to extraordinary events. They emphasize how actors in work settings make sense of their circumstances, and especially how they make their actions (and their outcomes) 'accountable' as rational, common-sensical, and 'in-accord-with-a-rule'.

Thus, they offer an approach to organizational analysis which is poles asunder from the structured nomothetic accounts typical of 'mainstream' organizational research. Rather than seeking to generalize causal relations, they highlight particular activities, and explain how they are created and sustained through the subjective definitions of competent actors. They unravel the complex negotiations which characterize everyday life, and the knowledge and assumptions that underpin the reproduction of 'normal' routine behaviours. Instead of viewing organization as a structure of explicit and accepted prescriptions, they make us aware of conflicting role orientations. They argue for an emphasis on the creative nature of organization, rather than on officially expounded rules and procedures.

CONCLUSION: ETHNOMETHODOLOGY – A NEW PARADIGM FOR ORTHODOX ORGANIZATIONAL ANALYSIS?

This chapter has attempted to give an introduction to ethnomethodology, and to illustrate the type of research conducted by ethnomethodologists in formal organizations. It has reviewed the basic theoretical principles upon which their approach to organization is built, and illustrated how these are 'operationalized' in empirical studies of bureaucracy. It has attempted to provide a basic guide for those wishing to consider ethnomethodology as a method for doctoral research.

In conclusion, ethnomethodology is without doubt one of the most original developments to emerge out of the so-called 'crisis' phase in Western sociology (see Friedrichs 1970, Gouldner 1971). This is mainly because it focuses on a set of questions that have been inadequately answered by traditional sociology, especially regarding how structured social relations find their way into everyday activity, and how individuals act out their lives 'contextually' according to specific rules of social conduct. Indeed, many ethnomethodologists go so far as to suggest that their concerns are separate from those of academic sociology; for them, ethnomethodology is not so much a development *in* sociological analysis, as an alternative to it.

This notion of separate identity has been reinforced by writers who (after Kuhn 1970) suggest that ethnomethodology represents a different 'paradigm' to traditional sociological analysis. Notable here are the theses of Bottomore (1975) and Burrell and Morgan (1979), both of which cite ethnomethodology as an 'interpretive' alternative to the 'functionalist' orthodoxy. Ethnomethodology is seen to differ from 'objectivist' approaches in that it refuses to allow for the existence of 'organizations' in any hard and concrete sense. Whilst accepting the *concept* of organization, and especially its use as an accounting practice for making sense of the world, it does not allow for the existence of organizations as such; structural absolutism is firmly rejected. Indeed, for the ethnomethodologist, mainstream organization theory is built upon extremely problematic foundations. Organizations are not definite, concrete, phenomena: the organizational world is not a tangible, static facticity – on the contrary it is processual; it is based upon the 'intentional' acts of creative participants. Consequently, as the ontology of organization theory is problematic, so are the concepts upon which the discipline trades (e.g. job satisfaction, organization structure, organization climate); they are mere reifications. In Bittner's terms they are used as technical 'resources', whereas they should be treated as 'topics' for analysis.

In sum, ethnomethodology offers a unique approach for conducting organizational research. It yields subjectivist, idiographic descriptions of everyday situations through moving 'closer' to the subject matter. Researchers attempt to assess interaction from the perspective of the participant actor rather than the detached (social) scientist. The emphasis is on unfolding social processes rather than on defining social structures. Organizations are seen as having no material existence of their own. Instead they are complex social constructions whose identities are only accessed through reference to the locations of their production. Meanings are conferred upon social activities by 'competent' actors who interpret events according to the social context in which they occur. Organizations are sanctioned, and made accountable, through the interplay of biography, situation, and linguistic exchange.

REFERENCES

Bittner, E. (1973) 'The police on skid row', in G. Salaman and K. Thompson (eds) *People and Organisations*, London: Longman.

Bittner, E. (1974) 'The concepts of organization', in R. Turner (ed.) *Ethnomethodology: Selected Readings*, Harmondsworth: Penguin.

Bottomore, T. (1975) 'Competing paradigms in macrosociology', in A. Inkeles *et al.* (eds) *Annual Review of Sociology*, New York: Annual Reviews.

Burrell, G. and Morgan, G. (1979) *Sociological Paradigms and Organisational Analysis*, London: Heinemann.

Cicourel, A. V. (1972) *Cognitive Sociology*, Harmondsworth: Penguin.

Douglas, J. (ed.) (1971) *Understanding Everyday Life*, London: Routledge & Kegan Paul.

Fairhurst, E. (1981) 'A sociological study of the rehabilitation of elderly patients in an urban hospital', Ph. D. thesis, University of Leeds.

Fairhurst, E. (1983) 'Organisational rules and the accomplishment of nursing work on geriatric wards', *Journal of Management Studies* 20: 315–32.

Friedrichs, R. (1970) *A Sociology of Sociology*, New York: Free Press.

Garfinkel, H. (1967) *Studies in Ethnomethodology*, Englewood Cliffs, NJ: Prentice-Hall.

Garfinkel, H. (1974) 'The origins of the term "ethnomethodology"', in R. Turner (ed.) *Ethnomethodology: Selected Readings*, Harmondsworth: Penguin.

Garfinkel, H. (forthcoming) *A Manual for the Study of Naturally Organized Ordinary Activities*, London: Routledge.

Garfinkel, H. and Sacks, H. (1970) 'On formal structures of practical actions', in J. C. McKinney and E. A. Tiryakian (eds) *Theoretical Sociology*, New York: Appleton Century.

Gephart, R. (1978) 'Status degradation and the organizational succession problem', *Administrative Science Quarterly* 22: 553–81.

Gouldner, A. W. (1971) *The Coming Crisis in Western Sociology*, London: Heinemann.

Kuhn, T. S. (1970) *The Structure of Scientific Revolutions*, Chicago: University of Chicago Press.

Lynch, M. (1979) 'Art and artefact in laboratory science: a study of shop work and shop talk in a research laboratory', Ph. D. Thesis, University of California at Irvine.

Madut, A. (1986) 'Phenomenology: an alternative research approach', *Graduate Management Research*, 2: 32–41.

McHugh, P. (1968) *Defining the Situation*, New York: Bobbs Merrill.

Phillipson, M. (1972) 'Phenomenological philosophy and sociology', in P. Filmer *et al.* (eds), *New Directions in Sociological Theory*, London: Collier-Macmillan.

Pollner, M. (1974) 'Mundane reasoning', *Philosophy of the Social Sciences* 4: 35–54.

Sacks, H., Schegloff, E. A., and Jefferson, G. (1974) 'A simplist systematics for the organization of turn-taking for conversation', *Language* 50: 696–735.

Salaman, G. and Thompson, K. (eds) (1973) *People and Organisations*, London: Longman.

Schegloff, E. A. and Sacks, H. (1973) 'Opening-up closings', *Semiotica* 7: 289–327.

Schutz, A. and Luckmann, T. (1974) *The Structures of the Life World*, London: Heinemann.

Silverman, D. (1975) 'Accounts of organizations', in J. B. McKinlay (ed.) *Processing People*, London: Holt Rinehart & Winston.

Silverman, D. and Jones, J. (1973) 'Getting-in', in J. Child (ed.) *Man and Organization*, London: George Allen & Unwin.

Silverman, D. and Jones, J. (1976) *Organizational Work*, London: Collier-Macmillan.

Sudnow, D. (1973) 'Normal crimes', in G. Salaman and K. Thompson (eds) *People and Organisations*, London: Longman.

Turner, R. (ed.) (1974) *Ethnomethodology: Selected Readings*, Harmondsworth: Penguin.

Weider, L. (1974) 'Telling the code', in R. Turner (ed.) *Ethnomethodology: Selected Readings*, Harmondsworth: Penguin.

Zimmerman, D. (1971) 'Record-keeping and the intake process in a public welfare bureaucracy', in S. Wheeler (ed.) *On Record*, New York: Russell Sage.

Zimmerman, D. (1973) 'The practicalities of rule-use', in G. Salaman and K. Thompson (eds) *People and Organisations*, London: Longman.

Zimmerman, D. and Pollner, M. (1971) 'The everyday world as a phenomenon', in J. Douglas (ed.) *Understanding Everyday Life*, London: Routledge & Kegan Paul.

9 The case-study: a vital yet misunderstood research method for management[1]

N. Craig Smith

IN RECOGNITION OF THE CASE-STUDY

What does the scientific method amount to in application to management? An examination of the content of many management journals containing empirical papers would suggest that being scientific means quantification within a hypothetico-deductive approach to science. Qualitative and inductive approaches are much less frequently reported, if at all (Bonoma 1985). Consideration of the contribution of this management research (the extent to which it is meaningful) is beyond the scope of this chapter. It would raise a number of major questions, particularly about the agenda for management research and who sets it. The concern here, however, is with whether in seeking to apply scientific method to management, researchers are using the most appropriate research methods and techniques. This clearly has some bearing on the potential contribution of research in management. The case-study, it is suggested, is deserving of greater recognition as a research method. Such a claim has to be made within the context of an appreciation of what management research is trying to achieve.

Within social science generally there has long been criticism of positivist research orientations (Silverman 1985). This is gradually being acknowledged within the management literature (see, for example, *Administrative Science Quarterly* 24 (December 1979) or Bonoma 1985). However, positivism continues to dominate, especially in the United States. Despite the leadership of the United States in management education, the traditional American research model might not be the most suitable one to emulate. Being scientific is not solely or necessarily the result of number-crunching. While this author would not deny a role for quantitative approaches within management research, qualitative approaches, including the use of the case-study method, are often more appropriate for tackling the important research problems of management.

In using any research method it is helpful to understand its epistemological underpinnings. By examining the relationship between epistemology and research methods further support can be found for the use of qualitative approaches such as the case-study in management research. It should be noted that all references to case-study research in this paper refer to the development of case-studies for research purposes. Teaching cases are developed to illustrate established theory. Research cases are used to build theory, though this does not preclude their later development into teaching cases.

EPISTEMOLOGY AND RESEARCH METHODS

Rigby's (1965: vii) observations on the failure of management researchers to address fundamental methodological concerns seem almost as valid today as they were twenty years ago. Such criticism is borne out by the reference above to the positivist orientations found in much published management research. Positivism can be defined simply as 'working as natural scientists are believed to' (Bell and Newby 1977: 21). It reflects, therefore, a belief that the social sciences can be investigated in the same way as the natural sciences. Many writers on research methodology have argued against positivism; the essence only of these arguments will be necessary here to demonstrate the relationship between epistemology and research methods and, as a consequence, the shortcomings of some of the more commonly adopted research approaches in management.

It should first be noted that positivists only rarely define themselves as such. Positivism is all but a term of abuse; though some would say rightly so, for in extreme cases it amounts to an ignorance of epistemological issues. Yet the waters beyond positivism are dangerous. They are best avoided by the faint of heart. In some respects, to operate within a positivist framework allows the researcher the luxury of not having to question whether the research is meaningful; the methodological concern of such research often focuses on internal rather than external validity. Ultimately, this is dysfunctional if social science is to advance.

There has been considerable debate about the 'scientificness' of the social sciences, including management (for example, Dainty 1983, Hunt 1976). Science aims to create order, to make sense of facts. It seeks patterns or regularities. In so doing, a process of systematic observation, description, explanation, and prediction is employed. At least this much can be agreed on. And all of this may be found within the social sciences. A reasonable position to adopt seems to be one of admitting the limitations to social science achievements while acknowledging the complexities of social science research. It may then be claimed that the social sciences are sciences insofar as they apply scientific method. But one must ask, what form of scientific method (if any) is appropriate to social science?

Consider the nature of this particular human activity known as science. Hughes (1980: 12) notes that 'scientific methods seek deliberately to annihilate the individual scientist's standpoints and are designed as rules whereby agreement on specific versions of the world can be reached: a distinction, in short, between the producer of a statement and the procedure whereby it is produced.' The outcome of these methods is scientific knowledge: 'a systematic body of concepts, theories, principles and laws or law-like statements designed to explain phenomena' (Hughes 1980: 1). This outcome is achieved where plausibility is recognized or where, as Hughes puts it, there is agreement on specific versions of the world. The problem for the social sciences (and hence some of the complexity of social science research as acknowledged above) is that this involves a human attempt to explain human phenomena. This is problematic because it is doubtful as to whether method can ever 'annihilate' the individual scientist's standpoint. Medawar (1967: 149) admits this problem within the natural sciences; he quotes Whewell: 'Facts cannot be observed as facts except in virtue of the conceptions which the observer himself unconsciously supplies.' Such is the dilemma posed for the social sciences, that Hughes (1980: 124) feels obliged to ask: 'Is a science of social life impossible?'

In reference to Schutz, Hughes (1980: 119) explains the dilemma of the social sciences in terms of the social construction of reality: 'Like all sciences they make objective meaning claims, or at least aspire to do so, but in the case of social sciences these have to be within the context of the human activity which has created them and which cannot be understood apart from this scheme of action.' As Berger and Kellner (1981: 68) put it, in a different context, 'Direct access to facts and laws ... is never possible, no matter what one's standpoint ... there is no magical trick by which one can bypass the act of interpretation.' This is the basic epistemological problem of social science. How can the human world be objectively known in subjective, human terms?

One may, indeed, go further, for scientific activity and what is associated with it, including the status of scientists and scientific knowledge is, after all, like the phenomena studied by social scientists, a social construction. As Ford (1975: 5) neatly observes, 'When academics take off their white scientific coats and funny philosophical hats they turn into ordinary people.' This is the problem, and one that social scientists cannot escape. Moreover, to echo an earlier and vital theme, if they didn't have their white scientific coats and other accoutrements of scientific activity – including titles and ivory towers – would the outcome of such activity, scientific knowledge, still have intellectual authority?

Clearly, at this juncture, the analysis of epistemological issues surrounding social science research has reached a point well within the maze of research methodology. The problems facing social scientists seem intractable. One might, therefore, take heart in the following words from the sociologist George Homans, quoted by Denzin (1978):

> You do not have to believe anything about theory and methodology that is told you pretentiously and sanctimoniously by other sociologists – including myself. So much guff has gotten mixed with the truth that, if you cannot tell which is which, you had better reject it all. It will only get in your way. No one will go far wrong theoretically who remains in close touch with and seeks to understand a body of concrete phenomena.

It is very easy to end up in a methodological maze. Providing the researcher has a basic grasp of the issues and remains close to the phenomena studied, meaningful research is likely to be conducted. Yet, within this sensible conclusion, lies a key to some resolution of the problem identified above as well, highlighting the principal weakness of positivist research. The superiority of scientific knowledge, its greater intellectual authority, stems from whether the scientist *qua* scientist was able to 'stand back a bit', achieve some measure of objectivity. Morally at least, there is an obligation on the scientist to do this if claims of superiority are to be made. But even though social science involves human attempts to investigate human phenomena, a natural science, positivist approach to the social sciences often ignores the inevitable act of interpretation by the scientist. It then becomes invalid because the attempt at objectivity is illusory. Moreover, because of this artificial distancing, the researcher is not sufficiently close to the phenomenon under investigation to understand it. So, just as there is a requirement 'to stand back a bit', there is an equal requirement not to stand back so far that the findings are distorted by distance as well as by the act of interpretation.

This argument about distance from the phenomenon under study and its impact on objectivity and whether research is meaningful can be expressed another way. It was earlier noted that science involves a systematic process of observation, description, explanation, and prediction. In applying natural science methods and techniques to social science problems, positivist approaches assume that social science is at a point of development whereby methods and techniques appropriate to explanation and prediction may be employed and that much of the complexity of social phenomena can be ignored. For much of social science, observation and description, with possibly limited explanation, are the requisite modes. Certainly, this is true of management. Accordingly, methods appropriate to this phase of development need to be employed.

Bonoma (1985), in one of the few papers in the management literature on the case-study method, covers this problem of positivist research orientations by referring to a trade-off between 'currency' and 'data integrity'. Currency pertains to generalizability of results, an amalgam of what is elsewhere termed external validity and pragmatic or ecological validity. Data integrity refers to those characteristics of research that affect error and bias in research results, an amalgam of internal validity, statistical conclusion validity and reliability. Bonoma notes that, ideally, high levels of both data integrity and results currency should be sought, but that it is not possible for any single research method simultaneously to minimize multiple threats to both data integrity and currency. So, for example, laboratory experiments offer high data integrity but low currency, in contrast to case research which offers high currency but low data integrity.

In making the trade-off, choosing the right method, Bonoma suggests the researcher has to consider the purpose of the research and nature of the phenomenon under investigation. On the former, Bonoma, in essence, notes that high data integrity methods (and, therefore, with low currency) cannot be efficiently applied to theory-building research; that is, research at the description end of a research continuum of description, classification, comparison, measurement/estimation, establishing association, and determining cause and effect. This is because 'either the power of deductive methods is underutilized, or theory and/or method are prematurely pressed into service when their underlying assumptions cannot be met'. Of course, the converse applies to high currency, inductive methods. In considering the phenomenon under investigation, he suggests the key issues are whether the phenomenon can be studied outside its normal setting (often requisite for high data integrity) and whether it is amenable to quantification. On the latter point, Bonoma gives the example of good practice in marketing management as a research topic which currently, at least, defies quantification.

In looking at the research conducted in marketing, Bonoma concludes that 'the apparent research bias towards types of investigation that preserve data integrity at the expense of currency results in a methodological one-sidedness that may impair the development and testing of sound theories'. This reiterates the concern earlier expressed about the research agenda for management. Some areas of management can quite legitimately be investigated using quantitative and hypothetico-deductive approaches. In such circumstances one might conclude that positivism is acceptable. However, to what extent are these areas more worthy of investigation than those demanding more inductive and qualitative approaches? One must certainly question a research agenda should it be determined by a requirement to use particular research methods.

In sum, an understanding of the epistemological issues surrounding social science research point to the requirement to use an appropriate method for the research problem; in other words, 'horses for courses'. The debate about positivism has illustrated the limitations of traditional research methods when applied to many social science problems. An alternative and seemingly more potentially fruitful path would employ qualitative and inductive approaches. The case-study is included in such approaches.

Epistemological issues as discussed above seem frequently to be considered irrelevant to the practice of research – to be ignored if the researcher can latch on to an appropriate research method, appropriateness usually stemming from prior use in similar circumstances. Yet, they have a direct consequence for the meaning which may be attributed to the research; meaningful research demands a sound epistemological base to the research methods. Epistemology and research methods are interrelated in a complex way. Despite the assumed division between the theory and practice of research, the two cannot be considered in isolation. There is, so to speak, a two-way street. Much of the criticism of the use of case studies in research stems from this misapprehension, the view that the relationship between epistemology and research methods is unidirectional, a one-way street.

IN REPLY TO QUESTIONS OF REPRESENTATIVENESS

The principal criticism of case studies in research is that they are unrepresentative. Theoretical conclusions derived from case studies are not considered to be valid unless the cases can be demonstrated to be 'typical' of the phenomena under investigation. The very word 'representative' implies recourse to survey research methods to demonstrate, via quantitative procedures, that the theoretical conclusions derived from the cases are applicable to the population as a whole. Qualitative research, according to the canons of positivism, is fine for exploratory studies, but quantification is necessary to establish the validity of any findings. But concerns with representativeness may be irrelevant. Some would argue this irrelevance is absolute. Others that it is only temporary, that – for the moment – representativeness can be ignored, but that it must be attended to eventually if generalizations – valid theoretical conclusions – are to be drawn. The next section, in examining theory building and the case-study method, is largely concerned with the former proposition that representativeness is absolutely irrelevant. Such a proposition rests on accepting the two-way street concept of the theory and practice of research, that there is an interrelationship between epistemology and research methods and hence concern with whether cases are typical or not is epistemologically erroneous. However, before explaining why this should be so, it is useful to consider the proposition that representativeness is only temporarily irrelevant. In so doing, the more conventional argument for the use of the case-study method may be briefly explored.

Perhaps surprisingly, there is not a great deal of literature on the use of the case-study method, at least not under that title. Yet, many researchers refer to case-studies. This imbalance seems to reflect the low status of case-study research (because of the representativeness issue) and the view that it is not a method as such. One can find references to research methods such as repertory grid or comparative analysis which then *produce* case-studies, but they are not conceived as forming a part of case-study method. Consequently, McClintock *et al.* (1979) refer to case-study 'strategies' rather than 'methods'. This would indicate that case-studies are an approach, rather than a method. As Goode and Hatt (1952: 331) put it over thirty years ago: 'The case study, then, is not a specific technique. It is a way of organising social data so as to preserve the *unitary character of the social object being studied.* Expressed somewhat differently, it is an approach which views any social unit as a whole'. Clearly, the case-study is not a technique, it is not a means for obtaining data. Yet, it may be described as a research method insofar as it is a method of organizing data. One may also refer to case-study methods, such as participant observation, content analysis, or repertory grid, by which data for case-studies is obtained. (However, it is simpler to distinguish between techniques and the method, particularly as techniques such as content analysis or repertory grid are not exclusive to the case-study method.)

Case-studies, as qualitative research, may be employed within a positivist perspective. One may seek to involve numbers and counting, as Jauch *et al.* (1980) suggest in advocating the structured content analysis of cases; or as McClintock *et al.* (1979) propose, apply the logic and method of survey research. The latter paper considers some of the literature on the use of case studies and qualitative versus quantitative approaches. It suggests a choice between 'thick', 'deep', and 'holistic', and 'thin', 'narrow', but 'generalizable'. In response to the question: 'What do you do if you prefer data that are real, deep *and* hard?' McClintock *et al.* favour the invention of research designs that incorporate qualitative and quantitative strategies. They seek (quoting Warwick), 'to wed the qualitative and historically attuned case study with representative coverage and quantification'. By incorporating elements of positivist research design (sampling, quantification, etc.), they absolve themselves from the charge that their cases are unrepresentative.

THEORY-BUILDING AND THE CASE-STUDY METHOD

So the problem of representativeness may become temporarily irrelevant either by choosing to view case-studies as appropriate to exploratory work only, or by making them representative through the application of quantitative procedures. However, both solutions still accept the epistemological requirement for representativeness. One may, alternatively, view it as absolutely irrelevant.

There are two reasons for this. First, one may have different intentions when using case-studies as opposed to survey research. One's purpose, for example, may be description rather than correlation. Second, and perhaps most importantly, there is the recognition that representativeness is irrelevant because it can be a spurious basis for claiming validity. As Worsley and others (1970: 112) write:

> The general validity of the analysis does not depend on whether the case being analysed is representative of other cases of this kind, but rather upon the plausibility of the logic of the analysis. The generality is of the same kind that enabled Sir Ronald Ross to announce the 'cause' of malaria when he found the malaria parasite in the salivary gland of a single female Anopheles mosquito in 1897.

Clyde Mitchell (1983) has expanded on this argument in a recent article which presents a particularly thorough and convincing submission for the case-study method. As he shows, 'Logical inference is epistemologically quite independent of statistical inference'. How he comes to this conclusion is worthy of close consideration. Mitchell starts by referring to an eclipse of interest in case-studies as a method of sociological analysis, which he attributes to the tremendous increase in quantitative studies following the development of statistical techniques and powerful computer technology. He suggests there is a consequent confusion about the use of case-studies, as indicated by the challenge frequently addressed to those who have chosen to pursue the deviant path of case-studies: 'How do you know the case you have chosen is typical?' Mitchell responds to this challenge by explaining the difference between making inferences from statistical data and from cases. In so doing, he provides guidelines for the use of case-studies in social investigation and theory building.

Mitchell defines the case-study as 'a detailed examination of an event (or series of related events) which the analyst believes exhibits (or exhibit) the operation of some identified general theoretical principle'. He notes that different types of case-study may be identified according to their complexity and their use. However, Mitchell's central concern and the 'fundamental problem' in case-studies is 'the basis upon which general inferences may be drawn from them'. He asks how ostensibly unique material can form the basis for interference about some process in general. The very word 'case' connotes this uniqueness and the implication of a chance or haphazard occurrence. Yet some social anthropological and much sociological theorizing is founded on case-studies. He suggests the difficulties in the practice of the case-study method arise out of the common assumption that the only valid basis of inference is that which has been developed in relation to statistical analysis. However, as Mitchell goes to great lengths to explain, statistical analysis merely permits the inference that characteristics within the sample may be expected within the population. Theorized relationships between the characteristics are the result of a separate procedure and not substantiated by statistical analysis.

Mitchell offers an interesting example of a study for which the author claimed validity on the basis of statistical significance, but which was rejected because it was not plausible. The findings were rejected, not because the variables failed to correlate statistically, but because they were not logically (or causally, if one prefers) related. The researcher had linked interpretations of Rorschach inkblots with dietary disorders. It had been found that there was a statistically significant difference between those with dietary disorders and those without, in terms of the former reacting to the blot with a 'frog' response. This the researcher attributed to an unconscious belief in the cloacal theory of birth, which involves oral impregnation and anal parturition. The cloaca of the frog (its excretory and reproductive canals) are common, a biological fact providing, it is assumed, the rationale for this belief. The researcher hypothesized: 'Since patients should be inclined to manifest eating disorders: compulsive eating in the case of those who wish to get pregnant and anorexia in those who do not ... such patients should also be inclined to see cloacal animals such as frogs on the Rorschach.' The response of other clinical psychologists to this, however, was 'I don't believe it', even after having seen the experimental results. The theory proposed was rejected on the grounds of plausibility, regardless of unimpeachable method. As Mitchell explains, 'While the clinical psychologists may well have accepted that more people with dietary disorders saw the blots as frogs than those without, they could not accept the *explanation* of the relationship between the two characteristics' (his emphasis).

He is not, of course, the first to recognize such a distinction. Glaser and Strauss (1967: 62), for example, make the distinction between theoretical and statistical sampling: 'Theoretical sampling is done in order to discover categories and their properties, and to suggest the interrelationship into a theory. Statistical sampling is done to obtain accurate evidence on distributions of people among categories to be used in descriptions or verifications.' Mitchell, in turn, recognizes the commonly accepted distinction between statistical inference and scientific or causal inference. The former is 'the process by which the analyst draws conclusions about the existence of two or more characteristics in some wider population from some sample of that population to which the observer has access'; whereas, 'scientific or causal – or perhaps more appropriately – logical inference, is the process by which the analyst draws conclusions about the essential linkage between two or more characteristics in terms of some systematic explanatory schema – some set of theoretical propositions.' Importantly though, Mitchell recognizes that the distinction is often absent in quantitative studies:

> In analytical thinking based on quantitative procedures *both* types of inference proceed *pari passu* but there has been some tendency to elide logical inferences with the logic of statistical inference: that the postulated *logical* connection among features in a sample may be assumed to exist in some parent population simply because the features may be inferred to *coexist* in that population (his emphasis).
>
> (Mitchell 1983)

More importantly, this distinction paves the way for illustrating the irrelevance of representativeness in case-studies, for the analyst, in using this method, is only concerned with logical inference. As Mitchell argues:

> The process of inference from case studies is only logical or causal and cannot be statistical and extrapolability from any one case study to like situations in general is based only on logical inference. We infer that the features present in the case study will be related in a wider population not because the case is representative but because our analysis is unassailable.
>
> (Mitchell 1983)

So, in summary of Mitchell's position on the extent to which case studies have validity, Silverman (1985: 114) writes, 'The claim, therefore, is not to representativeness but to faultless logic'. As Mitchell puts it, 'The extent to which generalizations may be made from case studies depends upon the adequacy of the underlying theory and the whole corpus of related knowledge of which the case is analysed rather than on the particular instance itself.'

Selecting cases for study will, as a consequence, not therefore rest on how typical the case may be, but on its explanatory power. Indeed, 'deviant' cases may be chosen, as analytic induction suggests, to demonstrate the limits to generalization. The presentation of the case will be limited to that material which most effectively reveals the theoretical principle investigated, for just as the 'best' cases are employed, so are the 'best' elements within each case. This atypical, selective quality to case-studies gives rise to their criticism as a basis for generalization, but this is ill-founded. Irrelevant elements, just as irrelevant cases, would merely serve to confuse; providing the analyst meets the *ceteris paribus* criterion they should be ignored. Mitchell explains: 'It is perfectly justifiable for the analyst to operate with a simplified account of the context within which the case is located provided that the impact of the features of that context on the events being considered in the analysis are incorporated rigorously into the analysis.' Much, of course, is left to the analyst, particularly his or her intimate knowledge of the circumstances of the case. Mitchell's observations on the logic of case-studies has been usefully summarized in a table by Silverman (1985) (Table 9.1).

Table 9.1 The logic of case-studies

	Survey research	*Case-studies*
Claim to validity	Depends on representativeness of sample	Only valid if based on articulated theory
Nature of explanations	Correlations not causes	Logical/causal connections
Relation to theory	Theory-neutral	Theory-dependent

In sum, it should be recognized that epistemology and research methods are interrelated. A position on the former does not simply give rise to the latter. Accepting this two-way street prompts a reappraisal of the accepted wisdom that the case-study method is inferior to quantitative methods because it lacks representativeness. Such a charge often prompts the response that representativeness is temporarily irrelevant; either because the case-studies are exploratory, implying survey research at some future date, or that quantitative and qualitative procedures may be combined to provide the 'best of both worlds', which, while acknowledging the usefulness of case-studies, still assumes the importance of representativeness. Alternatively, representativeness may be viewed as absolutely irrelevant. This position, contrary to accepted wisdom, reflects either an acknowledged difference in purpose, as in the concern of an ethnographer to describe a simple society as part of an anthropological study, or recognition of the epistemological distinction between statistical inference and logical inference.

CONDUCTING CASE-STUDY RESEARCH

The data collected frequently comes from both primary and secondary sources. Semi-structured interviews, using interview schedules, often provide much of the primary data. The interviews should, with the permission of the respondents, be tape-recorded and subsequently transcribed in full. Transcribing interviews is a lengthy process, but worthwhile in enabling the researcher to stay close to the data. Tape-recording ensures all data were noted and, in leaving the researcher free from the burden of making notes, allows concentration on the issues of concern and rapport to develop more easily. Data such as copies of letters, reports, and so on, may also be obtained from interviewees.

Interviews are problematic in a number of ways, as identified by many sources. These problems must, as far as possible, be controlled for, though the author has much sympathy with Silverman's (1985: 161–2) position that there is no bad way of doing interviews, there is only bad analysis of interviews. As he writes, 'for positivists, interviews are essentially about ascertaining facts or beliefs out there in the world', whereas (as an interactionist would argue) interviews may also be seen as social events in themselves, involving interviewer and interviewee in mutual participant observation. Interviews are not just about asking questions and taking the answer given, but also about interactions, as, for example, in how they reveal feelings or fears. So finally, before reviewing the strengths and weaknesses of case-studies, this section should make brief mention of the form of analysis which may be employed.

The more sophisticated sources on qualitative data analysis (such as Miles and Huberman 1984: 49–78, or Glaser and Strauss 1967: 101–15) refer to explicit coding and analytic procedures, whereby categories (concepts or relationships), and their properties are identified and analysed as they occur within the data. Some advocate quantitative procedures, from simply counting categories to statistical analysis. Ignoring the positivist overtones of coding and its analysis, there is the problem of specifying what to code. If the data alone are to generate theory then clearly categories cannot be specified a priori. This suggests either leaving the coding to the end of the data collection, which would deny flexibility such that interesting categories would only be recognized too late to prevent appropriate investigation within the study, or coding everything, a burdensome (if not impossible) task, as Glaser and Strauss (1967) acknowledge. They propose the constant comparative method, which, they suggest, incorporates an on-going explicit coding procedure and permits theory development during the study.

However, on the basis of this author's experiences of case-study research, this source and even the 'hands-on' manual by Miles and Huberman (1984), seem remote from the practice of research.[2] Research as lived, where interviews are a process of continual idea development; where theory is the outcome of a combination of studying other works, the data collection and chance occurrences and conversations; where as Latour and Woolgar (1979) comment on the natural sciences, order is brought forth from chaos; research as lived may not have the time or requirement for such fancy procedures. Coding, for this author at least, was satisfactorily achieved intuitively during the data collection. Only on writing up the cases was it thought necessary to code the data in any way, and then only to be certain of conveying key elements within the cases. This may, however, have had something to do with the partly deductive approach adopted or the research problem. However, the usefulness of explicit coding during data collection appears limited. If the researcher is close to the data, analysis, and theorizing is inevitably taking place. The value of such procedures may have more to do with making qualitative research appear acceptable and rigorous, than improving the method.

A further consideration is deciding how many cases to present, yet this may be out of the hands of the researcher. This author found that as each case progressed, as each interview was conducted, the data were found to be conforming to a pattern. In other words, a theory was emerging. The data became 'predictable' because they conformed with expectations. This is common to qualitative research and is sometimes referred to as 'saturation' (by Glaser and Strauss, for example). When saturation is achieved, the researcher may claim to have a sufficient number of cases.

STRENGTHS AND WEAKNESSES OF THE CASE-STUDY METHOD

The use of the case-study method can lead to charges of anecdotalism. Yet, for many research topics within management, this method is the most appropriate. However, case-studies need not be viewed as solely exploratory or tentative exercises in research. Their validity, when correctly understood, depends on how they are used and the logic of their analysis.

Yet it would be foolish to understate some of the weaknesses of the case-study method. As the earlier discussion has indicated, qualitative approaches do bring the researcher closer to the phenomenon under investigation and some might say too close. This raises two distinct problems. First, the problem of the dependence on the researcher's skills of clinical analysis in maintaining objectivity. Yet, as with quantitative research, judgement may still be passed on the validity of research results. (Indeed, this distinction between qualitative and quantitative research may be artificial in many ways. As the earlier discussion suggests, one might agree with Ratcliffe (1983) that '*all* approaches to inquiry are inherently qualitative in nature.') Second, there is the political consideration of the acceptability of case study research. As Bonoma (1985) somewhat drily observes – and this is a fitting conclusion to this chapter – 'Because the major thrust of most published marketing research *is* towards deductive, numerate, and causally directed research, the researcher may have a greater challenge in demonstrating the benefits and necessity of qualitative methods for the problem studied.'

NOTES

1 An earlier version of this paper was presented at the British Academy of Management Annual Conference, Cardiff, 1988. It was subsequently published in

Mansfield, Roger (ed.) (1989) *Frontiers of Management*, London: Routledge; as well as in *Graduate Management Research*.
2   Two excellent publications on the practice of case-study research have appeared since I first wrote this paper: Yin, Robert K. (1989) *Case Study Research: Design and Methods*, Newbury Park, London: Sage; and Eisenhardt, Kathleen M. (1989) 'Building theories from case study research', *Academy of Management Review* 14, 4: 532–50.

REFERENCES

Bell, C. and Newby, H. (1977) *Doing Sociological Research*, London: George Allen & Unwin.

Berger, P. L. and Kellner, H. (1981) *Sociology Reinterpreted: An Essay on Method and Vocation*, Harmondsworth: Penguin.

Bonoma, T. V. (1985) 'Case research in marketing: opportunities, problems, and a process', *Journal of Marketing Research*, xxii.

Dainty, P. (1983) 'Meaningful management research', *Graduate Management Research* 1, 1.

Denzin, N. K. (1978) *The Research Act: A Theoretical Introduction to Sociological Methods*, New York: McGraw-Hill.

Ford, J. (1975) *Paradigms and Fairy Tales: An Introduction to the Science of Meanings*, London: Routledge & Kegan Paul.

Glaser, B. G. and Straus, A. L. (1967) *The Discovery of Grounded Theory: Strategies for Qualitative Research*, New York: Aldine.

Goode, W. J. and Hatt, P. K. (1952) *Methods in Social Research*, New York: McGraw-Hill.

Hughes, J. (1980) *The Philosophy of Social Research*, London: Longman.

Hunt, S. D. (1976) 'The nature and scope of marketing', *The Journal of Marketing*, 40 (July).

Jauch, L. R., Osborn, R. N., and Martin, T. N. (1980) 'Structured content analysis of cases: a complementary method for organizational research', *Academy of Management Review* 5, 4.

Latour, B. and Woolgar, S. (1979) *Laboratory Life: The Social Construction of Scientific Facts*, Beverly Hills: Sage.

McClintock, C. C., Brannon, D., and Moody, S. M. (1979) 'Applying the logic of sample surveys to qualitative case studies: the case cluster method', *Administrative Science Quarterly* 24 (December).

Medawar, P. B. (1967) *The Art of the Soluble*, London: Methuen.

Miles, M. B. and Huberman, A. M. (1984) *Qualitative Data Analysis: A Sourcebook of New Methods*, Beverly Hills: Sage.

Mitchell, J. Clyde (1983) 'Case and situation analysis', *The Sociological Review* 31.

Ratcliffe, J. W. (1983) 'Notions of validity in qualitative research methodology', *Knowledge: Creation, Diffusion, Utilization* 5, 2.

Rigby, P. H. (1965) *Conceptual Foundations in Business Research*, New York: John Wiley.

Silverman, D. (1985) *Qualitative Methodology and Sociology*, Aldershot: Gower.

Worsley, P. and others (1970) *Introducing Sociology*, Harmondsworth: Penguin.

10 Management field research using repertory grid technique: problems and possibilities

Paul Dainty

INTRODUCTION

Repertory grid technique and personal construct theory (which has developed in relation to repertory grid technique) have grown in popularity over the last fifteen years. There is an increasingly broadening literature on the technique and construct theory, there is a regular conference held on personal construct psychology and, since 1988, there is a journal devoted to the subject (the *International Journal of Personal Construct Psychology*).

Repertory grid has been applied to research issues in several disciplines and has seen an increase in use in management research. Such a growth in popularity seems largely because it is a flexible instrument that can be used to investigate management topics as diverse as market opinion on dog foods, to issues concerned with interpersonal relationships in the work place. The technique does not need psychiatric skills to understand or administer, and once mastered is relatively straightforward. More writers have been prepared to explore possible areas of application of the technique and there has been considerable development in the range of computer analysis packages available for use with repertory grid.

Nevertheless, repertory grid technique is rarely considered in research texts. While there are several books devoted to the technique, there is value in highlighting for the management researcher some of the possibilities and pitfalls of repertory grid for field research before turning to the more specialized texts. Thus, the purpose of this chapter is to consider the theoretical background underlying repertory grid, outline the basic format of the technique, and address some of the issues the management researcher needs to consider in order to conduct field research successfully using the technique.

THEORETICAL BACKGROUND

An appropriate starting-point is the theoretical background. It is not absolutely necessary to understand the theoretical assumptions behind repertory grid to administer the technique. However, there are issues, particularly in relation to eliciting meaning from respondents which, if left unexplored by the researcher, may place him or her at a disadvantage in conducting research.

The theory developed by Kelly, which underlies repertory grid, is based on the assumptions that people actively engage in making sense of their world. They do this through a personal construct system which is a set of representations or a mental map of the world. The construct system is used to understand, construe, interpret, and evaluate incoming data and then translate this understanding into decisions on how to respond. The cognitive system originates because, according to Kelly, the individual can be seen as acting as a personal scientist who formulates hypotheses, tests them against experience and then reviews them depending on the outcome. Thus, our mental maps are not fixed but can be influenced by our interaction with our environment (Kelly 1955).

Since Kelly's original formulation of construct theory, development of the theory has been erratic. Subsequent writers have tried both to distance personal construct theory from other theoretical positions (e.g. Bannister and Fransella 1971) and also integrate the theory with the writings of a range of theorists from Freud to Piaget. There is a theme throughout the literature of encouraging other researchers to develop construct theory further, as Duck (1983) does in relation to issues in social psychology. But there are also others (e.g. Adams-Webber 1979) who are integrating their work with compatible philosophical traditions such as symbolic interactionism and phenomenology. However, personal construct theory still sits uneasily, even within the mainstream of psychology.

The end result is a loose theory concerned with understanding cognitive structure. This has enabled repertory grid to be applied to a wide range of research problems, including those within the management area, across all management functions. Yet an important part of Kelly's work is sometimes missed – that is, his epistemological orientation. The key to Kelly's approach is that the meanings (ways in which people construe/interpret their experiences) of the respondent rather than the meanings of the investigator are important. As Viney (1983) points out, Kelly is not alone in being concerned about meaning which is, for instance, an essential focus of phenomenological writers like Berger and Luckman (1972). However, the repertory grid technique developed by Kelly is unique in the way it assesses this meaning, in terms of the dimensions used by the subject rather than those imposed by the researcher. In fact, according to Dingemans *et al.* (1983) it was not since the word-association technique of Jung that there had been any significant development in this area.

Thus repertory grid differs from almost every other psychological method, according to Thomas and Harri-Augstein (1985), in being formally structured while remaining content-free. This allows broad applicability of the technique in terms of subject matter investigated, but in terms of the method, if used in its original form as developed by Kelly, the repertory grid has distinct parameters. Indeed, writers such as Thomas and Harri-Augstein (1985) condemn researchers who construct the grid in a way which reduces the scope the individual has for expressing his or her own meaning. The repertory grid can be constructed to act like a semantic differential with investigators completely imposing their interests. However, despite possible protestations from the purists, there is nothing wrong with this. What may be wrong is that the technique may be inappropriate for the research investigation. What is important is that the investigator is completely clear about his or her research purpose. There is nothing wrong with using the technique as a semantic differential, but there may be quicker, cheaper, and more appropriate methods available depending on what the research is trying to achieve.

REPERTORY GRID TECHNIQUE

So repertory grid is a technique for establishing an individual's mental map, with the unique quality of establishing meaning – and is probably best used for research with this as its purpose. However, as indicated, the technique can be constructed to be used in a number of different ways. The intention here is not to cover in detail the construction and analysis of repertory grid. There are already quite a number of good texts available, including Bannister and Fransella (1971), Ryle (1975), Slater (1976, 1977), Easterby-Smith (1981), and Smith (1986). The basic technique is outlined in this chapter, however, so that the researcher unfamiliar with repertory grid has a starting point from which to determine its usefulness before considering the more detailed texts, and also so that some of the limitations of repertory grid can more easily be explained.

There are three core areas that need to be considered when constructing a grid. They are: the elements, the constructs, and a method of linking these which is a grading system. Usually the elements are seen as the objects under consideration, while the constructs are the evaluations of those objects.

The elements

Depending on the investigation, elements can be objects as diverse as different products such as cars or paint, different departments within a firm, different companies, different people, or different activities. Elements can be generated through discussion, from a pool such as 'five colleagues', from role or situation descriptions, or they can be supplied. The most common method is through role descriptions. Figure 10.1 shows a role sheet which is typical of one used to investigate interpersonal relationships within the work place. Managers, as respondents, were given the role sheet and then asked to supply individuals familiar to themselves to fit each role. As a name was designated for each role, these people became each element and were written on to a grid sheet (see figure 10.3, p. 165).

Easterby-Smith notes that in generating elements it is important to ensure that the elements are as specific and homogenous as possible (Easterby-Smith 1981). That is, it is not possible to have people and activities as elements on the same grid because while you might describe an individual as being autocratic or less experienced it is difficult to evaluate an activity in these terms. Moreover, any role sheet should be comprehensive. It may cause considerable difficulties when it comes to data analysis to omit from the role sheet 'your manager' if you are concerned with significant others in the work place. Additionally, I have also found some managers who have difficulty with the role, colleague, or subordinate 'disliked' (role 4 and 8 in figure 10.1). I have been quite surprised at the number of managers who do not have anyone they dislike at work, which is either indicative of my own construct system or of their truthfulness.

There is little firm guidance about the number of elements necessary to complete a grid. Easterby-Smith (1981) argues that for industrial purposes you should generate as few elements as is necessary, although less than six may cause analysis problems. In industrial settings I have found that more than twelve elements can make respondents impatient.

Figure 10.1 Role sheet

1 Myself at work.
2 The person I report to (my manager).
3 The person my manager reports to.
4 A subordinate least liked.
5 A subordinate liked.
6 My best friend at work.
7 A colleague liked.
8 A colleague least liked.
9 An unsuccessful colleague.
10 A successful colleague

Source: Dainty (1984)

Constructs

The constructs are usually the evaluations or qualities attributed to the elements by the respondent. Again, these dimensions can be generated in several ways. They can be supplied by the researcher, though if they are all supplied as earlier explained, this largely negates the unique properties of a repertory grid. They can be elicited from diads or triads. They can also be generated through computer methods. The original method Kelly used, and possibly the one still most frequently used, is the triads method. This consists of writing the elements on cards and then using three cards chosen at random to elicit the construct. The elements are placed before respondents and they are asked which two elements are most like each other and least like the third. They are then asked, 'Why are the two cards you have chosen similar?' This generates the first part of the construct, the pole. Kelly argued that our construct system is bipolar, although quite a number of writers take issue with this both at a theoretical level (e.g. Shaw 1981) and a practical level, with Smith (1986) arguing that it causes confusion in industrial settings. The confusion may be more the result of the third question, 'Why are the two elements dissimilar to the third?' This generates the second or bipolar aspect of the construct and should be written down alongside the first pole to complete the construct elicitation. However I have found, in administering hundreds of grids in industrial settings, that respondents rarely have real difficulty in producing a bipolar construct. Indeed, there are other difficulties in administering the grid, noted later, which pose greater problems.

The process is repeated with different cards until the respondent is unable to generate additional constructs. A list of constructs generated from the elements in figure 10.1 are provided in figure 10.2. None of the constructs are the same and usually the researcher will encourage the respondent to try and produce a different construct if the previous one is repeated, as merely replicating constructs adds nothing to understanding the individual's mental map.

Easterby-Smith (1981) highlights additional pitfalls to avoid when generating constructs. Constructs to be avoided include situational constructs (such as 'lives in Wolverhampton'), excessively broad (such as 'is a woman'), excessively narrow (such as 'is a rat-catcher'), and vague (such as, 'not bad'). Perhaps the biggest pitfall that the researcher should counter, recalling that ideally a grid establishes individual meaning, is to prompt or give suggestions to the respondent. But while important in principle, in practice the repertory grid may create a degree of respondent dependency on the investigator, which is one of a number of contaminating factors rarely noted in the literature. This will be considered later. One variation of this approach is to supply some, rather than all, of the constructs. In figure 10.2 the construct 'Hard working

– Not hard working' was supplied by the researcher in order to investigate the meaning of hard work for the respondent and how it relates to other constructs.

There are no clear bench-marks about the optimum number of constructs to be generated and, indeed, there is some controversy. Smith (1986) argues that the minimum number of constructs is eight, though research by Chetwynd-Tutton (1974) suggest more than eight adds little to the researcher's understanding of an individuals' construct system. I have rarely found respondents in an industrial setting keen to generate more than sixteen constructs.

Figure 10.2 Sample constructs

Honest	–	Not straight
Uncaring	–	Professional
Easy going	–	Capable
Street-wise	–	Intellectual
Good communicator	–	Poor communicator
Poor leader	–	Good with people
Naive	–	Political
Tough minded	–	Tender minded
Hard working	–	Not hard working

Source: Dainty (1984)

Linking elements and constructs

The final major stage of administering the grid is to get the respondent to grade each element in relation to each construct. So, for example, a score is generated for 'myself at work' in terms of whether I am 'honest' or 'not straight'. Easterby-Smith (1981) notes that the most common methods of grading are ranking and rating, though 70 per cent of published studies use a rating method. According to Smith (1986) it is possible to have a scaling up to 100, although a five- or seven-point scale is more common. Figure 10.3 shows a completed grid combining the elements and constructs from figures 10.1 and 10.2. In this case, the respondent wrote his elements along the top of the sheet and then wrote in the constructs as he generated each one. He then rated each element in terms of the constructs moving down the page: that is, all the elements in terms of 'Honest – Not straight' were rated, then he moved on to the dimension 'Uncaring – Professional'.

GRID ANALYSIS AND INTERPRETATION

One reason for the growth in repertory grid is the availability of computer packages for grid analysis. However, there are disadvantages as well as

Figure 10.3 **The completed grid**

Name: Example Manager

Elements

Constructs (rated 1–7 from left pole to right pole)

Constructs	1 Myself at work	2 Margaret	3 Fred	4 Ron	5 John B	6 John R	7 Bob	8 Ivan	9 Kevin	10 Brian	11	12
1 Honest — Not straight	1	4	7	6	4	4	1	1	1			
2 Uncaring — Professional	5	5	5	1	4	1	1	5	6			
3 Easygoing — Capable	7	6	1	1	7	4	1	5	7			
4 Street-wise — Intellectual	3	2	4	5	5	4	3	5	2			
5 Good communicator — Poor communicator	3	2	3	4	4	4	5	4	7			
6 Poor leader — Good with people	6	7	2	4	4	5	2	4	6			
7 Naive — Political	5	7	6	4	5	5	5	2	5			
8 Tough minded — Tender minded	3	2	4	4	3	3	3	5	3			
9 Hard working — Not hard working	4	5	7	7	4	4	7	4	4			
10												
11												
12												

advantages to this computing power. As Easterby-Smith (1981) argues, the potential for quantification can exert a 'mesmeric effect' on the investigator and has led to two common misconceptions: that a grid cannot be analysed adequately without a computer and that computer analysis provides all the answers. Repertory grid has benefits in generating concepts – without conducting any kind of grid analysis at all – and, essentially, computers are needed only where a grid is large, where there is limited time, or where there is a need for extremely precise measurement. Computer output tells little more than what is written down on the grid, except where it highlights patterns or helps to establish clearer linkages. Yet there are a number of sources (e.g. Thomas and Harri-Augstein 1985) which explore equivalent manual techniques of interpretation and there are often benefits, even for those with some experience of repertory grid technique, in conducting a manual grid analysis before using the computer.

Nevertheless, there are excellent computing packages available. Some, such as Higginbotham and Bannister's GAB (1980) can be used on a personal computer, but the two main collections of grid programs need mainframe computers. The GAP programs which include INGRID and (more recently) INGRIDA are based on principal component analysis, while the FOCUS programs are based on cluster analysis. It is difficult to say which is better, though I agree with Easterby-Smith, who argues that the more complex INGRID program is best for research, while the more easily interpreted FOCUS analysis may be best for 'operational' activities.

The range of programs in the INGRID and FOCUS collections cope with different analytical purposes. In addition to INGRID and FOCUS there are the SERIES and CORE programs which combine grids with the same elements and constructs. PREFAN and SOCIOGRIDS are programs which combine several grids with the same elements and different constructs, while ADELA is a principal component analysis program which combines grids with the same constructs but different elements. Additionally there is a principal component program, called DELTA, which analyses the difference between grids with the same elements and constructs. In the UK, many central computing departments at the major universities have some or all of these programs and they are explained in detail in the various manuals accompanying the packages.

However, while there is a range of sophisticated computer software available to analyse grids, the analysis is really of no value until the researcher has interpreted it. Interpretation is very much an art rather than a science. Ironically, a technique which focuses on extracting meaning from the respondent rather than have it imposed, has as its outcome a whole range of possibilities for subjective interpretation by the investigator. Clearly there are ways of reducing this by, for instance, joint interpretation between the respondent and the researcher. But the fact that the technique permits data to be elicited in a value-free manner should not lead investigators to believe that the end result is value-free analysis.

Ways of interpreting grids, as with grid construction, are well outlined in the repertory grid texts (such as Ryle 1975, Slater 1976, 1977, and Stewart *et al.* 1981), hence I will only review the overall process.

The essential points about the print-out with, for instance, INGRIDA, are that, first, it enables the researcher, through the analysis of component space, to see to what extent an individual is cognitively complex: that is, on how many dimensions they view others or the issues under study. Second, the output shows how the individual relates elements together and which individuals, for instance, are seen as dissimilar or similar. Third, the output highlights the same associations for the constructs, and again which ones the individual sees as dissimilar or similar. The final important aspect of the output is how the constructs and elements relate to each other, and with INGRIDA a graphic mental map can be produced, as in figure 10.4

The map is of the manager whose elements and constructs were given in the previous figures. It shows the manager's elements inside the circle and the constructs around the circumference. By linking the elements together and noting their position in relation to the constructs it is possible to establish how this manager construes part of his interpersonal world at work. In brief, the map shows that the manager sees himself (1) as very similar to Brian (successful colleague, 10) and Bob (colleague liked, 7) with an emphasis on the constructs, capable (+3) professional (+2) and good with people (+6). However, he sees himself as very dissimilar to Ivan (colleague least liked, +8) and Ron (subordinate least liked, +4) both of whom he sees as more uncaring (-2) easygoing (-3) and not hard working (+9). Additionally, a number of other clusters can be identified and viewed in relation to the constructs, such as the similarity the manager sees between Margaret and Fred (my manager and the person my manager reports to) and their characteristics of being street-wise (-4) and tough-minded (-8).

This is not a comprehensive analysis and there are many other analytical avenues that could be pursued. But even if the investigator does pursue the analysis in more depth, a real difficultly is interpretation. For instance, one might expect that the way the manager relates to those people he sees as similar to himself, will be different to the way he relates to Ivan and Ron or anyone else he evaluates unfavourably. This is a reasonable assumption, but the researcher would benefit considerably from discussing the analysis with the respondent. However, this is not always possible and, accordingly, it is easy to make conclusive leaps from data which cannot support the assumptions underlying these conclusions. For instance, in repertory grid studies of consumer purchase behaviour, an individual may associate a Ford auto-

Figure 10.4 **A graphic mental map, showing how constructs and elements relate to each other**

Component 1 versus Component 2

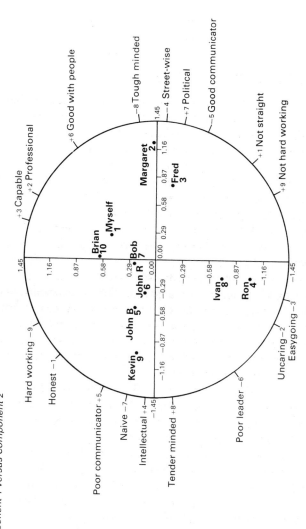

mobile with the constructs of 'economical', 'good value for money' and 'stylish'. But whether this gives rise to a decision to buy the vehicle is an entirely different matter and to some degree reflects the well-worn debate about the problematic relationship between mental predispositions, whether attitudes or constructs, and actual behaviour.

So while the output from the major computer programs is useful, it is still the researcher rather than the computer who has to draw the conclusions. For most research the range of possible avenues open for exploration is a positive advantage, but only if the investigator remains aware of his or her own construct biases and limitations.

REPERTORY GRID AND FIELD RESEARCH

Management research is not only conducted as field research. There are many problems relevant to management which can be explored in laboratory settings, such as the influence of incentives on motivation to perform a task. Moreover, the more traditional researcher, whose approach is closest to natural science methodologies, may prefer the possibility of a greater degree of rigour in laboratory research. However, while rigour is important, laboratory research may lack relevance because of the environment in which the research takes place. Field research is sometimes criticized for lacking rigour, but it is often seen as being more relevant. Indeed, there are many management issues which cannot be investigated except in the field. The whole notion of the manager is a role concept. If individual managers are taken out of their work environment, then in removing the setting, the investigator is changing, to a large degree, the phenomenon under study. Clearly there is no reason why one cannot combine methods, but management research will always be characterized by field investigations. Repertory grid technique used in management field research has advantages over some of the more traditional field research methods, but also suffers from some of the same problems.

On the positive side, in many ways repertory grid is an ideal technique for field research, assuming that the researcher is clear about his or her purpose and understands the mechanics of grid construction. It enables the researcher to establish a respondent's evaluations on a range of subjects. It taps information that is salient to the individual, is comprehensive, reduces the concern that important issues may have been missed and that the data have been gathered in a form that cannot be analysed by a computer. It is an excellent tool for exploratory research and can generate concepts and ideas which can be used in other field research forms. Moreover, the 'hard' computer data output may be seen as providing a degree of rigour in a field environment.

However, it is possible to be seduced into thinking that mastery of the technique alone (although important in itself) is enough for research purposes. This is clearly not the case. There are a number of problems both particular to the technique and also problems in common with other field research techniques which are worth highlighting.

Bouchard (1976) identifies five main field research methods: interviewing, questionnaire use, participant observation, systematic observation, and unobtrusive methods. Repertory grid, which Kelly (1955) considered to be a means of communicating by conversation, has some of the potential difficulties of 'communication' vehicles such as questionnaires, despite the distancing of the repertory grid technique from these methods. Repertory grid is a special form of communication which depends heavily on mutual trust and the goodwill of respondents. As with any serious research interaction, if the technique is to yield useful information, goodwill and trust must be maintained and cultivated by the researcher.

In looking at these issues in relation to repertory grid, it is useful to review the technique in the light of four conditions which Bouchard (1976) highlights for maximizing trust and motivation. First, the requirement to maximize privacy. A colleague once administered a repertory grid to landlords of public houses. On some occasions this had to be done in the public bar, which, with the continuing distractions, was not the best environment for clear thinking and grid construction.

Second, it is important to maintain neutrality. With the repertory grid perhaps the most critical point where this is likely to contaminate the data is during construct elicitation. Yet for reasons noted below maintaining neutrality is often much harder in repertory grid administration than the literature seems generally to acknowledge.

Maintaining confidentiality, the third of Bouchard's conditions, is particularly important in relation to repertory grid completion. I have found that the grid can seem very threatening to some people in a work environment. If a role element selection device is used which includes items such as 'subordinate liked', 'subordinate least liked', 'an unsuccessful colleague', 'a successful colleague', a high degree of trust has to be established before respondents will commit ratings to paper and for them to believe that the information will not be disclosed. In a recent study of a law enforcement organization, I received veiled threats, by quite powerful, senior personnel, of serious consequences should their repertory grid data be leaked. Some respondents were only prepared to use initials or code names for elements related to colleagues, and several insisted that names be erased from the repertory grid after completion and the element cards disposed of in their presence. This was despite a constant reassurance about confidentiality. This created significant problems. With no names (elements), it is difficult to produce a mental map, like that shown in figure 10.4. But, more importantly, it raises issues about the quality of the information gathered. Given the sensitivity of completing a grid in some circumstances, one has to be aware that there is no guarantee that respondents have been truthful. This applies to all paper and pencil instruments, but the neutral mechanics of the repertory grid should not blind the researcher to the possibility of this happening.

Fourth, Bouchard suggests it is important for the field researcher to be open, to identify him or herself, the research purpose and the amount of time needed from the respondent. I have found that these are also important issues for those administering repertory grid. Depending on its format the grid usually takes about an hour to complete and often longer. Some respondents may not be prepared to give this amount of time, or feel angry if the researcher has not detailed the time a grid can take beforehand. In addition it also requires a significant amount of a researcher's time. There are ways of reducing this, for instance, by providing the elements or constructs or both. But usually it demands face-to-face administration. I know of colleagues who have attempted repertory grid by mail but with little real success. Moreover, any attempts to use repertory grid as a survey method are fraught with analysis difficulties. For instance, it is possible to use the SERIES program to combine grids, but this is limited to small groups. With given constructs and elements it is also possible to use part of the data output of a grid such as element distances and combine these with other grids. However, attempting then to look at statistically significant relationships is plagued with other problems like the issue of interval as against nominal data.

Finally, repertory grid poses an additional problem for the researcher in terms of identifying the research purpose to respondents. It is not always an easy instrument to explain and it is important to think of ways to explain the technique in a simple manner. Repertory grid is straightforward to construct for the researcher who understands the mechanics. It is also straightforward to give instructions when administering the grid. But while it might be relatively easy to administer, it can be extremely difficult to explain to managers who have control over research access to their employees. Moreover, even when completing the grid, respondents may have difficultly in understanding what they are doing. It is interesting that a technique intended to tap meaning can leave respondents uncertain about what the technique is meant to do. This may cause particular problems for researchers trying to maintain neutrality and not prompt the respondent, as noted earlier. It is not unusual for respondents to start asking during construct elicitation whether their response is what you (the researcher) want. It does not seem surprising to me that research using repertory grid has been abandoned due to insurmountable 'administrator' difficulties (Keen and Bell 1981).

CONCLUSION

This chapter has outlined the theoretical background to repertory grid and the mechanics of grid construction. Many texts emphasize the importance of construction, and clearly this is important. However, as this chapter has shown, equally important is for the researcher to have an understanding of some of the difficulties of using repertory grid in the field. The problems which have been highlighted should not detract from the scope and flexibility of repertory grid. Moreover, despite the technique's wide use within management research there are still many areas which might benefit from being explored using repertory grid. However, as this chapter has emphasized, no matter how good a technique may be in itself, it cannot compensate for bad research preparation or for using a good technique inappropriately.

REFERENCES

Adams-Webber, J. (1979) *Personal Construct Theory: Concepts and Applications*, New York: Wiley.

Adams-Webber, J. and Mancuso, J. C. (1983) *Applications of Personal Construct Theory*, London: Academic Press.

Bannister, D. and Fransella, F. (1971) *Inquiring Man*, London: Penguin Books.

Berger, P. L. and Luckman, T. (1972) *The Social Construction of Reality*, Harmondsworth: Penguin.

Bouchard, T. J. (1976) 'Field research methods', in M. D. Dunnett (ed.) *Handbook of Industrial and Organisational Psychology*, Chicago: Rand McNally.

Chetwynd-Tutton, S. J. (1974) *Generalised Grid Technique and Some Associated Methodological Problems*, unpublished Ph. D. thesis, London University.

Dainty, P. (1984) *A Study of the Motivation of Managers in Manufacturing Organisations in Conditions of Contraction*, unpublished Ph. D. thesis, Cranfield Institute of Technology.

Dingemans, P. M., Space, L. G., and Cromwell, R. L. (1983) 'How general is the inconsistency in schizophrenic behaviour?', in J. Adams-Webber and J. C. Mancuso (eds) *Applications of Personal Construct Theory*, London: Academic Press.

Duck, S. (1983) 'Sociality and cognition in personal construct theory' in J. Adams-Webber and J. C. Mancuso (eds) *Applications of Personal Construct Theory*, London: Academic Press.

Easterby-Smith, M. (1981) 'The design, analysis and interpretation of repertory grids', in M. L. G. Shaw (ed.) *Recent Advances in Personal Construct Technology*, London: Academic Press.

Higginbotham, P. and Bannister, D. (1980) *The GAB Computer Program for the Analysis of Repertory Grid Data*, Computer Services Psychology Department: Leeds University.

International Journal of Personal Construct Psychology, 1988, New York: Hemisphere.

Keen, T. R. and Bell, R. C. (1981) 'One thing leads to another: a new approach to elicitation in the repertory grid technique', in M. L. G. Shaw (ed.) *Recent Advances in Personal Construct Technology*, London: Academic Press.

Kelly, G. (1955) *The Psychology of Personal Constructs* (vols 1 and 2), New York: Norton.

Ryle, A. (1975) *Frames and Cages*, London: Chatto & Windus.

Shaw, M. L. G. (1981) *Recent Advances in Personal Construct Technology*, London: Academic Press.

Slater, P. (1976) *The Measurement of Intrapersonal Space by Grid Technique, Vol. 1: Explorations of Intrapersonal Space*, London: Wiley.

Slater, P. (1977) *The Measurement of Intrapersonal Space by Grid Technique, Vol. 2: Dimensions of Intrapersonal Space*, London: Wiley.

Smith, M. (1986) 'An introduction to repertory grids', *Graduate Management Research* 3, 1 and 2.

Stewart, V., Stewart, A., and Fonda, N. (1981) *Business Applications of Repertory Grid*, London: McGraw Hill.

Thomas, L. and Harri-Augstein, E. S. (1985) *Self Organised Learning*, London: Routledge & Kegan Paul.

Viney, L. L. (1983) 'Experiencing chronic illness: a personal construct commentary', in J. Adams-Webber and J. C. Mancuso (eds) *Applications of Personal Construct Theory*, London: Academic Press.

11 Choosing a survey method in management research

David Jobber

A key issue in management research is the choice of the most appropriate survey method. A researcher has a choice of three methods – face-to-face, by telephone, or by mail survey. A wrong decision at this stage of a Ph.D., for instance, can cause frustration, disappointment, and a great deal of wasted effort. A mail survey with a response rate in single figures, for example, can prove disheartening to even the most resolute of researchers. Each method has its own strengths and limitations which must be borne in mind when making the decision. The objective of this chapter is to discuss the relative merits of the three methods so that the correct choice can be made by the researcher.

The main strength of the face-to-face questionnaire is its ability to cover complex issues. A researcher, particularly during the exploratory research stage, may prefer to use a semi-structured questionnaire with topics but not listed questions. This gives maximum flexibility to the interview: the length of time devoted to each topic can vary between interviews depending on the responses of interviewees, and new topics can be added as they appear relevant to the research objectives. The face-to-face interview allows the maximum degree of probing. Two types of probe are used. Clarifying probes (such as 'Can you explain what you mean by...?') help the interviewer to understand exactly what the respondent is saying. Exploratory probes ensure that the respondent gives as full an answer as possible (e.g. 'Are there any other reasons why...?'). A certain degree of flexibility and probing can be obtained with a telephone interview, but time pressure and the less-personalized situation will inevitably limit the extent of such practices. The mail questionnaire, on the other hand, must be fully structured. The exact wording and layout of the questions must be determined prior to dispatch and probing answers which are incomplete, ambiguous, or of little value are not possible unless a follow-up survey (perhaps by telephone) is conducted. The potential for using open-ended questions is more limited than with face-to-face or telephone interviews since their presence reduces response rates (Falthzik and Carroll 1971). Thus, where a complex issue is being researched (e.g. a detailed understanding of a decision process), a mail questionnaire is unlikely to be viable. Furthermore, when a large number of filter questions is necessary the questionnaire may be confusing to respondents if administered by mail. In such circumstances a face-to-face or telephone interview would be more appropriate.

The major drawback to the face-to-face survey is that it requires a higher level of resources per interview than telephone and mail surveys. The personal interview is both time-consuming and costly. Researchers with limited funds may find difficulty in obtaining the required sample size within budget. A compromise may be struck with face-to-face interviews being supplemented with telephone or mail questionnaires. This is not always possible, however, because the nature of the research may demand the more personalized approach. In this situation, there may be no alternative to the lowering of sample size to a viable level. Another limiting factor may be the time involved in travelling to interview. Management of time is of crucial importance to a doctoral student, and it may not be possible to obtain the necessary sample size because of time constraints. Telephone and mail interviews are much less time-consuming and must be considered very seriously when large samples are desired.

Two types of interviewer bias may arise in face-to-face and telephone interviews. First, bias may be caused by the respondent's perceptions of the interviewer, and second, bias may be due to the attitudes and perceptions of the interviewer. Interviewers can be different with regard to age, sex, race, physical appearance, voice, and behavioural mannerisms. These characteristics may provide clues to the socio-economic group, educational background, and group memberships of the interviewer. Wide differences between interviewer and respondent may hinder communication. For example, a respondent may feel inhibited if the interviewer is clearly better educated than him/her. Furthermore, if the respondent feels that he or she is being evaluated along some hidden criteria under certain conditions they may become apprehensive or anxious that they will be judged negatively in some way. In an attempt to receive a positive evaluation, responses may be distorted to correspond with what is believed to be an acceptable or correct answer in the eyes of the interviewer (Rosenberg 1969).

Interviewer attitudes and perceptions may also give rise to bias. For example, in a study of opinions about prefabricated housing it was discovered that interviewers who themselves had favourable attitudes to such housing reported more favourable responses (Ferber and Wales 1952). Recording answers on questionnaires provides the opportunity for interviewers to select passages which more closely follow their own attitudes, particularly with long or ambiguous statements. Another related source of error is the opinions held by the interviewer about the respondent. An interviewer may expect that the respondent will hold certain opinions or behave in a certain way on the basis of the respondent's appearance, role, or previous answers. Once more there may be a tendency to interpret and record long or ambiguous responses in line with such expectations.

The implication of these potential problems is that management researchers should be aware of the dangers which can arise, and consciously seek to avoid them. This normally means adopting a friendly, polite, but neutral manner. For example, interviewers should avoid approving facial expressions when respondents give answers with which the interviewer either agrees or expects, while also avoiding making disapproving gestures to unexpected or disagreeable responses.

The major strength of the mail survey is the ability to survey widely dispersed populations at low cost. When information from businessmen is needed, the mail questionnaire is clearly viable because the names and addresses of companies can be obtained quickly and easily from directories. If some questions require the respondent to consult files (e.g. to obtain turnover figures), then this can be done at the respondent's convenience. A telephone interview is much less likely to result in such consultation. The respondent is more likely to give a top-of-the-mind estimate than to interrupt the telephone interview to search through his files. There is a caveat to the advantages of the mail questionnaire – too many questions which require effort on the part of the recipient will result in non-response. The cardinal rule of mail questionnaire design is to make the questionnaire appear simple to complete. The psychological response from the recipient must be, 'This looks pretty straight-forward. I'll fill it in now', rather than 'This looks a bit complex. I'll fill it in tomorrow.' Wherever possible, questions must be pre-coded so that the respondent only has to tick a box or ring a number to record his answer. When open-ended questions are necessary, they must be kept to a minimum and appear towards the end of the questionnaire. These restrictions mean that the mail questionnaire should not be used when a deep understanding of complex issues is sought. But when data is required on, for example, business practices (e.g. the percentage of industrial market researchers who have used group discussions, or the extent of use of certain quality control procedures) a mail questionnaire can be used successfully.

A further characteristic of the mail questionnaire is that the respondent fills in the questionnaire without the presence of an interviewer. This has two benefits: first, the possibility of interviewer bias is removed, and second, the respondent is likely to answer certain questions – perhaps of a highly critical, sensitive, or embarrassing nature – more willingly than when face-to-face with an interviewer. For example, in a study by O'Dell (1962) 17 per cent of respondents to a face-to-face interview reported borrowing money from a bank, while 42 per cent admitted doing so when a mail survey was used. However, these benefits may be offset by the lack of control of the interview situation. The questionnaire may be completed and returned but the questions may be answered in a hurried, ill-considered way. Further, there is no control over who answers the questionnaire. It may be delegated to a subordinate, and the possibility of group rather than individual answers cannot be ruled out.

The most common criticism of the mail questionnaire is that, compared to face-to-face and telephone interviews, response rates are low. Certainly single-figure responses have been recorded. These are usually associated with complex questionnaires on topics of little interest to the respondent. But there is no reason why such poor response is inevitable, and in the next chapter, by Paul Cragg, these issues are explored in more detail.

The telephone survey is probably the least used of the three techniques among doctoral students researching managers. This is in stark contrast to professional industrial market researchers who use this technique extensively and increasingly.

The method combines a degree of flexibility and some ability to probe with convenience, speed, and reasonable cost. It is almost a half-way house between the face-to-face interview and the mail survey. Response rates can be expected to be higher than the mail survey, although frustration may be experienced in trying to contact some respondents. A major drawback is the inability to use visual aids with respondents. For example, the use of the semantic differential scale for measuring attitudes would be extremely difficult to execute over the telephone. Furthermore, the telephone interview must be kept relatively simple. The need to read both question and answer categories and to ensure that the question is short enough to be comprehensible places limits on question complexity (Dillman 1978). For example, questions which ask respondents to rank objects (e.g. brands or attributes) along some criterion (e.g. preference or importance) are difficult to execute over the telephone. However, using the telephone does ensure that the correct respondent answers the questionnaire, unlike mail surveys where interview control is lost.

A criticism of the telephone interview compared with the face-to-face situation is that the interview time is much reduced. Evidence suggests that with general-public surveys, twenty minute interviews are feasible with virtually no termination of interview (Dillman 1978). No evidence from industrial populations is forthcoming, but personal experience suggests that telephone interviews lasting up to fifteen minutes are possible. Face-to-face interviews can last much longer than this and this is one reason why they are preferable for complex research issues. Interviews which last over one hour are commonplace in both consumer and industrial surveys.

This review has demonstrated that it is impossible to say which method is superior in abstract terms. Each method has its own strengths and limitations. The task facing researchers is to assess each of them in the light of the survey objectives, the nature of the information required, and the resources available. Only then may the question of which is best be answered. In order to facilitate this process, table 11.1 summarizes the factors affecting choice, and the performance of each method for each of them. It should be noted, however, that combinations of the three methods can be highly effective. For example, a mail survey can be followed by telephone interviews of non-respondents (e.g. Hooley *et al.* 1988). This not only raises response rates (and hence sample size), it also allows calculation of non-response bias to the mail survey. Another variant is to interview a sub-set of mail survey respondents to obtain a greater depth of response.

Table 11.1 A comparison of face-to-face, telephone, and mail surveys

Factor	Method		
	Face-to-face	*Telephone*	*Mail*
Questionnaire			
1 Complex issues	Good	Medium	Poor
2 Use of open-ended questions	Good	Medium	Poor
3 Flexibility	Good	Medium	Poor
4 Ability to probe	Good	Medium	Poor
5 Use of visual aids	Good	Poor	Good
Resources			
1 Time	Poor	Medium	Good
2 Cost	High	Medium	Low
Sampling			
1 Widely dispersed populations	Poor	Good	Good
2 Delegation to subordinate	Good	Good	Poor
3 Response rates	High	Medium	Low
Interviewing			
1 Control of who completes questionnaire	High	High	Low
2 Interviewer bias	Possible	Possible	Not possible

RECOMMENDED READING

The following texts are recommended for those wishing to read further on this subject:

Dillman, D. A. (1978) *Mail and Telephone Surveys: The Total Design Method*, New York: Wiley.

Frey, J. H. (1983) *Survey Research by Telephone*, Beverly Hills: Sage.

Moser, C. A. and Kalton, G. (1975) *Survey Methods in Social Investigation*, London: Heinemann.

REFERENCES AND BIBLIOGRAPHY

Burns, A. C. and Hair, J. F. (1980) 'An analysis of mail survey responses from a commercial sample', *Proceedings of the American Institute for Decision Sciences* (12 meetings), November, 227–9.

Dillman, D. A. (1978) *Mail and Telephone Surveys: The Total Design Method*, New York: Wiley.

Falthzik, A. M. and Carroll, S. J. (1971) 'Rate of return for closed- versus open-ended questions in a mail questionnaire survey of industrial organizations', *Psychological Reports* 29: 1121–2.

Ferber, R. and Wales, H. (1952), 'Detection and correction of interview bias', *Public Opinion Quarterly* 16: 107–27.

Ferrell, O. C. and Krugman, D. (1983) 'Response patterns and the importance of the follow-up questionnaire in a mail survey of advertising managers', *European Research*, October, 157–63.

Gouldner, A. W. (1960) 'The norm of reciprocity: a preliminary statement', *American Sociological Review* 25: 161–78.

Gullahorn, J. and Gullahorn, J. (1963) 'An investigation of the effects of three factors on response to mail questionnaires', *Public Opinion Quarterly* 27: 294–6.

Heberlein, T. A. and Baumgartner, R. (1978) 'Factors affecting response rates to mailed questionnaires: a quantitative analysis', *American Sociological Review* 43: 447–62.

Hewitt, W. C. (1974) 'How different combinations of postage on outgoing and return envelopes affect questionnaire returns', *Journal of the Market Research Society* 16, 1: 49–50.

Hooley, G. J., Lynch, J. E. and Shepherd, J. (1988) 'The effectiveness of British marketing: resumé of preliminary findings', *Proceedings of the Marketing Education Group*, vol. 3, Huddersfield Polytechnic, July, 106–26.

Kimball, A. E. (1961) 'Increasing the rate of return in mail surveys', *Journal of Marketing* 25: 63–4.

Jobber, D. (1989) 'The effects of questionnaire factors on response to an industrial mail survey', *International Journal of Research in Marketing*, forthcoming.

Jobber, D., Allen, N., and Oakland, J. (1985) 'The impact of telephone notification strategies on response to an industrial mail survey', *International Journal of Research in Marketing* 2: 291–6.

Jobber, D. and Sanderson, S. M. (1988) 'The effects of a prior letter and coloured questionnaires on mail survey response rates', *Journal of the Market Research Society* 25, 4: 339–49.

O'Dell, W. F. (1962) 'Personal interviews or mail panels', *Journal of Marketing* 26: 34–9.

Paolillo, J. and Lorenzi, P. (1984) 'Monetary incentives and mail questionnaire response rates', *Journal of Advertising* 13: 43–8.

Rosenberg, M. J. (1969) 'The conditions and consequences of evaluation apprehension', in R. Rosenthal and R. L. Rosnow (eds) *Artifact in Behavioral Research*, New York: Academic Press, pp.279–349.

Scott, C. (1961) 'Research on mail questionnaires', *Journal of the Royal Statistical Association* 124, 2: 143–92.

Sletto, R. F. (1940) 'Pretesting of questionnaires', *American Sociological Review* 5: 193–200.

Swan, J. E., Epley, D. E., and Burns, W. L. (1980) 'Can follow-up response rates to a mail survey be increased by including another questionnaire?', *Psychological Reports* 47, 1: 103–6.

Tullar, W., Pressley, M. M., and Gentry, D. (1979) 'Toward a theoretical framework for mail survey response', *Proceedings of the Third Annual Conference of the Academy of Marketing Science*, pp.243–7.

Veiga, J. F. (1984) 'Getting the mail survey returned: some practical research considerations', *Journal of Applied Psychology* 59, 2: 217–18.

12 Designing and using mail questionnaires

Paul B. Cragg

This chapter offers advice on the design and use of mail questionnaires. It draws on the advice of very experienced users of mail questionnaires, showing that the design and use of a questionnaire is a complex process. A case-study is used to explore the reality faced by researchers when using the mail questionnaire approach.

STRENGTHS AND WEAKNESSES OF THE SURVEY STRATEGY

Before using any data collection method, a researcher should be convinced that the most appropriate methods are being used and this choice depends on the research objectives. Although research strategies like experiments and case-studies can utilize questionnaires, the survey strategy makes the greatest use of questionnaires. The major strength of the survey strategy is the ability to collect data from a large sample; thus allowing quantitative analysis in the testing of inferences, and also the potential to generalize the findings. One of the major disadvantages of the survey strategy is that the important variables must be known in advance. If this is not the case then considerable exploratory research must be conducted prior to the use of a survey.

DESIGN OF A MAIL QUESTIONNAIRE

There are many sources of advice on questionnaire design. Sudman and Bradburn (1982) provides comprehensive advice on both question design and questionnaire format. The book by Dillman (1978), on the Total Design Method (TDM), offers advice on the whole process of designing and using a mail questionnaire. Both books result from many years' experience of conducting surveys.

Determining questionnaire content

The preparation of a good questionnaire requires time and thought. The questionnaire must serve its goal of providing reliable and valid data in a usable form which meets the needs of the researcher. A questionnaire may go through as many as twenty revisions.

Other questionnaires can prove useful in preparing draft questions to gather the information that is needed. Better still, use an instrument which has been proven to be reliable and valid by other researchers. The initial draft of the questionnaire should be assessed by peers, and amendments made. Dillman (1978) recommends pre-testing by three different groups: colleagues, potential users of the data, and potential respondents. Furthermore, Dillman suggests this pre-testing should be observed by the researcher so that all difficulties are identified.

An important part of the pre-testing process is to make sure the questions provide the needed data. If hypotheses are being tested then the methods of analysis must be determined prior to data collection. If the data analysis is on a computer, then the questionnaire must be designed in such a way that coding and data input are both easy and error free. If another person is to input the data, then seek their views on the questionnaire layout. In addition, the questionnaire may need to be pilot tested not once but twice, on a sample of up to fifty respondents.

USING A MAIL QUESTIONNAIRE

Based on theories of social exchange, Dillman (1978) argues that there are three things that must be done to maximize survey response:

- minimize the cost for responding;
- maximize the rewards for doing so;
- establish trust that those rewards will be delivered.

As a result, Dillman proposes a method which pays attention to all the factors which affect both the quantity and quality of response. Thus Dillman offers advice on the envelope, the cover letter, mailing dates, and many dos and don'ts. The advice is very comprehensive and recommends procedures which make the use of a questionnaire no easy option. Dillman argues that to obtain a useful response rate requires considerable attention to detail. It is not simply a matter of putting together a questionnaire and sending it out. In the absence of an accepted theory of mail questionnaire response, some of Dillman's detail is possibly unnecessary. However, his approach has been shown capable of consistently producing response rates above 60 per cent in samples of the general public, and even higher in more specialized populations. Researchers may therefore be keen to utilize Dillman's approach, although the attention to detail is very demanding.

In Dillman *et al.* (1984), an analysis is given of eleven studies using the same questionnaire and covering letter, but with differing adherence to the TDM. Dillman concluded that the greater the adherence to the TDM, the higher the response. These findings suggest that researchers should use:

- individual, one page, dated covering letter printed on headed paper;
- blue ballpoint signature added to each covering letter;
- a booklet-type questionnaire with an attractive cover and no questions on the front and back covers;
- questions laid out spaciously in a vertical answer format;
- first class post on all mailouts;
- a postcard follow-up sent one week after the first mailout, with a date and signature in blue ballpoint pen;
- a second follow-up, three weeks after the initial mailout, a similar package to the original mailout, including a questionnaire, sent to all non-respondents;
- a third follow-up to all non-respondents, seven weeks after the initial mailout.

The approach advocated by Dillman pays considerable attention to detail, so is very demanding of researchers. These demands are discussed in the example below where an attempt was made to follow Dillman's advice.

A CASE-STUDY

A survey of small firms in the East Midlands region of England attempted to use Dillman's TDM (Cragg 1986 and 1990). The TDM was found to be very difficult to implement in full. In particular, three areas of difficulty arose: personalization, typing of envelopes, and reminder procedures. In addition, a number of other adaptations to the method were made.

Personalization

Dillman advises that both the envelope and cover letter should contain the name and address of the intended recipient. The advice comes from conducting social surveys of the general population, and is very dependent, as with all surveys, on a detailed, comprehensive, and up-to-date sampling frame. Such a sampling frame did not exist for small firms, so directories and other sources were used to create a list of firms in the region. However, it is a more difficult task to obtain the name of the individual you wish the questionnaire to go to. For the small firms survey, the questionnaire was aimed at the owner of the firm. Some sources gave the owner by name; others did not. As a result the survey could not be fully personalized, and many envelopes and letters were addressed to the 'Managing Director'.

Typed envelopes and letters

The TDM recommends that the 'package' that a recipient receives should seem like a 'business letter', and thus be worthy of attention. Hence Dillman argues that the address should be typed on a typical business envelope; self-adhesive labels are to be avoided. For the small firms survey, no easy alternative to typing 1,100 envelopes was found. With a database of names and addresses already on a computer it seemed expensive to type each envelope. Though printers are capable of printing on to envelopes, no available printing centre was found that had the necessary attachments to automatically feed and print on to envelopes. Direct mail companies with such facilities were located, but tended to consider minimum runs of 4,000. The study used the simple alternative of labels, utilizing the 'labels' routine within dBASE III. The survey failed to use typed envelopes, justifying the use of labels on practical grounds, and on the assumption that many recipients would have their mail opened for them.

Reminder procedures

The TDM advises the use of three reminders. The first reminder, after one week, is mainly designed as a very gentle prod, but also serves as a thank-you to those who have already responded. The second reminder, after a further two weeks, is a similar package to the initial mailing, including another questionnaire, a return envelope and an amended cover letter. The TDM recommends that a third reminder is sent by registered mail to all non-respondents after a further four weeks. The use of registered mail is to emphasize the importance of both the survey and the recipient.

For the small firms survey, no third reminder was sent, partly because a good response had already been achieved, but mainly because the researcher did not wish to harm the relationship between researchers and organizations. It was obvious from the initial responses that some respondents found the questionnaire an imposition. This was communicated by a small number of respondents by telephone or by letter, or more typically, through comments on the questionnaire. However, following the second reminder, an even larger number of disgruntled comments were received; these far outnumbered the few unsolicited offers of further assistance from owners. As over 500 replies had been received, it seemed unwise to risk being viewed as an annoyance and therefore possibly harming the relationship between researchers and small firms. The disadvantages for the small firms survey was that nothing had been heard from about 50 per cent of the listed firms, raising questions of possible bias. In order to find out a little of this unknown 50 per cent, a small and brief telephone survey was conducted, mainly checking the eligibility of non-respondents. As the telephone survey was very small and did not require the co-operation of an owner of the firm, the researcher viewed it as likely to cause little offence. Though some telephone respondents knew of the survey, the cordiality of the brief conversations suggested that the researcher had not been considered a nuisance.

Other necessary adaptations

The researcher was able to follow in spirit most of Dillman's other recommendations, though many minor details were not followed precisely. One example is on the size of the stationery to be used. Dillman advises on the use of monarch sized paper rather than A4. The reason for such a size was to keep within the USA's 1 oz weight limit for cheaper postal delivery. As the equivalent limit is 2 oz in the UK, no stringent controls were needed on weight. However, the advice on using a typical business envelope was followed, thus requiring folding of the booklet-type questionnaire. Dillman's advice on using lower than typical weight paper made it considerably easier to fold and insert the questionnaires. A small second batch of questionnaires was printed using standard weighted paper, and these questionnaires proved difficult to fold despite being only three sheets of paper.

RESOURCES REQUIRED FOR A MAIL SURVEY

Dillman's recommendations on using a detailed, personalized approach makes the mail questionnaire method very labour-intensive. Surprisingly, Dillman seems to have used the approach on surveys of thousands, rather than hundreds, of possible respondents. As a result, the university where he is based has established a survey centre to handle these large surveys. What resources does a mere research student need to utilize his personalized approach?

Money helps; the small firms survey was supported by a research grant, of which about £2,500 was spent conducting the study. Without such funding it would have been hard to justify certain items of expenditure. First class postage was used for all mailings, including the Freepost returns. Dillman argues that the use of first class post reflects the great importance of the study. In addition, it would have been hard to justify the acquisition of company names and addresses from the British Telecom Yellow Pages. (For a supposedly up-to-date, computerized list the data seemed just as inaccurate as other directories of small firms. Complete lists are not available for many reasons, but County Council Directories were found to be the most cost-effective means of compiling a sampling frame.)

The research grant enabled the researcher to employ part-time clerical assistance, utilized mainly to:

- computerize the name and address database;
- type occasional letters in response to requests from respondents;
- assist with the large task at each mailout, involving folding, checking, labelling, inserting, and sealing (though self-seal envelopes were used for greater convenience). Once all resources were gathered together, a mailout of 1,150 questionnaires required about 60 hours work.

Use of computers

Micro-computers were used to create and update a name and address database, as well as to print the labels and the standard cover letters. Here, dBASE III was found to be excellent at handling the major task of managing the database. Its features and its ease of use made the task quite simple. An indexed database of 1,150 records just about filled one 360K floppy disk; hence it was useful to have an IBM PC XT available to store some files temporarily. Each record consisted of the following fields; owner, company name, address (four fields), telephone number, source ID, and a response ID. As the database was being used for research purposes only, it was not considered necessary to register it under the Data Protection Act.

The database was used for three major purposes: to print labels for mailings, to create a file to mail-merge the cover letters (on a laser printer with form feed for fast printing), and to produce printouts to help control mailings and record responses to later amend the database.

Printing costs were another major expense. Along with postage and clerical help, the research funds were easily consumed. Thus the time spent searching and applying for research funds was a good investment.

PLANNING AND ORGANIZATION

Implementing the TDM requires careful planning. For each mailing, resources like envelopes, questionnaires, and cover letters must be available. The cover letter should carry the date of the mailing. (Dillman advises posting early in the week in the hope of avoiding the questionnaire being lost and forgotten over the weekend.) Thus printing requirements have to be determined well in advance and deadlines met. This involves a few forecasts with respect to the likely response rate. The system also requires a certain amount of continued monitoring of responses so that only non-respondents receive follow-up mailings. In order to check for possible response biases through time, all incoming questionnaires need to be dated. In addition queries, particularly by telephone, will need to be answered. Hence, the days between mailouts are far from idle.

IS THE TDM WORTH IT?

Even if a researcher decides not to attempt a full implementation of the TDM, the method contains many pieces of sound advice learnt through experience. The sections on questionnaire design, testing the questionnaire, and the discussion of the content of the cover letter contain excellent advice for the novice researcher. Whether the approach in full is worth following is debatable as no experiment has been conducted which could test every aspect of the TDM.

The approach does obtain useful response rates. For the small firms survey it was about 50 per cent, including refusals. However, similar response rates have been achieved by other small business researchers who have not used the TDM in full. For example, Delone (1983) used a very crowded questionnaire layout and obtained a response rate of 49 per cent. Dillman would no doubt argue that use of a very crowded questionnaire is likely to have resulted in a greater number of completion errors and omissions.

THE IMPORTANCE OF PERSONALIZATION?

The research study was not intended to be a test of the TDM. However, the importance of personalization was investigated both in the pilot study and in the main survey. A much higher percentage of named individuals, compared with letters addressed to 'Managing Director', responded to the pilot study. As a result, greater efforts were made to obtain details of named contacts. For some firms, no named contact was available and as a result many letters were sent to the 'Managing Director'. An analysis by degree of personalization is given in table 12.1 below, showing that a higher percentage of named owners gave useful responses, but overall, the less personal approach gained a higher response.

Using X^2, the differences in response rates are significant at the 0.1 per cent level. However, the less personalized approach obtained the greatest response, suggesting that the search for the names of owner-managers was not rewarded. The X^2 difference is primarily due to the differing responses for ineligible returns, possibly reflecting quality differences in the sources of company information, which varied in the level of detail, and by compilation date. Another variable could be the proximity of the firms to the university conducting the research, with response reducing with distance. The study

Table 12.1 Response by degree of personalization

Addressed to	Usable returns number (%)	Ineligible returns* number (%)	Other returns number (%)	No response number (%)	Total
'Managing director'	105 (28)	76 (20)	19 (5)	172 (46)	372
Named owner/manager	250 (31)	73 (9)	52 (7)	420 (53)	795
	355†(30)	149 (13)	71 (6)	592 (51)	1167

Notes
* Ineligible returns comprised firms which were too large for the survey, subsidiaries, and non-engineering firms. Other returns comprised refusals, incomplete return, ceased trading, and gone away.
† The total of 355 is 3 lower than the actual total response because 3 returns were anonymous.

was not designed as a controlled test of the TDM, but the data does not support the need for a fully personalized approach.

Rather than advise fellow researchers to implement the TDM in full, the above experiences suggest that the TDM has many merits. The work by Dillman *et al.* (1984) suggests that the greater the adherence to the TDM, the greater the response. However, his conclusion was partially based on a rather arbitrary scoring system.

THE IMPORTANCE OF REMINDERS

One of Dillman's conclusions which is strongly supported by the data is that the number of reminders is important. Dillman estimates that each mailing achieves a similar response, of about 20 per cent. Hence, the more reminders, the greater the response in total.

A breakdown of the returns for the small firms survey is given in table 12.2. Of the total response, 40 per cent were received within the first week. The second reminder, sent out on the Monday of week 4, made a significant contribution to the total response as returns were dwindling by week 3, but picked up considerably in week 4. A third reminder, as advised by Dillman, would have no doubt produced an even greater response.

With respect to the 'quality' of response, table 12.2 gives a breakdown and shows again how important the second reminder was in producing not just responses, but a large number of usable responses, i.e. responses from firms within the study's focus. (Questionnaires were sent to firms who were found to be ineligible, e.g. a subsidiary, or too big. This problem is associated with the studying of small firms where no sampling frame exists.)

Therefore, the results of the small firms survey give support to Dillman's TDM in that the mailing process is important in obtaining good response rates.

Table 12.2 Small firms survey – types of response by week

Week	Event	Usable returns	Ineligible returns	Other returns	Total	%
1	Initial mailing	147	55	27	229	40
2	Thank you/reminder	69	24	18	111	19
3		19	9	2	30	5
4	Second reminder	99	47	17	163	28
5		13	9	6	28	5
6	onwards	11	5	1	17	3
	Total	358	149	71	578	100

SUMMARY

The study attempted to use Dillman's Total Design Method (TDM) in carrying out a mail questionnaire survey of small engineering firms. The TDM could not be used in full, particularly with regard to the degree of personalization and a third reminder. However, many other aspects of the TDM were followed and a total response of 50 per cent was obtained. The usable response rate was 30 per cent, mainly due to a poor sampling frame with many responding firms being too large or subsidiaries, rather than through refusals and ceased trading. An analysis of the responses showed that the use of a second reminder significantly affected the response, while full personalization did not. As a result, it is recommended that other researchers adapt and use Dillman's TDM when using either mail or telephone questionnaires.

REFERENCES

Cragg, P. B. (1986) 'A study of the impact of information technology on the financial performance of small engineering firms: a progress report', Working Paper No. 132, Department of Management Studies, Loughborough University of Technology.

Cragg, P. B. (1990) 'Information technology and small firm financial performance', Ph.D. thesis, Loughborough University of Technology.

Delone, W. H. (1983) 'Determinants of success for small business computer systems', Ph. D. thesis, University of California, Los Angeles.

Dillman, D. A. (1978) *Mail and Telephone Surveys: The Total Design Method*, New York: Wiley.

Dillman, D. A., Dillman, J. J., and Makela, C. J. (1984) 'The importance of adhering to details of the total design method (TDM) for mail surveys', in D. C. Lockhart (ed.) *Making Effective Use of Mailed Questionnaires*, San Francisco: Jossey-Bass, pp. 49–64.

Sudman, S. and Bradburn, N. M. (1982) *Asking Questions: A Practical Guide to Questionnaire Design*, San Francisco: Jossey-Bass.

13 A first-time user's guide to the collection and analysis of interview data from senior managers[1]

Susan J. Hart

INTRODUCTION

As more and more publicity is given to the commercial benefits derived from the use of market research, so more and more companies carry out or commission market research studies (Jobber and Bleasdale 1987, Hart 1987a, Hart 1987b, Simmons 1982).

For a company operating in consumer markets, there is a vast amount of information regarding research methods, which can be used to initiate an in-house study, or at least to keep tabs on externally-commissioned field-work (Goodyear 1986, Fahad 1986, Smith 1972, Gorden 1969). Not so for the company in the industrial sectors, where fewer research studies are designed and implemented and where comparative inexperience, together with a lack of basic, useful information leaves the progressive manager vulnerable to the pitfalls that abound during the survey process (Hooley and West 1984, Foxall *et al.*1987). However, perhaps even more necessary than information about conducting interviews with business executives is advice about analysing the content of the interviews.

Indeed, this problem is exacerbated by the tendency to consider interview-data analysis as something of an art, and to stress the importance of researchers' intuition (Patton 1980). Further, since analytical methods are rarely reported in any detail, there is very little advice for newcomers to follow. A further general consequence of all this is the fact that the validity of qualitatively-derived findings is seriously in doubt (Dawson 1979, 1982, LeCompte and Goetz 1982). When one considers that of all the survey techniques, the most expensive is the face-to-face interview, it is apparent that a trial-and-error approach will probably result in a costly, irrelevant, and ineffective exercise that is unlikely to be tried a second time.

This chapter aims to help correct the shortfall in practical information for would-be industrial researchers, by focusing on the problems encountered when interviewing business executives. This is particularly important to industrial companies, since recently-collected evidence shows that it is the interview technique which is the most important survey method in industrial market research (Jobber and Bleasdale 1987).

The remainder of this chapter is based on the author's experience of conducting and analysing focused interviews with senior managers and other élite personnel, such as senior civil servants. The discussion centres on the administration and analysis of a *focused* or semi-structured interview which falls largely under the auspices of qualitative research.

THE INTERVIEW PROCESS

The entire question of access to business respondents is one area of industrial market research which has been given attention in recent years and there is a good deal of advice to be found regarding the improvement of response rates (Jobber 1986, Martin 1986). However, there is little point in spending time and money improving the response rates if the quality of interviewing and analysis of the interviews is substandard. An overview of the major texts which deal specifically with the mechanics of interviewing reveals the complexity involved in conducting a good interview (Dexter 1970, Bingham and Moore 1966, Gorden 1957, and Gorden 1969). Less well documented, however, are the logistics of arranging, timing, and handling an interview, especially with business executives. An attempt is made, therefore, to summarize the author's experience for the benefit of those wishing to carry out interviews with top executives. Five areas are worthy of specific attention: arranging dates, arranging times, the handling of the interview, timing the interview, and directing the content.

Arranging dates

In reporting their survey of élite personnel, Grøholt and Higley (1970) underline the problems of timetabling a series of interviews. Elite personnel are prone to last-minute changes in schedules; it is therefore important to build some 'slack' into a programme of interviewing. The above-mentioned authors suggest a maximum of two interviews per day, geographical spread permitting, but this author's experience would suggest that one or two free mornings or afternoons in a week of interviewing will be necessary to accommodate last-minute changes.

Interviews with business executives have to be arranged some time in advance, since the respondents can often be away on business (Kincaid and Bright 1957). This is even more important if the interviewer has to travel away from base to carry out the interview, or a series of interviews in a given area. It is recommended that initial contact is made three to four weeks in advance of the time the researcher wishes to conduct the interview. However, if interviews are carried out in or near the base area, this is not necessary.

Arranging times

It is unwise to arrange appointments shortly before lunch or at the end of the day unless the interview can be completed with *certainty*. The author's experience suggests that respondents' impatience can be problematic, and such arrangements are risky if the respondent is at all late for the interview.

A lunch appointment may be suggested. Although a common way of 'doing business', this usually proves to be an unsatisfactory arrangement because the attention of both interviewer and interviewee is not complete, following the interview schedule is impaired, and both note-taking and tape-recording are often rendered difficult.

Handling the interview

The following excerpt from Bingham and Moore illustrates the improbability of suddenly becoming a good interviewer:

> He should have good judgement, imagination under control and special education in business research so that he can be readily trained to digest facts as they are given to him and make deductions promptly [...] He must be resourceful enough to gain an interview yet avoid being so self-assertive that his attitude repels. He must know how to be diplomatic if the interviewee disagrees with him and never let a discussion become an argument. Another pitfall he must guard against is a know it all attitude...
> (Bingham and Moore 1966: 142–3)

Given this list of attributes, and those detailed by other authors (Gorden 1957, Dexter 1970), it is to be expected that the first few interviews will probably prove to be less successful than the latter ones. It is therefore apposite to make at least two visits to every company, so that missing information can be gathered, and points of uncertainty resolved. If only one visit is to be made, then the interviewer must listen carefully and understand what is being said, or the major advantages of conducting an interview survey will be lost. The advantage in question is that of being able to ask for clarification and explanation about comments, something which is impossible in a mail survey.

While it is something of a truism to say that the executive interviewer should be prepared, experience suggests that advantages are to be gained from preparation, and that certain penalties are paid for lack of preparation. As Kincaid and Bright have commented: 'Our experience proved that the respondents in many cases *expected* that we would be well-informed about their company, at least to the extent of having read the publicly available literature' (Kincaid and Bright 1957: 307).

An interviewer's task is facilitated where the respondent companies are large well-known names, about which a good deal is written. For the less well-known companies, a knowledge of the product range, the number of employees, the major competitors, the two years' sales turnover figures can prove highly beneficial in two important ways. First, it reveals the seriousness and professionalism of the research study, which helps overcome communication barriers and establish rapport. Second, it gives the interviewer not only the confidence, but the knowledge to probe past 'public relations answers' and help unearth what really goes on, and why. Without the knowledge, probing is difficult, and again, the very *point* of conducting an interview is lost.

Timing the interview

Generally arriving 'on time' is unsatisfactory where the interviewee's time is restricted. In many instances, the interviewee is not called until the interviewer has arrived, at which point the secretary or receptionist has to locate the respondent, who might often be in a meeting or making an important telephone call. Ten or fifteen minutes can often elapse before the respondent becomes free, which could cause problems where he or she has stipulated an hour for the interview. Arriving a quarter of an hour early compensates for this and allows extra time for gleaning valuable information at the reception.

The location of the interview is not without importance. Most interviewees will suggest a quiet office, but some propose that the interview take place in the reception area, the staff refectory, or an open-plan office. None of these locations is satisfactory since respondents can be more inhibited in these 'public' places, and if the interview is to be recorded, the quality of the recording is often impaired. It should be said, however, that a working lunch in an office is not as awkward, since the increased privacy and quiet provide the correct environment for the serious business of conversation handling. Once the respondent and interviewer are settled, it is important to explain the purpose of the interview. Although there will have been previous letters and telephone calls for this, it is important to reiterate that the respondent's views and comments are of interest, and to urge against the public relations response.

Directing the content

The precise nature of each interview will vary from company to company. The author's interviews, which have tended to be qualitative and focused, have lasted an average of two hours on each visit. Generally, interviews of this nature follow a simple pattern of three stages. In the first stage, the interviewer presents herself or himself and the study. As Dexter (1970) recommends, it is important (1) to stress the interviewer's definition of the situation, (2) to encourage the interviewees to structure their account of the situation, and (3) to let the interviewees introduce, to a considerable extent, their notions of what they regard as relevant. This introductory format helps accomplish three things. First, preconceptions the respondent may have harboured regarding the objectives of the study are dispelled. This reduces the likelihood of respondents giving what they consider to be the 'desirable' or 'right' answer. Second, it clarifies to the respondents that their perceptions and opinions are of greatest interest. Third, emphasizing the confidentiality of individual responses and promoting the respondents view helps reduce the amount of figurehead or public relations responses.

The second stage consists of asking respondents for easily recalled, factual information about the company, its products and markets. The main function of this short sequence is to put the respondents at ease by allowing them to talk generally about their domain. The third stage begins the interview 'proper', and the general pattern of the schedule should be followed. A note is usually kept of issues covered before the question is formally asked, to avoid duplication and time-wasting. Respondents, for the most part, speak freely about their activities and react well to requests for clarification and elaboration. It is advisable to ask for specific examples which might elucidate the points being made. Not only are the anecdotes useful for illustrative purposes, but recalling a specific instance often reveals undisclosed information, thus provoking greater exchange.

The willingness of respondents to give freely of their time and experiences greatly helps the interviewer, but the occasional problem should be signposted.

At the outset of the interviews, a few respondents will be wary and hesitant. While they have agreed to be interviewed, they are not entirely at ease. Introductory remarks often helped dissipate this tenseness, especially if the respondents feel that the researcher is interested in *their* company and in what *they* have to say. Good preparation helps to convey such interest, as does taking the time to ask conversational questions, in familiar language, about their business (Zuckerman 1972).

A second problem is the 'public relations answer'. As Kincaid and Bright suggest: 'considerable probing is needed to distinguish between what is company policy for creating desired public impression as against what actually happens' (Kincaid and Bright 1957: 309). This is a difficult problem to overcome – it may not even be recognized as a problem. Certainly, a familiarity with the language and tone of company documents gives the researcher a feel for the sensitive areas of corporate image, but this is not enough to elicit the truth. The two-visit system can prove useful for rephrasing and repeating questions and thus detecting discrepancies or 'rehearsed' answers. Of course, the possibility that respondents have 'learned' from the first interview cannot be entirely discounted.

A third problem is the tendency of some respondents to stray from the point and elaborate on a different element of their responsibility. If this happens frequently, or at great length, the interview may well finish before the desired information has been obtained. Such situations are not easy to handle, although persistent re-phrasing of the question can often elicit an answer.

Finally, accuracy in reporting the respondents' views is helped by the use of a small tape-recorder, an issue discussed in more detail later on.

ANALYSING THE INTERVIEW

While there are several texts dealing comprehensively with quantitative data analysis – and many of these are marketing research texts – there is a notable shortage of practical advice on interview data analysis: 'A few years ago, an examination of several well-respected textbooks on field methods found that less than 5–10 per cent of their pages were devoted to analysis (Sieber 1976)' (Miles and Huberman 1984: 16).

In a random selection of commonly used market research textbooks (Tull and Hawkins 1987, Kinnear and Taylor 1987, Crimp 1985, Chisnall 1986) the amount of attention paid to analysis of qualitative data is lamentably low. This perpetuates the tendency for analysis of qualitative data to be done badly (McDonald and Blyth 1971, May 1978), a flaw exacerbated by the apparent wish to keep the techniques arcane. Thus the qualitative researcher 'relies primarily on his own intuitive capacities for inference, empathy, perceptiveness and creativity' (Jones 1981: 27). This perpetuates the lack of rigour which Tuck (1976), Miles (1979), the R and D Sub-Committee on Qualitative Research (1979), and Leather (1985), to name but a few, have mentioned. (It is apposite to mention in passing, that quantitative analyses may *appear* to be better protected from the whims of subjectivity by 'reams of computer printout conveying the impression of independence and objectivity' [Leather 1987: 8], but they are not intrinsically free from the vagaries of personal interpretation and judgement.) However, qualitative researchers are trying to imbue their techniques with scientific respectability, an endeavour that is often hindered by the lack of guidelines for protection against over-interpretation and delusion. Methods of analysis are not well formulated, are infrequently reported and the researcher is left to shape and select material without any rules – or even precedents – to follow (Fineman and Maugham 1983, Van Maanen 1979). Notable exceptions exist; occasionally researchers detail their method of analysis so that others may benefit (Eden *et al.* 1979).

In this chapter we are concerned with the analysis of focused, or semi-structured interviews. Where a researcher is dealing with fully-structured interviews, be they in the street, on the doorstep, or in the boardroom, the task of analysis is simplified, and is usually contained within the design of the questionnaire. Thus the interviewer need only check the questionnaire as directed. However, we are dealing with a style of interviewing which is more fluid, probing, and qualitative and which is often the more meaningful approach in complex industrial markets.

The lack of guidance referred to above adds to the list of 'disadvantages' in carrying out qualitative research. Yet, by following a few basic rules, this seemingly unapproachable, rather esoteric technique soon becomes demystified.

As previously mentioned, in the author's experience, a tape-recorder is an invaluable tool, although it is recognized that some researchers prefer to take notes (Martin 1986). The usual disadvantages of recording an interview centre on the anxiety and nervousness provoked in the respondent. The accuracy of responses can be jeopardized since respondents do not want to be recorded saying 'the wrong thing'. Concurring with the experience of Zuckerman (1972) such fears appear to be unfounded when dealing with an 'élite respondent'. The respondents, in the author's experience, do not seem to be reticent and appear to ignore the machine. This has never seemed to be a problem in interviewing top executives who are often used to speaking publicly, and even to the media. In any case, they are all advised that, should they wish to disclose anything sensitive, the machine can be switched off. Indeed, the use of the tape recorder has proved to be vital to the success of the author's interviews, relieving the interviewer of the simultaneous tasks of listening, writing, and thinking of the next topic for discussion. In this way, a genuine exchange can take place, rapport can be built up, and the accuracy of complete transcriptions for analysis is obtained.

Note-taking can be troublesome, because it is nearly impossible to keep note of everything that has been said, due to the speed of the conversation. In addition, a good amount of on-the-spot selection of important points takes place, which puts in question the accuracy and reliability of the data being recorded. Finally, it is difficult to concentrate on what is being said, write down the essence and guide the conversation logically to the next topic. All in all, the tape recorder is useful, especially for the novice because, as Patton puts it:

> A tape recorder is part of the indispensable equipment of evaluators using qualitative methods. Tape-recorders do not 'tune out' conversations, change what has been said because of interpretation (either conscious or unconscious), or record words more slowly than they are spoken. In addition to increasing the accuracy of data collection, the use of a tape recorder permits the interviewer to be more attentive to the interviewee.
>
> (Patton 1980: 247)

If tapes are to be transcribed fully, which according to Patton (1980) yields the most desirable form of data, despite the time and/or expense that transcription may entail, researchers should allow four hours to transcribe one hour of tape. It is a wise precaution to make more than one copy of the transcript, especially if the data collection process has taken place over a long period of time. Where the method of analysis involves cutting and pasting, more than one copy of the original is suggested. The master copy can then be used to locate the source material in context while the first full copy can be used for writing comments and highlighting important areas. Once the transcripts are ready, a choice has to be made which impinges upon both the analysis and the presentation of the data. The choice is between using a 'case' analysis and presentation or a more issue-by-issue presentation (computer programs for analysing qualitative data are not dealt with here). Within these two broad classifications the emphasis is on classification of the raw data. Without classification there is chaos.

Yet there is no one correct way of organizing, analysing, and interpreting qualitative data. Assembling the data by specific cases permit an in-depth study of the cases. The case record must include all the information needed for subsequent analysis, but organize the information at a level beyond that of the raw case data. Both classification and organization of the raw data are required *before* the assembly of the case is complete, yet the case must be thorough and comprehensive in its descriptions: 'Thoroughness also implies that every phase of the problem must be studied and that it must be approached from every possible angle' (Jocher 1928/29: 205). The emphasis of the case analysis is to describe and analyse what has happened in a single, bounded context.

On the other hand, where there is a need to verify that events and behaviour are not merely the result of one idiosyncratic setting, researchers are turning to 'multisite, multicase designs' (Miles and Huberman 1984, Louis 1982). Indeed, systematic comparison of several groups is the essence of the argument formulated in *The Discovery of Grounded Theory* (Glaser and Strauss 1967). As with the case approach, there is a need to devise a system for classifying the raw data, since qualitative interview data are voluminous. The choice between an aggregate and a case approach is not an easy one, since the advantages and disadvantages of each are not directly comparable. Table 13.1 summarizes these.

Table 13.1 Advantages and disadvantages of aggregate and case analysis of qualitative data

	Advantages	*Disadvantages*
Case analysis	Less contamination by the researcher	Not appropriate for many cases
	Tableaux can be supplemented with published information	Not appropriate where many issues are covered
	Ensuing analysis is based on *full* raw data	Generalizability of the findings difficult due to small samples
Aggregate analysis	Vast amounts of data can be handled more economically	Researcher interference can distort results
	Large number of cases can be catered for	Analysis carried out on data that has already been doctored
	Results (from a larger sample) can be more generalizable	Loses the immediacy of specific examples

THE CASE ANALYSIS

Taking the case history approach, the basic idea is to assemble information as comprehensively and systematically as possible regarding the case: the company, represented by the respondent, a senior manager. This information may include the interview data, observational data, company information such as financial reports, and any other data of relevance. That said, the accumulation can be enormous, and where a large number of companies have been interviewed, this type of analysis is not really suitable. Although it is perfectly feasible to 'cut down' the amount of information included in the case record, this somewhat defeats the purpose of the focused interview.

While the case method of analysis is well suited to a small number of detailed instances, it does not suffer, to the same degree as aggregate content analysis, from the intrusion and contamination of the researchers. This is because their interpretation and evaluation can be separated from the mere writing down of all the information relevant to a case. Naturally, selection of 'relevant' information may well be subjective, but in keeping with the purpose of case reporting, the more comprehensive the case record, the less this can happen.

In the author's experience, assembling a case record of a company, based on a focused interview with a senior manager entails the five steps in the list below. These are offered to guide the beginner. (Technical names for the analysis have been left out, as they are rather verbose, but for those wishing to read further, Miles and Huberman (1984) and Van Maanen (1983) have details of the analysis strategies and titles.)

Basic steps in case analysis of interview data

1 Assemble all the raw material to be included in the cases (transcriptions, printed material from inside and outside the company).
2 Decide on a logical pattern of topics in which to present the material. This is best derived from the interview schedule, if one was used, with the extra (non-interview) data given the same place in each case.
3 Once the pattern is set, decide on the major sections or paragraphs, together with their titles, and write them down.
4 Review the material in each case and check for missing information. Where data are missing, make a note.
5 Develop a detailed case record, only now editing the language of the transcription, into a document guided by the paragraph headings. This document should be condensed, comprehensive, and detailed, and will be used for further analysis, for example cross-case analysis.

The key step in the entire process is step 2. Here the researcher must decide how to classify the raw data in the transcription and any additional material that has been collected. In the case of interviewing a senior manager, general preliminary questions (which may themselves be the main classification issues in the research) are best put at the beginning or the end of the case history, together with any similar extra material. This stage distils into a decision on the main subject areas to be reported from the field-work. Where qualitative data analysis has been described, it often entails some sort of qualitative 'coding' which attempts, in a concise way, to flag 'key issues' within each transcription or 'site' so that they can be compared. The coding frame will be derived from the overall conceptual framework which, in the case of focused interviews, should be in place before interviewing begins, to differentiate focused interviews from depth interviews and group discussions. The conceptual framework is what the interview focuses on, and should be consistent with the research objectives and stated information requirements. Thus, if the interview guide contained five, seven, or nine main areas of inquiry then this would be the first breakdown of the resultant data. It is helpful to categorize these topics physically – either in separate notebooks, loose-leaf binders, or folders. The choice is up to the individual researcher, of course!

Often, a sixth step is added to this sequence: the preparation of an edited, and often stylized account of the case (Becker 1986, Strunk and White 1981).

THE AGGREGATE ANALYSIS

An aggregate analysis is appropriate where a larger number of respondents' data are to be analysed, and where there are a large number of topics relevant to the analysis.

Opting for the aggregate approach means that great care has to be taken in order to avoid too much of the researcher's selectivity and subjectivity contaminating the report. The steps in this analysis resemble those used in the case analysis:

Basic steps in aggregate analysis of interview data
1 Assemble all the raw material for each site.
2 Decide on a logical pattern of topics related to the research objectives (derived from the interview schedules).
3 Once the pattern is set, decide on the major sections or paragraphs together with their titles, and assign them to folders, or to separate notebooks.
4 From each transcription, take the comments relevant to each section and assign them to the appropriate folder or notebook. (This stage may be executed in writing down the comments, or by cutting and pasting.)
5 Once the responses from all the transcriptions have been assigned in this way, duplication can be detected and eliminated. The respondents can then be assigned to the responses. (This stage can also be executed with the aid of a computer.)

Steps 1, 2, and 3 are taken from the case analysis procedure, as they help minimize the effect of researcher selection of the comments and areas of interest. The most important aspect of stage 4, however, is to ensure that all the relevant comments are assigned. Within each of the main topic areas, recurrent themes in cases may be allocated a 'sub-code', which might be denoted either by using decimal paragraph systems or, more simply, with different coloured pens.

An example will further explain the method. In a survey of industrial buyers' key purchase criteria, an interview guide might include the issues of price, delivery, quality, service etc. Within a broad area like delivery, respondents might then comment on a number of 'sub areas', for example, delivery lead times, regularity of delivery, just-in-time delivery, and reliability. Comments – the data – relating to any of these four could be colour-coded for easy recognition across sites. This helps *all* comments made on relevant areas to be incorporated into the analysis, wherever they occur in the manuscription. There is always a danger that since the transcription follows the same order as the interview schedule, the person collating the information will only look in one section of the transcription for comments. This is to be avoided, for often, throughout the interview, respondents pass remarks relevant to many aspects of interest.

Step 5 results in a very useful summary sheet of who said what, and can be used to analyse the data further. It is a step which begins to tabulate the data, and which entails, to some extent, a loss of information. As indicated in the above list, it can be carried out using a computer spreadsheet. The main purpose of this stage is to make the data accessible to more than one interested party – which can also be a good test of the reliability of the data.

In both these types of analysis, the emphasis is on lengthy preparatory stages, which attempt to introduce rigour and standardization into the way the information is presented. As a result, all subsequent interpretive analysis can be checked against relatively clean – but structured and comprehensible – raw data. It should, of course, be remembered that all qualitative data analysis is plagued with the hazards of researcher involvement.

CONCLUSION

This chapter is based on the premise that, as industrial market research becomes more and more popular, semi-structured and depth interviews will be the most widely-used means of data collection. This being so, the chapter presents the novice with some general advice about the collection and analysis of data using these techniques.

In conducting the interviews, five areas were given specific attention: arranging dates, arranging times, handling the interview, timing the interview, and directing the content.

In analysing the data, two approaches were discussed, based on the author's experience: case history and analysis, and aggregate content analysis. Basic steps in each analytical method have been given, together with an overview of the pros and cons of each.

NOTE

1 This chapter has also appeared in *Marketing Intelligence and Planning*. It is used here with permission.

REFERENCES

Becker, H. S. (1986) *Writing for Social Scientists*, Chicago: Chicago University Press.

Bingham, W. V. D. and Moore, B. V. (1966) *How to Interview*, Harper International Student, reprint, 4th edition.

Chisnall, P. (1986) *Marketing Research,* London: McGraw-Hill, 3rd edition.

Crimp, E. M. (1985) *The Marketing Research Process*, Englewood Cliffs, NJ: Prentice-Hall, 2nd edition.

Dawson, J. A. (1979) 'Validity in qualitative inquiry', paper presented at the annual meeting of the *American Educational Research Association*.

Dawson, J. A. (1982) 'Qualitative research findings: what do we do to improve and estimate their validity?', paper presented at the annual meeting of the *American Educational Research Association*.

Dexter, L. A. (1970) *Elite and Specialised Interviewing*, Evanston: Northwestern University Press.

Eden, C., Jones, S., and Sims, D. (1979) *Thinking in Organisations*, London: Macmillan.

Fahad, G. (1986) 'The use of focus-group discussion by first time users', in D. Cowell and J. Collins (eds) *Proceedings of the Marketing Education Group*, conference proceedings, Plymouth Polytechnic.

Fineman, S. and Maugham, I. (1983) 'Data, meanings and creativity: a preface', *Journal of Management Studies* 20, 3.

Foxall, G. R., Gutmann, J. N., and Moore, B. M. (1987) 'Man marketing and the role of consumer-style research in non-consumer markets', *Proceedings of the 30th Market Research Society Annual Conference*, London, MBS.

Glaser, B. G. and Strauss, A. L. (1967) *The Discovery of Grounded Theory: Strategia for Qualitative Research*, Chicago: Aldine.

Goodyear, M. (1986) 'Not sex again', *Market Research Society Newsletter* 243, June.

Gorden, R. L. (1957) 'The dimensions of the depth interview', *American Journal of Sociology*, 62.

Gorden, R. L. (1969) *Interviewing: Strategy, Techniques and Tactics*, Illinois: The Dorsey Press.

Grøholt, K. and Higley, J. (1970) 'National élite surveys: some experience in Norway', *Acta Sociologica* 15.

Hart, S. J. (1987a) 'The contribution of marketing to competitive success', *Management News*, July.

Hart, S. J. (1987b) 'The use of the survey in industrial market research', *Journal of Marketing Management* 3, 1.

Hooley, G. J. and West, C. J. (1984) 'The untapped markets for marketing research', *Journal of Marketing Research Society* 26, 4.

Jobber, D. (1986) 'Managing industrial mail surveys – a user guide', in D. Cowell and J. Collis (eds) *Managing Marketing*, Marketing Education Group conference proceedings, Plymouth, July.

Jobber, D. and Bleasdale, M. (1987) 'Interviewing in industrial marketing research. The state of the art', *Quarterly Review of Marketing*, January.

Jocher, K. (1928/29) 'The case method in social research', *Social Forces* 1928/29.

Jones, S. (1981) 'Listening to complexity', *Journal of the Market Research Society* 23, 1.

Kincaid, H. V. and Bright, M. (1957) 'Interviewing the business élite', *American Journal of Sociology* 63.

Kinnear, R. and Taylor, J. R. (1987) *Marketing Research: An Applied Approach*, New York: McGraw-Hill, 3rd edition.

Leather, D. (1985) 'The work of the advertising research unit: part II – methodology'.

LeCompte, M. D. and Goetz, J. P. (1982) 'Problems of reliability and validity in ethnographic research', *Review of Educational Research* 52.

Louis, K. S. 'Multisite/multimethod studies', *American Behavioural Scientist* 26, 1.

Martin, C. (1986) 'Accessing and interviewing senior managers', *Graduate Management Research* Autumn/Winter.

May, J. P. (1978) 'Qualitative advertising research: a review of the role of the researcher', *Journal of the Market Research Society* 20, 4.

McDonald, C. D. P. and Blyth, W. A. (1971) 'How to handle soft data – a linguistic approach', Thompson Awards.

Miles, M. B. (1979) 'Qualitative data as an attractive nuisance: the problem of analysis' *Administrative Science Quarterly* 24, December.

Miles, M. M. and Huberman, A. M. (1984) *Qualitative Data Analysis: A Sourcebook of New Methods*, London: Sage.

Patton, M. Q. (1980) *Qualitative Evaluation Methods*, London: Sage.

R. and D. Sub-Committee on Qualitative Research (1979) 'Qualitative research – 4, summary of concepts involved', *Journal of the Market Research Society* 21, 2.

Simmons, K. (1982) 'The image of the British market research industry in the business world', *Proceedings of the MRS Conference*.

Smith, J. M. (1972) *Interviewing in Market and Social Research*, London: Routledge & Kegan Paul.

Strunk, W. and White, E. B. (1981) *The Elements of Style*, London: Macmillan.

Tuck, M. (1976) *How Did We Choose?* London: Methuen.

Tull, D. S. and Hawkins, D. S. (1987) *Marketing Research: Measurement and Method*, New York: Macmillan, 4th edition.

Van Maanen, J. (1979) 'Reclaiming qualitative methods for organisational research', *Administrative Science Quarterly* 24, December.

Van Maanen, J. (1983) *Qualitative Methodology*, London: Sage.

Zuckerman, H. (1972) 'Interviewing an ultradite', *Public Opinion Quarterly* 30.

Part III
Research contexts

PART III: RESEARCH CONTEXTS

Whatever difficulties may be faced in selecting an appropriate research method, at least most researchers consider this in detail. There are, however, other areas of concern, which are rarely addressed to the same extent, but can have a major impact on the success of a research project. Certainly, they are rarely explicitly covered in research texts. We have called these 'other areas' research contexts. All research takes place within a context, or framework, of constraints, opportunities, and expectations. A context does not refer to a theoretical position or research methodology, though they might be affected by the context. It refers to the stage beyond these considerations and the framework within which research is actually conducted. Accordingly, in the model of the research process presented in the Introduction, we showed research contexts as enveloping research perspective and research methodology. A context will often modify an ideal way of carrying out research and can range from the restrictions set down by gatekeepers with access to research subjects, to the limitations imposed by funding or expectations of colleagues.

Misunderstanding a context can cause considerable losses of time, money, and, in extreme cases, career damage. This is particularly true of research for an academic degree such as a Ph.D., where a candidate may misunderstand the constraints placed on their research by the examination process. But the notion of context is not only of importance in conducting research which is formally assessed. Hart's chapter in part II (chapter 13) emphasizes that data collection techniques do not have the unbending properties of micrometers and have to be applied in various environments, such as the world of the senior executive, which can challenge normative presuppositions.

The intention here is not to comment on the value or otherwise of conducting research in various contexts, but to encourage researchers to look at ways of managing them better. Their mismanagement may be a reason why many Ph.D. candidates fail to complete theses, why team research often fails to be the energizing and motivating experience that might have been expected, and why research flounders amid disagreement between researchers and funding bodies. Indeed, the more important point may not be that we fail to understand a research context, but that we fail to understand that we may be operating in several contexts at once. So two issues in particular are worth highlighting in relation to context: first, identifying the context and, therefore, the limitations and possibilities of conducting research; and, second, how it may be managed. Identifying the context is addressed below through a fourfold classification of resource context, evaluative context, procedural context, and operational context. These categories are not all-inclusive and there is some overlap between them, but they do act as a starting point in considering research contexts and how they might be managed.

Resource context

Resource context refers to the constraints and opportunities provided by resources such as money and time. Research funding will place limitations on the researcher and the project. A grant given by a government body to pursue a subject will involve different constraints compared with funding from a commercial sponsor. Students funding themselves will be operating in a different context to students with a research award. Frequently, money and time constraints go hand-in-hand, but time may be a constraint in itself. Time limits are often imposed by external bodies independent of funding and research projects will often have an internally imposed time constraint. Certainly, professors with demanding teaching schedules who pursue research for career reasons, or those doing research degrees part-time, are operating in a very different resource context to 'full-time' researchers.

Evaluative context

Research usually takes place within an environment of assessment or evaluation. There will normally be success criteria which impact on the research and the way it is conducted. There will be personal criteria, but rarely is research evaluated solely in this way. For degree research, there will be an assessment by examiners, often both internal and external to the institution. For post-doctoral and faculty research, assessment will come from the academic community and journal editors. For consultancy research projects it may be a company or project co-ordinator. The researcher may not always agree with evaluation criteria; nevertheless, they constitute a context which has to be identified and understood.

Procedural context

The procedural context is the *internal* environment within which the research is developed, planned, and reviewed. One context of this nature is a research team where research is carried out with the backing, support, resistance, or agreement of group members. Other procedural contexts include the research assistant reporting to a research leader, or the doctoral candidate to a supervisor. Hence, on occasion and to some degree, procedural context may overlap with evaluative context. Often research is conducted in a negotiated way with other internal actors who can influence how the research proceeds. This does not just occur where there is an obvious relationship between, say, supervisor and student. The so-called 'independent' researcher, the career academic for instance, will often be influenced by colleagues, heads of departments, university traditions, and other norms.

Operational context

On the surface this may seem to be the most obvious context and refers, in the first instance, to the *external* environment in which the research takes place. This could be a laboratory, but with management research it is more likely to be in the field. Being in the field, however, can range from researching a small section of a company to surveying a population of thousands. It can also range from collecting historical factual data, such as financial information, to subjective predictions of the future through such techniques as Delphi studies.

However, the operational context is broader than this. Many researchers address the possible issues connected with these examples when looking at research methodologies. What is often missed, however, is not so much the issues surrounding the techniques of collecting data, but rather, issues such as the requirements, resistance, or enthusiasm of organizational gatekeepers. Their requests for 'project' reports, data on issues not part of the research, or even for confidential data, is often not anticipated. Again, there may be an overlap between this operational context, where the research is executed, and the procedural context mentioned earlier. The demands made within the operational context may require reviews back in the procedural environment, though this may not be a straightforward process, particularly if important actors within the procedural context (for instance, a Ph. D. supervisor) advise against agreeing to the demands made by those with access to data. Nevertheless, within the operational environment, acceptability to an organization, both in terms of what is done and how it is done, maintaining good relationships with all interested parties, and avoiding being used as a political pawn, are issues in this context which can make or break projects.

There is also the broader, operational environment which needs to be distinguished. Hart provided one example at the end of part II, contrasting industrial with consumer markets. Others include the small company environment as compared with that of multinational corporations, the public versus the private sector, and, as chapter 21, the last in this section, highlights, even industrialized versus developing countries; all of which provide great constraints and possibilities for the management researcher.

Below we have placed the contributors to part III under the research context emphasized in their chapters. We have also given examples of research context concerns.

Resource context	*Examples of context concerns*
Tomkins *et al.* (Chapter 18)	1 Research funding
	2 Time limitations

Evaluative context	*Examples of context concerns*
Smith (Chapter 14)	1 Degree examination
Phillips (Chapter 15)	2 Journal editors
Jeffcutt and Thomas (Chapter 16)	3 Valued members of the academic
Clark (Chapter 17)	community
Tomkins *et al.* (Chapter 18)	

Procedural context	*Examples of context concerns*
Phillips (Chapter 15)	1 Research group norms
Jeffcutt and Thomas (Chapter 16)	2 Ph.D. supervisor
Tomkins *et al.* (Chapter 18)	3 University research traditions
King *et al.* (Chapter 19)	

Operational context	*Examples of context concerns*
Tomkins *et al.* (Chapter 18)	1 Managers – respondents and others
Kakabadse (Chapter 20)	2 Organizations – type, size, etc.
Ramachandran (Chapter 21)	3 Geographic location

MANAGING CONTEXTS

Merely identifying the research context is not sufficient. Equally important is the management of that context. Moreover, there may be several contexts to be managed. Yet it is easy to dismiss a context as being obvious, with the danger that the context may not be fully understood and consequently may be managed ineffectively. This is most noticeable when research is being conducted for a degree award, and particularly for a doctorate. The major context here would seem, fairly obviously, to be that of an evaluative context; though there are other contexts, such as the resource context, which can place great demands on the doctoral student. Yet perhaps the most fundamental issue which research students have to come to terms with, is dealing with the implications of the evaluative context for their research. Considerable constraints are imposed upon student researchers because the criteria for assessing postgraduate theses are often unclear and the assumptions about the nature of, in particular, Ph.D. research, differ considerably. Is the process one of research training or the path to producing a *tour de force*? What does a contribution to knowledge mean and is the way the subject is researched more pertinent in terms of evaluation than its importance?

These are issues Smith tackles in the opening chapter of part III. It is one of a set of four chapters concerned with research for the award of an academic degree. As Smith indicates, understanding the evaluative context may be the difference between success and failure, but may also mean hard decisions and compromises which some researchers find difficult to make. However, while the evaluative context is a particularly important one in relation to degree research, it is not the only context that the researcher has to understand and manage. Chapters 15 and 16 look at doctoral research issues which relate to the procedural context. While the Ph.D. process is often seen as a lonely, isolated affair, it does, however, take place within a university context and a particular relationship, that of student and supervisor. Phillips identifies some of the important issues in this context in 'Learning to do research' (chapter 15). In a longitudinal study she looks at the attitudes of students toward supervision and their relation to their work, and how these changed during the research process and skill development. As well as examining context management this chapter also raises the issue of the impact of contexts on the researcher over time.

Jeffcutt and Thomas, in chapter 16, continue this theme of the student and supervisor by looking at a number of dilemmas posed by the relationship and consider how it might be managed better. With Clark (chapter 17), we return to an emphasis on the evaluative context. He tries to establish the boundaries of the evaluative context, outlining his view of a doctoral dissertation and the qualities a social science Ph.D. thesis should have. The message we are left with is that the evaluative context is perhaps paramount, but to forget, deny, or disregard other contexts, such as the procedural, is bad management.

The remaining four chapters of part III look at research issues broader than those concerned with completing a research degree, though they still have relevance to that process. Indeed, the contexts outlined earlier are evident whatever the research being conducted and degree research, while different, should not be seen as divorced from other management research activities. This is evidenced in chapter 18. It develops on the idea that several contexts often need to be identified and managed, and the implication of the preceding four chapters, that even research with 'rules' is far from straight-forward. The notion that research is concerned solely with a procedure which, in general terms, identifies a problem, collects and analyses data and then draws conclusions, is forcefully challenged by Tomkins *et al*. The chapter does not refer specifically to the contexts outlined above, but in looking at the social process of research it exemplifies issues within each of the four contextual categories. The chapter strongly emphasizes problems of the procedural context, considering issues which arise with a multi-disciplinary research team, of negotiating order, responsibilities, and control over a project. But other problems from other contexts are also highlighted, particularly the resource context with regard to funding, and the operational context of research within local government. As the authors argue, after reading this chapter one should become more aware of research as a social process – a theme we developed in the Introduction and evident in earlier chapters – and the management necessary for successful project completion.

Great benefits can come from multi-disciplinary research: development of a greater range of skills and knowledge, better integration of subject matter, and a possible spin-off of new ideas to each researcher's core discipline. However, readers in the human resource disciplines, at least, will be aware of the particular difficulties of getting teams to work well even where the objectives and procedures are clear. Where they are not clear, where there may be not a formal leader and where the energies of group members are diverted to other tasks, the difficulties are immense. The diversity would seem to provide great opportunities – but the reality may be very different, as chapter 19 shows. King *et al.* continue the theme of multi-disciplinary teams, concentrating on the procedural context. The chapter outlines the activities of a research team within a framework of group development, giving practical clues about the areas that should be addressed if projects are to be completed successfully.

The final two chapters, 20 and 21, look at issues arising in the operational context. As earlier noted, the operational context will throw up issues which may not always be obvious. One issue in particular is the external political environment of the research. The chapter by Tomkins *et al.* touches on some aspects of this, but Kakabadse (chapter 20) considers a range of political issues more thoroughly and in a different but thought-provoking way. He discusses an 'intervention' rather than the more traditional research approaches, and raises issues which some readers may be reluctant to consider. Outlined is an approach to gaining support and acceptance of a research project in an organization where there may be resistance. Faced with similar circumstances some readers may, for ethical reasons, feel obliged to go elsewhere rather than go along with Kakabadse's approach. However, the paper does raise often-ignored issues concerning the kinds of skills and influence processes that may need to be considered, not only within an organization, but also with sponsors and other interested parties. At the very least, an awareness of political processes may be necessary for a successful research outcome.

It was noted earlier that there are broad as well as more situation-specific operational contexts which the researcher needs to consider. Some of these broader contexts, such as the public and private sectors, have already been covered in the literature, but rarely considered is the context of developing countries and research in this situation. Ramachandran shows how methods such as interviews and questionnaires, with all the problems identified in earlier chapters, have an added dimension of complexity in an environment where literacy may be low, communication difficult, and some databases non-existent. We will not all have the experience – and rewards – of researching in this particular context, but the paper raises more general issues about the assumptions we make concerning the broader operational context. It should encourage researchers to reflect on their contexts, not only the limitations, but also the range of research possibilities available.

14 The context of doctoral research[1]

N. Craig Smith

The context of doctoral research places particular constraints upon the researcher, not least of which is the emphasis upon a positivist methodology. This chapter describes the author's perspective on the context of doctoral research and the conflict that may arise between such a context and the researcher's position on what constitutes sound academic research. Yet while dissatisfaction can result from this conflict, it is suggested that the researcher be prepared to compromise on his or her research ideals and aspirations and accept the doctoral process for what it is. The notion of the Ph.D. as a *tour de force* is considered in this regard and it is argued that such a notion may be a major cause of failure to complete; though this might well be unavoidable and even desirable.

A SCIENTIFIC ENDEAVOUR

The doctorate is viewed somewhat romantically – at least in the United Kingdom – by all but those who have been working on their thesis for more than six months or who have recently completed. One may be working on some 'lofty cause', as Victoria Bourne describes her 'close shave with the Russians in the ivory tower' (1983). One is at least attempting to further the frontiers of knowledge – an intrepid explorer on a scientific endeavour. After all, the principal criterion by which the work will be assessed is whether it is a significant contribution to knowledge.

This rosy idea of the doctorate seems commonplace, but most notably in the mind of the applicant to a doctoral programme. Indeed, this view of the doctorate as a scientific endeavour could well be a major reason for the applicant wishing to undertake the doctorate in the first place. But the romantic impression proves to be short-lived. As the new researcher comes to terms with the reality of research – an isolated exercise in self-deprivation, self-discipline, and self-denial – this image fades; a process of disillusionment amusingly described by Bourne (1983). However, the criterion of making a significant contribution to knowledge remains and the notion of the Ph.D. as a *tour de force* goes unchallenged.

RESEARCH CONTEXTS

Most doctoral students seem to perceive themselves primarily as researchers, not students. This is, perhaps, partly due to the contribution of knowledge criterion, but in essence it is the totality of the image of the Ph.D. that would seem to prompt this. Consequently, some doctoral students refer to themselves as doctoral candidates or research associates. Such titles, although harmless in themselves and occasionally useful for obtaining research access, emphasize the importance to the student of the sense of a research mission. Yet despite this perception of themselves as researchers *per se*, doctoral students must submit a thesis for examination if their research is to be viewed as successful. For this reason alone, the context of doctoral research is different to that of other research. The context of doctoral research also differs in a number of other ways – ways that place constraints on the research ideals and aspirations of the researcher. The more important constraints and the conflict that may result are explored in this chapter.

As an illustration of the doctoral student's perception of his or her role, consider an interesting taboo. 'Submission for the award of Ph.D.', or something similar, will be stated on the title page to a doctoral thesis. It is, however, unusual to come across any acknowledgement of this elsewhere in the thesis. It is almost as if the reader need be convinced that, in fact, the thesis is not reporting doctoral research at all. Although, of course, these would-be doctorates would proclaim themselves to be social scientists, who have no truck with taboos and the like. Moreover, as new researchers, they must surely be acquainted with the recent research methodology publications advocating explicit recognition of the circumstances of the research. As Rowan and Reason put it, the researcher should be 'making clear where one is coming from in taking a particular view' (1981: xiii-xiv).

Yet it is not suggested that doctoral research alone is influenced by the context within which it is conducted. All research is influenced by context, be it the social experience of the researcher or the ethos of the institution in which the research is undertaken. Rowan notes that 'a great deal of social science, as at present practised, may be a species of autobiography. And so long as researchers ignore the unconscious, and pretend that they can be totally objective, this will continue to be the case' (Rowan 1981: 77).

The context of the research will then, to some extent, dictate the research outcome. Influence by context can be minimized, though this cannot be discussed here except insofar as the researcher may seek to minimize external influences or constraints on the research. The influence of such constraints on research is recognized by many writers on research methodology. Glaser and Strauss, for example, make their position clear: 'Our criteria are those of theoretical purpose and relevance – not of structural circumstance. Though constrained by the same structural circumstances of research, we do not base research on them' (Glaser and Strauss 1967: 48). For the doctoral student, the context of the research is different to that for other researchers and therefore the constraints imposed will also be different. The constraints are likely to be greater and will at least be perceived as such by the doctoral student who will most probably have high research ideals and aspirations.

CONSTRAINTS IN DOCTORAL RESEARCH

Political, status, economic, and many other factors place considerable constraints on the doctoral researcher. As noted above, such constraints, as part of the research context, will influence the research outcome. It may well be that the constraints in doctoral research are so great that they preclude the achievement of a significant contribution to knowledge in most cases, the criterion by which the work is to be examined. There will at least be some conflict, paradoxically, between this criterion and the constraints imposed. However, this will vary from case to case and be particularly dependent upon the research topic and methodology of the researcher.

Support for this view can be found elsewhere, although much of the work – not surprisingly – is of American origin. Despite the differences between British and American doctoral programmes this does not seem to detract greatly from the points made. One such examination of doctoral research is by Joseph Katz. He at one point writes: 'So many dissertations and so much research are done out of duty – out of an enforced sense of what and how one should do it – rather than out of lively curiosity' (Katz 1976: 123). Often, this prescription comes from the research supervisor.

The student–supervisor relationship is a widely acknowledged problem in doctoral research (see, for example, Christopherson *et al.* 1983, Howard and Sharp 1983: 167–71), and the supervisor can be a constraint in doctoral research in a number of ways. The supervisor may have considerable impact on the research outcome. In a questionnaire survey of graduates of doctoral programmes at twelve American universities it was observed that:

> Despite general approbation for dissertation experiences, several respondents also pointed to a lack of realism on the part of dissertation advisors in demanding either a theoretical basis for research, undue use of statistical analyses, or excessive rewriting of the dissertation to accommodate

personal predilections as to forms of expression, organisation, and treatment and presentation of data.

(Dressel and Mayhew 1974: 103)

In another survey, one student commented:

Any kind of a jump or leap is too much for them. I mean they just don't have the courage, and they aren't stimulated at all. They don't give you a chance to engage in original research. You do what your graduate advisor tells you to most of the time.

(Taylor 1976: 137)

Of course, the supervisor's task is not easy and however creative students may be, they still must recognize the demands of the examination process. Moreover, students are often too demanding and depend too much on the supervisor and not enough on themselves. Yet the supervisor will still be a constraint on the research.

The position of the doctoral researcher in his or her department is another, related, consideration. Altbach reports the low status of the graduate research student (1971: 273–87) which can sap the confidence of the researcher. More generally, as Katz and Hartnett note on the position of the research student: 'The present ambiguity about the student's relation to authority creates ... a disposition towards constraining thinking in the direction of conforming with professorial ways of thinking' (1976: 269).

The student–supervisor relationship and the position of the researcher in his or her department are aspects of the political nature of doctoral research. There are others. Good research requires the researcher to be brutally honest with himself or herself, and with the research. Yet this is not always feasible in doctoral research where the researcher is required, in effect, to go through a series of hoops, each hoop having political ramifications. So, for example, is it sensible for the researcher to be brutally honest about the research, revealing all its flaws, at a formal review meeting where one can 'pass' or 'fail'? The same can be said of the meetings with research supervisors, others in the department and the thesis itself. It must be remembered that the primary objective in doctoral research is not research but to obtain a doctorate. Such considerations must inevitably be guided by this objective, even though they may conflict with the researcher's position on sound academic research.

There are many other constraints in doctoral research which may lead to conflict with the researcher's position on research and the attempt to make a significant contribution to knowledge. Some of the more important constraints have been discussed but one could also refer to others, such as time and money. However, they may all be reduced to a single common denominator, the reason for the research. Those research constraints particular to doctoral research are directly attributable to the objective of obtaining a doctorate, even though they may be at odds with the principal criterion by which the doctoral submission is assessed.

AN ORTHODOX APPROACH

The doctoral research context places some constraints on the research which are unlikely to be found in other research contexts and conflict with the doctoral student's perception of his or her role as a researcher *per se*. One likely effect of these constraints is that the researcher is pushed towards the more orthodox research topics and methodologies. The scope for employing a grounded theory type of methodology will be considered in illustration of this. First, however, it is worth considering some features of this pressure towards the more orthodox research topics and methodologies.

Much is made of the requirement for students to manage their research, it being argued that better management of the research would improve completion rates (Howard 1983). Yet this tends to posit a particular model of research – a positivist model, as will later be seen. Such a model is evident in the thinking of the Economic and Social Research Council (ESRC), which demands regular reports from the doctoral students it sponsors. At the end of the first year, the student completes a report answering questions such as, 'Have you completed your critical survey both generally and for your specific topic?' This assumes that research is a sequential process, the first step of which is a literature survey which should be completed within a year. Another report asks for 'a brief note on the hypothesis being tested', which assumes that all research is concerned with the testing of hypotheses. These reports and the suggestions for better management of the research are an attempt to ensure a timely completion. However, they do so by pushing the student towards the more orthodox approaches to research.

It may be that this hypothetico-deductive approach is not only the approach most likely to guarantee a timely completion but also the approach suitable for the topic and the researcher. At the Sixth National Conference on Doctoral Research in Industry and Employment, held at the London Business School, 1982, one facilitator argued that a study along the lines of 'Herzberg in St. John's Wood' was most likely to ensure successful completion. He too was advocating the hypothetico-deductive approach, but many of the delegates dismissed this as 'normal science', although what they expected to achieve other than this was not clear. Their response seems to support the notion of the doctoral thesis being perceived as a *tour de force* and indicate unrealistic research aspirations. Or can the doctoral student avoid the pressures towards an orthodox approach? It seems unlikely or, at least, difficult. There is, after all, the viva to consider, where orthodox approaches will at least be expected by most examiners, and perhaps demanded by some.

THE DANGEROUS WATERS BEYOND POSITIVISM

The model of research employed by the ESRC and appropriate to a 'Herzberg in St. John's Wood' study is drawn from the natural sciences. It is for this reason positivist, given Bell and Newby's brief definition of positivism as 'working as natural scientists are believed to' (Bell and Newby 1977: 21). But what of the waters beyond positivism? Many writers on research methodology have argued against positivism, a particularly thorough treatment being that by Hughes (1980). Hence the essence of the argument only will suffice for this paper.

Consider the nature of this particular human activity known as science. Hughes notes that 'scientific methods seek deliberately to annihilate the individual scientist's standpoint and are designed as rules whereby agreement on specific versions of the world can be reached: a distinction, in short, between the producer of a statement and the procedure whereby it is produced' (Hughes 1980: 12). The outcome of these methods is scientific knowledge: 'a systematic body of concepts, theories, principles and laws or law-like statements designed to explain phenomena' (Rigby 1965: 1). The problem for the social sciences is that this involves a human attempt to explain human phenomena. This is problematic because it is doubtful as to whether method can ever 'annihilate' the individual scientist's standpoint. Such is the dilemma posed, that Hughes feels obliged to ask: 'is a science of social life impossible?' (Hughes 1980: 124).

Perhaps the solution is to remain untroubled by such philosophical concerns. Certainly ignorance of the epistemology of science seems as prevalent today among management researchers as when it was noted by Rigby (1965: Preface). However, management researchers are not the only ones ignorant of such issues and, as Homans observed, it may not matter:

> you do not have to believe anything about theory and methodology that is told you pretentiously and sanctimoniously by other sociologists – including myself. So much guff has gotten mixed with the truth that, if you cannot tell which is which, you had better reject it all. It will only get in your way. No one will go far wrong theoretically who remains in close touch with and seeks to understand a body of concrete phenomena.
>
> (Denzin 1978: opening pages)

Yet if management researchers are to make the claim that management is a social science – if only in the use of scientific methods – and that their investigations are scientific, can these issues be avoided?

In reference to Schutz, Hughes explains the dilemma of the social sciences in terms of the social construction of reality: 'Like all sciences they make objective meaning claims, or at least aspire to do so, but in the case of social sciences these have to be within the context of the human activity which has created them and which cannot be understood apart from this scheme of action' (Hughes 1980: 119).

This is the basic epistemological problem of social science. How can the human world be objectively known in subjective, human terms? Indeed, scientific activity and what is associated with it, including the status of scientists and scientific knowledge, is, after all, like the phenomena studied by social scientists, a social construction. Ford observes that 'When academics take off their white scientific coats and funny philosophical hats they turn into ordinary people....' (Ford 1975: 5). This is the problem, and one that social scientists cannot escape. Moreover, if they didn't have their white scientific coats and other accoutrements of scientific activity – including the title of doctor – would the outcome of such activity, scientific knowledge, still have intellectual authority?

Can such questions be asked in doctoral research? There is obviously a case for raising these issues, as the above discussion indicates. For management research the case may be particularly strong and go beyond abstract philosophical concerns, because of the potential use of the research findings and the often managerially partisan nature of the research conducted.[2] Positivist approaches may not be acceptable to the individual researcher or suitable for the research topic, but other approaches may not be feasible because of the constraints in doctoral research. Grounded theory is one such approach. As will be shown, it can never be successfully and sensibly employed in doctoral research in its true form as espoused by Glaser and Strauss (1967).

GROUNDED THEORY IN DOCTORAL RESEARCH

Grounded theory is based on the notion that the theory emerges from the data, with the minimum of pre-existent conceptualizations imposed by the researcher. In this sense, it is unstructured and already, therefore, a high risk strategy for the doctoral student who is seeking to work within a time constraint. There are also various pressures on the student not to conform to this sort of model of research but to follow the positivist model and impose as much structure as possible. This, as earlier noted, is called 'managing the research'. Glaser and Strauss give some consideration to this problem of the lack of requisite (in some circumstances) structure. They refer to this as a problem of research tempo:

> The tempo of the research is difficult to know beforehand, because it is largely contingent on the tempo of the emerging theory.... This raises a problem: in presenting proposals for research grants, how does the sociologist who intends to generate theory anticipate the amount of time necessary, for data collection and for the whole project?
>
> (Glaser and Strauss 1967: 74)

The grounded theory approach is intrinsically problematic for any research context. Inevitably it is something that funding bodies or examiners will be suspicious of because of its abstract nature – even if they are fully acquainted with it as a methodology. The problem is that it does not offer the comfortable, concrete reassurance that the hypothetico-deductive approach offers. There is not the security of knowing precisely what the researcher is examining, because no hypotheses have been proposed or method suggested by which they should be tested. If the problem for established researchers is considerable, the problem for doctoral researchers is even more so. They do not yet have experience nor the credibility which, a cynic might observe, is suddenly realized the day after the successful doctoral viva. And, most importantly, their prime concern as already noted is to get the doctorate, not to do research – and within a time constraint!

The constraints within the doctoral research context militate against such an approach, even if the doctoral student is personally prepared to accept the uncertainty and risk that such an approach entails. The observation by Glaser and Strauss, quoted earlier, that they are not prepared to be constrained by the structural circumstances of research (Glaser and Strauss 1967), may be appropriate to established and experienced researchers. But can it realistically be considered appropriate to doctoral research? The dependence on what amounts to serendipity is unacceptable. In all research there is an element of chance, but if one is so unfortunate as not to substantiate the hypotheses under test, at least one has something to say. This is not the case if one is still waiting for a theory to emerge from the data, when there is nothing to report. Indeed, if the researcher follows the advice of Howard and Sharp, and ensures that the hypotheses are designed and tested such that there is a symmetry of outcomes, then the researcher's risks are minimized (Howard and Sharp 1983: 37–9). Although, one might also argue, so is the likelihood of having anything significant to say.

The solution to the problem posed by the intrinsic difficulties of grounded theory both for doctoral students and for academics who, if ambitious, want to be able to publish their research as rapidly and frequently as possible, is not to do it; as implied by Glaser and Strauss. Exercises in verification, such as Herzberg in St. John's Wood, are far easier, far more certain and lower risk – providing one can accept the positivist assumptions that may go with such a study. It seems that doctoral students, in the main, solve (or avoid) the problem by going out to get data with the intention either of explicitly or implicitly 'testing' hypotheses. Such hypotheses may not be stated as such, they may only be 'propositions' and the research described as exploratory, but, in effect, they follow the natural science/positivist route of formulating hypotheses which are then 'tested' to varying degrees of precision. There seems to be little alternative in the doctoral research context if the doctoral student wishes successfully to complete – other than relying on serendipity.

So, although critical of positivist approaches, this author does not reject them outright – least of all for doctoral students. The positivist approach is particularly comfortable if one can remain untroubled by issues of ontology and epistemology. It offers a certainty about social facts and the methods of social research that other approaches lack. The simplicity and structure that such an approach can bring may be essential for some students and may be the only possible approach for some research topics. Moreover, positivism is a matter of degree, not of absolutes. The point is that the constraints in doctoral research may conflict with research aspirations – such as to avoid positivism – as illustrated by the discussion of the applicability of a grounded theory approach.

Other examples, both of ways in which there are orthodox approaches to doctoral research which foster positivism and, more generally, other ways in which the constraints in doctoral research may conflict with research aspirations, can soon be thought of. Perhaps, however, the doctoral researcher identifying such a conflict is expecting too much. Perhaps he or she has unreasonable research ideals and aspirations – unreasonable, that is, if it is hoped that they can be achieved within doctoral research. Put another way, is the notion of the Ph.D. as a *tour de force* unrealistic? This notion, as the final section of this chapter shows, may be a major cause of failure to complete, as well as a constraint in doctoral research.

COMPLETION RATES AND THE *TOUR DE FORCE* PH.D.

A study of the Stanford Ph.D. programme suggests that the notion of the dissertation as 'a research *tour de force*' (Study of Graduate Education at Stanford (SGES) 1972: 102) has a major effect on completion rates. The authors thought it 'inappropriate to continue interpreting the Ph.D. (or pretending to interpret it) as the reward for a major, original contribution to knowledge' (SGES 1972: 101). As Mayhew and Ford have written: 'There is an inclination to accept the reality that a doctoral dissertation is not an original contribution to knowledge' (Mayhew and Ford 1974: 212). And such a view is not restricted to the United States, being evident in the United Kingdom Swinnerton-Dyer and Rothschild reports on the social sciences and with some people suggesting that the doctorate should be seen as a research training (Sayer 1984).

This author would not dispute the SGES conclusion that the notion of the Ph.D. thesis as a *tour de force* is both unrealistic and inhibits completion. Yet this does not mean that the objective of producing a *tour de force* thesis is unworthy, or that to achieve such is impossible in every case. The Stanford study observes: 'Many of our present graduate students do not have the creative capabilities of an outstanding Ph.D. candidate.' However, they do continue by noting:

> we do not think that the Ph.D. should be reserved for a few research stars. Instead, graduate education culminating in the Ph.D. should be recognized as a stepping stone toward a teaching career for many students, toward a professional non-academic career (e.g. in engineering) for others, and finally toward careers in basic research for others.
>
> (Study of Graduate Education at Stanford 1972: 101)

Unfortunately, perhaps, because of the reluctance by many to detract from the mystique of the doctorate it is still perceived as a *tour de force*, and only by looking at a number of completed doctoral theses will the student recognize the mystique for what it is and compromise unrealistic aspirations. This author would suggest that many students do not complete because either they do not recognize that a doctorate can be obtained without producing a *tour de force* (although there are plenty of examples of poor theses around which illustrate this quite convincingly!) or because they refuse to compromise their research aspirations.

And yet, it could be argued, not producing a *tour de force* thesis, does not necessarily prevent the research from making an original contribution to knowledge. It is merely that the scale of this contribution and the focus in the research are likely to be extremely narrow. For while a *tour de force* doctoral thesis is largely impossible, a small but original contribution to knowledge, although perhaps an unrealistic objective in some or even most cases, is not precluded altogether.

The idea of a doctorate as research training, rather than to produce an original contribution to knowledge is based on the recognition of the constraints of the doctoral research context. In this sense it is worthy, though somewhat questionable in that it is assuming that most doctoral candidates will go on to do research, whereas in fact they don't; as the previous Stanford quote implies, most will go on to teach. A doctorate is generally the first major piece of research a student will undertake; unfortunately, perhaps, it is also frequently the last. Of course, what is probably more questionable is the implication that a doctorate as research training does not involve an attempt to contribute to knowledge. This implication is rejected here, as although the researcher's aspirations may to some extent have to be compromised because of the virtual impossibility of producing a *tour de force* thesis, there may remain through the research, the objective of making some contribution to knowledge. This is thought to be desirable as a motivator; the idea of conducting some sort of exercise as 'training' seems futile.

So, in conclusion, while the doctoral student may for some time view his or her task as to produce a *tour de force*, this aspiration is both unrealistic and likely to impede completion. The researcher's aspirations are perhaps too high in this respect, but they are also constrained by the context of the research; the constraints in doctoral research examined earlier in the chapter may then conflict with the researcher's perception of sound academic research. It is suggested that the researcher be prepared to compromise, because his or her aspirations may be unduly high and also because the doctorate should be accepted for what it is, a research process involving particular constraints where the prime objective is to obtain a doctorate.

It may be that some view the notion of the Ph.D. as a *tour de force* as undesirable because it impairs completion rates. However, this is not the position taken here. Such a notion is viewed as a necessary device to motivate the student to achieve a high standard. Moreover, while only the odd Ph.D. thesis is ever likely to be a *tour de force*, more may be contributions to knowledge in a narrow sense, given the right aspirations. In other words, the target needs to be set sufficiently high. And there is always the possibility of a *tour de force* after the Ph.D., when 'real' research begins. Besides, who would want to detract from the mystique?

NOTES

1   This article was written when the author was a doctoral candidate at Cranfield School of Management, Cranfield Institute of Technology, UK.
2   If you have doubts as to whether management is a managerially partisan discipline, see Honour and Mainwaring (1982) and Andreski (1972).

REFERENCES

Altbach, P. G. (1971) 'Graduate students', in P. G. Altbach, R. S. Laufer, and S. McVey (eds) *Academic Supermarkets: A Critical Case Study of a Multiversity*, San Francisco: Jossey-Bass.
Andreski, S. (1972) *Social Sciences as Sorcery*, London: André Deutsch.
Bell, C. and Newby, H. (1977) 'Introduction: the rise of methodological pluralism', in C. Bell and H. Newby (eds) *Doing Sociological Research*, London: George Allen & Unwin.
Bourne, V. (1983) 'A close shave with the Russians in the ivory tower', *Guardian*, 16 August.

Christopherson, D., *et al.* (1983) 'Research student and supervisor: a discussion paper on good supervisory practice', *Graduate Management Research* 1, 2.

Denzin, N. K. (1978) *The Research Act: A Theoretical Introduction to Sociological Methods*, New York: McGraw-Hill.

Dressel, P. L. and Mayhew, L. B. (1974) *Higher Education as a Field of Study: The Emergence of a Profession*, San Francisco: Jossey-Bass.

Ford, J. (1975) *Paradigms and Fairy Tales: An Introduction to the Science of Meanings*, London: Routledge & Kegan Paul.

Glaser, B. G. and Strauss, A. L. (1967) *The Discovery of Grounded Theory: Strategies for Qualitative Research*, New York: Aldine.

Honour, T. F. and Mainwaring, R. M. (1982) *Business and Sociology*, London: Croom Helm.

Howard, K. (1983) 'Should Ph.D.s in management be managed?', *Graduate Management Research* 1, 1.

Howard, K. and Sharp, J. A. (1983) *The Management of a Student Research Project*, Aldershot: Gower.

Hughes, J. (1980) *The Philosophy of Social Research*, London: Longman.

Katz, J. (1976) 'Development of the mind', in J. Katz and R. T. Hartnett (eds) *Scholars in the Making: The Development of Graduate and Professional Students*, Cambridge: Ballinger Publishing.

Katz, J. and Hartnett, R. T. (1976) 'Recommendations for training better scholars', in J. Katz, and R. T. Hartnett (eds) *Scholars in the Making: The Development of Graduate and Professional Students*, Cambridge: Ballinger Publishing.

Mayhew, L. B. and Ford, P. J. (1974) *Reform in Graduate and Professional Education*, San Francisco: Jossey-Bass.

Rigby, P. H. (1965) *Conceptual Foundations of Business Research*, New York: John Wiley.

Rowan, J. (1981) 'From anxiety to method in the behavioural sciences by George Devereux: an appreciation', in J. Rowan, and P. Reason (eds) *Human Inquiry*, Chichester: John Wiley.

Rowan, J. and Reason, P. (1981) *Human Inquiry*, Chichester: John Wiley.

Sayer, D. (1984) 'A doctorate's new prescription', *Guardian*, 13 March.

Study of Graduate Education at Stanford (SGES) (1972) *Study of Graduate Education at Stanford*, Stanford University.

Taylor, A. R. (1976) 'Becoming observers and specialists', in J. Katz and R. T. Hartnett, *Scholars in the Making: The Development of Graduate and Professional Students*, Cambridge: Ballinger Publications.

15 Learning to do research

Estelle M. Phillips

This chapter deals with the development of research skills. Seven postgraduate students, based in two universities, were interviewed at monthly intervals during the three years of their Ph.D. registration. Their supervisors were interviewed every six months. Gradually a series of case studies was built up which showed that: (1) it was necessary for students to develop an ability to evaluate their own work; (2) the rate of this development appeared to be related to the degree to which the students were allowed to remain dependent on their supervisors; (3) the postgraduates' enthusiasm for their Ph.D. diminished due to the length of time they had to spend working on a single problem; and (4) writing helped to clarify thinking but was seen as a difficult activity and of minor importance. It is suggested that some kind of 'weaning' process should be introduced into the student/supervisor relationship as the postgraduates develop the self-confidence to monitor their own work.

INTRODUCTION

Seven postgraduate students from two universities were interviewed at monthly intervals during the three year period of their research degree. Their supervisors were interviewed twice a year, at six monthly intervals, over the same period. The students and their supervisors were from each of the following departments: nuclear physics, bio-chemistry, astronomy, and industrial chemistry in the Sciences and architecture, English literature and medieval history in the Arts.

The seven research students each completed a repertory grid at their first interview and subsequently at six-monthly intervals. The grids were unique for each student but some elements such as 'Reading', 'Writing', 'Seeing Supervisor' were given by all seven postgraduates.

The grids were analysed in such a way that the postgraduates could be presented with precise correlations and matching scores which were related to changes in the way they thought about particular aspects of their Ph.D. for a given period (Phillips 1980). These grid analyses were used to form the basis of a feedback interview during which the postgraduates could comment on the information presented. The results presented here are interpretations of the computer analyses, influenced by the interview data arising from the feedback sessions as well as the less structured interviews.

The precise question, based on the computer printouts, which the post-graduates were asked at the feedback session was: 'The way you think about ... has changed in the last six months, (or since you started your Ph.D. etc.) – can you account for it?' The postgraduates' replies were noted together with the discussion which sometimes followed their comments. By this means the changes in the students' views of their work, as they occurred during the three years, was monitored while the students explored certain issues of importance to them.

The study reported here was part of a larger project which attempted to understand how a small sample of postgraduate students construed their situation as they went through the process of learning to do research. Specific aspects of the project to be discussed in this chapter are those concerned with the students' attitudes toward supervision and their relation to their work, together with their perception of actually doing the Ph.D. and writing the thesis.

THE STUDENT AND SUPERVISOR RELATIONSHIP

Table 15.1 gives some examples of comments made by postgraduate students and supervisors when interviewed separately, with a guarantee of confidentiality. The students and their supervisors were talking about the same topic at approximately the same time during the students' three years of research for the Ph.D. degree.

The first two quotations illustrate the different ways in which the post-graduate and supervisor construe (a) their tutorial meetings and (b) the amount of attention given by the supervisor to the student's work.

The other two quotations illustrate (a) how supervision is experienced by postgraduates at different times during the process of learning to do research and (b) how supervisors construe the changing behaviours which result from these subjective experiences of their students.

Postgraduate students may eventually discover, at the time of their oral examination, what they have learned during the preceding years in terms of what it is that is needed to bring a research project to a successful conclusion. However, it is the end product which is being judged and upon which the decision concerning success or failure is taken.

Table 15.1 Student and supervisor comments

Student	Supervisor
6 months	
I haven't found a way of telling him how very frustrated I am with these meetings.	He always appears to go off in a more contented frame of mind than when he arrives.
1 year	
After seven weeks of writing he only talked about a very minor aspect of my paper.	Each time, I choose a single aspect from a paper he has written and suggest he develops it.
2 years	
The supervisor gets all the credit for the student's work and my supervisor should realize he's lucky I've got this far, given the way he supervises.	He suffers from periods of depression and I feel he hasn't put all the energy he might have into his work recently.
3 years	
I can see now that from a supervisor's point of view, if he thinks you have something to do he leaves you alone to get on with it.	He's become an independent research worker, he's doing original work all the time, but he wouldn't have got very far without the supervisor. But that's all part of the game.

In order to acquire some systematic information from the viewpoint of the students, rather than compare differences between successful and unsuccessful candidates, it was decided to pay attention to the process of research as it was experienced by the participants and not just to the final product. This is potentially a more illuminating approach, as it leads to an understanding of the requirements for completion of the research degree instead of merely revealing aspects of evaluation of the training based on eventual performance.

The data revealed that supervisory style directly affected the length of time it took postgraduates to become autonomous researchers. The three supervisors who kept themselves constantly informed of the progress of their postgraduates had students who continued to be dependent upon them for ideas and information well into the three-year period of the Ph.D. The reverse was also true, and of the supervisors in the sample who decided to leave the students alone to get on with their work until such time as the students asked for help, one had a student who dropped out of the higher degree course; while the other three became independent in their approach to their work very early in their training.

The length of time it took for the postgraduates to become autonomous with regard to their work, was largely a function of the amount of contact they had with their supervisors coupled with their expectations of what the role of supervisors ought to be. These results do not mean that student neglect is shown to be an effective method of postgraduate supervision, merely that a gradual 'weaning' process is necessary. It is important for supervisors to estimate the amount and type of intervention needed by an individual postgraduate at a particular time. As long as it was possible to do so, the students looked to their supervisors for information about how well they were doing. When this was not possible for any reason they were thrown on their own resources and had to make decisions on the basis of what they thought of the outcome of their efforts to date. The independence of the postgraduates was related to their understanding that their own actions could be used to monitor their performance. Analyses of the grids, the feedback sessions, and the regular interviews combined to reveal an inverse relationship between dependence on the supervisor and involvement with the work for its own sake (Phillips 1981).

An example to illustrate this comes from one of the science students. He said: 'I don't think that my early relationship with my supervisor was good and he wouldn't give me information first-hand. At first I had to do all the work without any leads, but later on that changed. If you begin to enjoy the relationship with your supervisor then positive feedback is obvious. Some supervisors would opt for the student to dig up the research themselves; it would make you approach the problem differently and is a better training for later work when you have to cope alone.'

This postgraduate had linked the amount of dependence on his supervisor with a lack of intrinsic satisfaction from and involvement with his work. He was explicit about the importance of external reinforcement and aware that his own training may not have been the most efficient for later autonomy in research.

As time passed, it became clear that other of the postgraduates expected less direction from their supervisors and more guidance, through negotiation of suggestions which originated from either the student or the supervisor.

This implies that, together with the importance placed on the need for information concerning progress which the students expected to receive from their supervisors, was the equally important need for the students to understand and accept the feedback which was constantly available in their own work. Perhaps it is this ability which is most needed in order to become an independent researcher.

The way in which the students learned to interpret the results of their work was a function of the way in which they were supervised (Phillips 1979). Originally it was to the supervisor that the students looked for feedback and information. The students learned to decide for themselves what actions to take, through the process of attending to the decisions made by their supervisors concerning which actions were appropriate for them. They set themselves short-term goals, so that their work was planned in such a way that, even when their overall plan for the three years was rather vague, they still knew what they would be doing in the immediate future.

When they were wrong in their estimation of what they could achieve in a given period, they adjusted their predictions in order to arrive at an intermediate goal within the next few months. This became apparent during the interview when postgraduates acknowledged that they had not completed the amount of work intended during the previous month.

Whether the deadlines were imposed by the supervisors, or internally constructed by the students themselves, it was usually the time-targeting of the plan of work that needed to be adjusted. The work not undertaken during the stated period was often included in, or substituted for, the plan of the following month. In this way, the students gradually imposed their own boundaries of action and time as they learned how to evaluate their work by interpreting the feedback for themselves instead of relying on their supervisors to do it for them.

At first the postgraduates had been unable to do this, but most of them gradually acquired the ability to perceive, interpret, and act upon the information contained in the feedback from operating on their plan of work. Once the postgraduates were able to make use of the information concerning progress which their own work contained, they began to reflect on their own performance and evaluate it. Not all the postgraduates in the sample managed to achieve this and so they remained dependent on their supervisors' assessments of their work.

PERCEPTION OF THE PH.D.

At their original briefing interview, when the postgraduates had first agreed to become part of the research sample, they had all been asked why they had taken the decision to study for a research degree. At that time they had said either that it would allow them to make a personal contribution to their field or that it would enhance the choices open to them for their future career, or both.

The postgraduates had commenced their three year course full of enthusiasm, but once the research had been completed and they had only to write the thesis in order to complete the Ph.D. they spoke of wanting 'to get it and forget it'. Their changing perception of their Ph.D. degree was mainly due to the monotony of concentrating on the same thing for an extended period of time. Remarks from both science and arts postgraduates were similar in their reference to the repetitive nature of the work. A science student said: 'I'm trying to finish off groups of experiments and say "that's the answer" rather than exploring it more fully, which is what I used to do; before, I was aiming for "the truth", now I'm aiming for results. I'm looking forward to finishing rather than doing the work for its own interest.'

This disillusionment was the rule rather than the exception with the postgraduates in the sample. An arts student who had originally seen his work resulting in a creative end-product which would emerge out of the mechanical process of collating manuscripts said, after two and a half years: 'I'm really fed up with it right now, doing the mechanical things just goes on.'

Another science student, at the same stage in his degree course, reported during the grid feedback session that he had become more remote and detached. He said, 'in the beginning I had to concentrate hard on what I was doing, it completely occupied my mind. In some ways I've got less enthusiastic, all I want to do is finish and get out.' Everything in the comparison of his first and latest grids pointed to the differences in his early and more recent perceptions of doing the Ph.D. He said, 'at first I was full of enthusiasm for work and work was going to be very important, but at the end other things gave me much more satisfaction. The work was boring and monotonous and I was waiting for it to be over and done.'

These remarks from both science and arts postgraduates are similar in their reference to the repetitive nature of the work. The regular interviews had established that there was a growing disillusionment with and disinterest in the programme on which they had embarked so enthusiastically. The reason for this disillusionment and unrest became clear when the discussion was based on the particular constructs that had changed within a certain period.

WRITING THE THESIS

Very little is known about the process of writing generally, and even less about the role of writing in research.

Conducting the research is, of course, very important, but needing to communicate exactly what has been done, and why, forces researchers to think about their work in a different way from that in which they think about a possible solution to a research problem. Cohen (1977) suggested that writing played an important part in the process of psychological discovery and that it merited serious study. He commented on a relationship between creativity and writing in psychology that seemed to be absent in other sciences.

But, no matter what the discipline, most writers experience some degree of discomfort or difficulty while trying to formulate clearly in writing, ideas which will be new to the reader but which will have become very familiar to the author. The writers' awareness that they are aiming to give information and knowledge that they already possess to others who do not yet have it means that assumptions have to be made explicit and ideas expressed clearly. The thinking that links one idea with others or that emerges from a particular assumption has to be unambiguously translated into the written language.

Remarks such as 'good writing can't cure bad thought' and 'I can't clearly express in words what I have in my head', from two of the postgraduate sample, are not dissimilar from comments made by university staff members in a survey conducted by Lowenthal and Wason in 1977.

Several of the eminent psychologists interviewed by Cohen (1977) said that the only time they think is when they write and Murray (1978) reports that this is also true of poets and authors. He suggests it may be true of all writing and the results of my research into the process of doing a Ph.D. indicate that this is a real possibility.

It may be that the difficulty in writing experienced by so many academics at both the student and staff levels is due to a strong link between written language and thought. Written language has been referred to as 'the means of discovery of new knowledge' (Olson 1975). If it is writing that leads to discovery and not, as is generally supposed, discoveries that merely need to be put into writing, this may in part account for the experience of writing an academic paper as the most difficult part of the work.

Several comments from scientists in the postgraduate sample showed quite clearly how they felt about the experimental and reporting aspects of their work. The bio-chemist said: 'If it's time-consuming and mindless, like just repeating experiments, I like it, but if it's difficult too, like writing an introduction and conclusion, then I don't like it.' The industrial chemist commented: 'I'd rather potter about in the lab. during working hours – it's less taxing mentally.' The nuclear physicist reported: 'I prefer to be working with my hands than writing, I don't like a lot of this book work.'

This preference, shown by all the scientists, for experimental work in the laboratory to occupy them during the working day, meant that writing was assigned to evenings, weekends, and holidays. It was not perceived as 'real work' and as it was of only secondary importance, was never undertaken at the time intended. One student said, 'I'm doing bits and pieces of writing-up whenever I get a minute,' but abandoned every piece of written work commenced during the period of study.

None of the postgraduates will receive their doctorate unless they present a thesis in writing; therefore, this aspect of their work is very important. However, people were reluctant to settle down to writing and delays in getting started were extremely common.

Acquiring the discipline to start writing means not only developing the necessary state of mind and motivation, but also making it legitimate for working hours to be spent in composition. Comments such as 'when I have the enthusiasm to sit down and write, it's not as frustrating as it used to be, the difficulty is actually getting the enthusiasm to sit down in the first place', and 'getting up the energy to tackle it was actually worse than writing it', are typical illustrations of the kind of discipline needed in order for 'getting started' not to become 'putting it aside'.

Once they had got down to it, students from both Arts and Sciences agreed that writing helped them to think. One postgraduate said that he found writing difficult because 'it's at the level of ideas'. Another said: 'When you start writing a paper you see how everything goes together.' A third, who insisted on planning everything in detail before commencing to write said: 'Obviously you don't formulate what you're going to say completely until you come to write it down ... it was only when I was writing it that I realized that in one section my interpretation was completely wrong. The point I was trying to make just wouldn't embody itself verbally, so I thought it out again and rewrote the whole section.' This was from an arts postgraduate, but a science student agreed: 'Writing up my experimental work helps me to see where I'm going.' It is the 'organizational' aspect of writing which seems to be particularly useful at this level of education.

Even when a link between writing and thinking was acknowledged, writing was not accepted as an integral part of research work. More usually it was perceived merely as the logical conclusion of months (or years) of data collection. The main point to come out of this investigation so far as writing at the pre-doctoral level is concerned, was that at least in the Sciences, writing is considered to be a secondary activity. However, if it is true that original ideas occur during the process of writing then perhaps there should be a re-emphasis on this aspect of learning to become a scientist.

CONCLUSIONS AND RECOMMENDATIONS

The process through which the students pass, and in which their relationship with their supervisors is an essential component, is as follows:

1 Early enthusiasm.
2 Increasing interest in their work.
3 Transfer of dependence from supervisor to information resulting from effort.
4 Generating their own ideas based on that information.
5 Frustration at not being able to develop these ideas.
6 Boredom with the original problem.
7 Determination to finish what they started.

There are indications from the comments of the students that the continuing use of the grid throughout their period of research helped them to isolate precise problem areas. This knowledge was often used by them either to decide upon a course of action or to define and understand the source of irritants which they had previously been unable to locate.

In addition, it appears that at present writing is largely ignored at all levels of scientific training, where it is considered to be 'not really science'. The Ph.D. thesis is expected to make an 'original contribution to knowledge'. It may yet be shown that a far greater amount of constructive, creative work is done at the desk by the scientist than had previously been thought. If this is so, then perhaps part of supervision should be to encourage practice in the development of this skill.

The results of this research into postgraduate education suggest that it is very important indeed for the students to learn to interpret and use the feedback which is contained within their own work and of which they are initially unaware. It may be that the supervisor is important in the early stages of the work to act primarily as mediator between the students and their output.

At first the supervisor is needed to direct the postgraduates' efforts and help them to formulate their ideas. Gradually the supervisor can 'wean' the student from this dependence by encouraging self-criticism and helping their students to develop their own thinking. This weaning process would need to include making the postgraduate aware that they have sufficient knowledge and ability to be able to trust their own judgement and so monitor their own performance.

Once students have learned the skills and acquired the confidence necessary to assess their own efforts, their dependence on the supervisor begins to be superseded by their reliance on their own ability to evaluate their progress.

It is at this point that the students' perception of the supervisors' role changes. Instead of seeing it as one of primarily generating external approval and information, the supervisor becomes somebody with whom they can discuss new ideas and develop earlier thinking. The supervisor is used as a sounding board, as an expert with the ability to proffer the reverse arguments to be countered. The supervisory role is changed from one of tutor to that of colleague through the developing autonomy of the postgraduate.

This comes about as a result of the students' increased ability to assess their own work. The teaching of the skill to interpret and judge the results of their own work, together with those skills needed to impose structure on the planning of projects, was what the postgraduates in the sample most needed at the start of their three-year training in research.

REFERENCES

Cohen, D. (1977) *Psychologists on Psychology*, London: Routledge & Kegan Paul.
Lowenthal, D. and Wason, P. C. (1977) 'Academic writing', *Times Literary Supplement*, 14 June.

Murray, D. M. (1978) 'Internal revision: a process of discovery', in C. R. Cooper and F. Odell (eds), *Research on Composing*, Illinois: N. C. T. E.

Olson, D. (1975) 'The languages of experience', *Bulletin of the British Psychological Society* 28: 363–73.

Phillips, E. M. (1979) 'The Ph.D.: learning to do research', *Bulletin of the British Psychological Society* 32: 413–14.

Phillips, E. M. (1980) 'Education for research: the changing constructs of the postgraduate', *International Journal of Man-Machine Studies* 13: 39–48. Reprinted in M. L. G. Shaw (ed.) (1981) *Recent Advances in Personal Construct Technology*, London: Academic Press.

Phillips, E. M. (1981) 'Gridding the grad', Fourth International Congress on Personal Construct Psychology, Brock University, Toronto, Canada. Published in M. Shaw and T. Keen (eds) (1982) *Practicalities of Personal Construct Theory*, Montreal: Cybersystems Publishing.

16 Understanding supervisory relationships

Paul Jeffcutt and Alan Thomas

INTRODUCTION

In institutions of learning all over the world, peculiar ceremonies occur on a regular basis. Students dress in medieval robes and are ritually given documents by tutors in similar dress. This exchange symbolizes the student's acquisition of knowledge and is a conferment of a level of expertise. The student has now qualified, graduating from one certified state of knowledge to another, this period of passage between states or degrees of knowledge being delineated by a supervisory relationship between tutor and student.

Unfortunately, not every supervisory relationship culminates in the ceremonials of degree-giving. Of those students who embark on postgraduate research, some will never make it to the finishing line. Perhaps because, like Tolstoy's unhappy families, every unhappy research experience is unhappy in its own way, it is difficult to generalize about the reasons why things go wrong. Yet it is hard to escape the conclusion that in many cases it has something to do with the relations which prevail between student and tutor.

Failure to complete should not, of course, always be seen in a wholly negative light. In the risky business of research it is inevitable that some will travel more in hope than in expectation of arrival. But failure necessarily involves costs, and although these tend to fall most heavily upon the student, tutors are by no means immune from the consequences. Recently some failures in supervisory relationships have been pursued through external avenues – notably by recourse to litigation alleging tutor negligence. There have also been examples of more extreme forms of behaviour; one American student is said to have shot his tutor after having failed his course!

Many, and perhaps most, supervisory relationships seem, however, to work tolerably well, and some appear to have been spectacularly successful. Recently, the 1984 Nobel prize for medicine was given jointly to Milstein and his former student Koehler. Some clues as to why some supervisory relationships are successful whilst others fail may come from an examination of the educational structure of a supervisory relationship.

THE SUPERVISORY RELATIONSHIP

Institutions of learning commonly define the successful completion of a course of supervised research as being 'judged to constitute an addition to knowledge' (University of Manchester 1981: 2). One may thus by inference assume that a successful supervisory relationship is one which engenders or facilitates such an addition to knowledge. However, since beauty is taken to be in the eye of the beholder, knowledge may also be in the eye of the perceiver. Such academic judgements are thus fraught with questions of hegemony and definitions of creativity.

On entering a supervisory relationship a student becomes aware of an established power differential. First, the tutor is an authoritative guide to the legitimacy of the activities to be undertaken – since the tutor is empowered to be an academic guide as to what constitutes knowledge and what may or may not be an addition to it. Second, the tutor's judgement in these respects is ultimately uncontestable, since the tutor is also an examiner of the student's activities. One immediately perceives the essentially medieval nature of this relationship; the tutor as a guardian of an élite, the student as an acolyte or neophyte. As a research student known to one of the authors recently observed, 'When my supervisor says jump, I just ask – how high?' The formal power of the student as regards the tutor is feeble by comparison. The enshrined independence of academic judgement means that internal avenues for exploring tutor accountability are virtual dead ends. It must be remembered, however, that the tutor is seldom an unfettered guardian, since he or she is constrained by the norms of the academic community whose shadowy presence is ultimately made manifest in the shape of the external examiner.

From, and even prior to, the first face-to-face interaction the tutor and student are developing a curriculum to structure the relationship's learning activities. From his position as formal academic guide, the tutor is able to legitimate certain learning strategies, and proscribe other activities as irrelevant or distracting. A curriculum is further constructed through the development of a research proposal which outlines the work to be done and the method by which it is to be achieved. Thus we have both a formal curriculum, the research proposal, and an informal curriculum, the tutorial interactions. At worst, the curriculum is totally imposed by the tutor, the student acceding and doing the 'donkey-work'. At best, the curriculum is an evolving structure that is negotiated between tutor and student, being flexible and responsive to the demands of developments in learning. Both approaches must be considered as possibilities in any real student–tutor relationship.

SUPERVISORY STYLES

Studies in the areas of leadership, management, and teaching have often used the concept of 'style' as a way of distinguishing distinct approaches to these tasks. The starting assumption is that if different styles can be identified, it may then be possible to relate these to some notion of 'effectiveness'.

Unfortunately, these issues have not received much attention in the case of research supervision. Even so, evidence from research into classroom teaching (Morrison and McIntyre 1970) and the folklore of postgraduate research lead us to expect that supervisors do differ in their methods, and that an important type of variation is the degree of 'directiveness' which the supervisor brings to the relationship. So, just as classroom teachers vary in the extent to which they emphasize discovery and self-direction, as opposed to teacher direction and control, so research supervisors may differ in much the same way. Understanding supervisory relationships might well depend on an appreciation of these differences.

Obviously, reality is more complex than our analysis would appear to make it. But let us assume for the moment that supervisors can be located on a continuum of directiveness, ranging from the highly directive supervisor at one end, to the highly non-directive supervisor at the other. And let us envisage the 'typical' research project as involving a sequence of stages such as problem selection, research design, data collection, data analysis, interpretation, and presentation. How might directive and non-directive supervisors approach the supervisory relationship?

Our imaginary directive supervisor might behave as follows. He or she would select the research problem, specify the research design, collect or provide some or all of the data, specify and process the data analysis, interpret the results and write up the thesis! Here, if the student does anything, it amounts to little more than doing as the supervisor tells. In effect, the student is cast in the role of research assistant or technician. The opportunities for independent work are low. On the other hand, the chances of a 'successful' piece of work emerging are high, always assuming, of course, that the supervisor is both willing and able!

By contrast, the non-directive supervisor is essentially reactive. He or she expects the student to select the topic, design the research, collect and analyse the data, make sense of it and write it up. In the extreme, this is the 'go away and come back in three years with the thesis' approach, in which the supervisor becomes simply the person whose name must be entered, somewhat grudgingly, in the acknowledgements. In this case the student is the independent learner with a vengeance. The risks of things 'going wrong' are correspondingly high.

We are not suggesting that any actual supervisor will bear a close resemblance to either of these polarities. But it might not be too difficult to place someone nearer to or further from one of these extremes. The point worth stressing is that these different styles carry with them different expectations about the kinds of behaviour which are legitimate within the student–supervisor relationship. If both parties share the same expectations, harmony may prevail. Where they do not, conflict, a souring of personal relationships and even a termination of relations may well result.

What happens, for example, when a directive supervisor is paired with a student whose own expectation is of non-directive supervision? The supervisor is likely to see the student's struggle for independence as indicating pigheadedness, and unwillingness to respond to 'advice', and a lack of trustworthiness: 'He simply won't do as he's told!' The student, on the other hand, is likely to regard the supervisor as overbearing, authoritarian, even exploitative: 'He's simply using me for his own ends!' Needless to say, as trust goes out of the window, acrimony comes in.

Similarly the non-directive supervisor charged with a student with a directive orientation is likely to see the student as demanding, dependent, and lacking in initiative and commitment: 'He wants spoon-feeding!' And the student is likely to reply with charges of unhelpfulness, lack of commitment, and the cry, 'I've been abandoned!'

Unfortunately, the likelihood of these kinds of mismatching taking place is heightened by the vagueness and ambiguity which is inherent in the supervisory relationship. When student and supervisor are brought together, they enter into a kind of contract, but the rights and obligations of the parties are usually ill-defined. Many of the expectations which each party has of the other are untested assumptions which are implicit and taken for granted, and the falsity of any one of them only comes to light after seemingly legitimate expectations have been violated. If this were not enough, the fact that the resulting tangles arise from contradictory expectations may never come to light. Opportunities for misunderstanding, therefore, seem as ubiquitous as those which foster mutual comprehension.

SUPERVISORY DILEMMAS

Like the policeman's lot, the supervisor's is not a happy one. At least, it isn't always a happy one. For the supervisor is faced with a number of critical dilemmas. Each of these serves to complicate the supervisory relationship.

The directiveness–dependency dilemma

Supervisors are aware of the fact that they carry a responsibility for directing their students' work. Yet they also know that one of the aims of postgraduate research is to develop independent scholars who are capable of pursuing their own research with an acceptable degree of competence. High directiveness tends to place the control of the research in the hands of the supervisor. At the same time it weakens the student's independence. At what point should the student's independence be sacrificed for the sake of increasing the chances of completion (if indeed, this follows)?

The trust–control dilemma

As Charles Handy (1981) has indicated, there is an inverse relationship between the degree of trust between a manager and a subordinate and the degree of control which the former exercises over the latter. Where trust is high, the subordinate's discretion is high. But the chances of making mistakes is correspondingly increased. And when mistakes occur, there is a temptation to increase the degree of control. Often the result is a regressive spiral of increased control, lowered trust, distorted communication, and growing interpersonal friction.

In the case of the supervisory relationship, this suggests that even if a supervisor perceives increasing intervention to be in the best interests of the student, this carries with it the implication that the student cannot be trusted. If it seems necessary to increase supervisory control, how can this be done without sparking off a vicious regressive spiral?

The teacher–examiner dilemma

This dilemma, which is faced by all teachers who also have a responsibility for the formal examination of their student's work, boils down to the question: Whose side am I on? As a tutor, the supervisor may develop a deep personal commitment to his student, a sense of ownership of the student's problems. The supervisor becomes an ally, supporting the student in his struggles to complete a satisfactory piece of research. He sees himself, if you like, as the second in the student's corner.

As examiner, however, the supervisor is required to take on a detached stance, to evaluate the student's work dispassionately, treating the thesis as a product of the student's unaided effort. Whilst he may not entirely relinquish his role as second, he is now primarily the judge examining the work in impersonal terms.

As most teachers are aware, these roles are in conflict. Students should not be surprised then if their supervisors seem to shift ambivalently between these roles, now shouting encouragement, then giving a kick in the pants. No supervisor can give unconditional support because this increases the risk of legitimating work which may fall below an acceptable standard – one which as an examiner he is required to enforce. If supervisors cannot afford to give too many hostages to fortune, can they ever then be thought of as wholly trustworthy?

MANAGING THE SUPERVISORY RELATIONSHIP

Are we able to identify particularly effective teaching/learning behaviours within a supervisory relationship? Research into adult learning in general, and individual learning styles in particular, indicates that there are no sure-fire formulae for success (Knowles 1973). There appear to be general individual proclivities for learning which will make individuals more receptive to certain strategies or more willing to undertake certain activities. Learning styles are behaviour stereotypes, however, and each individual is a complex and dynamic synthesis of all, rather than an adherent to any one style or another. Learners appear to be able to learn something from anything. We can postulate that there will be behaviours that are more appropriate for individual learning, but we are unable to describe any that are totally inappropriate. Hence, what may be 'timewasting' to one tutor or student, may well be 'freedom to learn' to another. The received wisdom of past or others' experience gives all sorts of indications of successful or inappropriate behaviour, for example:

'good students don't need supervisors'
'good dissertations follow this pattern'
'good tutors ensure their students submit on time'

and many more, too numerous to mention. Such models of behaviour will obviously shape the expectations of tutor and students alike.

Most definitions of success appear to encompass both 'formal' and 'informal' elements – both certification and learning. These, however, may be mutually incompatible objectives. To return to the analogy of the journey and the destination, it would appear then that most choose the safety of arrival rather than the uncertainty of travelling hopefully.

In research, as in life, there appears to be no guaranteed way of predicting successful pairings, for the most unlikely liaisons seem to bear fruit. Success appears to depend on the interaction of individual proclivities (compatibility), and the ability to develop a mutually acceptable framework for working together. The primary objectives that a student might bring to a supervisory relationship could be summarized as follows:

• To undertake a project that allows for self-expression and development, rather than doing someone else's 'donkey-work'.

- To develop a fruitful relationship with the tutor and receive encouragement and advice, rather than disinterest and detachment.
- To submit a good piece of work and pass the course, rather than drop out or fail.

And for supervisors:

- To supervise research which is personally interesting and within the range of the supervisor's expertise.
- To develop a productive relationship with the student in which commitment is reciprocated.
- To be associated with high-quality work which adds to the supervisor's knowledge and development.

These objectives suggest that negotiation between tutor and student is likely to be a prerequisite for the development of satisfactory supervisory relationships. This is not to say that no learning can come from an imposed curriculum, for every situation has learning potential. However, the student's internalization of the tutor's learning objectives (laudable as they may be), is certainly inferior to the development of his or her own awareness.

The formal power differential is such that the tutor and student are automatically cast in the roles of master and apprentice. Tutor pre-eminence is such that most students will adapt their hierarchy of needs and objectives to suit a more subservient role. A more emancipated relationship may be possible if the tutor is prepared to narrow the power differential, and institute a renegotiation of position. The potential for this boundary exploration from a student initiative is a more uphill and infrequent development. Both these strategies will require some initial processes of role re-definition, since apprentices require masters as much as masters require apprentices.

Additions to knowledge are often characterized by their challenging nature; innovation can be uncomfortable, particularly if this discomfort is experienced in respect of cherished views. Both tutor and student will certainly be presented with such challenges during the course of a supervisory relationship. An openness to negotiation of the curriculum requires the tutor's relaxation of the position of being the sole academic guide of the relationship. Since knowledge is not invested in any individual by divine right, a supervisory relationship has the potential for learning by both parties. This may be a challenging development to directiveness-orientated tutors since it not only requires the acceptance that learning is progressive, but that it also can come from 'inferiors'.

As in any long-term relationship, an awareness of your own needs as well as a sensitivity to others' needs is an important precondition for success.

REFERENCES

Handy, C. B. (1981) *Understanding Organisations*, Harmondsworth: Penguin.

Knowles, M. (ed.) (1973) *The Adult Learner – A Neglected Species*, Houston: Gulf.

Morrison, A. and McIntyre, G. (1970) *Teachers and Teaching*, Harmondsworth: Penguin.

University of Manchester (1981) *The Degree of Doctor of Philosophy: Ordinances and Regulations*, Manchester.

17 Writing up the doctoral thesis

Norman Clark

INTRODUCTION

This short chapter represents my *own view* of what a doctoral dissertation should consist of in terms of its scope, structure, style, and quality. I emphasize subjectivity advisedly, since to my knowledge there are no 'criteria of scholarship' laid down in tablets of stone which provide a generally accepted set of guidelines. Indeed, as with many other aspects of academic life, the rituals surrounding doctoral degrees carry all the hallmarks of a priestly cult in which novices are initiated into the necessary mysteries through a complicated process of training understood only by the chosen few (and *never* talked about). Students are expected to pick up what it is necessary to know through a process of unwritten diffusion mediated occasionally by a series of catchphrases of impressive vagueness, for example:

'you ought to have a "theory chapter"!'
or 'where is your "literature review"?'
or 'I understand that you are going to gather some interesting "evidence"!'
And so on.

Recently, however, there has been increasing pressure from grant-awarding bodies (like the Research Councils and the University Funding Council (UFC)) to tighten up the administration of postgraduate degrees, partly it is true to save money and partly also in an attempt to gear postgraduate training more directly to social goals. However, there is also a strong feeling abroad that social science Ph.D.s in particular are often badly administered, indifferently supervised, and of poor quality (when they are actually completed, which is not nearly as frequently as they ought to be), and there is every likelihood that in the coming years a much more stringent quality control will be exercised by those responsible for disbursement of funds.

Consequently, one purpose of this chapter is to help anticipate some of these developments through initiating a discussion of thesis specification. It provides some background information, attempts to define a thesis in terms of a sustained coherent argument, and summarizes many of the important qualities a thesis is supposed to exhibit. It also summarizes what the structure of a thesis typically looks like and finally concludes with an overall discussion in terms of the University of Sussex Social Policy Research Unit's (SPRU) own particular line with regard to scholarship, as I see it. Let me emphasize again, however, that many of these views are my own and need not command general agreement. They should, however, instigate debate.

THE RECENT UGC LINE

In 1984, Peter Swinnerton-Dyer, Chairperson of the UFC, addressed a special SSRC (ESRC) conference on the future of postgraduate research in the social sciences. His main point was that the Ph.D. degree had been imported originally from Germany to Oxbridge in the 1920s in order to provide an incentive for Britain's best young scientists to stay in this country, rather than go to the USA where opportunities were good. The three-year period, initially chosen on rather arbitrary grounds, gradually became a period during which the young scientist served an 'apprenticeship in research', culminating in the writing-up of a fairly limited project under the close supervision of a senior scientist who would ensure that the requisite degree was awarded if he/she felt the award were warranted by the general performance and capability of the student in question.

In the social sciences, however, the Ph.D. tended to follow a rather different line – one in which the Ph.D. thesis became in effect the candidate's first book and was seen directly as a work of scholarship which would permit, if successful, the launching of an academic career. Hence while the science Ph.D. has continued to act as a 'training in research', fitting the student for a wide variety of careers across education, industry, commerce, and government, the social science Ph.D. graduate has become fitted for very little other than teaching/research in higher education. And with the retraction in this area in recent years has come a concomitant retrenchment in the need for social science Ph.Ds. It followed therefore, according to the logic of Swinnerton-Dyer's argument, either that we should cease to produce them or that the *nature* of training should alter radically so as to fit students for a wider job market – in this case bringing the social science Ph.D. more into line with the natural science Ph.D. Although these views did not go down too well with the social scientists present, they deserve attention and discussion.

ARGUMENT

A thesis is essentially an argument developed according to a given tradition of scholarship. The candidate is persuading his/her reader that the proposition advanced is both important and tenable – *important* in the sense that it is of a non-trivial nature and drawn from an established body of knowledge, *tenable* in the sense that it is advanced in ways which give it the stamp of veracity. It should also be *comprehensible* to the intelligent reader – i.e. it should be written in such a way that the essential steps of the argument are readily followed, thus adding to its persuasiveness. Hence words such as 'well-focused' or 'tight' refer to how well the argument has been developed. The corollary is that the more descriptive and the more generalized it is, the poorer its value as a thesis. UN Reports, for example, do not make good thesis material. It follows also that the more narrowly the topic is defined to begin with, the easier it is to fashion it into a viable thesis at the end of the day.

QUALITIES

A number of *properties* appertaining to a good thesis follow from this very general set of specifications.

1 Clarity

The student should strive to keep the exposition as simple as possible. This means more than simplicity in written expression (a difficult enough task in itself). It also means: (a) not using technical concepts unless these are explicitly defined; (b) restricting the number of graphs and tables to the minimum required for efficient exposition of necessary detail; (c) avoiding the use of unnecessary mathematics; (d) restricting the use of theory to that minimum necessary to lay the analytical basis for the main argument.

2 Objectivity

The student should pay close attention to justifying each main strand of the argument through such mechanisms as sourcing, referencing, citing data, providing logical justification, etc. Thus the argument should avoid the use of unsubstantiated assertion as much as possible, hence minimizing its susceptibility to criticism on grounds of subjectivity. An associated point is the importance of being seen to take objectivity seriously.

Two common mistakes which students often make are, *first* to 'argue by weight of quotation' in the erroneous assumption that the greater the number of supportive quotes the stronger the argument, and *second* to append a blanket reference to an argument without telling the reader where in the text the appropriate support is coming from and what is the nature of this support. Crude referencing of these types serves merely to detract from the power of the argument and hence from the quality of the thesis as a whole. A final point here relates to one's own personal values which usually impinge in all kinds of subtle ways and can often vitiate the overall persuasiveness of the thesis. Two general rules to attempt to deal with this problem (complete success is rarely possible) are: (a) to make a conscious effort throughout the writing of the text to abstract from one's own value position, no matter how personally painful this is; and (b) to state one's own value position and how this may impinge on the thesis, early on in the text. The former is an important aid to intellectual development while the latter gives a clear signal to the reader on where the writer stands on these points. The reader may then discount accordingly.

3 Logical consistency

By logical consistency I mean *first* that the thesis should be written in such a way that each strand of the argument is consistent with preceding and succeeding strands. The greater the attention paid to this, the better the 'flow' of the overall argument will be. One useful technique to adopt to this end is to append a conclusion at the end of each chapter summarizing the argument at that point, and anticipating the development of the succeeding chapter. Similarly one may usefully do the same during the introductory passage of each chapter. Even a small effort in this direction can make life immeasurably easier for the reader. A *second* sense in which I use the term 'logical consistency' relates to the development of written argument where the capacity to write logically is of great advantage. Here the main problem many students (and faculty!) have is that of avoiding *non sequiturs* and other forms of illegitimate argument.

4 Economy

Every attempt should be made to make points in the shortest possible way, consistent with adequate treatment. External examiners tend on the whole to dislike repetition while re-enforcement of points may be made in concluding and introductory passages.

5 Evidence

Supporting data should be handled carefully in the sense that they should say clearly what you want them to say and not be subject to different interpretations. Where data *processing* is involved, of course, it is important that the methodology be legitimate.

6 Originality

The thesis should make a 'contribution to knowledge', although this is normally interpreted in an elastic fashion.

Each of the above 'qualities' are not 'absolutes' in themselves but should rather be seen as objectives to aim for. Sometimes they will tend to contradict each other, for example where the amount of necessary detail may preclude economy of exposition. The art of thesis writing lies essentially in a capacity to achieve the necessary balance consistent with the overall objectives of the thesis.

STRUCTURE

One very important technique which helps to produce a persuasively argued thesis is that of providing a clear structure. This is so because the *act* of thesis structuring helps to sort out the student's thinking – and hence improves the quality characteristics outlined above, *and* because it helps the reader to follow the argument more closely. Exactly how any particular thesis should be structured will depend upon the student and supervisor, and upon the subject matter itself. However it is possible to set out a 'model structure' which describes what a thesis typically looks like, as follows:

1 Introduction

In many ways this is the most important section of thesis (and should be written *last!*). It tells the reader what the student intends to argue, why the argument is important, how he/she intends to proceed methodologically and what the layout of the thesis will be.

2 Literature review

This section lays out the conceptual/analytical basis for the argument, through a 'state of the art' review of the literature, which will identify the gap(s) which the thesis will fill. It is in this section too that 'theory' appears, though more about this below.

3 Methodology

Usually a thesis will contain an account of how the student has gone about obtaining empirical evidence, what weaknesses such evidence manifests, how data have been processed, etc. The objective here should be to provide the reader with an honest account of the (potential) limitations of the overall argument. Sometimes the methodological section is included with the presentation of results or included as an appendix to the main text.

4 Analysis and presentation of results

This represents the 'core' of the thesis and can take many different forms depending upon its nature.

5 Conclusion

Finally the results are presented within the context of the problem as stated in the early sections. It is at this stage too that any policy implications and suggestions for further research are normally made (more about this below).

6 Appendices

A useful technique is to include as much detailed material as possible as appendices, thereby enabling the argument itself to be clearly developed, shorn of extraneous detail.

7 Notes and bibliography

This is a vital part of a good thesis, since it provides an account of the 'building blocks' in terms of literature and supporting evidence. Every effort should be made to make absolutely explicit the sources of the 'quotes', 'claims', 'facts', and 'arguments' culled from the literature, so that the reader (and the student) can see clearly what 'new knowledge' is being generated.

8 Sub-headings

It is often useful to split individual chapters/sections etc. into defined 'pieces of prose', signposted by headings.

SPRU (University of Sussex Science Policy Research Unit)

What I have tried to do up to this stage is to 'define' the nature of the thesis as clearly as I can in terms of what I understand to be normally expected by academic bodies. In reality, of course, theses will vary greatly depending upon the subject/department in question and how it pursues and evaluates scholarship. In turn this depends upon complex views (which are often internalized) about the nature of the scientific method and how it may be applied in specific contexts. Hence, although British universities normally operate under an 'external examination' system which is supposed to enhance the independence and homogeneity of academic assessment, there is often considerable latitude in practice regarding how such judgements are actually reached. Students would be aware of this.

A particular problem in the social sciences is how far to 'dress up' the thesis so as to conform to *disciplinary* canons – for example, how far to cite theoretical language, use technical discourse to describe phenomena, and employ empirical methodologies which are specific to the discipline in question (and indeed help to define it). I say 'particular problem' advisedly because as the world becomes a more complex place the isomorphism between the 'discipline' and the 'problem' is becoming less and less clear. Indeed the growth of multi-disciplinary schools and institutes is one consequence of this trend, and similar changes are taking place within the structures of research councils and other grant-awarding bodies and foundations. Students should take advice from their supervisors on this point, but at the same time remember that their theses will *ultimately* be judged not on elaborate technical window dressing, but rather on how well they are defined and how successfully their embodied arguments are demonstrated.

In my own institution, because we are a unit concerned with policy research of an interdisciplinary kind, this in itself defines the kind of thesis we expect from doctoral students. For example, we *do not expect* ritual obeisance to any given body of social science theory beyond what is necessary for providing a foundation for the argument. Hence the literature review should be seen as *contextual* and not as an opportunity to rewrite grand theory. Indeed 'theory' itself is a very undefined term and students should engage in it with great circumspection.

A second point concerns 'policy', since writing a thesis is essentially a diagnostic process involving *existing* evidence relating to *past events*. It follows that the conclusions reached will be concerned with what *has* happened in the past and how the student wishes to interpret these past events. It also follows, therefore, that the thesis is not a forecasting exercise and should not be written *directly* about policy. Rather, policy statements should arise as a natural consequence of the conclusions reached, given appropriate contextual conditions.

Finally, there is a premium on brevity. Theses should aim to be somewhere between 200 to 300 pages long (in terms of textual discussion). This is not to say that there *may* not occasionally be a need for a longer piece of work. On the other hand, students tend to over-write on the whole and, given current trends towards making the Ph.D. period a training in research lasting no more than three years, it is advisable to err, if anything, on the short side.

18 The social process of research: some reflections on developing a multi-disciplinary accounting project[1]

Cyril Tomkins, David Rosenberg, and Ian Colville

Beware of all enterprises that require new clothes.

(Thoreau 1854)

An underlying assumption behind this chapter is that social science and researchers would derive considerable benefit if accounts of how social science is carried out in the 'real world' were available as readily as formal textbooks on research methodology. It is, in fact, part of the common-sense occupational culture of the social sciences that a considerable discrepancy exists between how social research has actually been done and what is found in textbooks. Nevertheless, few accounts exist of the social processes involved in research and even fewer of the processes of accounting research. Recognizing this situation, this chapter aims to achieve four objectives:

1 to consider briefly in what respect reported research methodology does not describe the research process;
2 to consider the bureaucratic structure of much research conducted in universities and its implications;
3 to describe the research process in one multi-disciplinary project in which the three authors are jointly engaged; and
4 to derive some conclusions from that experience which may have relevance, for consideration by grant-giving institutions, research institutions, research grant holders, and individual research officers. It is stressed that the conclusions are very tentative and may be viewed by some as no more than indicating that the research process should itself be developed as a field of research.

Each of these objectives is dealt with in a separate section in the following text.

OMISSIONS IN REPORTED METHODOLOGY

Dissent from the procedural rules which prescribe a uni-directional sequence of axiomatic theory, hypothesis formation, observations, testing, and conclusion is quite common. Baldamus, for instance, argues 'side by side with the official methodology that one finds in systematic theory, formal logic, statistical methods, survey design or interviewing procedure, there exists a reservoir of unofficial non-formalised techniques of inquiry' (Baldamus 1972) and he continues:

> While there is a well established sociology of science, no systematic research has been done specifically on what would have to be called the 'sociology of *social* science'. It is surprisingly easy, nevertheless, to visualise the nature of unofficial techniques. What comes to mind are, for example, the exchange of personal experience, of 'gimmicks' and lucky 'hunches', of frustrations and unexpected insights, between researchers and or theorists when they meet privately, at conferences or in staff common rooms. In addition one could draw on the occasional autobiographical remarks in the preface to published works and, of course, one's own accumulated experience distilled from memory and introspection.
>
> (Baldamus 1972)

However, this 'common-sense' reservoir of research knowledge is very rarely articulated in published social science work and, as a consequence, one gets the impression from the literature that a set of standard techniques can be drawn from to provide a normative methodology of either a positivistic or phenomenological kind, irrespective of its wider social and historical context. Bell and Newby, who have edited perhaps the only English collection of field work 'accounts' in sociology, emphasize that for them contexts can mean everything from micro-politics of inter-personal relationships, through the politics of research units, departments, universities, and polytechnics to the various apparatuses of the state. All these contexts may vitally determine the design, implementation and outcome of social research (Bell and Newby 1977). Some aspects of the way in which these various 'contextual levels' can have an impact upon the research output are examined in the rest of this chapter. Following Platt (1976), it is felt that there is a need for a theorization of social science research production. She herself has written on the power relations in bureaucratic research. This chapter attempts to provide a more comprehensive framework.

THE BUREAUCRATIC STRUCTURE OF RESEARCH IN THE UK

As Platt suggested, the characteristic organization of the majority of funded research in the UK is as follows. The would-be project director develops a research proposal to receive a limited amount of grant support over a fixed period of time from a funding agency and this is used to defray the salaries of full-time or part-time research officers and the expenses incurred in the research activity. The research officers then work, with varying degrees of autonomy, under the supervision of the project director who is normally someone with various other commitments in higher education and unable to devote more than a minority of his time to the research in question. There is, therefore, a clear division of labour between the person who initiated the work, but who is not usually involved in it on a full-time basis, and the research officers who do the bulk of the day-to-day work. Platt stresses that the research officers come to the project with their own interests, expectations and motives and for them it is a 'work situation' as well as one of intellectual activity for its own sake.

Such a structure has several implications. First, the nature of the fund-giving agency may influence the nature of the research, its process and outcomes. Baritz has written on the history of the use of social science in American industry under the telling title of 'servants of power'(Baritz 1965). As research is normally funded by some government agency or private industry, at least one may conjecture that not all social categories will benefit from research work. In addition, various differences can probably be identified between most research funded by industry and by government agencies. Industry is likely to fund research of immediate relevance (though not necessarily with short-term impact), is likely to be less bureaucratic in drawing up the research contract and exercising control over the project, and is more likely to insist on a significant involvement by the senior researcher who designed the research proposal. In State-funded research, it is less likely that the funding agency wishes to dictate the theoretical pivots of the research, but research funded is usually closely related to the need for social prediction and control.

While the previous paragraph indicates that research output may differ in type according to the type of funding agency, in fact this simple State-private industry dichotomy is probably of limited value. Government departments funding research appropriate to their own activities and objectives may well take a line closer in thinking to that of private industry than a 'State-at-one-remove' organization like the Social Science Research Council (SSRC). Care is, therefore, needed in attempting to demonstrate the precise influence that funding agencies have and sweeping generalizations should be avoided. Moreover, the impact of the funding agency may also be contingent upon other structural factors in the research process. For example, one might hypothesize that State and industry funding of a problem-solving nature has led to an emphasis on positivism and follow Marcuse in arguing that positivism is a doctrine followed by rulers rather than the ruled (Marcuse 1965). However, given that most research proposals are constructed by academics, the dominance of positivism could be more a result of the need for credibility of emerging social science departments in the eyes of the more mature science departments of universities and the desire on the part of the former to be seen as 'scientific' (Glaser and Strauss 1968). On the other hand, the validity of this status-seeking argument is also probably not universal and may itself depend upon the maturity and status of the parent university to which a social science department belongs.

Coming down the contextual hierarchy one comes next to the grant holder. Given the way in which most grants are obtained and administered and the lack of the grant holder's full-time involvement, the question of the method of delegation to be employed arises. Basically there is the choice of two broad approaches: either the grant holder views the project as well-defined in terms of purposes and methods to be used and sets tight guidelines and targets to ensure he can retain control, or he or she adopts a method of 'loose delegation' based upon the notion that 'good people' have been hired and they will perform best if left 'to get on with it'. While tight control can be associated with a less structured research process which allows for modification of research hypotheses and methods in response to learning based upon early field-work, it will involve a much greater time commitment on the part of the grant holder than would tight control accompanied with a positivistic research design. In the latter case the grant holder needs merely to monitor reports from research officers that various pre-planned stages of work have been completed according to methods prescribed – although rarely would any grant holder be quite so detached as to do nothing except that. With unstructured research processes, however, tight control can only be maintained if the grant holder is able to spend a significant amount of time involved with the research officers in the field-work itself and insisting on very frequent feedback especially where hypotheses and procedures have to be modified. Therefore, while positivistic research does not have to be tightly controlled, it would seem that grant holders wishing to retain tight control will more often opt for a positivistic approach.

The inclination of the grant holder to adopt a tight or loose control may itself be a function of various influences including personality, professional training and culture, and the type of research project. It is also quite possible that professional cultures dominate in the sense that research attracts people from a broadly homogeneous personality group who will always prefer one or two types of research. Thus academic accountants and economists *may* be mainly averse to risk in research design and adopt project work which can be extensively pre-planned.

There may be other institutional effects which enable risk-aversion to succeed. For example, it seems that, in some social science disciplines, but certainly not all, it is just as acceptable to publish results which report the inability to find significant relationships between hypothesized relationships as it is to publish proven theories. A risk-averting grant holder can therefore avoid almost all risk by ensuring that a positivistic approach is carefully pursued, giving little regard to any learning process about his hypothesis formulation and research process as the research proceeds. Either way he or she can publish. Of course, this assumes that the main satisfaction comes from publication rather than the discovering of new valid theories and few academics would admit that. Nevertheless, the pressure to publish is significant, especially on younger academics, and so the point may have practical relevance.

It can also be argued, of course, that publication of the inability to find significant relationships helps other researchers to avoid 'blind alleys'. However, such an argument is only valid if the hypothesis tested is widely held or shown to be 'grounded in reality'. If the hypothesis is one of a vast number of possible relationships which one might concoct without reference to the decision context, publication that it does not hold may be of little relevance for explaining the world 'as it is' or devising policy.[2]

While it appears that there may be contextual pressures, as outlined above, which may lead to a positivistic research design, there are also pressures in the other direction. The grant holder who adopts such an approach with little contact with the research process provides a possible source of conflict within his team. Unexpected events and themes can be expected to arise during the research process which may lead research officers, who had no hand in preparing the research proposal, to believe that the proposal was inadequately formulated. Given the ethos that researchers are not just employees, but are also involved in the search for knowledge for its own sake, their compliance with the grant holder's wishes cannot be guaranteed. Formal power of enforcement may rest with the grant holders but, with current employment legislation and 'acceptable practices', such power may be more apparent than real; although the power derived through ability to withhold references for future posts should not be overlooked. Nevertheless, unless the project is very tightly controlled, once data collection commences, much power in determining the research outcome rests with the research officer. Most grant holders have neither the time nor inclination to analyse masses of data and may only have a general idea of the form in which it is stored – especially if computer facilities are used. In such a situation the grant holder may feel that the best form of control is to be very careful in appointing the research officers in the first place and then give them responsibility and discretion commensurate with 'data control power' and closer 'field knowledge'. While formally the research officers may only have discretion to *suggest* modifications in procedures to the grant holder, their degree of influence may be substantial.

Obviously, it would be foolish to argue that positivistic research which is tightly controlled should never be used. It would be contrary to the notion of contextual influences to adopt such a view. Where research officers are young and inexperienced and where grant holders and researchers have the same professional background, such methodology will probably be effective. However, there may well be an additional requirement and this is that the research field has been well trodden already (either generally or by the grant holder) such that only relatively marginal developments are being attempted where hypotheses are available which are 'visibly well grounded'. Where knowledge has not yet been so extensively developed, multiple disciplines and experienced research officers are involved, it may be more usually appropriate to adopt a 'loosely controlled' strategy in order to achieve success in social science research.

The above discussion points to the need for research to discover how far these theoretical arguments regarding contextual factors are important in determining the research outcome. Taking a broad contingency approach, such research might involve an analysis of the relationship between research outcomes and various types of financing, research institution, project control style, disciplines involved, etc. However, it is the interaction of these variables which influence the research outcome and it may make little sense to attempt to identify the separate impact of each one. Also, at the present state of knowledge, to proceed too rapidly in such a direction would be to fall foul of the argument to show the relevance of the hypothesis to reality before conducting widespread tests. At present it may, therefore, be more fruitful to build a data bank of descriptions of the social processes involved in specific research projects, perhaps supplemented by an analysis of expectations held by each party to the research (from grant giving body to research officer), at several stages of the work. The data collected should include each party's perceptions of expectations of other team members. Researchers will have to be confident enough to expose their activities, 'warts and all', for they will run the risk of accusations of incompetence from many social science researchers who still adhere strictly to a particular style of research, but this seems to be necessary if a sociological theory of social science research is to emerge.

Roth stated, over two decades ago, that researchers have given little thought to how to apply the hypothesis of the sociology of work and formal organizations to their own activities (Roth 1966). In social research, as in other organizational activity, there is a hierarchy of authority and the need to manage. Good management is dependent upon awareness of the impact that different managerial processes have upon organization members and this is gained to a large extent from experience. It is to this end that this chapter now turns to a description of the social process of a research project in which the three authors have been the principal actors. Moreover, the project has inter-disciplinary facets which further complicate the contextual analysis presented so far.

DESCRIPTION OF SOCIAL PROCESSES IN A MULTI-DISCIPLINARY RESEARCH TEAM

As this chapter is about technical and social aspects of a research process, it is relevant to describe how it came to exist. The research project, described later, contained no plan to produce a chapter like this.

Moreover, no formal research process was undertaken to produce it. As the project progressed the participants became more and more conscious of the difficulties they had faced and the various contextual influences which played a significant part in determining the eventual direction of the research and its likely results. At the time of writing it is felt that the major difficulties of operating as a multi-disciplinary team have been overcome, but the path to that situation was not an easy one. It remains to be seen whether these difficulties recur cyclically. With this experience, however, it is felt that later stages of this project and any multi-disciplinary project in which we are involved in future can be better managed and organized by explicit recognition of various characteristics encountered so far in this project which may tend to occur in many multi-disciplinary projects.

The 'data base' for this chapter was a collection of personal notes made by the researchers on their perceptions of the research process and several taped discussions between pairs of the three researchers, and between all three together. The recording of these notes was not planned with a view to publication nor organized systematically, the notes were prepared and discussions taped at different times during the last six months before writing this chapter as each researcher or pair of researchers felt inclined. Unfortunately no notes or taped discussions are available which were produced at the time the project faced greatest difficulties. The chapter is, therefore, based extensively on memory, perception of what happened, and introspection, albeit aided by discussion. If this chapter establishes that such research processes should themselves be researched, it will obviously be preferable for perceptions to be checked out at the time of difficulties and not afterwards.

A paper was drafted first by David Rosenberg (a sociologist) and then modified by him after taped discussion with the other researchers. The paper was then completely re-written and extended by the grant holder (an accountant) although various sections and many ideas of the original draft were retained. The paper was then further modified following suggestions by Ian Colville (an organization development analyst) and finally drafted after several further long debates between the three researchers regarding their actions as described and how they should be interpreted. This apparently tedious description is important as it indicates that each researcher has actually drafted or recorded his own perceptions and that this is not just the work of the grant holder drafting his view of the project. This is relevant information, given the different perceptions which seem to have been held as to what was happening in earlier stages of the project.

The grant holder, a member of the School of Management at the University of Bath, was awarded £37,585 by the SSRC to carry out research into the organization contexts of the use of accounting information in a social services and treasurer's department of a local authority and a police authority. Sufficient finance was given to enable the grant holder to employ two mature research officers for two years. The stages of the project will now be described in chronological order.

From conception of the project to the receipt of grant

For several years the grant holder, with a number of years' practical accounting experience in the public sector, had wondered why so little research had been done on how accounting information was used in decision-making in organizations and most of what had been done, while pioneering, appeared to him to be superficial. The grant holder mentioned this to an old friend of his who had recently become County Treasurer of a near-by local authority and the idea arose that, in view of the grant holder's experience in such an organization, some research on that question might be undertaken in that authority. Both agreed that the research would have to be based upon an intensive study of people in their worksetting in an attempt to acquire a deep understanding of their aims, problems, needs, and use of information, rather than an approach based on questionnaires or single interviews.

After gaining permission from the chief executive and relevant committees of the council, the grant holder set about the development of a research proposal. As already mentioned, he was familiar with the small amount of literature in the mainstream accounting literature which did not seem to help much and so he turned to an examination of some work in the field of psychology, believing that work on how individuals reacted to various stimuli might offer some ideas on methodology for the project. Some time was spent on such a search, but while the grant holder identified a number of different approaches, none seemed to him to be suitable for a longitudinal in-depth study of one local authority. He therefore drafted a research proposal which included a critique of existing studies and methodology and simply argued for an approach which involved a long stay in an organization observing practices, developing case studies and repeatedly interviewing personnel about their tasks and information requirements. Moreover, some quantitative modelling was not ruled out although work of that type when reviewed did not seem to offer much promise.

The grant holder had recently joined the school of Management at Bath University and, through both the way the school is organized and the way in which coffee and lunch breaks are taken, he was bound to meet someone from the Centre for the Study of Organizational Change and Development on most days. In this way he became aware of a dominant research thrust in that centre based upon phenomenology and, more particularly, that the grounded theory approach of Glaser and Strauss (1968) was held in high regard. From the grant holder's obviously initial superficial view of that material (which he had not even heard of before coming to Bath) it seemed at least to have some affinity to the research approach that he and the local County Treasurer had thought appropriate. The draft research proposal was, therefore, given to several members of the centre and many useful (and highly critical) comments were made, especially from Professor Mangham (the head of the centre) who directed the grant holder to a number of other references in the organization behaviour field which related to a number of the notions the accountant/grant holder had put into the draft on the basis of his 'common sense'.

This interaction was crucial in re-drafting the research proposal and enabling the grant holder to see what type of people he would need to undertake the research. It is absolutely certain that had the grant holder been at any of the previous (single discipline) departments where he had been employed, such a project would have had quite a different complexion in terms of research personnel and methodology. Moreover, just 'nodding acquaintance' with organization theorists within the same school would probably also have had little effect – the *social* interaction with at least four or five members of the centre was the all-important catalyst. This in turn may also be a function of the existence of a variety of disciplines within a relatively small school, but an argument based on that alone is probably too simple.

It is important for later discussion to note that the research methodology proposed by the grant holder arose from a 'general awareness' of what was required rather than from his own 'deeply rooted' experience of research of the phenomenological type.

The methodology outlined in the grant proposal stated that the grant holder would spend six months mapping formal information flows, defining and classifying types of accounting information and identifying key points in the organization decision network in order to select places where case-studies could be constructed. After six months two research officers would be appointed to commence the field-work which would involve repeated interviews over two years and the construction of some case studies based upon diaries kept by some officers regarding the use of accounting reports.

In the event there was a delay in getting an affirmative decision from the SSRC and the work could not commence at the proposed date. The research officers had to be appointed before hardly any preparatory work was done and, for reasons given below, this proved to be a lucky event which reduced the possible effect of problems which arose later in managing the research team.

The recruitment of research officers

The research submission provided for the appointment of two research officers: one with experience of analysing organization structures and behaviour and one accountant or systems analyst. During the nine months between submitting the research proposal and appointing the research officers, the grant holder decided that the project stood more chance of identifying the part that accounting played in achieving organization effectiveness if two research officers were appointed from the 'behavioural sciences' rather than one being an accountant. This was decided for two reasons. First, the grant holder began to become more closely acquainted with literature relating to organization effectiveness and realized that that side of the project work would be more extensive than he first imagined. Second, the SSRC wrote specifically advising him to appoint someone who could unravel the political aspects of local authority activities and resource allocation pressures. The latter advice has proven to be very sound as becomes clear later in this chapter.

The first research officer appointed had recently been a research student under the supervision of the head of the Centre for the Study of Organizational Change and Development and appeared to the grant holder easily the most appropriate of those short-listed and interviewed. Again the influence of the setting in which the project was based is shown here in terms of cultural dissemination. The head of the centre assisted with interviewing and pointed out differences between the research officer most preferred by the grant holder and the others (all rejected) in terms of research outlook and philosophy.

All those rejected were well qualified and apparently highly satisfactory candidates; one apparently ideal candidate was a qualified accountant who had just obtained a Ph.D. in organization behaviour and who would almost certainly have been appointed by the grant holder acting alone. It is stressed here that that candidate would probably have worked well with the grant holder and produced interesting results, but the research project would have developed quite differently and would not have identified the informal decision processes. More importantly if that candidate had been appointed, the grant holder can now see that it would have been an 'impossible fit' with the other research officer in terms of co-operation in designing and developing a research methodology. At the time of the interview the grant holder did not have sufficient awareness of the different schools of thought in what to him was an alien discipline which appeared on a 'common-sense basis' to contain one relatively homogeneous set of researchers.

Several weeks later another applicant was identified (i.e. the sociologist co-author of this chapter), and he seemed to display a similar research orientation as well as providing more appropriate skills for analysing the political content of decision-making. Indeed this applicant had come for interview in a very sceptical mind about the whole project, having read the proposal and observing what he saw as marked inconsistencies in it in terms of the call for in-depth longitudinal work and some of the proposed methodology. He was also suspicious of teaming up with an organization behaviour researcher trained in a school of management. His first fear was, apparently, quelled when he saw that, if appointed, he would be required to participate in helping an accountant take cognisance of social and political factors and that he would have room to manoeuvre the research methodology more to his liking – although he did not raise this at the interview. The second fear, he says, was laid when the other research officer, already appointed, referred to the work of Everett C. Hughes;[3] apparently, anyone who knew such work could not be completely impossible to work with even if from a school of management. The sociologist had himself held a stereotyped view of a school of management and says he did not realize that its culture was not 'one monolithic block', and he was encouraged to find this point of contact.

From recruitment to commitment (the first two and a half months)

In these initial stages of the research, the grant holder became aware of some uneasiness amongst the research officers in a series of meetings held to establish plans and procedures for the project. Both research officers seemed to the grant holder most reluctant to make plans at all and he puts this down to the usual feelings of uncertainty which often accompany the early stages of any, even single discipline, projects. However, although he did not know this until some time later, one of our research officers was very near to leaving the project and the other was very unhappy. Various lessons for inter-disciplinary work can be learned from this.

The research officers perceived the grant holder to be quite ambivalent about adhering to the grounded theory philosophy which they espoused and which had been referred to in the research submission, although the proposed methodology had not been so closely defined in the grant submission as to suggest that an exclusively grounded theory approach would be used. The research officers insisted that they could not focus directly upon the accounting information flows and financial controls if they were expected to identify the part these mechanisms played in achieving organizational effectiveness. In their view, entry had to be made into the organization at almost any point and then working outwards from that initial contact there would be a gradual build-up of the 'organizational picture', following important strands as they emerged, checking back (often many times) with people visited previously. The research officers strongly resisted the grant holder's attempts to set up case-studies relating to information use at points he perceived to be important and to follow through the formal information flows as specified at the initial research stage in the proposal. They argued that if accounting was important to organizational success it would emerge without forcing attention on to it. It must be remembered that the grant holder did seek mature researchers to help him apply a research paradigm which had not previously been used in his own discipline.

On the other hand, the grant holder was beginning to wonder whether he had not made a grave error in appointing two 'alien' research officers who appeared determined to study the organizational culture, management styles, and processes in the social services and the police authority while also seeming indifferent as to whether accounting information and financial control processes were studied or not. This was felt more strongly with regard to the sociologist who had said openly that he expected it to take six to nine months before he would have begun to 'penetrate the organization' and, with only a two-year project, the grant holder felt this would leave him nearly half-way through the project before he knew whether accounting processes would figure largely in the results or not. Incidentally, somewhat later the Director of Social Services himself expressed such fears while, paradoxically, also calling for a more extensive study of social and political processes. Subsequent discussion amongst the research team had made it clear that while the grant holder and research officers all realized that their clients were both the SSRC and the local authority officers, the grant holder placed rather more emphasis on the former than did the research officers. The research officers were much more concerned about their ability to convince local authority personnel, whom they would meet on a day-to-day basis at all levels, that their work was relevant to the problems they faced, whether predominantly financial in nature or not.

The grant holder's reaction to this situation was quite *consciously* to overplay his hand and act in a 'heavy-handed manner' (obviously without telling the research officers). By repeatedly stressing that the project was supposed to be concerned with accounting and financial controls, he intended to make the researchers see that he would be highly displeased if the project ended with an analysis of organization effectiveness and internal social processes with no reference to accounting procedures. Also, to try to get a greater financial emphasis from the outset, he reasoned that he had spent a number of years working in local government finance and, therefore, was already partially 'grounded' and so he could give some advice on where to focus enquiries. Moreover, he saw the researchers' stance as 'purist'. While intellectually accepting grounded theory as the basic methodology, he questioned whether the 'grounding' had to be so absolute as they proposed; he constantly asked himself 'How grounded does grounded theory have to be?'

In addition, an academic in the accounting field who had just completed a course in organization behaviour joined the project, supposedly on an almost full-time basis, while on sabbatical at the School of Management. The grant holder observed this accountant become so fascinated with the fundamental principles and origins of phenomenology that he appeared to sink deeper and deeper into fundamental theory. While the grant holder was reading some of the literature and fully recognized the intrinsic satisfaction coming from complete mastery of the origins of the research procedure being used, he was also absolutely clear that he could not slide down that 'slippery slope' or that he would be completely in the hands of his researchers with no control. Indeed, he would be unlikely to emerge in time to operationalize these concepts before the project period was concluded.

It appears, in retrospect, that just at that point of time in the project, the research officers, having an affinity to each other in terms of research methodology, saw themselves as reinforcing each other against a grant holder whom they could see had no experience of 'grounded theory field-work' (although he had undertaken various projects involving field-work based on interviews of both the structured and semi-structured type) and who *in their perception*, while accepting their methodology on an intellectual plane, did not internalize it. At the same time the grant holder was concerned at the inflexible attitude that the research officers adopted and wondered (especially with regard to one research officer) whether they were motivated to study accounting and financial control questions at all. It would be easy to oversimplify this situation; it was not a question of a significant rift between grant holder and researchers. At times other coalitions formed between the grant holder and one of the researchers as the grant holder paid attention in turn to the police and then the social services side of the project. However, the researchers tended to support each other, with varying degrees of intensity, when the question of fundamental research methodology was debated.

The obvious solution to such an impasse would be better contact and communication between the grant holder and the research officers. However, frequent meetings and, at that time, almost daily social interaction *did* occur. Moreover, at no time were personal relations between the three researchers anything but most cordial. The problem seems to have stemmed from the different academic backgrounds of the researchers which for several months made unambiguous debate difficult and which possessed different notions of proof. The accountant grant holder, while wanting immersion of the research officers into the organization to get a deep understanding, and being prepared for much qualitative research, was still inclined to want more structure and more measurement than did the research officers. It was not a question of outright conflict about basic methodology; it was a matter of differences in emphasis and feelings of comfort and unease of first research officers and then grant holder as different emphases emerged with each 'side' not clearly understanding why the other was uncomfortable.

Even so, it may not have been disciplinary differences, *per se*, which alone caused the difficulties experienced. The grant holder was engaged in teaching, university duties, other research, and some other activities while supervising this project. Moreover, he already had some degree of 'acceptability' amongst peers in his discipline. While not relishing the thought of failure in a major project, his position was, perhaps, not so exposed as that of the research officers, both of whom had not previously had an extensive publication record. At that stage of the project they found themselves apparently at the direction of an alien professional who was questioning the extent to which they should employ the only contribution they had to make – their particular brand of research methodology. If the research officers gave that up, they perceived that they would be in a 'finance project'. The point is that not only would they have been uncomfortable in such a situation, they would have undertaken severe risks of becoming marginal to their own chosen career while clearly not becoming accountants.

Fortunately the project design had been loose enough to 'go either way', i.e. to become more structured with semi-planned interviews and case-studies (albeit on a repetitive basis over time) or more open-ended involving a marked emphasis on observation of both informal and formal processes in the organization as well as unstructured interviews. It can now be seen that the delay which prevented a start on the first stage of the project was, in fact, vital to success. Had steps already been taken to establish the project structure in liaison with bodies being researched, it would probably have been impossible to have it changed and, perhaps, the research officers would not have joined the project at all, hence preventing a truly inter-disciplinary approach.

The turning-point for the project, as far as the research officers were concerned, came with the drafting and acceptance of the 'research contract' with representatives of the police authority and the social services and treasury department. The grant holder had decided from the outset that a formal document needed to be drawn up which would provide as explicitly as possible common expectations as regards research topics, process of investigation, access arrangements, and publication rights. This would serve as a basis of negotiation (persuasion) if difficulties with access, etc. occurred later on; although it was recognized that the authorities being researched could eject the researchers whenever they liked. As the drawing up of such a contract was fundamental to many organization behaviour projects, the task of drawing up the first draft of the 'contract' was given to the research officer from that field – the grant holder's confidence in the research officer grew as he saw that the contents of the contract was consistent with one or two texts on organization behaviour research (for example, Beckard and Harris 1977). In retrospect the monitoring of a skilled researcher by reference to textbooks seems absurd, but it highlights the problem of exercising control over researchers who come from different disciplines. This is problematic in particular when none of the researchers already know each other and so have gradually to negotiate some sort of order and responsibility for the project while building some confidence in each other's academic ability; the possession of paper qualifications was of little value in providing such confidence.

The research officer used this opportunity to ensure that a commitment to 'a grounded theory approach' was written into the contract document formally as the sole method to be used. At the same time this document recognized formally that the thrust of the project was to examine the way financial control was exercised and accounting information used, but stressing that this must be done within a review of the total context of organization effectiveness. The latter element also gave the grant holder rather more confidence in the research officers' motivation. He now saw that each research officer appeared far more committed to an action programme to which all three researchers could relate. No doubt the feeling of having a say in planning the research at a senior level by liaising (along with the grant holder) with the County Treasurer, Director of Social Services and Assistant Chief Constable also gave the research officers a greater feeling that they had some responsibility and control over their own future activities.

Two other events were probably more fundamental as a 'turning point' for the grant holder. First, the younger research officer agreed to his suggestion that the officer should read some of the 'behavioural accounting' literature to see what he thought of it. This officer's readiness to do this indicated clearly that he was prepared to make an effort to come to grips with management accounting processes. The same officer, aided by the visitor spending his sabbatical in the school, also carried out some enquiries relating directly to accounting information flows in the police authority. The sociology researcher, however, did not appear keen to read any accounting literature at that stage of the project, being more concerned to 'acclimatise himself' in the organization. The grant holder embarked on a series of joint interviews with this particular officer and provided some direction to financial matters in the enquiries. More particularly it helped the grant holder determine how far he could rely on the research officer.

The grant holder also now recognizes that he under-estimated the difficulties the research officers faced in getting to grips with accounting procedures. He knew from his experience that management accounting procedures were very straightforward in local authorities, involving little or no sophisticated 'accounting technology'. However, to the research officers, any accounting processes were seen to involve skills and a language they did not possess and, especially in the sociology researcher's case, there was a definite early reluctance to take his research in to the treasurer's department. (This was later more than adequately put right.)

The grant holder now recognizes the need for a far more explicit process of negotiating order and responsibilities when multi-disciplinary teams are involved. In addition, the need for establishing a means of controlling the project probably needs more delicate and explicit treatment where one has a mix of disciplinary backgrounds and activities in the team, than the relatively straightforward scheduling process which is probably adequate in most single-discipline projects.

Fieldwork

Beyond the 'contract stage', difficulties still occurred, but the researchers were now all committed to the project, saw it as a good one with many possible developments, and were enthusiastic about the work. Moreover, following the grounded theory philosophy, the grant holder was seen to be amenable to modifying research theories in response to data collected, although there was still sufficient coverage of the initial proposals. This gave the researchers added commitment both to him and to the project.

Following Oleson and Whittaker (1967), the subsequent research process can be divided into four sub-sections and each will be described briefly in turn.

The surface encounter

This stage refers to the initial attempts by the researchers to gain entry to the organization and there are various contextual points of interest here. Formally, entry had been agreed for the grant holder before applying for the grant, but the researchers still had to establish their own acceptability and it became clear that there must be some mutually satisfactory relationship between the body researched and the researcher and that academic discipline and previous background may be vital in gaining entry and determining acceptability.

In terms of research acceptability it appears that there are (at least) two dimensions which need to be considered: 'value fit' and 'personal fit'. By 'value fit' one means the degree to which the field researcher feels able to demonstrate some apparent sympathy with official goals. In the case of the researcher working in the social services this provided no problem – indeed the danger was rather that he might over-identify with them; this is something of which he is quite aware and attempts to guard against. Moreover, that research officer seemed to find it fairly straightforward to form 'warm' personal relationships with various social services officers, although he was 'mocked' by the Director for his unconventional dress.[4] In the case of the other research officer, he felt no previous 'value fit' but found his sporting passions gave him immediate 'rapport' with most policemen. Even so, the message was passed through that he would have to cut his hair much shorter if he wanted to get the co-operation of senior police officials and, while not getting rid of his beard, he did modify his appearance and dress to some extent. While the question of appearance and dress was, therefore, raised by both social services and the police and, in any case, some effort was made to comply with expectations, dress is only part of 'personal fit' and lack of appropriate dress may not be as important as other aspects of 'personal and value fit'.

It seems clear then that a potential always exists for the culture amongst social researchers, which stresses independence and role playing, to be regarded as threatening by an alien professional. In this instance, the fact that the research was conducted from within a school of management (rather than a department of sociology or social psychology) and that the team leader in all important negotiations was a professor from an apparently 'hard discipline', perhaps overcame initial doubts about the research officers – at least in so far as it gained initial entry for them; especially as formal agreement to entry was negotiated by the grant holder in his capacity as an accountant before it was known whom he would employ as research officers. Informal co-operation could still have been withheld, but at least there was already a written promise to 'give the researchers a chance'.

Another factor which arose on entry was the luke-warm attitude of the police to the project. Comments were made that indicated that they felt it was 'the County Treasurer's project' and that they had had the project foisted upon them. It is quite possible that a direct approach from the university, even as a school of management, would not have succeeded in gaining entry. However, once again, it is one thing 'to gain entry' and another to gain full co-operation, and the lack of a felt need for this research on the part of the police officers certainly placed stress on the research officer carrying out that side of the field work.

Proffering and inviting

Once some acceptable base was established in each organization, the research officers began the mutual exchange with the organization members – this involves offering definitions of 'self' while asking for such definitions from those researched. While both researchers were personally well committed to the project by this stage, their confidence waxed and waned. This was due partly to memories of the earlier difficulties in research design and the realization that the subjects being researched, who had some guiding power over the research through a steering committee which had been established, were also anticipating a more structured approach with initial direct emphasis on accounting information. In addition, the police attitudes, initially of a forebearing rather than positive nature, raised doubts about how far they would go along with the work. These pressures created an apprehension amongst the two research officers and several small events were interpreted as 'straws in the wind'. For example, failure to be given the time of an important meeting was viewed by the researcher of the police as hostility to the project. Similarly the failure by county council officials to inform the researchers that they had taken away the room initially allocated to the researchers (though little used) and given it to the NALGO branch representative was seen as added emphasis of the weak power base of the team and an indication of indifference at a time when few firm working relationships had been established. The grant holder's assurance that the researchers were over-reacting was interpreted as a lack of awareness of the difficulties of gaining a working base in this type of work. He had always achieved entry for his own style of research in the past and felt that there was little difference in establishing a basis of trust and co-operation in this project from work he had undertaken before, some of which involved data of a secretive nature (probably more so than the data requested in this project). The research officers, however, were perhaps partly conditioned by difficulties faced by other sociologists and social psychologists in establishing 'credibility' amongst businessmen and practitioners. In the event, both incidents were shown to be oversights quite unrelated to basic attitudes towards the research. Nevertheless, they highlight the way in which researchers from different research cultures can interpret events differently, and how this can lead to extra strains within the team.

The 'turning points' when the research officers believed that the social services and police were committed to the project occurred as follows. The hierarchy in one service was forced to reprimand one researcher for showing what was interpreted as being a lack of respect for committee members by a breach of etiquette at one meeting. A few days afterwards a senior official followed the 'stick' with a 'carrot' and explained that, while he sometimes had little confidence in the way public representatives took decisions, a deferential role presentation oiled the mechanism of local government re-source allocation. If the researcher recognized this, he was to be allowed to attend a closed and secret team session with the service organization.

In the other service, the crucial turning point occurred some time later when the research officer was virtually summoned to appear to present some initial research ideas to the organization's own research section. These ideas had been written down for a steering committee meeting which was to occur two days later. The researcher saw this as a clear sign that his presence was about to be terminated. Perhaps it was, but after an intensive session with the organization's research unit response was that his proposals were very warmly welcomed. From that point on there seemed to be a recognition throughout the organization that time should be found for the researcher, although the interviewees had almost always insisted beforehand that their time was scarce.

Incidentally, both research officers have had to be very flexible in terms of times and places that they could conduct interviews. This has involved weekends and one interview with a public representative in a car parked in a remote place!

Selecting and modifying

After mutual and general acceptance of each other by researchers and organization members being researched, there seemed to be a stage where a reciprocal selection of meaningful and viable positions of each other's roles occurred. The researchers and the researched gradually established boundaries as to what could be tackled and what could not; who would help, when, and in what way.

In line with the grounded theory approach this was the key stage for setting the direction of the research. The organization officers and members were very willing to co-operate where they perceived the research to focus on something meaningful for them or the organization – in other words where it related to their own problems in being efficient and effective. The rich flood of data along these lines and the impact of the recent change in government forced the researchers to redefine the emphasis of the research. While information on the use of accounting information and the exercise of finan-cial control was still a main goal of the project, the process by which resources were allocated through the budget was itself seen to be of crucial importance and failure to pursue this research theme in more depth than planned would have certainly resulted in the researchers being seen as of marginal significance.

Once again the different research traditions of different disciplines could create difficulties for a multi-disciplinary team. In this project this problem had already been foreseen and to a large extent resolved at the beginning of the project, as described earlier. Nevertheless, the problem still arose as to how far the budget should be analysed as a social and political process. The SSRC had indicated that some attention to such questions would be needed. Indeed it was fairly obvious that the use of information in a local authority would depend upon social and political processes, but the grant holder was unsure as *to what extent* the social/political interactions had to be studied and described in order to do this. It became clear that there was no easy answer to such a question on a priori basis; one has to explore the elements seen to be important in determining effectiveness and see where it leads, backing off if the research brief is being violated too much. However, a grant holder can only allow such an approach if he trusts the research officers' own judgement on when to proceed and when to back off. Unfortunately, trust does not occur just because it is needed and, with multi-disciplinary work, it may take care and effort to create despite the desire 'to believe'.

The grant holder agreed to adopt a fairly liberal interpretation of the project boundaries, but again a contingent factor emerged from one of the departments being researched which insisted that the social and political processes of the resource allocation system must be fully probed. Of course, this particular department saw some benefit to itself from such a study and the conventional response from researchers would be that 'we are not interested in that' and that 'we must not be "used"'. However, non-compliance with this request could have meant exclusion from topics which the team did want to research. It must, therefore, be recognized that, with this style of field-work, there may have to be negotiation of research boundaries with the organization researched and events can occur in mid-project which call for boundary modification. However, this must not be allowed to compromise the researcher's adherence to strict impartiality in terms of data collection and analysis: there can be no negotiation at that level.

Stabilizing and sustaining researcher/researched relationships

The team feels that it took about nine months before this stage of the research was reached. From that point no major problems have been encountered and co-operation by officers in all departments and the few public representatives approached, has been very open and warm. The research officers are now fully integrated into the authority's managerial processes. Indeed both research officers are now 'told off' if they occasionally miss a meeting, as though the organization officers have an obligation to see that the researchers 'do their work properly'. These meetings include the internal management committees and sub-committees of both the police and social services which are usually closed meetings – for example, the treasurer's representative can only attend if invited and there are occasions where the nature of agenda items would mean that he definitely would not be invited.

At present, all is running smoothly except that, with local authority officers and members seeming to want to co-operate, there will be a time problem in completing all the analyses. Moreover, the researchers now seem, at last, to have become a team reinforcing each other rather than reacting to, and sometimes from, each other and moving back to keep some strong contact with their parent discipline.

Finally, it should be stressed that, while the above sections reflect the general flow of research role-making, the boundaries between each stage are fuzzy; they may even exist simultaneously. Consequently, researchers and researched may not experience the phases simultaneously and such discrepancies may also be influenced by structural and situational factors. Moreover, with a research method like that employed in this project, the researcher is expected to become part of the organization (albeit retaining his own independent research stance). In this setting not only must the researcher successfully conduct his research role, but his life role as it is apparent to the organization, may also affect the research outcome. In addition, through near-constant immersion the researcher cannot separate the formal research process from the informal interactions. There is no way the researcher can justify 'switching off' over comments exchanged over lunch in contrast to revelations in a formal interview as the researcher's objective is to discover what happens. It follows that even if the relatively formal research roles of researcher and researched are 'in phase', there can still be discrepancies between phases of life roles. Both types of roles need to be managed successfully and particularly in the last two phases of the research process outlined above.

TENTATIVE CONCLUSIONS AND EVALUATION

Observations from the project description suggest various aspects which should be considered if undertaking research into research activity in the social sciences. At the level of the research process generally, there were clear contextual influences at a number of stages in the project, where the impact of the SSRC, the School of Management, the professional orientation of the research officers and grant holder and the organizations being researched has been shown. In addition, the change of government early in the project radically affected the willingness of everyone to talk about his or her problems. In times of crisis everyone needs a friend and a platform. However, there are also possible lessons to be derived for the organization of future *multi-disciplinary* research teams.

First, considerable problems can occur within a research team when a relatively senior member of one discipline tries to import research paradigms from another discipline, if the research officers coming from that discipline have not had a direct hand in designing the research on a relatively equal footing with the grant holder. Failing the ability to do this before obtaining a grant, there should be the clear recognition that the development of the research design and topic will be a first major stage of the research process itself and that tight adherence to a pre-determined research proposal will probably limit the success achieved and may even be disastrous. In the grant submission there should be a greater emphasis in setting bounds around the research field rather than precise hypotheses and methodology. If the grant-giving body feels uncomfortable with this, it would probably be better to arrange a more sophisticated scheme of feedback with the researcher as a means of retaining control rather than insist on a priori hypothesis formulation. To its credit the SSRC did not insist on a tighter design at the outset of this research.

Next, just saying that the researchers should have an equal say in research design does not go far enough. There has to be a clear recognition of why each has joined the project, what risks each faces in terms of peer assessment and career development and the ambiguous nature of communication which can occur at the outset. Terms apparently quite clear and precise to one may hold many hidden meanings for the other. In a single-subject project such matters can usually be taken for granted, but in multi-discipline projects there must be greater scope for negotiation. In order to get the consensus needed for team building, one needs to have each researcher's perception of the negotiation boundaries, the negotiation process and his fears openly discussed. Even open discussion may not guarantee a researcher shifting his fundamental beliefs about research procedures, carefully nurtured for years by his training and background which may vitally affect his self-respect. This may suggest that when new multi-disciplinary lines are established, work is likely to be more successful if there is the explicit intention to import research paradigm from one discipline 'lock, stock and barrel' to apply to problems in another discipline which has had little experience of them before, rather than attempting to merge research philosophies to produce new inter-disciplinary paradigms. People from different disciplines need to learn more about each other before more fundamental changes can occur. This also suggests, perhaps, that multi-disciplinary projects can run into considerable difficulties (greater than those encountered in this project) if the research officers who are expected to co-operate more closely come from disciplines with different research cultures. At least in this project there was a need to solve one major difference of focus (between grant holder and research officers). If a systems analyst had been appointed, instead of one of the research officers, the whole project might have fragmented.

The contract drawn up specifically for getting agreement between the researchers and the researched in fact probably played a more important part in creating research team consensus. For multi-disciplinary teams, especially where the grant submission was made by one person or more from a single discipline, a formal 'internal contract' may focus attention on potential misunderstandings at the outset of the project. Moreover, while the close physical proximity of staff rooms and frequent meetings did not avoid such problems in this project, it is certain that the problems would have been far more severe, perhaps insurmountable, if it had been otherwise.

A single-discipline grant holder should also recognize that he is dependent on trust. He will be more at the mercy of his research officers than in a single-discipline project. It is in everyone's interests if actions are taken to build up this trust as quickly as possible. The 'internal contract' is probably not sufficient for this purpose. Where doubts exist, the grant holder must be prepared to enter into the field-work fairly extensively in the early stages of the project on a joint basis with the research officer. This will aid the building up of understanding and then the grant holder can back off from field-work later on. Of course, joint field-work may result in the lack of trust being heightened; in which case it is better to identify this as soon as possible and face up to the problem. Fortunately, this did not occur in this project.

On appointment of staff, it seems imperative for the single-discipline grant holder to have advice from a senior person from the research officers' own discipline. The grant holder may think that he knows exactly what he wants, but he may be unaware of subtle distinctions between different schools of thought in other disciplines. Fortunately, such advice was close at hand and willingly given in this project. It might be desirable for such an adviser/consultant to continue into the project up to the 'internal contract' stage. This did not occur in this project, but it could have helped with initial difficulties.

Next, all three researchers recognized that the building of a team and relationships with the researched organization were dependent on a series of interactions, but all participants have little difficulty in pointing to single events (turning points) which settled their doubts. A study of 'turning points' in other projects may indicate key matters of concern to grant holders/subordinates of different disciplines. The notion of a 'turning point' may also suggest that some sign clearly visible to all (i.e. to oneself and known to be visible to others in the team) is crucial in building teams from different disciplines.

Explicit consideration should also be given to the extent of the value gap which may exist between the researcher and the researched organization. Similarly, entry may be better negotiated by some members rather than others as the organization may have stereotyped ideas as to certain disciplines, which may also be enforced by appearances. Some types of establishments, perhaps only by virtue of their name, may be able to negotiate entry easier than others.

In multi-disciplinary teams, researchers may react differently to the pull an organization attempts to command over researchers. Co-option of research and researcher into the 'world view' of the organization and its command structure is a common problem for researchers, but in multi-disciplinary projects there may be no common basis to enforce each researcher's standpoint. In this project the grant holder clearly has a more problem-solving/policy-making orientation to his broad area of research than the other researchers.

Members of multi-disciplinary teams who come from accounting or economic backgrounds may well find it difficult to internalize the premise that the researcher can never switch off, as his field-work tradition is of a different variety. As a consequence, researchers from these traditions may divide time up between 'research time' and 'private time' when they are in the field and fail to recognize information given in an informal setting. This can take the form of jokes, attitudes, and physical gestures as well as direct statements which would probably be taken at face value unless trained to note and relate to the total task and position of the subject. Certainly the sociologist researcher has found his lunches in the staff canteen with professionals from the social services department to be the time and place where many useful cues can be obtained. The formal interview, structured or semi-structured, may induce a guarded response and this will probably be even more marked in a written response to a postal questionnaire. At informal gatherings, guards may be relaxed. The accountant, for example, investigating personal perceptions of organizational effectiveness, must realize the doubtful correspondence between verbal statements and overt acts. The research technology traditionally employed in accounting scarcely recognizes this and makes few or no proposals for overcoming it despite the behavioural impact of this work.

A problem not yet faced, but foreseen, affects disclosure of information. With the heavy emphasis on this research on observation of officers and local authority members in informal and formal settings, as well as frequent interviewing and re-interviewing of the same people, a wealth of information is being collected of a highly sensitive nature. In fact many of the researched do not seem to realize how vulnerable they can be if private knowledge becomes public through publications. This problem can arise in a single-discipline setting and will probably be dealt with mainly in this project by each researcher (the two research officers and the grant holder) self-censuring the material they have, i.e. perhaps even from each other. Moreover, the police authority and social services have rights to examine documents before publication. However, in disciplines so divergent as sociology and account-ancy, the conceptual division between 'public' and 'private' information is of dubious value and may prove to be another cultural difference. The grant holder and the research officers recognized this problem early in the field-work. It remains to be seen whether several difficulties will arise and, if so, how they will be resolved.

Finally, it should be recognized that the process described in this chapter refers to setting up the project and essentially finding out how things work. If the project proceeds to an action stage (and it is not clear yet whether it will) there is the possibility that the differences between academic disciplines and cultures may become even more problematic in terms of gaining client organization acceptability. It is one thing to be 'oggled' and quite another to go beyond that!

To conclude we quote from the work of Benton who carried out statistical tests based on questionnaires sent to eighty-four professionals involved in six multi-disciplinary projects on the Colorado State University campus. At the end of his article he says:

> the most important factor related in inter-disciplinary is team-work – a willingness to co-operate.

and

> success of IDR (inter-disciplinary research) is not guaranteed by mere assemblage of an impressive set of names ... if the results are to show a large degree of inter-disciplinarity, the project has unique management requirements.
>
> (Benton 1976)

Given the virtual non-existence of descriptions of multi-disciplinary work, it was thought that some exposure of our experiences and aspects of both our managerial success and our mis-management might be helpful in providing flesh instead of the bare bones of statistics. In this way, if others follow suit, insight into the best practices for managing multi-disciplinary projects may emerge.

NOTES

1 Reprinted with permission from *Accounting, Organizations and Society* 5, 2 (1980), Pergamon Press PLC.

2 Social science journal editors, which do not already do so, might therefore consider whether they ought not to urge their reviewers to check carefully whether the hypotheses tested have themselves been adequately based on real world events rather than desk-bound deductions. It is stressed immediately that desk-bound

deduction is *not* to be despised; indeed it should be encouraged and is a vital part of the academic's role, but should tests based upon theories established that way only be published if they show significant relationships?

3 Founder of the Chicago School which played a big role in the formulation of the sociology of work.

4 Very lightweight suits acquired by the researcher in a previous employment at an East African university.

REFERENCES

Baldamus, N. (1972) 'The role of discoveries in social science', in T. Shanin (ed.), *The Rules of the Game*, London: Tavistock.

Baritz, L. (1965) *The Servants of Power*, New York: John Wiley.

Beckhard, R. and Harris R. T. (1977), *Organizational Transactions: Managing Complex Change*, Reading, MA: Addison Wesley.

Bell, C. and Newby, H (1977), 'Introduction', *Doing Sociological Research*, London: Allen & Unwin.

Benton, D. A. (1976), 'Management and effectiveness measures for inter-disciplinary research', *S. R. A. Journal*, Spring.

Glaser, B. G. and Strauss, A. L. (1968) *The Discovery of Grounded Theory*, New York: Weidenfeld & Nicholson.

Marcuse, R. (1965), *Reason and Revolution*, London: Routledge & Kegan Paul.

Oleson, V. and Whittaker, E. (1967) 'Role-making in participant observation', *Human Organisation*, Winter.

Platt, J. (1976) *The Realities of Research*, Brighton: University of Sussex.

Roth, J. A. (1966) 'Hired hand research', *The American Sociologist*, August.

19 Researching in teams: lessons from experience

M. King, R. Lee, J. Piper, and
J. Whittaker

This chapter is a short record of the experiences of a research team based in the Department of Management Studies at Loughborough University. The main objective of the chapter is to provide a single case-study about group research which may be of interest and use to those currently engaged in, or about to embark on, such an exercise. It is also hoped that we will be able to provide some level of analysis of our experiences which will not only help practitioners but also those who study research processes. Third, it is possible that the act of reporting and analysing our experiences will actually lead us to better practice within the current project.

When this chapter was written, the team had been working together for eighteen months and it was our intention to revise this paper at appropriate times during the remaining two years of the project.

Little will be said here about the detail of the research itself except insofar as it is necessary to explain events. The research team is engaged on a management research project involving case studies within commercial organizations. Although those who know us will be aware of the specific area in which we are working and the sponsoring organization, since we have tried to be as frank as possible about our activities, we feel it necessary to retain at least some measure of anonymity. This will be less important when the research findings have demonstrated the worth of our efforts.

There are two obvious ways to structure a chapter such as this. It could be done in terms of issues such as:

What methodologies work best?
What are the problems of communications?
How should conflicts be managed?
How do you manage time?

and so on. These are all vital issues which will not be ignored. However, we are aware of the temptation to whitewash our failings and fall into the trap of offering prescriptions when we are not qualified to do so. Therefore we have chosen to tell the story of our project so far in chronological order whilst attempting, at this stage, only a limited analysis.

Seven stages in the project's development have been identified:

- obtaining the funds
- getting going
- stuck in neutral
- getting going again
- finding second gear
- high revving in second
- finding third, or is it top?

We make no apology for the motoring analogy, which we feel is entirely appropriate. Every new research team will have to start as learners and improve through a series of developmental stages.

OBTAINING THE FUNDS

Our recollections of this vital first stage in the process are already rather blurred. Ours was not a meeting of minds which spontaneously arose out of existing research passions. We had all been departmental colleagues for some years and had collaborated in different groups on various projects. We were all experienced researchers but the level of prior involvement with team research within the group was limited.

The sponsoring body advertised for proposals to do research within their specific area of interest. One individual asked another if he was interested in responding, they contacted a third and then approached the fourth and final member. Choices were made on the basis of technical knowledge which was perceived to be appropriate at the time, they were not made on the basis of friendships or personalities. At least, they were not positively made in that way. However, there were exclusions of certain individuals who, whilst perceived as technically appropriate, were seen as potentially uncooperative or lacking in commitment to work with others.

Our lack of positive focus on personality may help to explain some of the conflicts which emerged later, but we are now convinced that our, albeit imperfect, use of expertise rather than other considerations as the primary basis for selection has been a beneficial factor in the team's longer term development.

The short time available before application meant that there was little time to reflect and work creatively. Instead, we drew on our previous experience and expertise, and after a few discussions parcelled out tasks to individuals. The final document was a careful welding together of these individual contributions, which is not to say it was not a strong proposal, it was! We had to defend it at interview with the funding body and were chosen from the shortlist of four.

GETTING GOING

After the initial elation had worn off the doubts began to set in. The prize which we had won was a large research grant plus a great deal of work, plus, we soon began to realize, a large number of headaches.

There was a short honeymoon period before the money arrived. During this two months we *thought* there were only two major problems to tackle:

1 Converting a convincing research proposal into a practical plan of action; and
2 Recruiting a research assistant.

From proposal to plan

We were all agreed from our previous experience that it pays to be clear at the outset about concepts and how they are linked together in a conceptual framework. In the proposal we had used certain technical and common usage terms as though they were straightforward and unambiguous. It soon became clear that we each had different interpretations and when we began to consider practical problems of identification and measurement these would then have to be resolved.

Even more fundamentally problematic were the different views of the business organization which we brought to the project. None of us represented extreme conflict or unitarist perspectives nor were any of us dogmatically attached to social systems or social action frames of reference, but there were awkward differences which emerged along these and other dimensions. Perhaps inevitably, this was one of the factors which drew personality issues out into the open. This will be returned to later.

To say that the honeymoon was spoiled by endless discussions of a philosophical and methodological nature would be wrong; many of them were intellectually valuable and stimulating, and some have made a lasting contribution to the project. Nevertheless we all now look back with some feeling that time and energy could have been used more effectively.

Recruiting a research assistant

We discussed briefly the sort of qualities and qualifications we would like the research assistant to bring to the project. For the salary we could offer it was obvious that no multi-disciplinary professor would be likely to apply!

We devoted a full day to the interview process and took time to get to know the candidates. After much consideration, and bearing in mind the qualities of the short-listed candidates, we decided that we did not need technical expertise because that was already present within the team in abundance. What we needed was an experienced researcher with the ability to learn and whose personality would not add to the tensions within the group.

STUCK IN NEUTRAL

January 1986, the official start of the project, came and went, the research assistant was in post and the funds were available. Why were we making slow progress despite considerable amounts of effort?

There were three main problems at that time:

1 The decision-making issue.
2 The intellectual issue.
3 The learning curve.

The decision-making issue

Charles Handy (1976) discusses four phases in the development of groups:

Forming
Storming
Norming
Performing

We had now moved out of the 'forming' stage and were struggling with the storm. No formal decision-making process for the project had been established. Were we a democracy? Was there anyone with all-round ability who would be acceptable as a 'leader'? Probably all of us would have liked the title and perhaps it would have helped the project if one individual could have clearly emerged to take the reins. But this was absolutely impossible given the multi-disciplinary basis of the project, the equal standing of the team members, and the nature of the promotion process within the university.

To avoid what might have become an acrimonious issue we made a decision to work together on the basis of discussion and consensus. Given the dynamics of our group this was the only possible way forward. It may have served to slow us down in some ways but none of us regret the decision and we feel it has prevented us taking actions which might have lead to less effective research in the long run. There is no doubt that the decision to operate on the basis of consensus lead to a few delays in the early stages; however it also lead to a strong feeling of shared responsibility which has been a major positive influence on the project. We should note at this stage that the decision was not made with these positive benefits in mind – it was made because it was the only way we could agree to work together.

The decision-making issue, combined with some frustration at our intellectual struggle, served to highlight personality differences. Emotions became heightened too easily and there was too little listening. All of us suffered a lowering of enthusiasm and morale.

The intellectual issue

The continuing discussions about research frameworks and key concepts were both stimulating and disheartening. Perhaps with more skilled management of the process we could have been more concise in our efforts. There is no doubt that we indulged ourselves in trying to resolve conceptual points at this early stage which would have been better left until they were confronted in the field. We were trying to cross too many bridges before we had even set foot outside the door. As individuals we would not have prevaricated, but because we were working in a group we had fallen into a trap of believing that everything had to be properly understood and agreed before we started field-work.

The learning curve

By now we were all struggling individually to overcome our deficiencies in one or more of the disciplines relevant to the project. Why were we not making more efforts to use the strengths within the team to teach each other? The answer lies in the foregoing discussion, we were clearly *not* a team.

If *we* were struggling at this time, pity the poor research assistant. We all had strengths in at least one discipline; for her there were several new disciplines as well as the specifics of the project. We had perhaps paid too little attention to the problems which she had in grasping all this in a short time.

The picture at this stage should by now be fairly clear. Lots of effort being made, much time being spent, but not much happening which the outside world would benefit from. We were stuck in neutral and something had to change.

GETTING GOING AGAIN

There was no instructor to help us find first gear, we had to work out something for ourselves. Even if we could not agree on a complete conceptual framework at this stage we could still get out into the world and start gathering some data.

During the, albeit incomplete, conceptual discussions we generated a list of hypotheses which we would like to examine. Some of these came from our individual studies, some emerged during group discussions, and others were drawn from the literature. We brainstormed and created categories of hypotheses. It seems that we were in agreement about the sort of questions we should be trying to answer; this was a considerable leap forward.

Methodologists may debate the merits of this approach, but we believe it will prove effective. Clearly there is a conceptual framework underlying the hypotheses; this may not be entirely complete or coherent but it can be (is being) identified and developed during the field-work. Its completion is not possible before the research is started and its detailed identification is not a prerequisite.

Once we had established our hypotheses we worked on interview schedules and other data collection instruments; at the same time we were now warming up our pilot case. We deliberately selected a company which some of the team had worked with before and which we knew would be tolerant if we had to make repeated requests for data as we developed both our concepts and our instruments.

FINDING SECOND GEAR

So the field-work commenced, we were in first gear and moving, albeit rather slowly. Progress was difficult because we were uncertain of the research concepts as well as the research process. This was normal and would happen with any individual project. However, with a group project there are additional difficulties related to:

1 Literature
2 Communications
3 Meetings

There are, of course, related subjects, but we will discuss them separately.

Literature

How should we cope with the vast quantity of potentially relevant literature? All researchers are insecure about this, but when a project is interdisciplinary and involves a multi-disciplinary group the problems are much greater.

We started simply by circulating everything to everybody. Apart from the inevitable bottlenecks it became clear that there were other problems. Many specialist papers were almost unintelligible to some team members and even when they could be understood what was to be done with relevant ideas? And anyway time is short and we would spend most of our research time reading if we were serious about keeping up with all the literature. For a period all papers were circulated and salient points were noted and kept in a folder. The research assistant was asked to try to extract key points and summarize them before circulation. When they eventually returned she was to make a note of all relevant points and file these under the hypothesis to which they referred.

This was fine in principle but it overlooked two problems. We were too busy to read all the papers and the research assistant was not yet sufficiently expert to identify and record the salient points.

It has to be said that this problem has not been completely resolved and will require further effort in the near future as we pursue the publication of our early findings.

Communications

A group project by definition, involves communication problems. Team members have to let each other know about both practical and conceptual developments. With five in a group, four of whom are part-time and extremely busy with other work, often of high priority, communication has to be a managed process. This realization arrived quite early; the complete solution is still awaited but progress has been made.

One obvious method of communication is meetings. These are important and will be discussed below. But meetings are time consuming, difficult to arrange, and not always appropriate.

The simple memorandum is a useful device but is too easy to put on one side. We soon learned to use 'the assertive memo', which states specifically what type of response is sought, when it is wanted, and what will be done if no response is received.

Another useful device has been the 'position paper'. It has been necessary to produce a series of written statements about our methodology, or, more usually, parts of it. These have mainly been restatements of the hypotheses, discussions of the rationale behind them, and deeper papers in pursuit of an overall conceptual frame-work. Some have simply been comments on our use of particular terms and ideas.

In the long term these are one of the best measures of the project's progress. Our confidence in the project has been closely related to our level of satisfaction with the current state of these position papers *plus* our contentment with the 'operational instruments' in use at any point in time.

By 'operational instruments' is meant the introductory letters, background questionnaires, interview schedules, transcript formats, and so on, which guide us when we are gathering data. These have to be continually refined and are a powerful cohesive force – provided we are happy with them. One problem is that any change which one individual feels should be made in terms of either concepts or data collection has inevitable ramifications for a number of documents. They thus tend to be always slightly out of phase; a rewording of a hypothesis means that an interview question requires modification, a clarification of a concept requires the reformulation of a hypothesis, and so on. This is inevitable, it is progress, but it makes it very important to date documents and make sure everyone accepts and is working with latest versions.

Meetings

We had all spent plenty of time in meetings before embarking on this project and considered ourselves pretty good at managing them. By this stage of the project, however, we realized that we would have to improve our skills.

There are plenty of excellent texts on the management of meetings (see, for example, Fletcher 1983) and we will not attempt to repeat their material here. For the most part they are full of common-sense prescriptions such as:

- Always have a chairperson
- Have a clear agenda
- Manage time
- Allocate tasks

and so on. Simplistic maybe, but if you are agreed on your objectives and are prepared to leave personality clashes at the door, they work. We have made great efforts in this respect and have found that well-managed meetings can be both pleasurable and effective.

We now always set strict time limits on meetings but nevertheless they can still take up a lot of time. To reduce the time spent by individuals we often work without the whole team present, it is too easy to just assume that the whole team is required for every discussion.

HIGH REVVING IN SECOND

In retrospect we probably spent about four months in second gear! The project was moving forward, two cases were almost completed and two others underway, but we were still putting in a disproportionately large effort for our return.

We hoped that our techniques would become sharper, our knowledge of the intellectual and methodological issues would improve, and things would happen faster. Undoubtedly there was some increase in pace but nowhere near what was needed if we were to achieve our target without five nervous breakdowns.

At this point we had our first major progress meeting with the research committee of the sponsoring body. We hoped to persuade them to accept fewer case-studies. They were adamant, however, that twenty was the target; the draft cases received were excellent but they wanted a wide spread of organizations to be covered.

Our discussions with the sponsors were invaluable. On the train home we thrashed out the issues which had emerged. Were we being seduced into consultancy? Were we going into too much depth? Could we improve our procedures? To the first question a clear 'no'. To the second, 'yes', but we could not simply produce a series of superficial cases. Small savings in time by researching some hypotheses in less detail could, however, be made. The third question was dealt with as part of a much larger issue. On that train journey we resolved to cease being a research group and to become a research team.

FINDING THIRD, OR IS IT TOP?

When it became clear to us that we could not reduce our obligations we were forced to look again at our activities. We had made progress in important ways but we could not claim to be highly effective as a *team*. It is not that we were unaware of the major benefits of a team-working philosophy, it is just that the research situation can be an exceptionally difficult one in which to make it happen. But all managers say the same about their situations! The truth is that, as with most areas in management, the theory is much easier than the practice. One way in which the theory oversimplifies is in assuming that people want to work together; well now at last we had realized we would have to if we were to fulfil our commitments.

TEAM-WORKING

As with meetings, the basic ideas of team-working are simple. The guidebook we used to initiate our development was that of Hastings *et al.* (1986). Their model did not fit our situation exactly: nonetheless it was extremely useful. We held a superteam meeting and resolved to make some significant changes:

- clearer objectives
- managing the outside
- better planning
- being a team

Establishing *clearer objectives* involved identifying who were the main parties with a stake in the team's performance and being aware of commonalities, differences, and conflicts. The main parties were: ourselves as individuals, the sponsoring body, our university department, the case companies, the academic world, and, of course, ourselves as a research team pursuing a reputation. A long look at the different criteria by which these groups would judge us was most enlightening.

We identified our own hitherto hidden agendas. We also highlighted where we had been pursuing academic objectives which fell outside the requirements of our sponsoring body. *We agreed on the paramount importance of the research team, as an academic institution which could serve all the other parties.* These steps lead to an acceptance that decisions should be made for the good of the team. We did not all forswear our personal goals but we asserted the need to sacrifice them on occasion for the long-term advantages which the team's success would confer on us all.

Discussing our objectives thus had several useful effects; it lead to some redirecting and simplification of our research process. It served to clear the air, and it had a positive impact on morale – not knowing where you are going makes you less happy about hurrying there!

Managing the outside more effectively requires the process of clarifying performance criteria described above to have been carried out, but there is more to it. A major issue is that of *image*. We agreed that wherever possible we would all try to be ambassadors for the project and the institution. We also resolved to take positive steps to publicize our achievements and identified key ways of communicating progress to particular individuals and groups.

One of the consequences of clearer objectives is the potential for *better planning*. We developed a simple but comprehensive planning chart which could be used as the basis for discussion at our progress review meetings. This chart shows when activities have to be started and finished and who is responsible for what. Planning is inevitably a problem with a complex three-year team project. Possibly there will be crises in the future if certain cases cause significant delays or if there are other unforseen problems, but at least the chart will highlight the extent of the problem and we will be able to consider its resolution in the light of our objectives.

Being a team, whether a research team or any other, involves more than just clear objectives, good external relationships, and planning. Synergy results from putting together the expertise and effort of individuals skilfully. It requires a continuous commitment from all and a high level of morale bolstered by the celebration of every success. The ideal is a shared set of values and a shared vision of the team's contribution. We cannot claim to have achieved this ideal but we are working well towards it.

CONCLUSION

None of us in the research team really believe we are in top gear yet. The pull of other tasks and priorities make it difficult to maintain the effort and enthusiasm that a 'superteam' demands. None the less we are still learning and progress is continuing. No doubt there are plenty of challenges still to come!

REFERENCES

Fletcher, W. (1983) *Meetings, Meetings*, Sevenoaks: Hodder & Stoughton.

Handy, C. (1976) *Understanding Organizations*, London: Penguin.

Hastings, C., Bixby, P., and Chaudry-Lawton, R. (1986) *Superteams*, London: Gower.

20 Politics and ethics in action research[1]

Andrew Kakabadse

In a paper I wrote (Kakabadse 1982), I made the point that simply doing a 'good job' and hoping that promotion is likely, or at least the sack is unlikely, is an unrealistic hope. For people with some ambition and certain survival instincts, attaining professional competence is only the first step. To achieve high office relatively rapidly requires skills in negotiation, skills in forward planning, skills in making projects work, skills in getting on with people, in fact skills in being different and yet ironically in being able to fit with superiors, colleagues, and subordinates. The reality of working life is that a substantial number of individuals spend their time at work vying for limited resources, competing for limited status positions, attracting the attention of senior executives, producing competent task work, assisting others, and paying attention to home life. The working situation induces a wide range of experiences.

With so many different forces operating in any work situation what behaviours should a third-party interventionist enter into and what ethical standards or guidelines should he/she adopt? In this chapter an attempt is made to explore the position of the third-party interventionist. The experiences and views of a process-orientated consultant (works with the client on his problems rather than trying to impose predetermined solutions) are explored. His activities in one intervention are discussed. It is indicated that the consultant considered it necessary to act 'politically' due to the circumstances of this particular case. The intervention is still currently active and whether the consultant will eventually be 'successful' is open to conjecture.

It is concluded that perceived political interactions are a natural everyday experience for most people in any organizational setting. Whether attempting to resolve open conflict or to introduce changes in an organization, third-party interventionists should be aware that certain 'political strategies' need to be adopted to try to reach some sort of mutually acceptable solution.

THE CASE

A police organization in the USA has recently faced substantial criticism for its handling of various community problems. In response, the organization has attempted to examine how and why certain problems have arisen.

As part of the examination process, the director of the police department decided to initiate a study of career development and motivation within this organization. The brief to undertake the study was passed down to the Assistant Director, Personnel, who decided to call a meeting of the various interested parties in the organization. After a limited number of meetings, the interested parties decided to form themselves into a steering committee. They recognized that they neither shared the expertise nor insights to conduct a study of motivation and career development in their organization. They obtained the assistance of a consultant (to be known as John), but he could only offer a limited amount of time as he was fully employed as an internal consultant by a large multinational company. John and the steering committee met on a number of occasions for a period of a year but made only limited progress. Eventually, John suggested that a project team should be formed to carry out an in-depth study of career development.

The steering committee agreed and formed a project team consisting of three senior officers, two middle-ranking officers and one sergeant who acted as the secretary/administrator to the team. The steering committee decided that a second consultant should be hired to act as adviser to the project team. A second consultant was eventually hired. The intervention described below is centred on the activities of the second consultant (to be known as Steven).

THE INTERVENTION

A number of individuals were approached to see whether they would be interested in acting as consultant to the project team. A favourite candidate was eventually identified. He is an academic who had been used as a visiting speaker at the organization's police training college. He had already established a reputation as a good lecturer on their senior management programme and his experience as a researcher and consultant made him attractive to the organization. In addition, both the manager of the training college (a senior police officer), who was shortly to be promoted to a top management position in the organization, and the senior management programme tutor favoured the individual and argued for his acceptance.

The chairman of the steering committee, a senior police officer and an exceptionally influential individual, invited the academic (Steven) to act as second consultant to the project team. Steven agreed, if the fee was right. The director of the police department found Steven's fee acceptable but did not have the authority to issue payment. A central servicing unit alone could authorize payment. They stated that they would have to be convinced that the money was to be spent wisely. This proved embarrassing for the client. Both client and Steven recognized that the central servicing unit were unlikely to make a quick decision. In addition, the director of police was demanding results and had already indicated a deadline for the project team, one year hence. The central servicing unit could well have delayed the proceedings for up to six months. Steven indicated that he would do the job on the understanding that he most likely would eventually receive his fee. The chairman gratefully agreed, thanking Steven for taking the risk, and organized separate meetings of the steering committee and project team in order to introduce him to the parties involved.

At Steven's first meeting with the project team, the atmosphere was tense. Steven gave a brief résumé of his past work experience and indicated that he looked forward to working with the team. The most senior man on the team welcomed Steven but stated that the team had not expected as many problems as they currently faced when they first agreed to take part in the project. As the conversation developed, it became clear that the project team had had no real guidance, nor had any real experience of working on people- and manpower-orientated problems. The members of the team shared an additional anxiety. Recognizing their lack of knowledge and experience in the area, they questioned whether they could produce any meaningful results, and if that happened, would that be to the detriment of their careers? Steven listened and agreed with the team that at this early stage, a number of meetings would have to be held to identify what direction the team should take.

A number of meetings were held between Steven and the project team. Steven stated that he would not wish to work with the team if they established any processes of formality such as an agenda. Protests were pushed aside by Steven, who stated that he was taking over the running of the team and anyone who felt they could not continue would always be free to leave. Steven knew that no one dare leave because of career implications. The meetings quickly became brainstorming sessions, exactly as the consultant desired.

The team, influenced by Steven's view, decided that simply examining career development systems in operation in other public service and private organizations was insufficient. A study would have to be conducted examining the existing career development system in the organization. Some members of the project team were against the idea, stating that the study could uncover views held by members of the organization that would be highly critical of senior management. How could the project team feed that information back? Steven advised them not to concern themselves with the results of the study before they had even planned the structure of the study.

The chairman of the steering committee approached Steven enquiring as to progress made. He indicated that the other members of the steering committee would wish to meet Steven, and, even if it was early days, be given a brief report of developments to date. Steven readily agreed, stating that he would wish to meet John before the steering committee meeting. The two consultants arranged to meet.

The meeting between the consultants was polite but tense. Steven concluded that John would probably be in favour of a study. It also became clear that John had not really identified the direction the intervention should take. John could be given some role in the study, then he would argue in favour of the study at the steering committee meeting. By probing John, Steven concluded that various members of the steering committee were anxious about the results of the whole intervention. The senior managers on the steering committee also felt their careers to be potentially in jeopardy if the eventual results produced were considered unsatisfactory. The two consultants agreed to support each other at the steering committee meeting.

Before the steering committee meeting, Steven decided that the intervention had to be concerned with substantial changes in the organization. Steven also recognized that he had begun to behave in ways that could be considered, if not unethical, at least on the borderline. The values of working with your client at his pace in his territory, being open and sharing information were unrealistic in the situation. The only clear policy the consultant could identify was to pursue the diagnostic study of career development in the organization, whether the client wanted it or not. Steven concluded that change was needed at the subsystems level in the organization. To accommodate that, some form of data was required.

Steven's first meeting with the steering committee was uneasy. The consultant was introduced by the chairman of the committee who then asked the consultant to address the members. The consultant offered his view of his role in the intervention and went on to explain the various ways of examining career development in any organization. He indicated that the various approaches had been fully debated by the project team and that the only sensible direction to take would be to undertake a study of career development in the organization. It would not make sense to develop policies for the future without understanding how people felt about their jobs, their level of work satisfaction, their views on promotions and methods of appraisal. At this point, both Steven and the chairman sensed that the other members of the committee seemed restless and anxious. The chairman confronted the group by stating that if others were perturbed about what was said and wished to ask questions, they should feel free to do so. Steven agreed, stating that he preferred this to be an open and honest meeting and that the members should feel free to ask any questions.

Certain minor questions were asked concerning how such a study could be conducted. After half an hour's discussion, one member stood up stating that he was not in favour of such a study. What use would such information be to the organization? Steven responded by asking what alternative approach could be undertaken, bearing in mind the organization's director's demand for results. The member (a senior and influential police officer) stated he did not know but there must be some other way. However, he said he could not remain to discuss the matter as he had other meetings to attend. He added that this one seemed to be a waste of time. Steven thanked him for his valuable input and when he had left the room, the consultant asked the others whether they could offer any alternative suggestions to examining career development.

Another member stated that Steven was right. The only way to begin to examine career development would be to analyse peoples' views about their jobs, work, promotion prospects, and the management styles adopted by their superiors. With the one member leaving the meeting, and the other seemingly in favour of some sort of study, the other members seemed to visibly relax. Steven capitalized on the pro-study contributions by asking the others for their suggestions on how they would go about organizing such a study. Numerous contributions were made and even the most nonsensical was warmly praised by the consultant.

After one hour's discussion, Steven felt confident that he had managed to turn the mood of the meeting in his favour. He dramatically stopped the conversation and turned to John (who had remained silent throughout) and asked him to give his expert opinion on whether a study on career development should be undertaken. John stated that he could see no alternative. Steven, dramatically turning to the other members, asked whether anyone was in favour of the one dissenting voice that had left the room. No one was, and in fact considered his objections to be destructive. The meeting unanimously concluded that the study be carried out.

Reflecting on the meeting, Steven decided to take the following steps:

1 reduce the level of anxiety amongst the members of the steering committee and project team;
2 isolate and reduce the level of influence of the steering committee member who objected to the study;
3 develop a warm and positive relationship with each senior police officer in the organization.

Steven became more proactive with the project team. He paid less attention to their needs and issues and more to the mechanics of conducting a study. Steven organized a series of workshops on research methodology and interviewing techniques. In addition, more brainstorming sessions were held exploring how to conduct the proposed research. During this time, one of the members of the project team was identified by the consultant and the other members of the team as being unsuitable. Steven approached the chairman of the steering committee to discuss the unsuitability of the one project team member of the study. To the approval of all (including the project team member), the individual was transferred out. The consultant wanted him replaced by the senior management tutor currently at the training college. After a number of telephone calls and informal one-to-one discussions with influential senior officers, the senior tutor was appointed to the project team. Steven agreed that once the senior tutor was in post, he would spend substantial time coaching him into the project at no extra cost.

Steven, together with the senior tutor, agreed that a pilot study was necessary. The pilot study should be conducted as a series of semi-structured interviews. A sample was identified and members of the project team were each given particular sample populations to interview. Steven stated that he alone would interview very senior officers as he would be seen as least threatening.

Steven used the opportunity to develop friendly relationships with the senior police officers that he could arrange to see. Some of the managers sat on the steering committee. Not only did they offer information about their job, task activities, and motivation, but were encouraged by the consultant to discuss the project at length. Fears and anxieties that individual senior officers held were reduced through discussion with the consultant. The one member of the steering committee who objected to the study refused to be interviewed. His superior also refused to take part in the study. In discussions with the chairman of the steering committee and his superior, the consultant emphasized the co-operation he had received from most members of the organization, except from the one who objected, and that person's superior. Slowly the word got round that only one group in the total organization were difficult and unco-operative in a project that was now recognized as important to the future of the police organization.

Throughout this time, the members of the project team met to discuss the data being gathered in the pilot study. In the opinion of all, the data was more valuable than originally expected. A steering committee meeting was held to discuss progress to date, which both the consultants and project team members attended. It was agreed at the meeting that the pilot study results were valuable and that the main study should be started. The individual who had originally objected to the study was not present, nor had he attended the last few meetings. Steven, at the end of the meeting, invited the steering committee members and the members of the project team to his university for lunch to celebrate the successful completion of stage one of the study.

Most of those invited attended the lunch, which turned out to be a success. By now Steven was viewed as acceptable to the organization.

IDENTIFYING THE POLITICAL STRATEGIES

The project team is ready to embark on the main study. The actual results of their studies so far, or even what they intend to do, are irrelevant so far as this chapter is concerned. What is of importance is to identify and examine the strategies adopted by Steven in the intervention. The strategies are outlined below.

Identify the stakeholders

It is imperative in any intervention to identify those individuals who have an interest or stakeholding in the situation. Whether their interests are compatible or incompatible with those of the individual, all the stakeholders have to be approached in order to identify their intentions in the situation. In the case above, Steven identified all potential stakeholders. With those whose views were not acceptable, attempts were made to isolate them from their colleagues and hence reduce their capacity to influence others.

Working on the comfort zones

In order to influence anyone effectively, work on the other person's comfort zone unless it is absolutely necessary to do otherwise.

An individual's comfort zone consists of those behaviours, values, attitudes, drives, and ideas that the person in question can accept, tolerate, and manage. The reason the comfort zones are emphasized is that every individual has developed a range of values and behaviours which they find acceptable and wish to put into practice. The range of values and behaviours is their identity. The person concerned may call it his personality. Something unique that is them.

Hence, people will pay attention to the concerns of others as long as their own are not threatened. Once an interaction with another concentrates on the issues important to only one party and is threatening to the other party, that interaction is likely to be terminated. And why not? People meaningfully interact when they have sufficient interest in a situation.

People hold two interests in any situation:

- the final objective, i.e. what is in it for them;
- the manner in which the final objective is achieved, i.e. the process.

People are as much concerned with both processes and outcomes. By handling the interactions so that the process feels comfortable to the receiving party, outcomes can be managed in a way that satisfies most parties.

Steven used this strategy more than any other. At this moment in time, he is generally recognized as being a friend to most of the stakeholders.

Networking

Organizations are a mixture of various cultures and group identities. The group identities may or may not coincide with the hierarchical structure of overt objectives of the organization. In terms of what really does and does not get done, the network may often be a more powerful force than superior/subordinate relations. For any outsider entering a situation that they wish to influence, it is necessary to identify the networks that exist and the individuals who are generally recognized as upholding the values of the network. These individuals are then influenced by working on their comfort zone. Steven identified a number of networks and gained access to most. He plans to utilize his access to the key stakeholders in the networks in part two of the study.

Making deals

Making a deal with other individuals or groups is common practice in most large organizations. Whether resources are limited or not, different individuals or groups may agree to support each other to achieve a common purpose as long as there are benefits for them. It is realistic to expect individuals and groups in the organization to wish to promote their own goals, which may be at the expense of others. Consequently, coming to some sort of agreement about common policies, or at least not disturbing each other's aims, may be necessary.

Two deals were made by Steven. First to continue on the project without fully agreeing the financial side to the contract. For his own career ends, Steven wanted the contract and was therefore willing to take the risk of doing work which may have gone unpaid. By making such a deal with the chairman of the steering committee, it was hoped that the chairman would argue forcefully to have Steven's financial terms accepted.

The second deal was to coach the senior tutor, who was a latecomer to the project team, for no extra payment. Apart from the fact that the tutor and consultant were personal friends, the tutor also possessed substantial knowledge and experience in the 'people management' type subjects which made him the most important member to the project team.

Withholding and withdrawing

It is impossible to satisfy the needs of all parties in any large, diverse organization. One way of ensuring that certain groups do not overreact to issues which they recognize as important, is to withhold information. By preventing certain information from becoming common knowledge, the manager is able to achieve whatever objectives he has identified without facing opposition that could destroy his plan. In such circumstances, the manager should be fairly convinced that his plan is valuable, even if others have not or will not recognize its worth. However, to constantly withhold information is not recommended, for such behaviour is indicative of a manager who cannot confront certain problems. Continuously withholding information is a means of protecting the manager and not the policy.

Withdrawing from a situation is at times necessary. There are times when the presence of a manager in a dispute or negotiation is of no help. To withdraw and allow the different factions to negotiate their own terms, or for management to withdraw an unpopular policy and shelve it for the time being, are common practices. The larger and more diverse an organization becomes, the more important is the timing of actions. When to introduce or withdraw plans and information are important considerations for policy implementation.

Steven used the strategy of withholding information and withdrawing from potentially difficult situations, on numerous occasions. Criticism of particular individuals or of the organization which the consultant felt would be unacceptable to the project team or members of the steering committee was withheld. In fact, the project team has no knowledge of the data the second consultant gathered in his interviews with senior management.

Throughout the intervention, Steven was consistently not presenting the full picture to the senior officers he met. Each was told a slightly different story to the other as to the objectives and expected outcomes of the study, according to what the consultant considered would be acceptable. In addition, if a slightly unpleasant situation required attention, Steven would approach one of the senior officers, offer him information and advice on how to handle the situation, and then withdraw so that he would not be implicated in the outcomes of the interaction.

If all else fails

Practising any one or more of the above strategies will not guarantee success. It is necessary to identify some fallback strategy if all else fails. Each person concerned would have to identify his own fallback strategy according to the demands of the situation and what he or she could personally handle. In this intervention, the second consultant identified two fallback strategies.

First, if this particular intervention failed, or if the consultant was not chosen to work with the project team, then at least Steven had negotiated warm and friendly relations with important people in the organization who could call him in at a later date on other projects or refer him to other organizations where he could get work.

Second, Steven had only just begun to work on the comfort zone of the boss of the chairman of the steering committee. This person was the former manager of the training centre and now promoted to a senior position in the organization. It was predicted that the individual would be the next-director-but-one. Whether these rumours turn out to be true in the future is unimportant. The fact that he was currently considered as important and influential was sufficient reason to nurture his favour.

REFLECTIONS

Certain questions arise out of this case. What of developing trust, trying to establish a common understanding, and treating others as human beings instead of levers for self-betterment? In fact, for anyone holding a third-party role, whether it be an intervention into an organization or a conflict resolution situation, should questions of ethics ever arise? From this case in this chapter, three ethical issues are identified below.

When is sharing feasible?

Sharing of information, opinions, or even anxieties is only feasible when people identify with certain common elements in the situation such as tasks, team identity, traditions, and personal interdependence. However, concerns such as having one's policies adopted and developing long-term organizational plans are unlikely to be comfortable shared experiences. When a number of individuals are involved in the process of generating and implementing longer term plans, it becomes as much a trial of strength and wit as to whose predominant values will eventually be accepted. Senior organizational personnel may sit in the same room debating issues, but that is all they share. For any third party involved in such a situation, how much information and opinion to disclose is dependent on what is feasible in the situation.

Who is your client?

Developments in any intervention may bring both client and consultant to a different point from that they had first expected. Not only may plans and expectations have changed, but further, the very need for the client and consultant to work together. Certainly any intervention that concentrates on the longer term strategic issues in an organization may well lead to rapid changes of expectations both for client and consultant. From the consultant's point of view, the client he first started with may not be the client with whom he should interrelate.

Changing clients in the same organization may not be easy. By switching clients, the consultant could damage his original client's position, his own position, or may even leave both parties exposed to other vested interests in the intervention. The ethical issue is to what extent can the change practitioner be open, sharing or even feel responsible for his original client whilst knowing that client and consultant may have to part because the situation may change.

When eclectic; when humanistic?

In any organization, there is always an uneasy balance between outcomes and process, between achieving objectives and the way in which they are achieved. In my paper (Kakabadse 1982), I indicate that third-party resolution technologies have arisen out of the OD (organizational development) movement. OD seems to have concentrated on processes, the way things are done, and has only really entered into outcomes in particular areas such as job redesign or data feedback surveys. As a consequence, third-party strategies for handling long-term strategic change have been left relatively unexplored. Approaches to OD and third-party intervention/conflict resolution have only been developed to cope with the micro side of change.

This case indicates, if nothing else, that macro change requires both a new philosophical base as well as alternative strategies for action.

NOTE

1 This chapter is adapted from an article in *Power, Politics and Organizations*, edited by Andrew Kakabadse and Chris Parker. Reproduced by permission of John Wiley and Sons Ltd.

REFERENCE

Kakabadse, A. P. (1982) 'Politics in organisations: re-examining OD', *Leadership and Organisational Development Journal*, Monograph 3,3.

21 Data collection for management research in developing countries

Kavil Ramachandran

In 1966 a young economist from the USA went to Nigeria to study the factors affecting agricultural production. He selected a 'national' sample of thirty villages, hired a crop of Nigerian interviewers, and sent them off to gather data on lengthy interview schedules from 900 farmers. Problems began immediately. The interview questions, which asked for details on farm acreage, number of livestocks, and crop yields per acre, did not make sense to the village farmers. Since the postal services were as unreliable in transmitting paychecks as field instructions, several of the interviewers quit having never seen either their pay or their paymaster.

(Cesar and Roy 1976)

Thus began a book on Third World surveys edited by Cesar and Roy. More than a decade later things remain almost the same with social science research in many developing countries.

The objective of this chapter is to highlight some of the issues pertaining to sound research methodology in the context of a developing country. One has to realize that while both developing and advanced countries are on the same 'development continuum' they are at different points and they differ in terms of research awareness and sophistication of people, availability of infrastructure facilities for living and communication, and a system of data storing. Also there are vast differences among the so-called developing countries, for instance between Malaysia and Malawi, and therefore any generalization has its own limitations. The issues discussed, however, are relevant to all the developing countries to different degrees. Again, the term management, even if limited to business enterprises, covers a whole spectrum of firms including giant manufacturing companies and very small informal enterprises.

This chapter discusses availability of reliable and accurate secondary data, the factors to be considered in the designing and administration of questionnaires, the role, responsibilities, and qualities of an investigator, and finally some of the key aspects of conducting surveys. Their relevance to large and small firms is highlighted wherever felt appropriate.

MANAGEMENT RESEARCH

Recent years have seen management as a discipline growing and acquiring widespread interest in developing countries. Policy makers in these countries have started realizing the need to promote strong management systems in all sectors. Changing competitive situations are also forcing multinationals to understand the factors influencing their market shares and profits. Not much research has, however, been done in this area and management practices in these countries are not adequately recorded. As a natural corollary, sufficient attention has not been given so far to methodological issues pertaining to management research in developing countries as different from those in advanced countries.

Field research has taken three distinct, though closely related forms (Balakrishnan and Prahalad 1973):

1 *Case research* Here the research takes an in-depth look at a single unit of analysis without any specific hypothesis for testing. The unit of analysis could be an individual, a group, or firms.
2 *Project research* Here one organization, or a few, are studied in depth with a view to understanding the process and interrelationships of the subject under study. Generally the focus here is on the development of concepts and hypotheses.
3 *Population studies* Here, as in the other cases, the focus is on empirical investigation to delineate patterns through comparing and contrasting several individuals/groups/firms. A large number of observations made under this method enable hypotheses to be validated. Population studies can be based either on primary or on secondary data.

Management research following any of the above three forms, depending on the research objective, can focus on widely diversified aspects, such as large or small enterprises, located in urban or rural areas, and using modern or traditional technology. The data collection process will be different in each case.

Field survey research is the most widely used research method in management. According to Herzog, Stanfield and Cesar,

Survey research is a process whereby in a relatively minimum period of time of relatively maximum disruption of the environment, a relatively large amount of relatively superficial information on a relatively large number of characteristics of a relatively large number of people/units in a relatively large number of places can be collected relatively accurately, for the purpose of making relatively precise statements for the larger population of which the units are a relatively good representation, and at a relatively low cost-per-unit of usable information.

(Herzog *et al.* 1976:)

Beyond the lighter side of this definition, survey research has its own limitations especially when the conditions in developing countries do not always facilitate easy and reliable data collection. Developing countries face many constraints in their environment compared to advanced countries. The question is how to go about collecting research data there.

DATA SOURCES

Data bases are required either for developing sampling frames or for testing hypotheses. In research involving field-work for primary data collection, data bases are useful for generating hypotheses and developing sampling frames. There are three kinds of issues related to databases:

1 Systematic collection of data is not widely practised in most developing countries. While there could be census data on the population, there may not be adequate data collected and preserved on industry.
2 Existing data may, however, not always be easily available. Data collection is often done as an end in itself and is not published in report form. When a report is published it is always delayed, making any analysis of it of little use. For instance, Sukumaran (1989) had to contend with the 1979 figures for total capital employed in public sector companies in Kerala, India for his study of profit planning completed in 1989. Moreover, when data are collected they can often be inadequate for research purposes. Saluja raises another problem. Several agencies of the Government of India collect data on different segments of small-scale enterprises. However, because of ineffective central direction and co-ordination, these agencies use varied concepts and definitions, leaving serious gaps in data collected for analysis. As a result, comparability of the data over time as well as between various segments is vitiated (Saluja 1988).
3 Accuracy and reliability of available data poses another problem. For instance, inter-country trade statistics collected from some countries in Africa were not found to be reliable by Peil *et al.* (1982). The World Bank and International Monetary Fund face the same problem of reliability. Berg noted that their data often lacked subsistence and reality; the margin of error in such statistics could be 20 to 25 per cent (Berg 1975).

Compared to small-scale enterprises, there are usually a greater number of data bases on large firms which are incorporated under company law or similar legislation. Trade associations and stock exchange directories are possible sources of secondary data on large companies. Most of the developing countries have government controls on newly established large firms and so have reasonably effective mechanisms to monitor operations of large companies, although these are not in very large numbers. Industrial financial institutions may also be able to supply some financial and technical information on firms.

Maintaining data on key variables of small-scale enterprises is laborious and most of the developing countries do not have either the motivation or systems for it. Besides, unlike large firms, their smaller counterparts do not in general have to register with any government department to start a business. Although departments such as those concerned with collecting sales taxes can attempt to compile useful data, they rarely do this. Personnel in, for instance, industrial development departments are often motivated to maintain statistics on new firms established and to project a glorified picture of a developing economy; there are hardly any statistics maintained on firm mortality. It is also to be borne in mind that entry and exit barriers for small firms are very few. Also, the mobility of small enterprises makes the task of keeping records on some of them even more difficult.

QUESTIONNAIRES

One of the most effective means of recording data is by questionnaire. Designing a questionnaire and ensuring it has high reliability and validity is fundamental to high-quality research based on field data. All questionnaires should be pre-tested and piloted to confirm their reliability and validity. Pre-testing a questionnaire should be done in the same kind of conditions under which the main survey will be carried out. The investigators who would be collecting data in the field might also be asked to do this under the supervision of the researcher. This enables the researcher to sort out in good time problems of a general nature that might crop up during the main survey. Such an approach is especially useful in developing countries where investigators may not be able to contact the leader of the research team while the survey is in progress, for clarification of issues that might arise in the field.

Data collected during questionnaire piloting should be analysed completely as if it is a product of the main survey. In fact, in this way all methodological issues can be sorted out prior to commencing the main survey. In the absence of this, the researcher may be forced either to go back to the respondents, or to forego analysis of some incomplete data. Going back to the respondents is not easy in a developing country where there are often transport and communication problems.

There are dangers involved in administering a questionnaire prepared in a non-local language such as English. One of the problems is that the field investigators may not be equipped to interpret the questions correctly and fully, and would thereby threaten the reliability and validity of the questionnaire. Another problem is that not all respondents will be familiar with the questionnaire language, and so whatever they answer may not fully reflect what they would have liked to have said. Also, even if the response is in the local language, the investigator may not be able to translate and record it in the questionnaire language. Thus there are several possible ways of losing useful data by using an inappropriate language. Such problems crop up more in small enterprises than in large companies.

Researchers in developing countries often fail to translate questionnaires in full, partly because they assume that the investigators will be able to 'manage' to speak either the questionnaire language or the local language. Also, researchers may be reluctant to take the trouble of translating first the questionnaire and later both the questionnaire and responses back to the original language.

This is a dangerous path to follow as it may defeat the whole objective of research. It is therefore suggested that the questionnaire should be translated into the local language in developing countries where the respondents may not be very familiar with the language in the questionnaire, for instance, English. The questionnaire should be first translated into the local language and later back to the original language. Bilinguists should do this exercise independently so that any variation that might arise could be corrected before finalizing the questionnaire.

Designing a good questionnaire is not easy. The content, language, length, and format are all important aspects to be taken care of. A questionnaire should be designed to suit a given research situation. The complexity of questions should be in relation to the level of understanding of the respondent class. For instance, a multi-point scaling method which may be effectively used in the case of company executives to discover their attitudes and attributes, may be a very poor instrument if used among rural entrepreneurs in an attempt to discover their attitudes and attributes. It is often found that demonstration aids are useful in surveys among poorly educated people.

Researchers have to decide in advance the expected duration of each interview, and formulate questionnaires accordingly. A researcher must be able to retain a respondent's interest in providing data from beginning to end. Also, the availability of time depends on the type of respondents. For instance, company executives may not have long hours to spend with a researcher, while respondents in rural areas sometimes may be able to spare more time. A small-scale entrepreneur may be able to answer questions while operating his machine. Where surveys are carried out rather frequently and the same respondents are approached for data by several researchers, they may not be inclined to entertain yet another researcher.

INVESTIGATORS

Field data are collected either by individual researchers themselves or by investigators, depending on the volume of work and resources available. As the quality of data depends to a great extent on the quality of investigators, care has to be taken to recruit and train suitable investigators. The nature and content of training depends on the target group of the survey.

Field investigators very often tend to interpret questions and give a lead to answers, thereby creating 'Investigator Bias' in the responses (Hershfield *et al.* 1976). They occasionally interpret respondents' views also. Apparently, investigators tend to do such interpretation when they are more educated than the respondents. In such cases, there are possibilities of respondents becoming mere listeners to what investigators say. Thus where respondents seek clarification on several unrelated issues the investigators will have to tackle them carefully. Also, investigators have to be careful not to disrespect local culture and practices.

Field investigators may not always record responses clearly and legibly. Some may note down only the main points of discussion, assuming that they will develop the points later. In both cases, the researcher is likely to lose valuable data in the process and may have to contact the respondents again. While it may not be very difficult to do so in advanced countries having well developed transport and communication facilities, the same may not be so in developing countries. Therefore every effort should be made to collect data in full during a field survey.

Investigators should have a comprehensive understanding of the research topic, as respondents are likely to ask them about the objectives of the research. Investigator training has to incorporate this also. While clarifying research objectives, investigators should take care not to promise to do things to solve respondents' problems unless that itself happens to be an objective.

In certain cases, respondents will be unwilling to co-operate if promises made by earlier researchers did not come true. In a study of the impact of a marketing assistance scheme for weavers, field investigators promised to offer better assistance once the data had been collected. Based on this assurance, the weavers co-operated with the investigators. But the study, which was sponsored by the government, did not lead to any policy changes. Later, another study team attempting to assess the financial requirements of weavers had difficulties in collecting data. So it is important that researchers do not make false promises. If respondents are unwilling, researchers will have to spend more time in convincing them about the importance of the project.

Investigators may have to use personal and informal approaches to gather data. Personal networking is sometimes a stronger and more useful mechanism than formal networking in developing countries. Even in large companies access to a potential respondent is very often easier and faster through personal contacts. The main reason for this could be a lack of awareness and appreciation of management research. People respond to oblige friends or relatives in such circumstances. In small enterprises located both in urban and rural areas establishing such contacts may not be required or possible, but a personal friendly approach to them is found to be effective in collecting data.

Field investigation is generally tough, especially if the weather is bad and transport, communication, food, and accommodation facilities are not very good. Street maps do not exist for most of the cities, apart from rough sketches for the use of tourists. Such obstacles gradually increase as one moves from metropolitan centres to interior places. Long hours of work, often starting early in the morning and stretching into late evenings, may put many investigators off. There are different ways of tackling such situations. Monetary incentives may be an attraction if remuneration rises gradually as the survey progresses. There could be weekend or fortnightly get-togethers of investigators at certain places at the expense of the researcher. Such meetings could also be used to review progress and to sort out any outstanding problems.

Considering the various constraints involved, investigators should be prepared to spend an additional 15 to 20 per cent of 'normal' time to complete the survey. When the sample frame is to be prepared in the field itself, more time will be required to select samples.

SURVEY APPROACH

Identifying and approaching potential respondents may pose two types of problem. First, availability of a sample frame at least in some crude form is essential to start collecting names and addresses of potential respondents. This may be possible to some extent in urban areas where telephone and telex facilities are available, especially in the case of large firms. In small towns and rural areas, data available with government departments may be a starting point.

Even when a sample frame is available, the investigator may fail to locate a few respondents, in which case substitute samples may have to be drawn. The second type of problem posed is in terms of getting access to the executives of large firms, by giving satisfactory replies to their secretaries. A researcher once mentioned his difficulties in contacting senior executives of large companies in India. Every time he telephoned an executive, his/her secretary would want to know who the caller was and why they were calling before disclosing whether the executive was available or not. Although the researcher got irritated with such behaviour, he could do nothing but learn to live with it.

In the absence of a sample frame, collecting data from firms which should at the end neatly fall into a stratified sample may not be easy. Government departments may be useful contacts. For instance, a survey of small-scale enterprises in a remote area may require samples to be drawn based on first-hand information available from the officials in the local industrial development agency. As mentioned earlier, survey research has several limitations, and therefore the researcher should try to do the best possible. Implementing sample selection as prescribed in the theory may not always be feasible. In such circumstances, the researcher should make the best efforts to stick to the theory as far as possible, and clearly describe the limitations in the report.

A survey can either be via the invasion method or via the immersion method (Hershfield *et al.* 1976). In the former, the investigator visits respondents without notice, finishes his/her work and goes away quickly. This is advisable if 'interviewee bias' is likely to be high in cases such as a survey to find the effectiveness of family planning devices. Also, if camping facilities are limited, and the researcher has to complete the work in one go, the invasion method may be appropriate. This is also useful for large-scale surveys. It has, however, weaknesses such as lack of opportunities to gather in-depth understanding of the problems in certain cases.

The immersion method is appropriate for case-studies involving in-depth interviews and action research. In such cases the investigator is advised to live and spend a lot of time with the respondents to record their attitudes, views, aspirations, etc. Where an investigator spends a long time in a specific area to record longitudinal data, it is advisable that the researcher has adequate resources. This method is ideal for qualitative research.

Another problem is 'courtesy bias' of respondents which originates from their desire not to offend their visitor. In such cases, respondents give answers designed to please the investigator. Another related bias is to give socially acceptable or popular answers. Another bias is in the nature of 'self-lifting' by respondents when they feel their replies would enhance their status in the eyes of the investigator. In instances where the respondents do not really know the answers they may give some answer to save face.

CONCLUSION

Management research in developing countries throws up its own challenges, especially for data collection. While every effort should be made to adhere to the theory, it may not be easy to follow it completely in practice under conditions which have several constraints.

It is often found that, besides unknown cultural heterogenity, there are problems of transportation and access to people, and their lack of familiarity with answering strangers' survey questions, especially those of an intimate nature. In such circumstances the modern research methods developed in advanced Western countries may not be readily applicable, and variations from theory may be unavoidable. In such circumstances intensive pre-study, exploration, and pilot study may be highly valuable to enable the researcher to gather insights into the critical aspects of research design.

Finally, there is a need for more qualitative than quantitative research in developing countries. There is still very little known about the needs, aspirations, attitudes, and attributes of individuals and the key factors influencing their behaviour which are important pieces of knowledge to management science. For instance, Ramachandran found that some of the regional development incentives which were presumed to influence location selection of industries which were offered in India, were in fact inappropriate to Indian conditions. Those schemes had been copied from the advanced Western countries (Ramachandran 1986). This is true of all contexts, but perhaps particularly in the Third World. One has to really understand the structure of an organization or country, before talking about changes therein.

REFERENCES

Balakrishnan, K. and Prahlad, C. K. (1973) 'Methods and strategy for research in business administration', Graduate School of Business Administration Working Paper, Harvard University, Boston, MA.

Berg, E. (1975) 'The recent economic evolution of Sahel', Ann Arbor Centre for Research on Economic Development, University of Michigan, Michigan.

Cesar, G. H. and Roy, P. (1976) *Third World Surveys: Survey Research in Developing Nations*, New Delhi: Macmillan.

Hershfield, A. F. *et al.* (1976) 'Problems in interviewing', in G. H. Cesar and P. Roy (eds) *Third World Surveys: Survey Research in Developing Countries*, New Delhi: Macmillan.

Herzog, W., Stanfield, D., and Cesar, G. H. (1976) 'Problems in measurement', in G. H. Cesar and P. Roy (eds) *Third World Surveys: Survey Research in Developing Nations*, New Delhi: Macmillan.

Peil, M., Mitchell, P. K., and Rimmer, D. (1982) *Social Science Research Methods – An African Handbook*, London: Hodder & Stoughton.

Ramachandran, K. (1986) 'Appropriateness of incentives for small scale enterprise location in less developed areas: the experience of the United Kingdom, Japan and India', unpublished Ph.D. thesis, Cranfield Institute of Technology, UK.

Saluja, M. R. (1988) 'Data base of the unorganised manufacturing industry: an appraisal', in K. B. Suri (ed.) *Small Scale Enterprises in Industrial Development: the Indian Experience*, New Delhi: Sage.

Sukumaran, A. (1989) 'Budgeting in selected private and public undertakings in Kerala', unpublished Ph.D. thesis, University of Calicut, India.

Index

Note: Figures are shown in **bold** numbers. In some cases there are also textual references on these pages.

a priori analytical categories 3–4, 13, 14, 15, 90–1, 273
accounting project 258–76
action research 75; politics and ethics in 289–99
actors and ethnomethodology 135, 137–43
Adams-Webber, J. 160
Adler, F. 34
Africa 302
Agar, M. H. 112
aggregate analysis **198**, 200–1
Allen, V. L. 29, 34
Allison, G. T. 38
Allport, G. W. 16
Altbach, P. G. 218
Althusser, L. 29, 35
analysis: of interviews 195–7, **198**; of journals reviewed 114–**115**
applied research 74–5
appropriateness 83
Argyris, C. 45
Arkes, H. R. 121
Augustyniak, S. 115

Baggaley, A. R. 114
Balakrishnan, K. 301
Baldamus, N. 253
Balsley, H. 91
Bamforth, K. W. 17
Bannister, D. 160, 161
Baran, P. 35
Baritz, L. 34, 254

Barley, S. R. 126
Barnard, C. I. 9, 17
Barnes, B. 23
basic objective research 74
Bateman, T. S. 196
Beckard, R. 266
Becker, H. S. 200
Bedeian, A. G. xiv
Behling, O. 45, 49
Bell, C. 146, 220, 253
Bell, R. C. 171
Bennett, R. 85
Benson, J. K. 23
Benton, D. A. 276
Berelson, B. 44, 45
Berg, E. 302
Berger, P. L. 147, 160
Bernstein, R. J. 19
Berra, S. M. 108
Beynon, H. 33
Bingham, W. V. D. 191, 192
Bittner, E. 133, 136, 137–9
Bixby, P. 286
Blackstone, G. 36
Bleasdale, M. 190, 191
Blumer, C. 121
Blyth, W. A. 195
Bobbitt, H. R. 44
Boehm, V. 106
Bohrnstedt, G. 115
Boje, D. M. 23, 38, 39, 47
Bonoma, T. V. 145, 149, 157

Bottomore, T. B. 23, 60, 142
Bouchard, T. J. 170
Bourgeoise, V. 23, 24. 28
Bourne, V. 215
Bowen, B. D. 96
Bradburn, N. M. 181
Braithwaite, R. 44
Brannon, D. 151
Braverman, H. 35
Bray, J. H. 114
Bright, M. 191, 192–3, 194–5
Britain *see* United Kingdom
Brown, R. 46
Bryant, C. 23
bureaucratic structure of research in United Kingdom 253–7
Burrell, G. 4, 7, 132, 142
Burrell and Morgan model 24, **25, 26,** 27–39
Bynner, J. 64

Campbell, D. T. 10, 44, 46, 51–2, 53
Campbell, J. P. 104, 107, 108, 118
Carjaval, R. 24
Carroll, S. J. 174–5
case-studies 82, 93, 94–5, 301; analysis 197, **198,** 199–200; conducting research 155–7; epistemology and research methods 146–50; logic of 153-**155**; political issue 290–9; representativeness 150–1; strengths and weaknesses 157; theory-building 151–4, **155**
Cesar, G. H. 300, 301–2
Chandler, A. D. 94
change in methodologies 125–7
Chaudry-Lawton, R. 286
Chetwynd-Tutton, S. J. 164
Chisnall, P. 195
Chomsky, N. 16
choosing: research method 88–99; survey method 174–80
Christie, R. 122
Christopherson, D. 217
Churchill, G. A. 117
Cicourel, A. V. 133, 134
Clark, D. L. 23, 73
classification level of research 86
Clegg, S. 31, 33, 34
Clover, V. T. 91
Coe, R. 108

Cohen, D. 232, 233
Cohen, D. K. 17
Cohen, J. 114
Cohen, P. 114
college students as subjects for research 122-**123,** 124
comfort zones 295–6
communications 284–5
completion rates for doctoral research 223–5
components of research relevance xv
computers: packages for grid analysis 104–5, 164–9; use in surveys 186; *see also* analysis; data
constraints in doctoral research 217–19; 222, 223
constructs, repertory grid 161, 163, **164, 165,** 166–9
contexts: developing countries 300–9; doctoral research 215–26; evaluative 208, 210, 211; operational 209, 210, 212; politics and ethics 289–99; procedural 209, 210, 211, 212; resource 208, 210, 212; social process xvi, xviii, 252–77; student-supervisor 211, 217–18, **288, 229,** 230–1, 234–5, 237–44; team research 278–88; writing theses 232–4, 245–51
conventional method 89–93
Cook, T. D. 44, 51–2
countries, developing 212–13, 300–9
Cousins, C. 36
Cragg, P. B. 183
Crick, B. 60
Crimp, E. M. 195
criteria for choice of research method 88–99
Crombie, A. 35
Cromwell, R. L. 172
Cummings, L. L. 107, 113, 114
Cunningham Report 33
currency 149

Dabbs, J. M. 112
Daft, R. L. 104, 107, 108, 118
Dahrendorf, R. 26
Dainty, P. 146
data: analysis of interviews 195–7, **198;** integrity 149; sources in developing countries 302–3; *see*

also analysis
dates, arranging for interviews 191–2
Dawes, R. M. 47
Dawson, J. A. 190
decision-making issue 281–2
deductive method of reasoning 92
Delone, W. H. 187
Denzin, N. K. 148, 220
description level of research 86
descriptive relevance xv
detachment of researcher 9, 10, 11, 12, 15
developing countries 212–13, 300–9
development of research skills for Ph.D. 227–36
Dewey, J. 16, 20
Dex, S. 35
Dexter, L. A. 191, 192, 194
Dickson, W. J. 53
dilemmas in supervisory relationships 240–2
Dillman, D. A. 177, 181–9
Dillman, J. J. 183, 188
Dilthey, W. 19, 20
Dingemans, P. M. 161
Dipboye, R. L. 107
dissertations *see* theses, doctoral
Dobbelaere, K. 24
doctoral research 5; contexts 215–26; ethnomethodology and 132–44; writing theses 232–4, 245–51; *see also* Ph. D.
Donaldson, L. 31
Douglas, J. 134
Dressel, P. L. 217–18
Driggers, P. F. 38
Dubin, R. xiv
Duck, S. 160
Duncan, G. J. 115
Dunkerly, D. 31, 34

Easterby-Smith, M. 161, 162, 163, 164, 166
Eckburg, D. 24
Economic and Social Research Council (ESRC) 219, 220
Eden, C. 196
Eilon, S. 24
Eldridge, J. 35
elements, repertory grid 161, **162**, 164, **165**, 166–7, **168**

Emory, C. W. 92
empirical research 47–8, 108, 134, 135, 137–9, 142
epistemology 8, 11–12, 20, 25, 29; and research methods 146–50; differences 47, 52–4; of science 220–1
ethics 289–99
ethnographic research 4, 63–5
ethnomethodology 82; definition 132–3; forms and orientations 134–6; method for doctoral research 132–44; organizational analysis 136–42; versus meta-analysis 119–21
evaluation research 74
evaluative contexts 208, 210, 211
Evans, J. 63–4
Evered, R. D. 16, 23, 106, 107
experiments 97–9
explanation level of research 86–7

face-to-face surveys 174–7, **178**, 179–80; *see also* interviews
Fahad, G. 190
failures in supervisory relationships 237–8
Fairhurst, E. 136, 139
Falthzik, A. M. 174–5
Faulkner, R. R. 112
Ferber, R. 175
field experiments 99
field research: and repertory grid 169–71; in accounting project 267–72
Filley, A. C. 45
Fineman, S. 196
Fire Brigades Union 36
Fire Service study in United Kingdom 29–39
Flanagan, M. F. 107
Fleishman, E. A. 115
Fleron, F. 34
Fleron, L. 34
Fletcher, W. 285
Fonda, N. 167
Ford, J. 147, 221
Ford, P. J. 223
Foxall, G. R. 190
Frankfurt School 33
Fransella, F. 160, 161
Friedheim, E. A. 28, 29

Friedrichs, R. 23, 142
functionalist paradigm **25**, 26–7, 30, 31–2, 36–7
funding: agencies 253–4; obtaining 279–80

Ganster, D. C. 124
Garfinkel, H. 37, 132–3, 134, 135, 136, 139
Garland, H. 115
Geertz, C. 16
Gephart, R. 136
Gergen, K. J. 46, 49, 50
Giddens, A. 29
Gieri, R. N. 121
Glaser, B. G. 153, 156, 157, 197, 217, 221–2, 255, 260
Glass, G. V. 112
goal relevance xv
Goetz, J. P. 190
Goffman, E. 133
Goldstein, K. 16
Goode, W. J. 151
Goodrich, C. 34
Goodyear, M. 190
Gorden, R. L. 190, 191, 192
Gordon, M. E. 45, 107, 122, 124, 126
Gospel, H. 35
Gouldner, A. W. 142
Government of India 302
Gramsci, A. 33, 34
Grant, J. H. 107
grants for research 245, 253–7, 258–60
Graves, P. 122
Griffiths, D. 28
Groholt, K. 191
grounded theory: in accounting project 260, 262, 264, 266, 267, 270; in doctoral research 221–3
Guba, E. G. 107, 120
Gutmann, J. N. 190
Guzzo, R. S. 112

Habermas, J. 11, 14, 20
Hackman, R. 32
Hall, E. T. 16
Hambrick, D. C. 113
Hamner, W. C. 44
Handy, C. B. 241, 281
Hanie, C. A. 43, 106
'hard approaches' 4; *see* inquiries from outside
Harris, R. T. 266
Hart, S. J. 190
Hartnett, R. T. 218
Harvey, L. 24
Hassard, J. 24, 29, 30, 31, 38, 39
Hastings, C. 286
Hatt, P. K. 151
Hawkins, D. S. 195
Hawthorne effect 50, 53, 99
Heidegger, M. 11, 14, 20
Hennessy, H. W. 124
Hershfield, A. F. 305, 307
Herzog, W. 301–2
Heyl, J. 23
Higbee, K. L. 122
Higginbotham, P. 166
Higley, J. 191
Hill, L. 24
Hirsh, H. R. 112
historical research 93–4; *see also* case-studies
Holbrook, M. xv
Homans, G. C. 46, 148
Hooley, G. J. 178, 190
Hopper, T. 28
House, R. J. 45, 87
Howard, G. S. 108
Howard, K. 217, 219, 222
Huberman, A. M. 156, 195, 197, 199
Hughes, J. 147, 220, 221
Hulin, C. L. 104, 107, 108, 118
human action science 20
Hunt, S. D. 146
Hunter, J. E. 112
Husserl, E. 11, 19, 20, 32
hypothetico-deductive approach 219, 222

identifying political strategies 295–8
ideographic research 16
indexicals 133, 134, 135
India 302, 307, 308
inductive method of reasoning 91
industrial market research, interviews for 190–201
innovations, adoption 119–21, 125
inquiries: from inside and outside 7–22; differences **13**; linking **19**; versus each other **12**
instability 46, 48–9

interpretive paradigm **25**, 26, 27, 30, 32–3, 37
intervention in action research 290–9
interviews 101–2, 140, 141, 155–7, 174–7, **178**; aggregate analysis 200–1; analysis 195–7, **198**; data from senior managers 190–203; process 191–5

Jackson, G. B. 112
Jackson, J. H. 44
Jackson, S. E. 112
Jacoby, J. 117
James, W. 9, 16, 20
Jauch, L. R. 151, 158
Jick, T. 38
Jobber, D. 190, 191
Jocher, K. 197
Jones, J. 32, 136, 139, 141–2
Jones, S. 195, 196
journals reviewed 108–18; constructs validation **117**, 118; dependent variables **113**, 114; level of analysis 109, **110**; means of data collection 111, 112; primary location of data collection 109; research using college students 122, 123, 124; results verification 116, 117; sample characteristics 110, 111; time frame of study 115, 116; types of analyses 114, 115; *see also* literature

Kahneman, D. 53
Kakabadse, A. P. 289
Kaplan, A. 7, 16, 46, 106
Katz, J. 217, 218
Katzell, R. A. 112
Keen, T. R. 171
Kehoe, J. 112
Kellner, H. 147
Kelly, G. 160, 163, 170
Kerlinger, F. N. 7, 44, 114, 116
Kerr, S. 45, 115
Kidder, L. H. 124
Kilmann, R. H. 106
Kim, J. 116
Kimberley, J. R. 115
Kincaid, H. V. 191, 192–3, 194–5
Kinnear, R. 195
Kirk, J. 112
Kisiel, R. 19

Kleiman, L. S. 45, 106
Knowles, M. 242
Kockelmans, J. 19
Koontz, H. 45
Kuhn, T. S. 7, 23, 125, 142

La Piere, R. T. 61
laboratory research 98, 149, 169
lack of realism 46, 50–2
Latour, B. 156
learning curve 282
learning to do research 227–36; perception of Ph. D. 231–2; repertory grid 227–8; student-supervisor relationship 211, 217–18, 228–31, 234–5; writing theses 232–4; 245–51
Leather, D. 195
LeCompte, M. D. 190
Leighton, A. H. 53
Lenz, R. T. 113
levels: of research 85–7; of rigour 87–8
Levine, M. S. 114
Lewin, K. 14, 16, 20
Liker, J. K. 115
Lincoln, Y. S. 38, 107, 120
Lindblom, C. E. 17
linguistic ethnomethodology 134, 140–1
literature 81, 283–4; journals reviewed 108–18;
Littler, C. 35
Locke, E. A. 126
Lockwood, D. 26
logical consistency of theses 248
logical inference 152–4, 155
Lord, R. G. 107, 126
Lott, W. J. 122
Louis, K. S. 197
Louis, M. R. 9, 23
Lowenthal, D. 233
Luckmann, T. 133, 160
Lundberg, C. C. 45
Luthans, F. 44, 124
Lynch, J. E. 178
Lynch, M. 136

McClintock, C. C. 151
McDonald, C. D. P. 195
McGaw, B. 112
McGuire, J. B. 106, 107, 120
Machiavelli, N. 119

McHugh, P. 134
McIntyre, G. 239
McKelvey, B. 48
Madut, A. 132
mail surveys 174–7, **178**, 179–80; *see also* questionnaires
Makela, C. J. 183, 188
management research: case-study 145–58; choosing a survey method 174–80; field research 159–73; in developing countries 300–9; meaningful xiv–xvi, 57–66; methods used 89–99; process 69–70, 71, 72
Mann, P. 58–9
Marcuse, R. 254
marketing research xiii, 149–50, 190–201
Martin, C. 191, 196
Martin, J. 23, 24, 36, 38
Martin, T. N. 151, 158
Maruyama, M. 29, 38, 39
Marx, K. 19, 20, 29, 30, 35
Mason, R. O. 24
Masterman, M. 24
Maugham, I. 196
Maxwell, S. E. 108, 114
Mayhew, L. B. 217–18, 223
Mead, G. H. 133
meaningful management research xiv–xvi, 57–66; meaning and social research 61–3; positivism 59–61, 62, 63; science and social research 57–65
Medawar, P. B. 147
mental map 160, 161
Merton, R. K. 47
meta-analysis techniques 119–21
methodologies 104–31: and circumstance 63–5; Burrell and Morgan model 24–39; case-study 145–58; choosing a survey 174–80; criteria for choice 88–9; ethnomethodology 132–44; field research and repertory grid technique 159–73; interview data 190–203; mail questionnaires 181–9; overview 105–8; principal methods 89–100; resistance to change 118–21; techniques of research 100–3

methods: of authority 90; of intuition 90–1; of knowing 90–1; of tenacity 90
Miles, M. B. 156, 195
Miles, M. M. 195, 197, 199
Miliband, R. 35
Miller, M. L. 112
Mills, C. W. xviii
Mills, J. S. 58
Mintzberg, H. 17, 24
Mitchell, J. C. 152–3, 154
Mitchell, P. K. 302
Mitchell, T. R. 107, 108, 117
Mitroff, I. I. 24, 45–6, 48
model building 92
modes of inquiry 20
Moody, S. M. 151
Moore, B. M. 190
Moore, B. V. 191, 192
Morgan, C. P. 44
Morgan, G. 106, 107, 132, 142
Morrison, A. 239
Mouzelis, N. 35
Muchinsky, P. M. 107
Mueller, C. W. 116
multi-disciplinary accounting project 258–76; teams 212, 278–88
multiple paradigm research and analysis 23–43
Murray, D. M. 233

Nagel, E. 46, 49
natural science model 3, 5, 44–56; instability 46, 48–9; lack of realism 46, 50–2; sensitivity 46, 49–50; uniqueness 46, 47–8
nature of social science: assumptions 26
networking 296
'new paradigm' research 75–6
Newby, H. 146, 220, 253
Newell, A. 47
nomothetic research 16
non-obviousness xv
Nord, W. R. 34
Nyland, C. 35

objectives: establishing for teams 286–7; of students and supervisors 242–3
observation techniques 100–1

O'Connor, J. 36
O'Dell, W. F. 176
Oldham, G. 32
Oleson, V. 267
Olson, D. 233
ontology 25, 28
operational contexts 209, 210, 212
operational validity xv
organization: alternative perspectives
    7–22; analysis 136–42; behaviour
    44–56; ethnomethodology 132–44;
    research methods 104–31
orthodox approach to doctoral research
    219–20
Osborn, R. N. 151, 158

paradigms 23–43; Burrell and Morgan
    model 24–39; comparisons 36–7;
    ethnomethodology 132–44;
    functionalist **25**, 26–7, 30, 31–2,
    36–7; inquiries from inside and
    outside 7–22; interpretive **25**, 26, 27,
    30, 32–3, 37; new research 75–6;
    prospects for 38–9; radical humanist
    25, 26, 27, 30, 33–4, 37; radical
    structuralist **25**, 26, 27–8, 30, 35–6,
    37
Patton, M. Q. 190, 197
Pearlman, D. 112
Pedhazur, E. J. 114, 116
Peil, M. 302
Peirce, C. S. 19, 20
personal construct theory 159
personalization for questionnaires
    183–4, 187, **188**
perspectives: inquiries from inside and
    outside 7–22; meaningful
    management research 57–66;
    multiple paradigm analysis 23–43;
    natural science model 44–56
Pettigrew, A. 17
Ph. D. research 207, 210, 211; context
    of 215–26; learning to do 227–36;
    writing theses 232–4, 245–51
Phillips, D. 60, 61
Phillips, E. M. 228, 230
Phillips, J. S. 107, 126
Phillipson, M. 134
Piaget, J. 20
Picou, J. 24
Pike, K. L. 16

Pinder, C. 23, 24, 28
Piore, M. 35
Platt, J. 253–4
Polanyi, M. 12
politics and ethics 289–99; case-study
    290–8; identifying strategies 295–8;
    intervention 290–4; reflections 298–9
Pollner, M. 133–4, 135, 138
Pondy, L. R. 23, 38, 39, 45–6, 47, 48,
    107
Popper, K. 24, 44, 46
positivism 4, 16, 108, 145–51, 254–6;
    dangers in 59–61, 62, 63; in doctoral
    research 219–23; *see also*
    case-studies
postgraduate research *see* Ph. D.
    research
Powell, A. 28
Prahalad, C. K. 301
praxis 14
prediction level of research 87
principal research methods 89–100
procedural contexts 208–9, 210, 211,
    212
pure basic research 73–4
Pym, D. 39

qualitative research 87, 112, 121,
    145–6, 150–1, 157, 195, 198, 308;
    see also case-studies; interviews
qualities of good theses 247–9
quantitative research 87–8, 108, 145,
    149, 150–1, 156
questionnaires 95–6, 102–3, 174–80; in
    developing countries 303–5; mail
    181–7, **188**, 189

R and D Sub-Committee on Qualitative
    Research 195
radical humanist paradigm **25**, 26, 27,
    30, 33–4, 37
radical structuralist paradigm **25**, 26,
    27–8, 30, 33–4, 37
Radnitzky, G. 19
Ramachandran, K. 308
Ratcliffe, J. W. 157
Reason, P. 216
reasoning process 91–2
Reed, M. 23, 31
reflexivity 65n
relevance in research xv

reminder procedures, survey 184–5, 188

repertory grid technique 82–3, 159–73, 227–8, 235; analysis and interpretation 164–9; constructs 161, 163, **164**, **165**, 166–9; elements 161, **162**, 164, **165**, 166–7, **168**; theoretical background 160–1

research contexts *see* contexts

research methods *see* methodologies

research perspectives *see* perspectives

research techniques 100–3

resource contexts 208, 210, 212

Rex, J. 35

Rigby, P. H. xv, 220

rigour, levels of 87–8

Rimmer, D. 302

Ritzer, G. 7, 23, 28

Roberts, G. K. 58

Roethlisberger, F. J. 53

Rogers, C. R. 15

Rogers, E. M. 119–20, 121, 125

role descriptions 162, 169

Rose, M. 23

Rosenberg, M. J. 175

Rosenthal, R. 112

Rosnow, R. L. 108, 125–6

Roth, J. A. 257

Rowan, J. 216

Roy, D. 53

Roy, P. 300

Russell, B. 12

Ryle, A. 161, 167

Sabel, C. 35

Sackett, P. R. 112

Sacks, H. 132, 133, 134, 135

Saluja, M. R. 302

Sanday, P. 23

Sapsford, R. J. 63–4

Sashkin, M. 115

Sayer, D. 224

Schegloff, E. A. 134

Schlenker, B. R. 46, 49, 50

Schmidt, F. L. 112

Schmidt, N. 107, 112, 122

Schneider, B. 113

Schriesheim, C. A. 115

Schutz, A. 16, 20, 33, 37, 133, 147

Schwab, D. P. 107, 117, 118, 126

science: and social research 57–65;

definition 5; meaning 19, 57; role in organizational behaviour 44

scientific inference 153–4

scientific method 89–93

Sears, D. O. 105, 107

sensitivity 46, 49–50

Shapers, D. 24

Shapiro, M. 45, 49

Sharp, J. A. 217, 222

Shaw, M. L. G. 163

Shepherd, J. 178

Sieber, K. 195

Siehl, C. 38

Silverman, D.: methodology 145, 154, 155; organizations 136, 137, 139, 141–2; paradigms 23, 28, 29, 31, 32, 38

Simmons, K. 190

Simon, H. 47

Sims, D. 196

Sims, H. P. 124

situational ethnomethodology 134, 140–1

Slade, L. A. 107, 122

Slater, P. 161, 167

Smart, R. G. 122

Smircich, L. 106, 107

Smith, J. M. 190

Smith, M. 161, 164

Smith, M. L. 112

social process of research xvi, xviii, 252–77

Social Science Research Council (SSRC) 254

'soft' approaches 4; *see* inquiries from inside

Space, L. G. 172

stakeholders, identifying 295, 296

Stanfield, D. 301–2

Stanfield University Ph. D. programme 223–4

Stanley, J. C. 10, 44, 51

statistical inference 152, 154

statistical sampling 153

steering committees 290–9

Steiner, G. A. 44, 45

Steinle, C. 38

Sternitzke, M. E. 108

Steward, V. A. 167

Stirner, M. 33

Stone, E. F. 7, 50
Storey, J. 35
Strasser, S. 106
Strauss, A. L.: doctoral research 217, 221–2; grounded theory 153, 156, 157, 197, 255, 260
Stribley, K. M. 64
structure of theses 249–51
Strunk, W. 200
student-supervisor relationship 211, 217–18, **228, 229,** 230–1, 234–5, 237–44
Study of Graduate Education at Stanford (SGES) 223, 224
styles of supervision 239–40
Sudman, S. 181
Sudnow, D. 136
Sukumaran, A. 302
supervisors: constraints on research 217–18; relationships 237–44
surveys 95–7, 174–7, **178,** 179–80, 181–9; in developing countries 306–7
Susman, G. I. 16, 106, 107
Sweezy, P. 35
Swinnerton-Dyer, P. 223, 246

tape recorders 155, 196–7
Tatsuoka, M. M. 114
Taylor, A. R. 218
Taylor, J. R. 195
team research 278–88
techniques of research 100–3
telephone surveys 174–7, **178,** 179–80
Tenopyr, M. L. 112
theoretical sampling 153
theoria 14
theory building and case study 151–5
theses, doctoral: context of 215–26; definition 247; qualities 247–9; structure 249–51; writing up 232–4, 245–51
third-party interventionist 289, 290–9
Thomas, K. W. xv, 106, 107
Thompson, B. 114
Thompson, P. 35
Thoreau, H. D. 252
Thorndike, R. M. 114
timeliness xv
Tosi, H. 107

Total Design Method (TDM) 181–9
'tour de force' 216, 219, 223–5
translation of questionnaires 304
triads method 163
Trist, E. 17
truth 76
Tuck, M. 195
Tversky, A. 53
Tymon, W. G. xv, 106, 107

uniqueness 46, 47–8
United Kingdom 140–2, 253–7; funded research 253–7; study on Fire Service 29–39; *see also* case-studies
United States of America Ph. D. programme 223–4, 290–9; positivism 145
University Grants Committee (UGC) 246
University of Manchester 238
usefulness approach 76

Van Maanen, J. 17, 112, 196, 199
Venkatraman, N. 107
Viney, L. L. 160

Wales, H. 175
Wason, P. C. 233
Watkins, J. 24, 29
Weber, M. 20, 35, 52–3, 138
Weick, K. E. 47, 51
Weider, L. 136
Weinstock, I. 108
Weisburg, H. F. 96
Wells, R. 24
West, C. J. 190
White, E. B. 200
White, O. 23, 24
Whittaker, E. 267
Willmott, H. 23, 24, 38
withholding information 296–7
Wood, S. 35
Woolgar, S. 156
Worsley, P. 152
writing up theses 232–4, 245–51

Zimbalist, A. 35
Zimmerman, D. 133–4, 137, 138, 139–40, 141–2
Zuckerman, H. 194, 196